THE
UNIVERSITY OF WINNIPEG
PORTAGE & BALMORAL
WINNIPEG, MAN.   R3B 2E9.
CANADA

DISCARDED

Paradise Lost
and the Rhetoric of
Literary Forms

PR
3562
·L385
1985

Paradise Lost

and the Rhetoric of

Literary Forms

Barbara Kiefer Lewalski

PRINCETON UNIVERSITY PRESS

PRINCETON, NEW JERSEY

Copyright © 1985 by Princeton University Press

Published by Princeton University Press, 41 William Street,
Princeton, New Jersey 08540
In the United Kingdom: Princeton University Press, Guildford, Surrey

All Rights Reserved

Library of Congress Cataloging in Publication Data will be found on the
last printed page of this book

ISBN 0-691-06642-6

This book has been composed in Linotron Galliard

Clothbound editions of Princeton University Press books are printed on
acid-free paper, and binding materials are chosen for strength and durability

Printed in the United States of America by Princeton University Press
Princeton, New Jersey

IN MEMORY OF
Rosalie L. Colie

Contents

Preface

THE TITLE of this study points to its central thesis. My first proposition, that *Paradise Lost* incorporates paradigms, topoi, and allusions from a great many literary genres, modes, and exemplary works is not in itself especially novel—save as the study demonstrates the range and comprehensiveness of the forms so included. My second proposition is that Milton makes constant, complex, and highly conscious use of the Renaissance genre system, and the cultural significances and moral values associated with the several kinds, as a means of imagining his unimaginable subject, and as a rhetorical strategy to educate his readers and to guide their responses. This study undertakes to read *Paradise Lost* as a rhetoric of literary forms, shaped to the special needs and purposes of a Miltonic Bard who sees himself as prophet-poet.

Like the heroic songs of the fallen angels, critical studies of *Paradise Lost* are inevitably partial, able to treat only certain aspects of that great work. But unlike those angels, Miltonists can engage in antiphonal exchanges with each other, and can hope to contribute to some larger harmony. The strain I undertake here is central to Renaissance and Miltonic poetics: the poet as prophet, maker, and teacher; his aesthetic and rhetorical intentions; and his deliberate genre choices and transformations.

My largest debts are to the many scholars who have illuminated aspects of Renaissance genre theory and practice, and to the many Miltonists who have studied various generic elements in *Paradise Lost*. Some of those debts are recorded in the following pages; others, less direct but not less important, are not. Participants in my NEH Seminar (1981-1982) on Renaissance Genre Theory and the Renaissance Genres helped me think through several of these issues, as did panelists in related MLA sessions, colleagues at several universities who

PREFACE

heard early versions of some chapters as lectures, and students in graduate seminars at Brown and Harvard. I am especially grateful to Mary Ann Radzinowicz, Janel Mueller, and Edward Weismiller for reading the manuscript with characteristic generosity and rigor. The faults that remain are of course my own.

Much of the research was carried out with the aid of a Guggenheim Fellowship in 1980-1981. I want to thank the librarians and staff of the British Library, the Widener and Houghton Libraries, the Henry R. Huntington Library, the Folger Shakespeare Library, and the Brown University Libraries for assisting my research. Mrs. Arthur Sherwood and Marilyn Campbell of the Princeton University Press gave painstaking attention to the editorial and publication process. I am grateful to the University of Pittsburgh Press, the University of California Press, and the editors of *Philological Quarterly* respectively for permission to use some materials from the following essays: "The Genres of *Paradise Lost*: Literary Genre as a Means of Accommodation," *Milton Studies* 17 (1983), 75-103; "Innocence and Experience in Milton's Eden," in *New Essays on Paradise Lost*, edited by Thomas Kranidas (1969), pp. 86-117; and "Structure and the Symbolism of Vision in Michael's Prophecy, *Paradise Lost*, Books XI-XII," *PMLA* 42 (1963), 25-35.

This book is dedicated to the memory of Rosalie L. Colie, in gratitude for many years of colleagueship, friendship, and colloquy about literary matters, especially Renaissance genre. As always, my greatest debt is to Kenneth F. Lewalski, whose "meet and happy conversation" sweetens every labor, however arduous, in the groves of academe and in the byways of daily life.

Providence, Rhode Island
May 15, 1984

Abbreviations

Hughes   *Complete Poems and Major Prose of John Milton*, ed.
         Merritt Y. Hughes (New York: Odyssey Press-
         Bobbs-Merrill, 1973). All citations and
         quotations of Milton's poetry are from this
         edition.

CPW   *Complete Prose Works of John Milton*, ed. Don M.
         Wolfe et al., 8 vols. (New Haven: Yale Univ.
         Press, 1953-1982).

CL   *Comparative Literature*
CLS   *Comparative Literature Studies*
CSEL   *Corpus Scriptorum Ecclesiasticorum Latinorum*
EIC   *Essays in Criticism*
ELH   *Journal of English Literary History*
ELR   *English Literary Renaissance*
E&S   *Essays and Studies by Members of the English
         Association*
HLQ   *Huntington Library Quarterly*
HTR   *Harvard Theological Review*
JEGP   *Journal of English and Germanic Philology*
JHI   *Journal of the History of Ideas*
MLQ   *Modern Language Quarterly*
MP   *Modern Philology*
PMLA   *Publications of the Modern Language Association*
PQ   *Philological Quarterly*
SEL   *Studies in English Literature, 1500-1900*
SP   *Studies in Philology*
SAB   *South Atlantic Bulletin*
TSLL   *Texas Studies in Literature and Language*
UTQ   *University of Toronto Quarterly*

Paradise Lost
and the Rhetoric of
Literary Forms

ONE

Paradise Lost as Encyclopedic Epic: The Uses of Literary Forms

Paradise Lost is preeminently a poem about knowing and choosing—for the Miltonic Bard, for his characters, for the reader. I intend to argue that the ground for many of these choices is Milton's own choice and rhetorical use of a panoply of literary forms, with their accumulated freight of shared cultural significances.

Readers have long recognized that *Paradise Lost* is an epic whose closest structural affinities are to Virgil's *Aeneid*, and that it undertakes to redefine classical heroism in Christian terms.[1] We now recognize as well the influence of epic traditions and the presence of epic features other than Virgilian. Among the poem's Homeric elements are its Iliadic subject, the death and woe resulting from an act of disobedience; the portrayal of Satan as an Achillean hero motivated by a sense of injured merit and also as an Odyssean hero of wiles and craft; the description of Satan's perilous Odyssey to find a new homeland; and the battle scenes in heaven.[2] The poem also incorporates a Hesiodic gigantomachy; numerous Ovidian metamorphoses; an Ariostan Paradise of Fools; Spenserian allegorical figures (Sin and Death); a romance garden of love in which a hero and heroine must withstand a dragon of sorts; and a poetic hexaemeron in the tradition of Du Bartas.[3] Moreover, because heroic values have been so profoundly transvalued in *Paradise Lost*, the poem is sometimes assigned to categories beyond epic: pseudomorph, prophetic poem, apocalypse, anti-epic, transcendent epic.[4]

Dramatic elements have also been identified within the epic form: some vestiges of Milton's early sketches for a drama

3

entitled *Adam Unparadiz'd*; some structural affinities to contemporary epics in five "acts," such as Davenant's *Gondibert*; and tragic protagonists who fall from happiness to misery through *hamartia*. Other dramatic features include the tragic soliloquies of Satan and Adam, recalling those of Faustus and Macbeth; the morality-play "Parliament of Heaven" sequence; the scene of domestic farce in which Satan first vehemently repudiates and then fawns upon his reprehensible offspring, Sin and Death; the scenes of domestic tragedy that present Adam and Eve's quarrel, Fall, mutual recriminations (and later, reconciliation); and the tragic masques or pageants portraying the sins and miseries of human history.[5]

The panoply of kinds includes pastoral: landscape descriptions of an Arcadian "happy rural seat of various view" (4.247); ecloguelike passages presenting the *otium* of Heaven and unfallen Eden; scenes of light georgic gardening activity.[6] Also, the several varieties of embedded lyrics in the poem have received some critical attention: celebratory odes, psalmic hymns of praise and thanksgiving, submerged sonnets, epithalamia, love lyrics (*aubade*, nocturne, sonnet), laments, and complaints.[7] There are also many rhetorical and dialogic kinds which have not been much studied from the perspective of genre: Satan's several political orations; God's judicial oration defending his ways; the parliamentary debate in hell over war and peace; the Satan-Abdiel debate over God's right of sovereignty; a treatise on astronomical systems; a dialogue on human nature between God and Adam and another on love between Raphael and Adam; a lecture on Christian historiography; Satan's temptation speech to Eve in the style and manner of "some Orator renown'd / In *Athens* or free *Rome*" (9.670-71).[8]

If we ask why Milton incorporated so complete a spectrum of literary forms and genres in *Paradise Lost*, a partial answer must be that much Renaissance critical theory supports the notion of epic as a heterocosm or compendium of subjects, forms, and styles. According to the major Renaissance genre theorist, Julius-Caesar Scaliger, epic is both a mixed form and "the chiefest of all forms"; it is "catholic in the range of sub-ject-matter," and it supplies "the universal controlling rules for the composition of each other kind."[9] Homer's epics, as Rosalie Colie has reminded us, were widely recognized as the source and origin of all arts and sciences—philosophy, mathematics, history, geography, military art, religion, hymnic praise, rhetoric, and much more—and, accordingly, as the source of all literary forms.[10] Out of Homer, said his great English translator George Chapman (citing Petrarch), "all Arts [are] deduced, confirmed or illustrated," and by reason of this inclusiveness, Homer can best instruct all kinds of people—kings, soldiers, counsellors, fathers, husbands, wives, lovers, friends.[11] Scaliger, on the other hand, considered the *Aeneid* to be the supreme epic, presenting the very "*ideas* of things . . . just as they might be taken from nature itself," only more perfect.[12] Moreover, ancient and Renaissance tradition recognized the Bible as epiclike in its comprehension of all history, all subject matters, and many genres—law, history, prophecy, heroic poetry, psalm, allegory, proverb, hymn, sermon, epistle, tragedy, tragicomedy, and more.[13]

Many Renaissance theorists also called attention to specific amalgams in the great poems of the tradition. The close parallel Aristotle drew between epic and tragedy, and his description of the plot of the *Iliad* as "pathetic," laid the groundwork for the common Renaissance view of it as a tragic epic. In this vein, William Webbe traced the origins of tragedy to the *Iliad* and the origins of comedy to the *Odyssey*. Giraldi Cinthio identified romance elements (characters, wonders, *copia*) in the *Odyssey* and the *Metamorphoses*, and Jacopo Mazzoni discussed Dante's *Commedia* as both comedy and epic. Puttenham (following Scaliger) emphasized the historical dimension in the epics of Homer and Virgil and classified them as one species of a larger category of historical poems.[14] And Sidney, the major literary theorist in Renaissance England, attributed a specific moral effect to each of the poetic kinds and defended their mixture: "if severed they be good, the conjunction cannot be hurtfull."[15]

5

Responding to this tradition, Renaissance poets devised epics on inclusivist lines. Noting that Homer and Virgil had intermingled all forms and styles in their great epics, Tasso (with obvious reference to his own *Gerusalemme Liberata*) claimed that Renaissance heroic poems incorporated an even greater range and variety of subject matter, imaging that of the created universe itself:

> The great poet (who is called divine for no other reason than that as he resembles the supreme Artificer in his workings he comes to participate in his divinity) can form a poem in which, as in a little world, one may read here of armies assembling, here of battles on land or sea, here of conquests of cities, skirmishes and duels, here of jousts, here descriptions of hunger and thirst, here tempests, fires, prodigies, there of celestial and infernal councils, there seditions, there discord, wanderings, adventures, enchantments, deeds of cruelty, daring, courtesy, generosity, there the fortunes of love, now happy, now sad, now joyous, now pitiful.[16]

And the major sixteenth-century English narratives with claims to epic status—Sidney's *New Arcadia* and Spenser's *Faerie Queene*—were quite obviously mixtures of epic, romance, pastoral, allegory, and song.

Contemporary theory and practice, it seems clear, gave Milton ample warrant to conclude that an epic comprehending the entire spectrum of kinds and subjects would be most doctrinal and exemplary to a nation, and would also have best claim to inclusion in the company he expressly sought for such a work—the *Iliad*, the *Odyssey*, the *Aeneid*, the *Gerusalemme Liberata*, and the Bible.[17] In this study, however, I do not undertake to enumerate and extend the list of kinds that can be located in Milton's epic, but rather to address the more important question of just how Milton employs generic inclusiveness to accomplish his poetic purposes. I shall be attending to the ways in which Milton uses topoi, thematic and structural signs, and allusions to particular exemplars to evoke a very broad spectrum of kinds and modes.

My central proposition is that genre choices, changes, and transformations provide a range of culturally defined perspectives upon the matter of the poem, and thereby serve Milton the poet in several ways: as an indispensable vehicle for his own artistic perception; as a fundamental means of accommodating his subject to his audience; and as a major rhetorical strategy for educating that audience. This argument engages some major issues in contemporary Milton criticism—intertextuality, the springs of poetic creativity and authority, the responses of the reader—but in terms supplied by Renaissance poetics and rhetorical theory. This vantage point invites revision of some current views of Milton and his epic.

Though I consider many specific allusions, and the subtexts and "infracontexts" they invoke,[18] I do not employ the contemporary vocabulary of intertextuality to discuss such allusions because I am concerned here with conscious artistic choices, with Milton's deliberate orchestrations within the echo chamber of language. Also, my argument proposes that the manifold allusions in *Paradise Lost* function most significantly as generic topoi, to activate and develop various generic paradigms within that poem. To use Thomas Greene's terms,[19] I argue that Milton's imitative and allusive strategies are essentially heuristic, and that the conventions of literary genre and mode constitute a primary element of his poem's "*mundus significans*"—the rhetorical and symbolic vocabulary shared by poet and reader.

In addition, though I focus upon Milton's engagement with literary precursors I do not find that engagement characterized by anxiety, struggle, transumption, or triumph.[20] And though I take Milton's conception of himself as poet-prophet to be central to his poetics, I do not find him claiming the direct divine inspiration or the transcendent visions afforded the biblical prophets.[21] Again, though I analyze readers' responses to *Paradise Lost*,[22] my emphasis falls upon the author as rhetor, employing carefully designed literary strategies to elicit these

7

responses. But I do not see Milton as a rigorous and punitive teacher, forcing readers into frequent and inevitable mistakes in reading and thereby causing them to recognize and reenact their own fallenness. To my mind, he embodies instead the pedagogic ideal in *Of Education*, advancing his readers' understanding through a literary regimen at once intellectually demanding and delightful.[23]

Milton's heuristic use of the literary tradition can in fact be argued from texts often cited as evidence for those other positions. One is the summary of Mulciber's fall (1.738-48) incorporated in the description of Mammon's activities in hell and heaven, which concludes, "thus they relate, / Erring; for he with this rebellious rout / Fell long before." Another is the description of Edenic fruit with reference to the fabulous golden apples of the Hesperides: "fruit burnisht with Golden Rind / Hung amiable, *Hesperian* Fables true, / If true, here only, and of delicious taste" (4.249-51). To be sure, these lines supply a correction to the classical fables. But the important point in both cases is that the Bard can only imagine and render his ineffable truths by recalling those fables, and that the reader is also led by these fables to imagine truths that transcend them. The story of Mulciber's fall is false as to its time and manner, but the pathos of the classical narrative reveals a moral truth—humankind's perennial disposition to romanticize Mammon. And the indescribable Edenic fruit can be best imagined as the true embodiment of the marvellous golden apples in Ovid's fabulous gardens of pleasure and delight.

This argument pertains even more clearly to Milton's use of literary forms. The formidable array of conventional genres and modes in *Paradise Lost* testifies to Milton's awareness that he can only see and tell of things invisible by using the familiar forms which literary art supplies to his own imagination and that of his readers. It testifies also to his belief that he can teach most effectively by building upon and letting his readers refine their developed responses to the values and assumptions about man, nature, language, heroism, virtue, pleasure, work, and love that have long been associated with the several genres and literary modes.

GENRE SYSTEMS AND NORMS:
RENAISSANCE AND MILTONIC GENRE THEORY

Exploration of Milton's ways with genre in *Paradise Lost* must begin with some working definitions, since critical terms pertaining to genre are invested with very different meanings by different critics, Renaissance and modern.[24] It also necessitates some prior attention to ideas about genres and genre systems which classical and Renaissance theory supplied to Milton, and which were of central importance to him in crafting his great epic.[25]

The familiar classification of literary works into the broad categories of narrative, dramatic, and lyric (to which many add nonfiction prose) has become a commonplace of modern literary theory. But valuable as this schema is in highlighting some important literary affinities, the problems attending its use as a universal system of genre classification have become increasingly apparent.[26] For one thing, the designation of narrative, dramatic, and lyric as foundation genres became widespread only in the nineteenth century. In Renaissance theory an analogous triad was derived from and understood in terms of Plato's and Aristotle's three kinds of imitation or representation: dramatic, in which the characters alone speak (tragedy and comedy); "narrative," in which the poet alone speaks or recites (Plato instances the dithyramb); and mixed, combining the former two (Homer's epics).[27] A few Renaissance theorists transformed the classical triad into something closer to the modern one, though still based largely on manner of imitation or presentation: Minturno proposed epic, dramatic, and melic or lyric as the three general "parts" of poetry, and Milton invoked the same broad categories in his *Reason of Church Government*.[28] In consonance with this Renaissance usage I refer to narrative, dramatic, and lyric as *literary categories* or *strategies of presentation*, not genres.[29]

9

I use the term *generic classes* to refer to the very influential genre system deriving from the Alexandrian *Canons*, Horace, Cicero, and Quintilian.[30] In that system, a few major classes of poetry and prose are identified by canonical lists of writers, on grounds of poetic meter (where relevant), structure, and purpose. Quintilian's classes are: epic (including didactic, historical, and pastoral poems written in hexameters), elegy, lyric, iambic, satire, tragedy, old comedy, new comedy, history, philosophy, oratory. This tradition strongly influenced Scaliger, who distinguishes a few major classes and, within them, literally hundreds of historical genres and subgenres, both poetic and rhetorical.

I reserve the term *genre* (or *kind*, the Renaissance term) for the historical genres—epic, tragedy, sonnet, verse epistle, funeral elegy, hymn, epigram, and many more—that are identified in classical and Renaissance theory and poetic practice by specific formal and thematic elements, topoi, and conventions. The historical genres are my major concern here, for it is they that constitute, in Claudio Guillén's happy phrase, problem-solving models for the poet, invitations to match experience to form in a specific yet undetermined way.[31] With Alastair Fowler, I approach the historical genres as families whose members share several (but not always the same) features drawn from a given generic repertoire. Such generic indicators or features include: formal structure, meter, size, scale, strategy of presentation, subject, values, mood, occasion, attitude, style, topoi, etc. *Subgenres* are formed from genres by further specification of subject matter and motifs (e.g., the piscatory eclogue evolved as a subgenre from the pastoral eclogue).[32]

I use the term *mode* for several expressive literary kinds—pastoral, satiric, comedic, heroic, elegiac, and tragic, among others—that are identified chiefly by subject matter, attitude, tonality, and topoi. Modes seem to have evolved from certain historical genres (heroic from epic, pastoral from idyl and eclogue), and may interpenetrate works or parts of works in several genres. For example, in Renaissance as in later literature we may find a *pastoral* comedy or novel or song, a *heroic* tragedy or ballad or sonnet, a *satiric* verse epistle or epigram or comedy. Mode is not a Renaissance term (any more than genre is), but Sidney anticipates the concept in his treatment of the eight major "parts, kindes, or species" of poetry: "Heroick, Lyrick, Tragick, Comick, Satyrick, Iambick, Elegiack, Pastorall, and certaine others." Though these classes derive from the Alexandrian tradition, Sidney does not describe them by meter or form but by modal qualities of tone, attitude, and effect: the "lamenting *Elegiack*"; the "bitter but wholesome *Iambick*"; the "*Satirick*, who . . . sportingly . . . make[s] a man laugh at follie"; the "*Lyricke* . . . who with his tuned *Lyre* and well accorded voice, giveth praise."[33]

Milton's Preface to Book Two of the *Reason of Church Government* provides some indication of his complex approach to genre and genre systems. He refers to the epic-dramatic-lyric triad, identifying within each of these categories several historical genres and notable models—classical, biblical, or contemporary:

> Time servs not now, and perhaps I might seem too profuse to give any certain account of what the mind at home in the spacious circuits of her musing hath liberty to propose to her self, though of highest hope, and hardest attempting, whether that Epick form whereof the two poems of *Homer*, and those other two of *Virgil* and *Tasso* are a diffuse, and the book of *Job* a brief model: or whether the rules of *Aristotle* herein are strictly to be kept, or nature to be follow'd . . . Or whether those Dramatick constitutions, wherein *Sophocles* and *Euripides* raigne shall be found more doctrinal and exemplary to a Nation, the Scripture also affords us a divine pastoral Drama in the Song of *Salomon* consisting of two persons and a double *Chorus*, as *Origen* rightly judges. And the Apocalyps of Saint *John* is the majestick image of a high and stately Tragedy, shutting up and intermingling her solemn Scenes and Acts with a sevenfold *Chorus* of halleluja's and harp-

11

ing symphonies: . . . Or if occasion shall lead to imitat those magnifick Odes and Hymns wherein *Pindarus* and *Callimachus* are in most things worthy, some others in their frame judicious, in their matter most an end faulty: But those frequent songs throughout the law and prophets beyond all these, not in their divine argument alone, but in the very critical art of composition may be easily made appear over all the kinds of Lyrick poesy, to be incomparable.[34]

Since Milton treats here only those genres he considered attempting, his epic-dramatic-lyric categories may not be all-inclusive. He does, however, deliberate about a wide range of genre choices and models within these categories. Renaissance theory and practice illuminate Milton's assumptions about these categories, and about the choices available to him.

Renaissance critics generally thought of epics as long poems treating heroic actions or other weighty matters in a high style, thereby evoking awe or wonder. Milton is typical in using the term "epic" to refer in the first instance to the specific genre for which the poems of Homer and Virgil were normative. He is typical also in using the modal term, heroic poetry, as a synonym for epic. And his reference to Tasso's *Gerusalemme* reflects that poem's status as the most influential contemporary epic, having a Virgilian subject and an Aristotelian epic structure. However, controversy raged throughout the Renaissance over the epic claims of quite different sorts of poems: romantic epics such as Ariosto's *Orlando Furioso*; allegorical romantic epics such as Spenser's *Faerie Queene*; philosophical poems such as Lucretius' *De Rerum Natura*; historical poems such as Lucan's *Pharsalia*; allegorical dream-visions such as Dante's *Commedia*; hexaemeral poems such as Du Bartas' *Divine Weeks and Works*; and biblical poems on Old and New Testament topics, such as Vida's *Christiad*. Sidney even included the prose romance, describing Xenophon's *Cyropaedia* as "an absolute heroicall Poeme"—a designation he would probably extend to his own *Arcadia*.[35] Milton's reference to

12

the Book of Job as model for the brief epic, and his acceptance of epics that follow "nature" rather than Aristotle (the allusion is to Cinthio's defence of Ariosto and the romantic epic)[36] indicate that for him the epic category is very broad indeed. He draws upon all these epic kinds and many epic models in devising his own encyclopedic epic.

The dramatic category or strategy of presentation included, for Renaissance as for modern critics, the two primary genres of tragedy and comedy with their several subgenres and related kinds. Renaissance critics commonly discussed tragedy in terms of Aristotle's famous definition and stated preference for a plot in which a hero better or greater than ourselves falls from happiness to misery. The Italian neoclassical treatises analyzed in great detail such Aristotelian concepts as complex and simple plots, peripeteia, discovery, *hamartia*, pity and terror, catharsis. It is significant, however, that Milton designated as models for tragedy not only Aristotle's preferred example, Sophocles, but also Euripides (and later Aeschylus as well),[37] thereby recognizing the very different varieties of tragedy they represent. Moreover, his reference to the Apocalypse of St. John as tragedy (reiterated in the Preface to *Samson Agonistes*) points to a distinctively Christian subgenre of tragedy, with biblical models. The Elizabethan stage afforded other concepts and models of tragedy, e.g., revenge tragedy, and tragedy involving an evil protagonist (*Richard III* or *Macbeth*).[38]

Lacking an authoritative Aristotelian treatise on comedy, Renaissance critics usually invoked the inclusive formula of the ancient grammarians, that comedies begin in troubles and end in peace and happiness.[39] To define one prominent variety, the comedy of intrigue in which the vices and follies of type characters are exposed to ridicule, Renaissance neoclassical critics appealed to the examples of Plautus and Terence (and such contemporaries as Ben Jonson).[40] Milton's reference to the Song of Songs as pastoral drama obviously looks to a very different concept, the notion of comic delight or *admiratio* originating with Demetrius of Phalareum and elab-

13

orated by Tasso and Sidney.[41] This concept provided the theoretical basis for several Renaissance comic kinds, distinguished by noble characters and a graceful and charming style: entertainments, masques, pastoral interludes, pastoral comedies, romantic comedies, Shakespearean romances. Some critics also recognized a species of philosophic comedy: Dante gave his *Commedia* its generic title because it begins with the horrors of hell and ends with the joys of heaven, and certain Neoplatonic critics identified Plato's dialogues (with their *eiron* Socrates) as comedy.[42] Also, though Renaissance neoclassical critics roundly denounced tragicomedies, this hybrid kind in which good characters confront genuine dangers but at the last moment are almost miraculously delivered from them was extremely popular on both the Italian and the Elizabethan stage.

In the passage quoted from the *Reason of Church Government*, Milton refers only to the noblest genres in the lyric category: classical hymns and odes, biblical hymns and other songs. We cannot know, therefore, whether his idea of lyric could include the vast array of poems modern critics designate as lyrics according to such criteria as brevity, subjectivity, and expressiveness. Those Renaissance Aristotelians who defined the lyric category by the object of imitation ("the affections and manners") and the mode of presentation (the poet speaking in his own person) could indeed accommodate such inclusiveness. Extending that definition, Minturno also assigned to lyric the entire province of demonstrative rhetoric (the awarding of praise and blame), and both he and Viperano suggested that the full tonal range of the tragic and the comic modes pertains as well to lyric.[43]

On the other hand, many Renaissance theorists reserved the lyric designation for stanzaic or monostrophic poems having some association with music and song, notably, for members of the ancient class of lyric or melic kinds originally accompanied by the lyre, cithera, or similar instrument, and written in the lyric meters.[44] So understood, the category was still very broad. Citing Pindar, Callimachus, Anacreon, Horace, and Catullus as normative, Scaliger identified hundreds of lyric genres and subgenres—hymns, dirges, songs, celebratory and Anacreontic odes—for many occasions and purposes, and on all kinds of subjects.[45] Many critics (like Milton) also included biblical psalms and songs, and others specified contemporary lyric kinds such as sonnets, canzoni, and ballads.[46] By this definition, however, certain brief genres were perceived as not, or not fully, lyric: epigrams (despite the close relation of epigram and sonnet in the Renaissance); the iambic and satiric classes; and elegies—both love laments and funeral poems— which in classical times had been written in elegiac meter and accompanied by the flute rather than sung to the lyre.[47] Both the broader and the more restricted definitions of lyric pertain to Milton's epic and the several lyric genres it incorporates.

Milton also includes many kinds of formal discourse in *Paradise Lost*, prompted perhaps by the notion that rhetoric had its origin in Homer's epics. Some of the rhetorical speeches— challenges, vaunts, exhortations to battle—are the distinctive topoi of epic, while others are heavily indebted to the soliloquy of Elizabethan tragedy. Still others follow the normative prescriptions and models that all Renaissance schoolboys studied assiduously: Aristotle, the author of the *Rhetorica ad Herenneum*, Quintilian, and especially Cicero.[48] *Paradise Lost* contains speeches in all three classical genres of rhetoric: judicial (forensic), involving legal pleas pertaining to past actions; deliberative (political, advisory), involving advice to political assemblies or rulers regarding future actions; and demonstrative (epideictic), involving praise or dispraise, usually in connection with ceremonial occasions. Such speeches often represent familiar Renaissance adaptations of the three classical species: e.g., the formal apology as a subgenre of the forensic oration; *suasoriae* directed to individuals as a subgenre of the deliberative oration; the encomium and the invective as subgenres of the demonstrative oration.[49] These rhetorical speeches develop arguments from the recognized topics of invention and employ the three kinds of proof—ethos (the moral character exhibited by the speaker), pathos (the emotions evoked in the audience), and logos (reasoning, examples, authorities). They also call upon the three styles as decorum requires: Plain (Attic, terse, low), customarily used for instruction; Middle (graceful, sweet, flowing), used chiefly to delight and charm; and Grand (high, copious, vehement), used to move and stir an audience to action.

Paradise Lost also includes several kinds of Renaissance dialogue, for which Plato, Cicero, and Boethius provided normative models. Renaissance dialogues generally explored a topic for some educative purpose, though they seldom attempted a Socratic dialectic in which the responses are progressively refined through rigorous criticism until the truth is apparent to all.[50] Plato's example gave rise to at least two distinctive varieties: the sharply focused two-party dialogue in which an ironic questioner uncovers by sharp probing the folly of an erring or naive respondent (Plato's *Meno*); and the informal dialogue in a social setting, during which several friends state partial truths that are at length ordered in relation to a more exalted or more comprehensive vision (Plato's *Symposium*, Castiglione's *Courtier*, Walton's *Compleat Angler*). In form, Ciceronian dialogue resembled the Platonic (especially the second kind), but used the form rather as a method of exposition than of philosophical inquiry. In Boethian dialogue, typically, an exalted authority educates an erring novice both by eliciting and challenging his notions and also by providing lengthy answers to his questions (Boethius' *Consolation of Philosophy*, Petrarch's *Secretum*).[51]

The Bible provided other models of dialogue for *Paradise Lost*, in the verbal encounters of the great Old Testament prophets and mediators (Abraham, Moses, Job) with God. And Milton's poem also incorporates formal debate, a prominent medieval-Renaissance genre drawing upon both dialogic and rhetorical traditions, in which more or less evenly-matched speakers argue opposed positions and an audience is expected to judge which has the better case.[52]

But for all this, *Paradise Lost* is hardly a mausoleum of dead forms. If Milton constructs it from many literary genres and modes devised in accordance with normative Renaissance models and critical precepts, he also invests those forms with an imaginative energy which profoundly transforms them. And as many critics have noted, these transformed Miltonic literary kinds themselves became models with enormous influence upon English and American writers for more than two centuries.[53]

LITERARY FORMS AND HUMAN VALUES

Despite the density and multiplicity of literary forms in *Paradise Lost*, there is nothing random or casual about their use. Interestingly enough, Milton's poem manifests many of the characteristics the Russian genre theorist M. M. Bakhtin finds in the emerging Renaissance novel, in sharp contrast to ancient epic: multiple genres, including extraliterary kinds, which create multiple perspectives upon the subject; the dialogic interaction of forms; the "polyglossia" of several generic languages within the work; strong connectives linking the poem to contemporary reality; the valorization of process.[54] But *Paradise Lost* is neither ancient epic nor modern novel. Multiple genres give Milton's modern epic great complexity, but not the indeterminacy and inconclusiveness Bakhtin identifies as the product of generic multiplicity in the modern novel. To the contrary Milton employs literary forms with great care and deliberateness, as a primary means of representing and discriminating among several kinds of life, action, and speech, and the values pertaining to each. Only through such forms, which embody the shared imaginative experience of Western man and woman, can the Bard realize and articulate his own vision of the truth of things. And only through such forms can he accommodate that vision to readers present and future, educating them in the complex processes of making moral discriminations.

Several of Milton's early poems reveal his use of literary genre and mode as a system indicative of style of life and choice of values. In "Elegy 6" he suggests that the "gay elegy" (such as his friend Charles Diodati was presumably writing) and the lofty hymn (such as his own "On the Morning of

Christ's Nativity") are countergenres, arising from and expressive of contrary life styles.[55] And in the companion poems literary kinds carry much more sweeping significances, as emblems of alternative ways of life.

Pastoral is the dominant mode in *L'Allegro*, embodying the essence of youthful gaity. An extended description of a rural English landscape established that mode by invoking pastoral topoi of several kinds: the whistling plowman, the singing milkmaid, the shepherd telling his tale "under the Hawthorn in the dale," the "nibbling flocks," Corydon and Thyrsis dining on herbs, Thestylis binding the sheaves, songs and dances on a "Sunshine Holiday" (ll. 41-99). Then the portrayal of L'Allegro's pleasures and values is completed by reference to several genres shown to be harmonious with pastoral: In the narrative category he enjoys fairy and folk tales; in the dramatic category, court masques and pageants, Jonsonian comedy, and Shakespearean romantic comedy of the green world; and in the lyric category, "soft *Lydian* Airs, / Married to immortal verse"—songs in the Greek musical mode associated with sweetness and enervating love.

Romance is the dominant mode in *Il Penseroso*, which describes a solitary scholar-errant wandering through a muted, mysterious, gothic landscape characterized by romance topoi: a melancholy nightingale, a "high lonely Tow'r," a drowsy bellman, "arched walks of twilight groves," brown shadows, a cloister with "high embowed Roof" and "dim religious light," and a hermitage with mossy cells. Il Penseroso's pleasures and values are further revealed by reference to his favorite literary kinds, all presented as harmonious with the romance mode: the idealist philosophy of Plato and Hermes Trismegistus; allegorical romance narratives; "gorgeous" Greek tragedies; the hymns of Orpheus and Musaeus and the divine anthems of Christian ritual. At the last, the romance mode modulates for Il Penseroso into "something like Prophetic strain."

Milton's early poems display another generic strategy that looks forward to *Paradise Lost*: the movement from less to more noble genres (or varieties within a particular genre) as an emblem of a parallel movement in moral understanding. The progression from the less exalted genres of *L'Allegro* to the higher kinds of *Il Penseroso*—from folk tales to allegorical romance, from comedy to tragedy, from Lydian airs to hymns— affirms the greater nobility of Il Penseroso's life. In *Comus* also, the Lady refuses to participate in the perverse masques the enchanter presents to her, but dances in a masque of virtuous pleasure at her father's house. Again, the uncouth swain in *Lycidas* tries out and rejects various versions of pastoral that cannot accommodate evil and untimely death, but his vision of the perfected pastoral of heaven enables him at last to accept the flawed world of postlapsarian pastoral: "Tomorrow to fresh Woods, and Pastures new."

In *Paradise Lost* we find similar but much more comprehensive generic strategies, which present and promote more complex and rigorous moral discriminations. That claim must be substantiated by detailed analysis in the following chapters, but the broad outlines of the argument may be sketched here, to suggest just how Milton incorporates literary categories, modes, and genres in *Paradise Lost*, and how their presence and progression serve as guides to interpretation.

Milton employs specific literary modes in *Paradise Lost* to characterize the various orders of being: the heroic mode for Satan and his damned society; mixed for the celestial order; pastoral (opening out to georgic and comedic) for prelapsarian life in Eden; tragic (encompassing at length postlapsarian georgic, pastoral, and heroic) for human life in the fallen world. These modes are made to govern the relevant segments of the poem through the use of appropriate subject matter, topoi, tone, and language. Also, each mode is introduced by explicit signals. As the narrative begins, the epic question and its answer (1.27-54) present Satan and hell in heroic terms. The Edenic pastoral mode is introduced by reference to the garden as "A happy rural seat of various view" (4.247). The forthright announcement "I now must change / These Notes to Tragic" (9.5-6) heralds the Fall sequence. And the affirmation that a tragic subject may be more heroic than traditional epic

19

themes leads into the mixed modes of postlapsarian but regenerate human life.

These several modes import into the poem the values traditionally associated with them: great deeds, battle courage, glory (*aristeia*) for the heroic mode; love and song, *otium*, the carefree life for pastoral; responsibility, discipline, and the labor of husbandry for georgic; the easy resolution of difficulties through dialogue and intellect for the comedic; the pity and terror of the human condition for the tragic. These contrasting modes and their modulations, together with the mixed modes that present the celestial order, engage us in an ongoing critique of the various perspectives on human life that they provide.

The distinctive mode pertaining to each segment of the poem is adumbrated through various narrative, dramatic, lyric, and discursive genres. The longer narrative and dramatic kinds—epic and romance, tragedy and comedy, and certain of their subgenres—are incorporated through references to their generic paradigms, structural and thematic, and their characteristic topoi. These generic paradigms and topoi are further reinforced by verbal, thematic, and structural allusions to specific works or episodes. By this means we are invited to identify certain patterns and certain poems as subtexts for portions of Milton's poem, and then to attend to the completion or transformation of those allusive patterns as the poem proceeds.

This strategy is common among epic poets. Virgil modelled his antagonist, Turnus, on Homer's primary hero, Achilles, offering thereby a critique of the Homeric heroic ideal. Dante's persona was guided through hell and purgatory by Virgil, whose epic hero had also descended to the underworld to learn about his life and destiny—but Dante required a better guide to the celestial regions. Spenser's Bower of Bliss is a reprise in much darker tones of the love gardens in Ariosto and Tasso. However, *Paradise Lost* far surpasses other epics in the comprehensive array of such paradigms and the thematic significance of them all. To take one example: Satan's adventures reflect the paradigms of one after another of the heroic genres (epic of strife, quest epic, romance, tragedy, history), and are measured against the actions of the most notable heroes in all these kinds, thereby promoting an exhaustive examination of the meaning of heroism. Again, Milton presents the Fall (and its aftermath) in terms of three successive paradigms of tragedy, arranged according to an ascending scale of worth—Satanic revenge tragedy, Aristotelian tragedy, Christian tragedy.

The lyric genres are present in Milton's epic through another strategy of inclusion. Lyrics of various kinds are embedded in the narrative, set off by specific generic conventions, signals of commencement and closure, and integrity of structure, tone, and subject matter. Embedded lyrics are common in epics early to late, chiefly hymns of various kinds, prayers, laments, love lyrics, and encomia. In certain epics the dominance of a single lyric genre serves important thematic functions: for example, the frequent laments and funeral dirges in the *Iliad* intensify the tragic tone; the continual love-complaints voiced by all the characters contribute to the pervasive irony of the *Orlando Furioso*; and the entire absence of lyrics in Dante's *Inferno* (contrasting sharply with the continuous hymnody in the other regions) comments on the nature of the damned consciousness.

Milton's epic employs a much more complete spectrum of lyrics, for a larger array of purposes, and in a more complex and conscious way than does any previous epic. The Bard voices numerous apostrophes, hymnic proems, blasons, and an epithalamion. Satan and the fallen angels often fall into laments but cannot sustain them long, and they can only pervert lyrics of praise. The angels celebrate all divine activities with hymnic praises, but they produce their most elaborate and most exalted hymns when divine creativity and divine love are manifested. And pre- and post-lapsarian man and woman exhibit their psychological and spiritual states through a great variety of hymns, odes, love songs, laments, complaints, encomia, and more. In *Paradise Lost* characters reveal their na-

21

tures and the values they espouse through the lyrics they devise.

Rhetorical and dialogic genres are also embedded in *Paradise Lost*, and again epic tradition affords precedent for that practice. Quintilian identified many kinds of speeches and all three styles of oratory in Homer; also, the Homeric councils of war gave rise to a plethora of scenes in later epics in which opposing counselors argue their cases in the forms of deliberative rhetoric.[56] Milton's epic is remarkable, however, for the inclusion of all the rhetorical genres (judicial, deliberative, demonstrative), several kinds of dialogue (Platonic, Boethian, biblical), and also formal debate, engaging us in careful discriminations concerning the uses and the perversions of speech and language.

For Milton this is not simply a matter of validating dialectic and discrediting rhetoric, as some have suggested.[57] It is true that Satan and his followers prove to be brilliant deliberative rhetoricians in the Council in Hell and in the temptation of Eve. It is also true that dialogue is the principal kind of discourse in Milton's heaven and in unfallen Eden, a circumstance that accords with the Platonic Socrates' view of dialectic as the best means of searching for truth and making it live in the mind. However, the Miltonic dialogues are of several kinds, most of them bearing little formal resemblance to Socratic dialectic. Also, there is formal rhetoric in heaven, notably the Father's judicial oration and apologia for his justice in sentencing humankind, and his demonstrative praise of the Son and of Abdiel.

Rather than posing a simple dichotomy of rhetoric and dialogue, Milton invites an assessment of many kinds of formal and informal speech and the values traditionally associated with them. For the various rhetorical genres, one standard is the moral goodness demanded by Cicero and Quintilian, who called for rhetor-statesmen with profound knowledge of and lived experience of moral goodness.[58] Another standard is the truth and justice held forth by the Platonic Socrates in his trenchant criticism of sophistic rhetoric, and in his description of a phil-

22

THE USES OF LITERARY FORMS

osophical rhetoric grounded upon true knowledge and always striving for justice.[59] In *Paradise Lost* the Socratic standard for dialogue presupposes shared assumptions and common purposes in seeking and understanding the truth.

Paradise Lost is, then, an encyclopedia of literary forms which also affords a probing critique of the values those forms traditionally body forth. Though that critique is grounded upon Renaissance concepts of generic decorum and hierarchy, the Miltonic version of the generic hierarchy (like the Miltonic version of the hierarchy of being) is flexible, complex, and open to the processes of development and transformation. Most literary forms are present in *Paradise Lost* in several versions—celestial and infernal, pre- and post-lapsarian, Christian and pagan—inviting discriminations that are at once literary and moral.

Some kinds are closely associated with the Satanic order and the diabolic consciousness—classical epic, deliberative rhetoric, soliloquy, Petrarchan sonneteering. However, this association is not exclusive. All these kinds have also their nobler versions: Christ is an Achillean hero in the Battle in Heaven; Christ's speeches in the Dialogue in Heaven have a persuasive dimension; Abdiel soliloquizes just before engaging Satan in battle; unfallen Eve composes a magnificent love sonnet to Adam. But some literary kinds and their values are not available to Satan—true dialogue, hymnic praise, the *otium* of pastoral—and that literary deprivation testifies to the impoverishment of the damned consciousness. By contrast, Milton suggests the plenitude and abundant life of the highest orders of being, the angels and most especially God, through the mixture and multiplicity of the genres and modes associated with them. And he indicates humankind's potential for growth and development both in the prelapsarian and the postlapsarian states as Adam and Eve take on the languages and the life styles pertaining to one after another of the literary genres and modes.

The mixture and multiplicity of literary forms in Milton's

23

epic are an index of its comprehensiveness and vitality. They also provide an important key to its interpretation. No poet has exploited such forms more extensively and more deliberately than Milton, as cultural signposts common to author and reader. This study is an attempt to follow those signposts.

TWO

Inspiration and Literary Art:
The Prophet-Poets of *Paradise Lost*

THE FACT that Milton in *Paradise Lost* gives constant attention to the choice of literary forms and the uses of literary art may seem incongruous with the fact that he also presents himself in that poem as a prophet-poet, an inspired bard. There is, however, no contradiction. Indeed, the relationship between conscious art and divine inspiration is a major theme of the Bard's personal proems to Books One, Three, Seven, and Nine, and the issue is also explored through the roles he creates for the subordinate narrators, the angels Raphael and Michael. All three narrators are poet-prophets who must seek out appropriate literary forms to embody the truths they receive in various ways from the divine source of truth.

Milton's assumptions about the prophetic role accord generally with those of the seventeenth-century Cambridge Platonist John Smith, for whom the term encompasses all forms of divine illumination of the mind. Smith's lucid summary of Hebrew tradition identified many kinds of prophets: those of the highest rank who (like Moses) were illuminated by direct impression upon their intellect; those several varieties of "true" prophets who received their revelation through the imagination—in visions or the lower mode of dreams; and those who (like David the Psalmist and other biblical poets) spoke "by the Holy Spirit," as enlightened but not directly inspired.[1] Prophets of all kinds were alike, however, in having to devise appropriate conceptual and stylistic forms for the revelations they received in their several ways from God:

> God made not use of Idiots or Fools to reveal his Will by, but such whose Intellectuals were entire and perfect;

25

and . . . he imprinted such a clear copy of his Truth upon them, as that it became their own Sense, being digested fully into their Understandings; so as they were able to deliver and represent it to others as truly as any can paint forth his own Thoughts. . . .

Besides, we find the Prophets speaking every one of them in his owne Dialect; and such a Varietie of Style and Phraseologie appears in their Writings, as may argue them to have spoken according to their own proper *Genius*. . . . *The things themselves they saw in Prophesie, but they themselves did explain and interpret them in that Dialect which was most familiar to them.*[2]

Milton presents his three narrators as different kinds of prophet-poets, standing in different relationships to divine revelation and speaking to quite different audiences. He does not, as is sometimes supposed, place his Bard on a par with the biblical prophets[3] or with his own prophet-angels, though all share the problem of finding appropriate literary forms to present divine truth. Rather, he uses the differences as well as the similarities among his three narrators to explore and to dramatize the process, the problems, and the purposes of creating divine poetry.

In his first three proems the Miltonic Bard implores, but does not claim, assured and continuous experience of the Muse's inspiration and of divine illumination; he makes that claim only in the fourth proem. The proems incorporate many literary forms, in part to highlight generic strategies prominent in the portions of the poem they introduce, but also as a means of self-discovery. They present the Bard engaging with his sacred subject by using the terms and the conventions of traditional literary genres and modes. For the Miltonic Bard, literary forms are at once a means of apprehending his subject and his prophetic role, and also of fulfilling that role by accommodating subject to audience, so as to educate that audience in knowing what is true and choosing what is good.

The functions of accommodation and education are also explored through the subordinate narrators Milton creates, Raphael and Michael. They are prophet-poets of a higher order than the Miltonic Bard, in that they know themselves to be mediators of revelation, sent directly by God to humankind. Divine illumination therefore poses no problem for them. Accommodation, however, does. As John Smith notes, prophets had the difficult task of conveying spiritual things in sensible terms to vulgar audiences: "Hence is that Axiome so frequent among the Jewish Doctors . . . Great is the power of the *Prophets*, who while they looked down upon these Sensible and Conspicable things, were able to furnish out the notion of Intelligible and Inconspicable Beings thereby to the rude Senses of Illiterate people."[4]

Both Raphael and Michael have to teach and to mediate divine truth to a sometimes not-so-fit audience, Adam and Eve, and both of them do so by literary accommodation, "inventing" precisely those literary genres that are best suited to their own capacities, to the height and variety of the several subjects they treat, and to the special needs and conditions of the audience. Though prophets, they are also Renaissance poets who believe that decorum is the grand masterpiece to observe. They combine both roles as they invent (so to speak) the prototypes of various literary kinds and set them forth in their pristine, ideal forms to teach, delight, and move Adam and Eve in the ways commonly attributed to those kinds. The literary genres, modes, strategies, and conventions in the Bard's proems and in the angelic narratives provide an important guide to the way in which literary forms function throughout the poem to mediate sacred truth to the Bard's own imagination and that of his readers.

THE MILTONIC BARD'S PROEMS

The four proems—to Books One, Three, Seven, and Nine—are personal, self-enclosed lyrics in which the Miltonic Bard analyzes poetic prophecy and poetic creation, and defines his own role as poet-prophet.[5] He also explores the difficulties a divine subject poses for a fallen poet addressing a fallen audience, and seeks solutions to those difficulties both in divine illumination and in literary art.

The Bard's first proem (1.1-26) is an epic proposition and invocation, in the form of an invocatory hymn to the Heavenly Muse and the Spirit. In it he places his poem in the epic tradition and engages himself to work out against that reference point the nature and scope of his subject and the sources of his poetic power. By verbal allusion to many epic poems—the *Iliad*, the *Odyssey*, the *Aeneid*, the *Divine Weeks and Works*—he indicates that the universal and true story of humankind must necessarily contain, subsume, and endeavor to surpass the greatest poems we know.

The proposition echoes that of the *Iliad*, indicating that the tragic subject of each is a human fault and its terrible consequences: "the anger of Peleus' son Achilleus / and its devastation, which put pains thousandfold upon the Achaians";[6] "Man's First Disobedience," which "Brought Death into the World, and all our woe." However, the allusion identifies the Fall as a tragedy more enduring and universal than the anger of Achilles, being the cause of "*all* our woe." The reference to "Man" in the Bard's epic proposition alludes to the openings of the *Odyssey* and the *Aeneid*—"Tell me, Muse, of the man of many ways"; "Arms and the man I sing"—thereby evoking medieval and Renaissance interpretations of Aeneas and Odysseus as figures of everyman encountering the trials of human life.[7] We are, however, to recognize that Adam as father of humankind is everyman in very truth and not in figure.

Moreover, the turn in Milton's epic proposition from death and woe to restoration of lost paradise—"*till* one greater Man / Restore us, and regain the blissful Seat"—recalls Virgil's double subject: Aeneas exiled from Troy and buffeted by many trials, "*till* he should build a city . . . whence came the Latin race, the lords of Alba, and the walls of lofty Rome."[8] But whereas the Virgilian city is founded by the hero at the end of the poem, the complete restoration of the Miltonic paradise must await the action of a greater Man at the end of time. The contrast reinforces the implications of the title: *Paradise Lost* has a tragedy at its center and undertakes a complex fusion of the heroic and tragic modes.

Other allusions point to other dimensions of the Bard's subject. By referring to that subject in Ariosto's very words— "Cosa non detta in prosa mai ne in rima";[9] "Things unattempted yet in Prose or Rhyme"—the Bard points to the romance elements of his poem, which treats of greater marvels than those in Ariosto or Tasso or Spenser. Also, by the somewhat surprising reference to Moses as "That *Shepherd*, who first *taught* the chosen Seed, / In the Beginning how the Heav'ns and Earth / Rose out of *Chaos*,"[10] the Bard affirms the relevance of the pastoral and didactic modes, and of hexaemeral epics such as Tasso's *Il Mondo Creato* and Du Bartas' *Semaine*. More important, by quoting the opening words of Genesis— "In the Beginning"—he suggests that *Paradise Lost* is a reprise of that book and indeed of the entire Bible: whereas Moses the shepherd-poet first taught this subject, the Miltonic Bard does so now. And his reference to a "great Argument" intended to "justify the ways of God to men" focuses attention upon the importance of rhetoric to the poem's overall design and to many of its episodes.

Formally, the entire proem is an invocatory hymn. The Bard's epic proposition, like Homer's, is formally part of the invocation—"Of Man's First Disobedience . . . / Sing Heav'nly Muse"—suggesting that the poem is the Muse's song and not his own. But he also offers the Virgilian formula, according to which the song is his and the Muse merely an assistant: "I thence / Invoke thy aid to my advent'rous Song." By this fusion the Bard not only proclaims himself heir to both Homer and Virgil as R. W. Condee suggests,[11] but also underscores the paradox of his role as prophet-poet. In his invocatory hymn the Bard recognizes and apostrophizes the two sources of his poetic power—the Heavenly Muse as source of inspiration for sacred art, and the Spirit of God as agent of divine illumination and creativity. The Muse is a figure for the artistic inspiration traditionally seen as requisite for the creation of great poems on lofty themes: to achieve his Christian epic the Miltonic Bard recognizes his need for poetic inspiration from a Heavenly Muse who embodies the principles of sacred art. The Spirit of God is the source of illumination, providing spiritual understanding of divine truth which alone can enable the Bard to conceive his great argument.

By the epithet "Heav'nly" the Bard identifies his muse with Urania, Muse of Astonomy, baptized by Du Bartas a century earlier as Muse of Christian poetry, and continually invoked thereafter (in place of Clio or Calliope) by poets undertaking religious subjects.[12] But he explicitly dissociates her from Du Bartas' "heedful Muse"—restricted to the "Middle Region" of God's created universe lest she sin by presumption[13]—when he urges her "with no middle flight . . . to soar / Above th'*Aonian* Mount." Her true meaning is suggested by her habitations and her functions. The Bard calls her forth not from Helicon and Aganippe but from biblical mountains and streams: Mount Oreb and its spur, Mount Sinai where she inspired the hexaemeral shepherd-poet Moses; Mount Sion, the location of the Temple with its sacred songs and psalmody; and Siloa's Brook, associated by the Bard with the "Oracle of God." She is, then, the source of inspiration for biblical poetry, the Muse of a biblical poetics. By invoking her the Bard places himself in the tradition of Moses, the Psalmist, and the prophet-interpreters of the divine oracles, as one treating the same sacred and true subjects and therefore needing artistic inspiration from the same Muse.

But for the Miltonic Bard the Muse's assistance is not enough. He also invokes the Spirit of God to illumine his darkness and instruct him with the Spirit's own knowledge so that as prophet-poet he may comprehend his sacred subject. More fundamentally, he addresses the Spirit as the great creating female and male force that brooded upon and impregnated the primordial chaos, ordering it and causing it to bring forth living forms.[14] Since he is himself fallen he cannot rise to the height of his "great Argument" unless the Spirit will reorder his chaos and raise his lowness, creating in him a new nature able to produce the universe of his poem.

The references in the proem to all *our* woe and the greater man who will redeem *us* incorporate the Miltonic Bard and his audience within the epic subject. Also, the Bard himself is here identified as one model of the Christian heroism the poem explores, in that he willingly embraces the tension and paradox created by his prodigious endeavor to soar above the Aeonian mount despite his admitted personal insufficiency and entire dependence upon divine aid. In his first proem the fallen poet heroically takes on the overwhelming task of writing for a fallen audience the true epic story of our fallen world.

The proem to Book Three, "Hail holy Light" (1-55) is the Bard's own literary Hymn to Light as primary manifestation of God and emblem of divine illumination. Conjoining high hymnic praise and reflective passages in several modes, this proem prepares us for the mixed genres of heaven and the generic progressions of Eden. Also, it again presents the poet's own experience as part of the universal story he tells. As a Christian version of the third kind of hymn in Scaliger's classification (those celebrating the *numen* of a god), it exhibits the tripartite structure common in the longer hexameter hymns of "Homer," Callimachus, and Scaliger: exordium, narrative myth, peroration.[15] And it contains conceptual and verbal parallels to several Renaissance exemplars, especially Spenser's *Fowre Hymnes*.[16]

The exordium of a hymn characteristically invokes the god in terms of several epithets indicating his attributes. This exordium apostrophizes light in biblical and Neoplatonic terms, according to its several ontological states: as first created of all things ("offspring of Heav'n first-born"); as an aspect of God's own nature ("since God is Light"); and as an eternal emanation from and manifestation of him ("And never but in unapproached Light / Dwelt from Eternity").[17] Such language prepares us for the multivalent light that emanates from God's throne and suffuses Milton's heaven.

The second hymnic element, the narrative myth of the god's

actions, is here replaced by a personal myth of the Bard's own "heroic" poetic journey, "taught by the heav'nly Muse to venture down / The dark descent, and up to reascend, / Though hard and rare."[18] In developing that myth the Bard invites but quickly dismisses parallels with Satan and Orpheus. Like Satan he has escaped the "*Stygian* Pool" and made his way through the darkness of hell and Chaos, but unlike Satan he has returned "safe" to the regions of light. Like Orpheus he has sung of "*Chaos* and *Eternal Night*" though with "other notes than to th' *Orphean* Lyre," for he has not sought love or esoteric knowledge in the dark places: instead of an Orphic "Hymn to Night" he offers his "Hymn to Light."[19] He resembles instead the pilgrim-poet Dante, who also undertook his journey under the guidance of a heavenly lady-muse, who also made his way from "the lowest pit of the universe" to the divine source of light, and who also apostrophized light as the manifestation of God.[20]

Then the Bard recasts his voyage as a psychological journey, exploring a succession of emotional states through the topoi of several literary modes. A brief, pathetic complaint that the light of God "Revisit'st not these eyes" gives way to a hauntingly evocative pastoral description of the sites, classical and biblical, of poetic and prophetic inspiration: Parnassus, "where the Muses haunt / Clear Spring, or shady Grove, or Sunny Hill"; and Sion with its "flow'ry Brooks" that "warbling flow." These pastoral *loci amoeni* also recall Virgil's Elysian Fields and Dante's Limbo, as the poet imagines himself frequenting such places in company with the great blind bards and prophets of Greece—"Blind *Thamyris* and blind *Mæonides*, / And *Tiresias* and *Phineus* Prophets old." Changing his notes to pathos, the Bard then voices a poignant pastoral lament for his own paradise lost—the light and beauty of the natural world, and the access to wisdom and human companionship that nature offers. The pastoral topoi anticipate the Edenic pastoral, and suggest that the Bard's tragic loss replicates, foreshadows, and derives from that of his protagonists, Adam and Eve:

Thus with the Year
Seasons return, but not to me returns
Day, or the sweet approach of Ev'n or Morn,
Or sight of vernal bloom, or Summer's Rose,
Or flocks, or herds, or human face divine;
But cloud instead, and ever-during dark
Surrounds me, from the cheerful ways of men
Cut off, and for the Book of knowledge fair
Presented with a Universal blanc
Of Nature's works to me expung'd and ras'd,
And wisdom at one entrance quite shut out.
(3.41-50)

The hymn's peroration implores the presence of the Celestial Light, the divine illumination which will be especially requisite for the Bard's portrayal in Books Three to Eight of unfallen Eden, heaven, and the Godhead—"things invisible to mortal sight." His stance is petitionary here: he seems confident of receiving the needed illumination, but he does not claim the extraordinary visions of a John of Patmos. Rather, he hopes for the mediated poetic vision of Dante who, in his dream, imagined himself blinded at first by the dazzling light of God but then accorded stronger vision; and for the clear understanding of Moses, who through the cloud and mist of Sinai encountered the light of God's Word.[21]

The Proem to Book Seven (1-39) is a complex invocatory hymn to the Heavenly Muse, welding together elements from epic invocation, Horatian ode, and Psalmic lament-prayer, and drawing upon Ovid and biblical wisdom literature to develop a personal myth of the poet's perilous situation.

Most obviously, as an epic invocation introducing the second half of Milton's epic, it recalls the brief invocation to Erato almost at the beginning of Virgil's Book Seven (37-44), proposing a rising action and a greater theme: "I will tell of grim wars, will tell of battle array, and princes in their valour rushing upon death . . . Greater is the story that opens before me; greater is the task I essay."[22] By contrast, the Miltonic

Bard proposes at this juncture a safer, more familiar, earth-bound subject, and his constantly reiterated terms—descend, fall, fallen—point not only to the catastrophe of his plot but also to the structure of his epic as a falling action, a tragedy.

In formal terms the proem is also a species of Horatian ode, specifically, a reprise and revision of the longest and most Pindaric of Horace's odes, the fourth of the Third Book. The Bard's opening words, "Descend from Heav'n *Urania*," echo Horace's invocation, "*Descende caelo . . . Calliope*.²³ The two odes also contain the same structural elements—prayer and praise to the muses and the gods, myths from the heroic past, personal references—and they explore the same themes: the poet's calling, the muse as embodiment of wisdom, light, and reason, the muse as guardian of the poet against the forces of chaos and disorder. Horace proclaims himself Calliope's darling, miraculously protected from several near-catastrophes in childhood, and ready to dare future exploits with full confidence in her continuing protection.²⁴ The Miltonic Bard credits his muse Urania with even more wonderful protections: "Up led by thee / Into the Heav'n of Heav'ns I have presum'd, / An Earthly Guest, and drawn Empyreal Air, / Thy temp'ring." But he is anxious about the imminent dangers of his "descent" to earth, and alarmed about the future—"fall'n on evil days, / . . . In darkness, and with dangers compast round."

Horace's ode recounts a public and political myth of Jove defeating the Titans whereas the Bard applies to himself two ancient myths of the fate of poets. He presents himself as a successful Bellerophon, favored by God in his Pegasean ascent to the heavens, but yet in danger of Bellerophon's ultimate fate as he returns to a fallen world, blinded and all too susceptible to erroneous wandering.²⁵ Also, like Orpheus he now sings among contemporary Bacchic revelers (the licentious Restoration court) who might well turn upon and destroy him.²⁶ But he takes comfort from his relation to a different Muse: while Horace's mythic Calliope could not save her poet-son Orpheus, Milton's Urania is both real and powerful. He therefore concludes with a fervent prayer that she find for his poem "fit audience . . . though few" and give him her protection: "So fail not thou, who thee implores: / For thou art Heavn'ly, shee an empty dream."

The Bard's hope of protection finds further basis in the other lyric genre this proem incorporates, the biblical psalm of lament and prayer. In passage after passage, the Psalmist calls for or rejoices in God's protection as he is beleaguered by darkness, dangers, and many enemies: "Hide me under the shadow of thy wings / From the wicked that oppress me, from my deadly enemies, who compass me about"; "For the mouth of the wicked and the mouth of the deceitful are opened against me: they have spoken against me with a lying tongue"; "thou hast visited me in the night."[27] Echoing such verses, the Bard claims similar experiences: he too is "fall'n on evil days, / On evil days though fall'n, and evil tongues; / In darkness, and with dangers compast round, / And solitude; yet not alone, while thou / Visit'st my slumbers Nightly." After associating himself with the chief classical archetypes for the poet and their sad fates, the Bard at length identifies himself with the better biblical paradigm, the historical David, whom God sustained in all adversity.

In this ode-psalm, the Bard also defines his Muse with greater precision by devising a true myth of her origin, building upon the allegory of Wisdom in Proverbs 8:22-31:

22. The Lord possessed me in the beginning of his way, before his works of old.
23. I was set up from everlasting, from the beginning, or ever the earth was.
. . . .
27. When he prepared the heavens, I was there: when he set a compass upon the face of the depth:
. . . .
30. Then was I by him, as one brought up with him: and I was daily his delight, rejoicing always before him.

35

Calling upon "the meaning not the name" of his Muse Urania, the Bard makes her the sister of Eternal Wisdom, ever conversing and playing with her "in presence of th' Almighty Father, pleas'd / With thy Celestial Song." As "daughter" of God and sister of Eternal Wisdom, the Muse is the principle of divine art, celestial song—and thereby of sacred poetry on earth. She has visited the Bard's nightly slumbers and he implores her continued aid: "still govern thou my Song."

The Bard's fourth proem (9.1-47) is, formally, a verse epistle on the poetics of the Christian epic, which makes explicit Milton's basic assumptions about true heroism, about the appropriateness of tragic subjects in epic, and about the relation of this poem to classical epic and to romance. Milton's critical statement recalls comparable prefaces in prose or verse prefixed to many Christian epics, from Juvencus' *Evangeliorum* in the fourth century to Cowley's *Davideis* in the seventeenth.[28] Its rather unusual placement here strengthens the connection developed throughout the four proems between the poet's creative act and the poem's unfolding action.

For one thing, Milton evidently wished to defend the appropriateness of a tragic argument in epic poems just before presenting his own tragic catastrophe, the Fall. His position could claim support from Aristotle's discussion of epic according to the norms of tragedy; from Italian neoclassicist theory asserting the close relation of epic and tragedy in subject matter, plot disposition, and emotional effect; and from contemporary poems fusing the two genres—Davenant's *Gondibert* (with its influential Preface) and Agrippa d'Aubigné's *Les Tragiques*.[29]

Insisting that his tragic argument is "not less but more Heroic" than those of the great classical epics, Milton focuses attention on various epic heroes as they propel tragic catastrophes or give voice to the tragedy of human existence. He points to Achilles' pursuit of Hector around the walls of Troy as the episode in which Achilles and Hector lock themselves into the fatal choices and courses which bring about their own destruction and that of Troy.[30] And though the overall argument of the *Aeneid* is not tragic, the Bard singles out a tragic dimension of it, Turnus' furious wrath for the loss of his bride, causing devastating wars between Latins and Trojans and resulting in Turnus' death.[31] He alludes as well to the extended tragic narratives within the *Odyssey* and the *Aeneid*, in which the heroes themselves recount to their hosts, Alkinoös and Dido, their manifold and persistant sufferings and calamities.[32] Like those heroes, the Miltonic Bard here formally accepts the "sad task" of narrating a more terrible fall than that of Troy, a more awesome divine wrath than that of Neptune or Juno, and sufferings more pervasive and more enduring than those of the Argives or the Trojans—woes that he necessarily shares since they extend to all mankind.

In this proem also, Milton assesses various faulty and false critical positions regarding heroism and the heroic poem just before his epic protagonists confront the complex arguments and choices upon which their own and all mankind's future depends. But unlike Adam and Eve's impulsive choices, the Bard's are judicious, reasoned, well considered, "Since first this Subject for Heroic Song / Pleas'd me long choosing, and beginning late." His assured tone here arises in part from his right choices regarding heroic subject and literary mode. His change of mode from pastoral to tragic is decorous for the new matter of distrust, revolt, disobedience, wrath, and woe. And in opposing conventional neoclassical dicta identifying war as the necessary heroic subject, and celebrating instead "the better fortitude / Of Patience and Heroic Martyrdom," he allies himself (as his hero Adam will at last learn to do) with the heroic standard defined by the Son of God.[33] Judging by that standard, he disparages the romance matter and topoi by which some Renaissance critics defined the modern heroic poem,[34] and claims that title instead for his higher argument. His proposition is that in the fallen world human heroism must perforce be exhibited under the tragic conditions of existence caused by the Fall. On that understanding, the Fall of Man and its tragic aftermath is at once the quintessential tragic subject and the quintessential heroic subject available to the modern Christian poet.

The Bard gains confidence also from the confirmation of his role as prophet-poet. The Muse's aid remains indispensable, but he need not invoke her here for she now comes "unimplor'd," and "dictates to me slumb'ring, or inspires / Easy my unpremeditated Verse." This does not mean that the Bard is a secretary transcribing divine dictation: that is not the way of prophecy according to John Smith, nor does it square with the Bard's presentation of himself in this very proem as a poet-critic making complex literary judgments and decisions about his art. Rather, while the choice and the development of the argument are his, the argument itself is a given of sacred history, whose true interpretation must be revealed to him (as to every person of faith according to Milton's theology) by divine illumination.[35] He evidently now believes that the requisite divine illumination informs his poetic dreams. His claim to prophecy, we should note, is here limited to the lower prophetic mode of dreams—the same dreams through which the Muse of sacred poetry works on his imagination. Assured now of her continued presence, he can hope to overcome the tragic conditions of the fallen world which might otherwise overwhelm his poetic flights: his own advanced age, England's cold climate, the degeneracy of the times. And he can hope to obtain from that celestial patroness of sacred poetry a style "answerable" to his argument precisely because he has chosen the proper tragic subject for heroic song, and because he has thought rigorously and reasonably about the literary forms that can best embody it.

Yet for all that, the language and imagery of these proems resist full explication as does the topic they treat, the springs of Milton's poetic creativity. The Miltonic Bard invites us to recognize that such a gift is finally mysterious, and, in some meaning of the term, divine.

Like the Miltonic Bard, the two subordinate narrators of *Paradise Lost* are also imagined as prophets and poets. They share with all intelligent creatures a need for divine illumination in order to understand truly the things of God, but they receive this illumination by distinct and characteristic means: Raphael (usually) by direct enlightenment of his understanding, Michael by visions.[36] As prophets, they are charged to accommodate divine truths to others and, like the Miltonic Bard, they do so through literary art, inventing ideal forms of several literary genres so as to educate Adam and Eve, unfallen and fallen, in the values pertaining to those kinds. The Bard's audience, with its awareness of literary tradition, is expected to learn from the angelic narratives in more complex ways—by comparing the ideal angelic prototypes to their flawed literary progeny. What Harold Bloom calls "transumption" in Milton—the claim that *Paradise Lost* is somehow prior to its sources[37]—pertains in the strict sense to the portrayal of the angels as primordial poets. Yet for all that, Milton presents those angelic poems, and his own, by means of familiar genres and texts in the literary tradition.

RAPHAEL'S PROTOTYPICAL GENRES

Raphael is a prophet in John Smith's most general and most exalted sense: he knows things divine and human, not by vision or dream but by the direct and continuous illumination of his understanding.[38] Dispatching him to his prophetic mission, God gave him general directives concerning his manner, tone, and basic purpose: to advise Adam about his own happiness and the threat to it from Satan. But God permitted the angel artistic license in devising appropriate forms of discourse: "Go therefore, half this day as friend with friend / Converse with *Adam*, in what Bow'r or shade / Thou find'st him . . . / and such discourse bring on, / As may advise him of his happy state, / Happiness in his power left free to will, / . . . tell him withal / His danger, and from whom" (5.229-39). As a skillful teacher will, Raphael allows Adam's questions and initiatives to determine the particular subjects discussed, and as a true poet must, he finds for those subjects fitting literary forms.

THE
UNIVERSITY OF WINNIPEG
PORTAGE & BALMORAL
WINNIPEG, MAN.   R3B 2E9
CANADA
DISCARDED

Adam accords Raphael the title "Divine / Historian" (8.6-7), evidently perceiving that he treats chiefly of past events and the nature of things. Though illumined by God, the angel usually draws upon his own firsthand experience and observation, supplemented, we may suppose, by the reports of others and by divine revelation for some aspects of the war in heaven and the Creation. Raphael is usually confident, therefore, that his knowledge is adequate to his chosen subjects, though worried at times about how to accommodate them to his intelligent but inexperienced audience. As we shall see, he invents prototypes in miniature of several epic kinds and of scientific dialogue, kinds that are linked to their progeny by characteristic themes, motifs, and topoi though not, of course, by close structural similarities.

Responding to Adam's hospitable offer of food and queries about the comparison of earthly and heavenly food, Raphael devises his first literary work, a brief philosophical poem on ontology, the nature of things (5.404-33, 469-505). Its concepts derive from Plato's *Timaeus*, Lucretius, Lipsius, Fludd, and others,[39] but the topoi and motifs associate the work most closely with Lucretius' *De Rerum Natura*, often classified as epic by reason of its elevated subject and hexameter verse form.[40] Lucretius' poem is a passionate and eloquent argument for the philosophy of Epicurus, grounded upon a version of Democritean atomism. As its proposition indicates, the *De Rerum Natura* explains the nature of the universe, the origins of all life and change, and the human condition by the constant, fortuitous collision of atoms which, in varying degrees of refinement, make up the substratum of all being, including the gods and the soul.[41] Lucretius' purpose is to free his addressee, Memnius, from superstition about the gods and from fear of death, so that he will base his choices in life upon a true and profound understanding of man's place in nature's eternal processes of change and continuity.[42]

Raphael's miniature *De Rerum Natura* also emphasizes the heavenly source of all life, the common material substratum of all being, and the continuous processes of change in the universe. And Raphael also intends to lead his addressee to make sound choices in life, based on a true apprehension of his place in nature. But Raphael's prototypical philosophical epic is founded on teleological rather than atomistic principles, recognizing God as source and end of all the natural processes, and emphasizing human choice rather than the fortuitous collision of atoms as a principal determinant of the direction of change:

> O *Adam*, one Almighty is, from whom
> All things proceed, and up to him return,
> If not deprav'd from good, created all
> Such to perfection, one first matter all,
> Indu'd with various forms, various degrees
> Of substance, and in things that live, of life;
> But more refin'd, more spiritous, and pure,
> As nearer to him plac't or nearer tending
> Each in thir several active Spheres assign'd,
> Till body up to spirit work, in bounds
> Proportion'd to each kind.
> (5.469-79)

Raphael's poem, like that of Lucretius, couches philosophical and scientific precepts in vibrant imagery and relates them directly to the experience and observation of the addressee. Both, for example, use a plant topos to illustrate the composition of matter—Raphael pointing to the root, stem, and blossom as evidence that all things are constituted of "one first matter," which is capable of various degrees of refinement as it nourishes progressively higher forms of life.[43] The point of this is not direct borrowing, since the plant topos had become a commonplace in philosophical-scientific discourse. Rather, we are meant to see that Raphael "invents" this topos (brilliantly suited to Adam in his garden), that he uses it to better purpose than later philosopher-poets will, and that his own act of eating the Edenic fruit exemplifies this principle graphically.[44] We are to recognize that Raphael's prototypical phil-

41

osophical epic far surpasses that of Lucretius in teaching human beings their true place in the nature of things.

Raphael next devises the genre of the classical epic, in response to Adam's request for a "full relation" of the story about the disobedient angels (5.556). In doing so he confronts a difficult problem of literary accommodation. The subject is "High matter" involving "th' invisible exploits / Of warring Spirits" while the audience is limited to "human sense." The narrator himself may have difficulty controlling his emotions: "how shall I relate / . . . without remorse / The ruin of so many glorious once." And the very relation of these "secrets of another World" may be unlawful. That last problem is met by a divine dispensation allowing the revelation for Adam's good, and Raphael proposes to deal with the limitations of his audience "by lik'ning spiritual to corporal forms"— leaving open the question of whether such corporal forms are in fact Platonic shadows of spiritual reality or not (5.563-76).

Acting upon this decision, Raphael presents the war in heaven as a miniature *Iliad*, based upon a true history yet with large scope for invention; the choice was probably dictated by the theory that Homer provided the original *paideia* for Western man.[45] Raphael's epic, like Homer's, begins with a ceremony (the elevation of the Son) at which an Achillean hero feels his honor affronted, and withdraws his forces to his own region. The warfare in heaven is chiefly Homeric, complete with single combats, epic boasts, mockery of foes, flytings, chariot clashes, legions attacking legions with spears and shields. But the hill-hurlings are suggestive of Hesiod's *Theogony*, and the diabolical cannon and gunpowder are from later epics such as Valvasone's *Angeleida* and the *Faerie Queene*[46]—identifying this celestial battle as the source of the epic warfare topos in literature, wherever it is used. This strategy directs the Bard's audience to compare later epics with Raphael's original—recognizing, for example, that Satan is a debased Achilles,[47] and that God's omnipotence is out of all comparison with the power of Hesiod's Zeus. But Adam learns from Raphael's epic directly: whereas Homer's *Iliad* held forth the ideals of battle prowess and individual glory, Raphael creates, as it were, the prototype of that epic, designed to lead Adam and Eve to a sounder view of heroism, power, and glory.

As an epic narrator who was also a participant in the struggle, Raphael's tone is in the main heroic, with occasional mock-heroic overtones as he (infrequently) associates himself with the perspective of the omnipotent God who holds his foes in derision. Raphael accords certain of his companions in arms—Gabriel, Michael, and especially Abdiel—their moments of *aristeia* during the first day's fighting, which begins with a blow from Abdiel that brings Satan to his knees, and ends with Michael shearing Satan's side with his sword. But unlike the Homeric Bard, Raphael declines to "eternize" all those who did wondrous acts of war. The rebels deserve to remain in oblivion for there is nothing praiseworthy in "strength from Truth divided and from Just"; and the elect angels, "contented with thir fame in Heav'n / Seek not the praise of men" (6.373-83).

In Raphael's epic, the angelic warriors are severely tested during the celestial battle. Though sent forth by God as an invincible army charged to cast the rebels from heaven, they find they cannot fulfill the charge, they are subjected to ridicule and humiliation, and their own warfare contributes to the near-ruin of heaven.[48] Yet, though they do not win decisive victories through martial prowess, their loyalty, obedience, courage, and faith are tested in battle and found heroic. Therefore, they are all accorded true honor by the Son of God: "Faithful hath been your Warfare, and of God / Accepted, fearless in his righteous Cause, / And as ye have receiv'd, so have ye done / Invincibly" (6.803-806). In its essence, then, though not in its martial manifestation, their heroism is a useful model for Adam and Eve.

The primary emphasis in Raphael's epic falls upon two heroes whose deeds flank and thereby provide a touchstone for the military action. The first is Abdiel, the moral hero who alone defended the right in the camp of the enemy, and who attempted by heroic argument to turn his fellows from their evil course. The other is the Son, the agent of God's omnipotence, who conquered the entire Satanic army in single combat even as he scorned them for measuring worth by physical strength (6.818-22), and who prefaced that combat with a more excellent display of power, the restoration of the heavenly landscape. By its conception and design Raphael's prototypical epic (like Milton's own) undertakes to display to its audience—Adam and Eve—the dangerous lure of evil, the deceptive rhetoric of temptation, the danger of power severed from right, the chaos attendant upon sin, and the nature of true moral heroism and true epic glory.

Adam's next query concerns the origin of heaven and earth, and it elicits additional "revealed" knowledge—the creation story from Genesis. Adam explains that his question is motivated by a desire to praise God's works, not invade his secrets, but the terms show him making a precarious beginning in theological speculation: "what cause / Mov'd the Creator in his holy Rest / Through all Eternity so late to build / In *Chaos*" (7.90-93). Besides the implication of divine mutability and laziness in these words, questions about God's activity before the Creation had long been taken as a flagrant example of presumptuous inquiry into God's hidden mysteries.[49] The genre Raphael chooses for his response is nicely calculated to lead Adam away from such fruitless and dangerous inquiries, by underscoring the necessarily radical accommodation of all knowledge of God to human understanding. Eschewing simple biblical paraphrase, he creates a brief hexaemeral epic which the Bard's readers should identify as a prototype of Tasso's *Il Mondo Creato* and especially of Du Bartas' *La Semaine ou Creation du Monde*, termed by Susan Snyder "an epic of the divine plan in the physical universe, with God the Maker as its epic hero."[50]

The language with which Adam initiates his query—"Deign to descend now lower" (7.84)—reveals his neoclassical assumption that the subject he here proposes is less exalted than the martial exploits of angels and the Divine King. But Raphael declares the creating work of God to be the highest of all subjects, far exceeding Adam's limited capacity and straining (for the first time) his own adequacy as prophet-poet: "to recount Almighty works / What words or tongue of Seraph can suffice, / Or heart of man suffice to comprehend?" (7.112-14). This subject (like that of the Miltonic Bard) requires him to soar "with no middle flight," and at the same time to achieve a radical theological and literary accommodation to the audience.

Raphael's prototypical hexaemeral epic meets this formidable challenge with a design vastly superior to that of its literary progeny and precisely suited to Adam and Eve's situation. He eschews the lengthy catalogues and the encyclopedic lore characteristic of the genre, offering instead a sharply focused description of the wonders and processes of creation. Raphael's poem presents as it were the original from which many passages describing nature's luxuriant creativity in Lucretius, Ovid, and Sylvester's Du Bartas were derived.[51] But Raphael's poem surpasses all of them in its pervasive and vibrant imagery of procreation and generation, here used to render the divine creative power. The Spirit broods and infuses his vital virtue and vital warmth into the fluid mass; the earth is first an embryo in the womb of waters, and then itself the womb which brings forth the "tumid Hills," the "tender Grass," and all manner of vegetation, bursting with life and the seeds of new life (7.234-36, 276-82, 320-26). The sea generates "Fry innumerable," the caves and fens hatch a numerous brood of birds from an egg "Bursting with kindly rupture," and then the Earth "Op'ning her fertile Womb teem'd at a Birth / Innumerous living Creatures" (7.400, 419, 454-55, 463-73). By couching his poetic hexaemeron in the imagery of sexual generation, Raphael accommodates it brilliantly to Adam and Eve, and at the same time reinforces their dignity and happiness as imitators of and participants in the divine creativity through their own sexual acts.

Also, Raphael's ideal hexaemeral epic avoids the biblical literalism and strident apologetics that often characterize Du Bartas[52] by its clearly acknowledged status as an accommodated poem. At the outset Raphael distinguishes sharply between the immediacy of God's creating act, "more swift / Than time or motion," and his own narrative of a six-days' creation, unfolded by "procéss of speech . . . / So told as earthly notion can receive" (7.176-79). The Bard's audience will better understand the ways of angelic accommodation if they compare Raphael's account of creation to the description Uriel addresses to a supposed Cherub, the disguised Satan. Uriel's is not a hexaemeron and it is devoid of imagery of generation, focusing rather upon what is most apparent and most important from an angelic perspective—the elements, the place and course of the stars and planets, and "this Ethereal quintessence of Heav'n" (3.694-735).

The last genre Raphael invents is a version of the scientific dialogue-treatise, a prototype in verse of Galileo's *Dialogue Concerning the Two Chief World Systems—Ptolemaic & Copernican*.[53] Adam poses to Raphael a query concerning the design of the cosmos and its motion which, he says, "only thy solution can resolve" (8.14). Adam's question was commonly treated in the hexaemeral literature as an aspect of the fourth day's creation of the planets, and was usually resolved in biblical literalist terms by an appeal to divine authority. Raphael, however, declines to provide an answer on his angelic authority. Instead, he invents a form that will *not* resolve the issue but that will provide a model for scientific inquiry, then and later. He thereby removes astronomy from the province of revelation and places it squarely in the realm of human speculation. This accords with his "Benevolent and facile" opening words to Adam: "To ask or search I blame thee not, for Heav'n / Is as the Book of God before thee set, / Wherein to read his wond'rous Works" (8.66-68).

In Galileo's dialogue-treatise, three friends meet together to discuss the two systems in a spirit of friendly inquiry. Salviati supports the Copernican system with cogent reasoning, careful astronomical observation (aided by the telescope), and elaborate mathematical calculations.[54] Simplicio supports Ptolemaic astronomy, grounding his arguments upon piety and the ancient authority of Aristotelian physics. Sagredo is an urbane, open-minded, intelligent layman who desires to be informed about the two systems so that he may decide rationally which to credit. Salviati's arguments clearly carry the day: the inconclusiveness of Galileo's ending is a transparent and in the event futile attempt to satisfy the censors.

In Raphael's prototypical dialogue-treatise, these positions are all represented, but with large differences in the substance and manner of the arguments. Adam initiates the dialogue from the perspective of a Sagredo, striving to make sense of the cosmos and fully conscious of the irrationality and absurdity of the geocentric planetary system as the naked eye (and Ptolemy) perceive it. He wonders why the entire firmament moves with incorporeal speed through incomprehensible space,

> merely to officiate light
> Round this opacous Earth, this punctual spot,
> One day and night; in all thir vast survey
> Useless besides; reasoning I oft admire,
> How Nature wise and frugal could commit
> Such disproportions, with superfluous hand
> So many nobler Bodies to create,
> Greater so manifold to this one use,
> For aught appears, and on thir Orbs impose
> Such restless revolution day by day
> Repeated, while the sedentary Earth,
> That better might with far less compass move,
> Serv'd by more noble than herself, attains
> Her end without least motion.
> (8.22-35)[55]

Raphael explores Adam's inquiry through what is formally an evenhanded dialogue of one, in which he plays both the Ptolemaic and the Copernican roles—though his perspective is as clearly Copernican as Galileo's. He begins by stating the issue to be discussed, "Whether Heav'n move or Earth" (l. 70)—though Adam has not actually supposed that the Earth might move. Establishing the context for the discussion, he observes that resolution of the issue as stated "Imports not" to the recognition of God's wondrous ways, and notes that some other cosmic matters have been wisely concealed from man and angel—presumably, God's ways toward other worlds and other creatures in the universe (8.169-76).

Raphael then develops a Ptolemaic argument that is a far cry from Simplicio's. Indeed, Adam's reasoning leads Raphael to associate the follies of Ptolemaic apologetics with Adam's progeny, guessing "how they will . . . / build, unbuild, contrive / To save appearances, how gird the Sphere / With Centric and Eccentric scribbl'd o'er / Cycle and Epicycle, Orb in Orb" (8.80-84). Raphael merely points out the false values implicit in Adam's comments about disproportion in a geocentric universe, and the unintended aspersions he thereby casts upon the Creator. The angel's "Ptolemaic" arguments are these: The greatness and brightness of the other planets do not make them superior to the fertile earth. The noble planets do not serve the earth as such but man who is more noble still. Yet man is not at the center of the cosmic system (as Simplicio supposed); he lodges only "in a small partition, and the rest / Ordain'd for uses to his Lord best known" (8.105-106).[56]

Raphael then takes on his Copernican role. As he does so he suggests that the cosmic system one credits depends on one's vantage point, and he explains that his defense of the Ptolemaic cosmos was designed simply as a corrective for Adam's false assumptions: "Not that I so affirm, though so it seem / To thee who hast thy dwelling here on Earth" (8.116-17). To angels who move among the planets the cosmos evidently seems Copernican, and Raphael describes such a cosmos in a series of provocative suggestions akin to those of Salviati: the sun may be a stationary center to the world; the seemingly steadfast earth might move "Insensibly three different Motions," fetching day and night by her travels; the earth might enlighten the moon by day as the moon enlightens earth by night; the spots on the moon might be atmospheric clouds providing food for moon-dwellers, if any; there may be life on other planets and unknown galaxies throughout the universe. This last dizzying speculation is quite beyond Adam's wildest imaginings (or Salviati's), though it is couched in animistic and sexual imagery precisely suited to Adam's comprehension:

> and other Suns perhaps
> With thir attendant Moons thou wilt descry
> Communicating Male and Female Light,
> Which two great Sexes animate the World,
> Stor'd in each Orb perhaps with some that live.
> (8.148-52)

Raphael's prototype of the scientific dialogue-treatise is not designed (like Galileo's) to demonstrate and defend a theory, but rather to help Adam discover, as no other form could, the terms that should govern scientific inquiry into the cosmos. Raphael's sudden shift from human to angelic perspective should encourage Adam to distrust naive sense impressions, and to abandon the notion that human concerns must be the focus of the entire cosmos—attitudes Salviati also pronounced essential to scientific discourse.[57] Adam's sons must wait some centuries before the telescope—or space probes and moon landings—bring them somewhat closer to Raphael's angle of vision (itself limited). Raphael's dialogue of one, in which he plays the roles both of conservative apologist and radical theorist, makes Adam and his progeny confront human limitation, teaching them not to conclude God's ways imperfect on the basis of the scientific orthodoxy of the moment, and not to assume that that orthodoxy can explain the entire order of things for all time.

Finally, Raphael's choice of genre reinforces the scale of human values. By at once indulging and refusing to satisfy Adam's scientific curiosity, while at the same time demonstrating the limitations pertaining to the human condition, Raphael indicates that Adam's primary attention, care, and joy, should be directed to human things: "thy being," "this Paradise / And thy fair *Eve*" (8.170-74). His point is that the scientific speculation and activity carried forward by Adam and his sons should not displace or violate the human person, the human environment, and human society.

MICHAEL'S PROTOTYPICAL GENRES

The archangel Michael is a prophet-poet of a specifically biblical kind, to accord with the nature and needs of fallen man. Like Raphael, he has from God a general charge as to his mission and manner: to drive Adam and Eve from Paradise "not disconsolate" and to reveal "what shall come in future days, / As I shall thee enlighten," especially the covenant renewed in the woman's seed (11.113-16). But unlike Raphael, Michael is to treat a subject unknown to him—the course and meaning of biblical history. God displays that history before him in visionary scenes and enlightens him as to their meaning, which he then mediates to Adam. Michael thereby enacts quite precisely the prophetic role of Isaiah, Elijah, Ezekiel, and especially John of Patmos, as John Smith described it:

> In all proper *Prophesie* . . . they supposed the *Imaginative* power to be set forth as a *Stage* upon which certain *Visa* and *Simulacra* were represented to their Understandings, just indeed as they are to us in our common Dreams; only that the Understandings of the Prophets were alwaies kept awake and strongly acted by God in the midst of these apparitions, to see the intelligible Mysteries in them, and so in these Types and Shadows, which were Symbols of some spiritual things, to behold the Antitypes themselves.[58]

Adam addresses Michael as a prophet, terming him "Seer blest" (12.553). In Book Eleven, Adam himself is portrayed as a seer of sorts, though at the lowest level Smith describes: some visions were presented dramatically to his fancy, but "his Mind was not at the same time capable of the mystical meaning, [which] . . . was afterward made known to him, but yet with much obscuritie still attending it."[59] However, the revelation that both Michael and Adam experience as prophecy

the Miltonic Bard and his audience perceive as history—the
biblical record of all our woe and of the course of providential
history through the ages.

Like Raphael also, Michael is poet as well as prophet and
must invent appropriate literary forms to accommodate his
received subject to his audience. In its essence that subject is
a version of the Apocalypse, as Renaissance readers under-
stood it—a series of emblematic pageants presenting epic
struggles, tragic sufferings, and ecclesiastical history.[60] Ac-
cordingly, Michael couches it in terms of the literary genres
associated with the Apocalypse. A formal statement of theme
identifies the entire prophecy as a species of epic, a counter-
point to Raphael's Homeric epic and a manifestation of the
"better fortitude / Of Patience and Heroic Martyrdom" which
the Miltonic Bard claimed as the true heroic subject: "Expect
to hear, supernal Grace contending / With sinfulness of Men;
thereby to learn / True patience" (11.359-61). Within this
epic frame, the material is disposed into two segments, differ-
entiated as to genre and manner of presentation.

Michael first describes the visions as tragic masques or pag-
eants, analogous to the apocalyptic visions characterized by
David Pareus (and Milton) as "diverse *shews* and *appari-
tions.*"[61] But whereas the visions recounted in the Book of
Revelation are symbolic, Michael's are historical (except for
the lazar house scene). And whereas angels presented the
apocalyptic visions to John of Patmos without elucidation,
Michael offers his tragic masques as moral emblems requiring
explication, and takes occasion from Adam's misunderstand-
ings to educate him in true interpretation.

Because Adam has been blind to sin and its effects, Michael
leads him to the Hill of Speculation, purges his eyes, and then
points out to him several scenes from antediluvian history: the
murder of Abel; a lazar house full of loathsome diseases; the
deceptively attractive but actually sinful society of the sons of
God and the daughters of Cain; the wholesale destruction
wrought by the giant offspring of that union; the luxurious
riot of the ensuing generation; and, finally, God's destruction

of the entire world by flood, saving only Noah and his family. Michael's interpretations are not overtly typological in this segment: though the Bard's audience understands the world's destruction by flood and its subsequent renovation to be a type of apocalypse and millennium, Adam simply learns to lament the world's wickedness and rejoice over the just Noah, from whom God will raise another world. But Michael does foster apocalyptic interpretation of the pageants as emblems of a world given over to sin, divine judgment, and the ravages of the Four Horsemen: Death, War, Pestilence (the lazar house filled with the diseases of intemperance), and in place of Famine, Flood.

Specifically, Michael orders his account of these tragic scenes into a biblical brief epic which is in some ways a prototype of Agrippa d'Aubigné's epic-tragedy, *Les Tragiques* (1616). That work links the events of the French religious wars, the persecutions of Protestants throughout Europe, and the trials of the biblical Children of Israel as aspects of a single story, the apocalyptic conflict of Christ and Antichrist.[62] In the fifth book, "Fers," D'Aubigné's speaker views (in heaven) a series of tableaux recording scenes of suffering and persecution, painted by the angels and interpreted by commentaries. Similarly, Michael presents several historical pageants, intended to teach Adam to view all history from the perspective of apocalypse.

The second segment of Michael's epic is a narrative of biblical history from Abraham to the end of time. Though Michael himself continues to receive his subject from God in the visionary mode of prophecy—"I see him, but thou canst not" (12.128)—Adam only hears about subsequent events in Michael's narrative summary of scripture. Michael's new manner of presentation accords with a change in Adam's condition and also with the demands of his new subject, biblical history: "I perceive / Thy mortal sight to fail; objects divine / Must needs impair and weary human sense: / Henceforth what is to come I will relate" (12.8-11). In some respects Michael's narrative is an expansion of Hebrews 11, presenting the typological progression of exemplary Old Testament heroes of faith—Abel, Enoch, Noah, Abraham, Moses, the warring judges

52

and kings—as culminating in and fulfilled by Christ's redemptive sacrifice.[63] The change to narrative accords with Michael's Pauline purpose of teaching Adam the new heroism by example, and leading him to comprehend the typological pattern of history by faith. Adam now stands before Michael as any Christian stands before the interpreters of scripture; he hears an account of biblical history, he often responds to it inappropriately, and he advances under constant correction "From shadowy Types to Truth" (12.303).

But this accommodation is literary as well as theological. Michael does not offer a commentary on Hebrews 11, but a historical poem which may be seen as a prototype and brief epitome of that classic of Christian historiography, Augustine's *City of God*. Nimrod and Abraham receive special emphasis in Augustine's history,[64] and Michael begins his historical narrative by presenting these two personages as earthly, political embodiments of the two cities: Nimrod the "mightie Hunter" who instituted tyrannical government on earth; and Abraham the man of faith who founded the elect nation covenanted to God and saved by faith in the Promises. Also, in keeping with the typological thrust of the *City of God*, Michael leads Adam by stages to understand the covenant of grace, and to read in the Old Testament types their Christic and apocalyptic fulfillments. Michael's account leads Adam at last to eschew the values Augustine identified with the City of Man—love of self, pride in human strength, glory, or wisdom—and to seek the contrasting virtues pertaining to the City of God:

Henceforth I learn, that to obey is best,
And love with fear the only God, to walk
As in his presence, ever to observe
His providence, and on him sole depend,
Merciful over all his works, with good
Still overcoming evil, and by small
Accomplishing great things, by things deem'd weak
Subverting worldly strong, and worldly wise
By simply meek; that suffering for Truth's sake

Is fortitude to highest victory,
And to the faithful Death the Gate of Life;
Taught this by his example whom I now
Acknowledge my Redeemer ever blest.
(12.561-73)[65]

More precisely, Michael presents here a prototype of the
brief epic based on biblical history—a miniature and com-
pleted version of Du Bartas' incomplete *Seconde Semaine*, which
was intended to trace the providential history of the Church
from Paradise to the Last Judgment in seven historical ages,
paralleling the seven days of Creation.[66] That pattern was
blurred by the fragmentary state of Du Bartas' poem, by its
diffuseness and digressions, and by its pervasive and often in-
appropriate use of epic and romance topoi: epic warfare, chal-
lenges, vaunts, councils of war, allegorical interludes, apos-
trophes, catalogues, epic similes, and the like. By contrast,
Michael's prototypical *Seconde Semaine* eliminates conven-
tional epic apparatus and achieves conceptual rigor and struc-
tural cohesion. It thereby provides a fitting counterpoint to
Raphael's prototypical *Semaine* treating the seven days of Cre-
ation. It is also a true counterpoint to Raphael's Homeric brief
epic in Book Six—a fully achieved epic of providential history
in which all the elect are called upon, in tragic circumstances,
to display some version of the new heroism: unwavering faith
and love, moral courage, "the better fortitude / Of Patience
and Heroic Martyrdom."

The Bard's four proems and the several prototypical genres
ascribed to the angelic narrators direct our attention to Mil-
ton's use of genre changes and permutations throughout the
poem, to provide multiple perspectives upon the various per-
sonages and incidents and to engage his readers continually in
the process of comparison and evaluation. Essentially, Milton
calls upon humanistic and literary means to imagine and ac-
commodate the subject matter of divine revelation, and to lead
his readers from partial to more complete, from simple to more
complex understandings of the human condition.

THREE

"Argument Heroic Deem'd": The Genres of the Satanic Heroic Mode

THAT MILTON PORTRAYS Satan largely in terms of the heroic mode is a commonplace of criticism, as is the idea that the Satanic heroic is a debased version of the classical heroic ethos.[1] Readers readily perceive that those parts of *Paradise Lost* concerned with Satan's activities are replete with epic matter and motivations, epic genre conventions, and constant allusions to specific passages in famous heroic poems, recalling thereby the glorious deeds, the heroic virtues, and the characteristic emotion—wonder—which Renaissance critics identified with these genres and these poems.[2] Even so, we need to observe more precisely the very comprehensive range of heroic genres that Milton associates with Satan, including all the chief varieties of epic, romance, and heroic tragedy. And in doing so we need to examine just how he makes such links, and why.

Milton begins to develop the Satanic heroic mode in the opening books of *Paradise Lost* by associating with Satan generic topoi from one after another of the heroic genres. Also, by specific allusions to the *Iliad*, the *Odyssey*, the *Aeneid*, and other heroic poems, he identifies these poems as subtexts for the Satanic episodes. We are thereby alerted to attend to the generic paradigms which take shape gradually as the poem proceeds, and to trace the analogies to major heroic poems through the continuing verbal allusions, plot analogies, and references to scenes and motifs. The dynamics of the poem lead us to trace each of these patterns to its completion.

To develop the story of Satan, Milton invokes the generic paradigms and primary exemplars of the major epic and tragic kinds and their permutations, interweaving them and at the

55

same time showing Satan's continued declination from higher to lower heroic kinds and models. Specifically, Satan's nature and role are analyzed through the debased, perverse, or parodic analogies they offer, first, to characters from the epic of strife and from the biblical "Exodus" epic; then from heroic tragedy; then from various forms of quest epic and romance; then from Ovid's *Metamorphoses*. This generic strategy is obviously addressed to an audience whose "fitness" is (in part at least) a function of their considerable literary experience and cultural sophistication.

Milton's intention is not to condemn classical epic or romance or tragedy; nor is it to exalt Satan as hero. Here as elsewhere literary genre is a vehicle of artistic imagination and of accommodation, making primordial evil comprehensible to poet and reader in all its attractiveness, complexity, multiplicity, and familiar local manifestations. Milton uses genre also for educative purposes: to lead readers to measure Satan against a great range of heroes and heroic actions, and against all these standards to find him wanting. We are to recognize— by degrees, and through a process of comparison, contrast, and judgment—just what the Satanic heroism is, as we find that it involves the perversion of *all* the heroic values that we have admired in literature and throughout history. At length, having refined our concept of the heroic, we are asked to measure that concept against a divine standard of action and speech which incorporates but transforms and transcends the highest human heroism.

Epic of Wrath and Strife

By the formal epic question about the cause of Adam and Eve's revolt, and the answer relating it to Satan's guile, envy, revenge, ambition, and the "Battle proud" he raised in heaven, Milton initiates the first generic paradigm, the epic of wrath and strife. In the opening scenes in hell he employs the distinctive topoi and conventions of that kind—Homeric catalogues, epic games, a council of war, exhortations to armies—

with specific reference to the two major epics of wrath and strife in the classical canon, the *Iliad* and the *Aeneid*. These references involve us immediately in a process of discrimination regarding Satan's heroic virtues.

As every reader has recognized, Satan appears more heroic and attractive in these scenes than ever again in the poem—a warrior indomitable in the face of defeat and staggering obstacles, manifesting the fortitude, determination, endurance, and leadership of the greatest epic heroes. But even as the deliberate parallels invite comparisons of Satan with Achilles, Agamemnon, Aeneas, and Turnus, they underscore differences. Satan, like Achilles, prides himself on his obduracy, his "fixt mind / And high disdain, from sense of injur'd merit" (1.97-98), and he commits himself, like Turnus, to revenge, immortal hate, and "eternal War / Irreconcilable" (1.121-22). But we soon see that Satan does not have genuine wrongs, as they did: he has not been insulted or dishonored by his leader as Achilles was, or deprived of a promised bride and kingdom as was Turnus.[3]

Other parallels focus attention upon Satan's heroic leadership. The description of Satan's forces scattered over the burning lake of hell recalls the description of Aeneas' fleet shipwrecked and scattered off the coast of Libya. In addition, the scene in which Satan sheds tears over his fallen armies evokes Aeneas' emotion on that occasion and also Agamemnon's bitter tears when the Trojans reached the Greek ships. We note that Satan masters himself and rallies his forces with more resolution than Aeneas or Agamemnon do, but we also recognize his very different motives: Aeneas and Agamemnon speak poignantly of peace, rest, and fulfillment of the gods' will, whereas Satan offers his forces only unrelenting and perpetual warfare against God.[4] Again, Satan's comment on his responsibilities as king—"Wherefore do I assume / These Royalties, and not refuse to Reign, / Refusing to accept as great a share / Of hazard as of honor" (2.450-53)—echoes Sarpedon's address to Glaukos: "Glaukos, [since] . . . you and and I are honored before others / with pride of place . . . /

Therefore it is our duty in the forefront of the Lykians / To take our stand. . . ."[5] However, Sarpedon's speech exhorts his comrade to share in the duty and glory of leading their troops to battle, whereas Satan's speech is designed to prevent anyone else from sharing in his perilous mission to earth and its honor. The contrast underscores the fact that Satan as leader grants no genuine collegial role in counsel or in action to others, but merely uses them as his instruments.

For specific plot analogies, we are directed first to the *Aeneid*, and invited to recognize Satan as a debased Aeneas enacting a parody of that hero's struggle to found a new kingdom. This pattern begins with Satan's first words to Beelzebub, "If thou beest hee; But O how fall'n! how chang'd"—a clear echo of Aeneas' words to the ghost of Hector come to bid him flee the destruction of Troy.[6] Like Aeneas who led his party of defeated Trojans from burning Troy to seek the kingdom ordained to him by fate, Satan calls his conquered legions forth from the burning lake of hell—though with nothing of the *pietas* that characterized Aeneas' exodus, carrying his ancient father on his shoulders and his household gods. Like Aeneas and his Trojans who settled for a time in Dido's Carthage, enjoying its splendid buildings, its harbor and roads, its glorious brazen temple, its laws and institutions,[7] so the fallen angels mine gold, construct a magnificent golden capitol, hold councils, and seek to establish a glorious city and society in hell (1.670-798). And like Aeneas who set forth from Sicily with a small remnant, leaving behind as settlers all those "with no craving for high renown," so Satan set forth alone from hell to seek a better kingdom, leaving his war-weary followers behind to settle and improve hell.[8] Aeneas, however, won his destined kingdom by heroic warfare, and his marriage to Lavinia established a new society linking Trojans with Latins, whereas Satan destroys by fraud the paradise destined for Adam and Eve. Yet like a perverse Aeneas he ironically and maliciously proclaims his desire to link himself with them in the closest societal bonds: "League with you I seek, / And mutual amity so strait, so close, / That I with you must dwell, or you with me / Henceforth" (4.375-78).

In the *Aeneid*, the founding of Rome and its projected glorious history are ordained by fate, and are achieved through the noble character and actions of the *pius* Aeneas and his descendants. Similarly, in *Paradise Lost* the several realms are created by God to conform to the natures of their inhabitants, and those inhabitants then produce material and social structures suited to those realms and consonant with their natures. Satan, cast into hell, seeks to persuade himself that his nature ordains him to another kingdom—"this Infernal Pit shall never hold / Celestial Spirits in Bondage" (1.657-58); "I give not Heav'n for lost. From this descent / Celestial Virtues rising, will appear / More glorious and more dread than from no fall" (2.14-16). But immediately upon arrival in Eden he finds that hell *is* his proper kingdom, that his nature is of the essence of that place: "Which way I fly is Hell; myself am Hell" (4.74). Accordingly, in Book Ten when Satan returns to hell to fulfill his role as an Aeneas, offering to lead his followers forth to possess as lords the realm he has won for them, the entire company is abruptly transformed into serpents and tormented by a thirst like that of Tantalus in the Virgilian underworld— in graphic testimony that hell is the only kingdom they are fit for. Satan's parodic and futile effort to lead his followers from a burning city to a new kingdom also alludes to the true fulfillment of this pattern, when Christ the true Aeneas will lead forth his redeemed to the heavenly kingdom ordained for them.

Next, we are directed to consider Satan's actions in terms of the *Iliad*. This pattern often produces mock-epic overtones as Satan is linked with unworthy prototypes or contrasted sharply with that foremost exemplar of physical courage and battle prowess, Achilles. The Iliadic paradigm begins with Satan's dark references to his "injur'd merit"; and it is developed in several scornful flyting matches recalling exchanges between heroes prior to single combat—Tlepolemos and Sarpedon, Euphorbos and Menelaos, Achilles and Hector[9]—as well as in the scenes of epic warfare.

Interrupting Satan and Death as they prepare for a mighty duel (2.681-726), Sin appeals to her dastardly family to avoid combat—"O Father, what intends thy hand . . . / Against thy only Son? What fury O Son, / Possesses thee to bend that mortal Dart / Against thy Father's head?" The scene provides a grotesquely comic reprise of those tender and pathetic scenes of familial love in the *Iliad* in which Andromache, Thetis, and Hecuba plead with their warrior husbands and sons to avoid battle.[10] But whereas Hector and Achilles always resist such pleas from motives of duty and honor, Satan heeds Sin's warning that the dart wielded by Death would be mortal to him, and promptly turns from insult to flattery. The bathos of Satan's *volte-face* is reinforced by a simile describing him moments before as a fiery comet portending fierce destruction, and also by the narrator's conditional syntax: "and now great deeds / Had been achiev'd . . . / Had not . . ." (2.722-24). In a later flyting match between Satan and Gabriel (4.878-976) Satan vaunts excessively but then foregoes single combat when Gabriel points to the sign of his impending defeat in the heavenly scales. To Satan's discredit, this circumstance recalls several occasions in the *Iliad* in which Zeus indicates the outcome of a battle in the celestial scales, after which the battle nevertheless takes place: we remember that in the *Iliad* a hero's proud words are followed by great deeds.[11]

In the narrative sequence, the Battle in Heaven serves as the climax to the Iliadic pattern, though chronologically it marks the first stage in Satan's career as a debased Achilles. As Martin Mueller observes, the three days of fighting in *Paradise Lost* "mirror the fighting in the *Iliad* from the initial encounter of Paris and Menalaus through the nocturnal council of the Achaians to the final confrontation of Achilles and Hector."[12] As we have seen, Raphael's account of the war to Adam and Eve is essentially heroic in tone, but the Miltonic Bard's allusions to the *Iliad* provide for his audience an overlay of mock-heroic ironies. The battle is filled with the Homeric heroic activities we expect—single combats, chariot clashes, legions fighting legions—but their significance is deliberately undercut. The terrible Homeric carnage is wholly absent, the good forces are never in any real danger, and even the wounded rebels (like Homeric gods rather than Homeric heroes) bleed "nectarous humor" rather than blood and heal promptly.

Moreover, in this warfare Satan's posture as Achillean hero is wholly deflated. Achilles, slighted by a leader inferior to himself in many respects, responded by simply withdrawing his allegiance and his support in battle. Satan, falsely imagining himself impaired by the elevation of the Son and preposterously claiming equality with God, makes treasonous war upon his erstwhile Lord and his comrades. And though Satan shows great strength and courage on the battlefield, he cannot match Achilles' prowess as warrior in his comparable scale. The first day's battle begins with Satan forced to his knees by a blow from the physically unremarkable Abdiel, whose sword bears the power of truth; and it ends with Satan's right side almost sheared off by Michael's invincible sword.

The Iliadic Battle in Heaven also supplies a corrective to Satan's description of God as a divine tyrant, superior to the angels only in physical strength. In the *Iliad* Zeus indeed appeals to his superior strength as the source of his right to govern the Olympian deities: "I could drag you up, earth and all and sea and all with you . . . / So much the stronger am I than the gods and stronger than mortals."[13] But in the Battle in Heaven it is Satan, not the Father, who makes martial prowess the test of worth: "Our puissance is our own, our own right hand / Shall teach us highest deeds, by proof to try / Who is our equal" (5.864-66). And when the Son as bearer of God's omnipotence echoes Zeus' claim before undertaking his single combat with the entire rebel host, he makes quite clear that battle prowess is the rebels' measure of heroic worth, not his own: "they may have thir wish, to try with mee / In Battle which the stronger proves, they all, / Or I alone against them, since by strength / They measure all, of other excellence / Not emulous, nor care who them excels" (6.818-22). Then the Son supplants Satan as a better Achilles. "Full of wrath," and "Grasping ten thousand Thunders" he exercises the Father's just wrath rather than his own, and wins thereby the true glory that God alone can bestow.

The final scene in the Miltonic epic of wrath is Satan's would-be triumph: he vaunts before the fallen angels as he describes his easy victory in Eden, and expects from them "universal shout and high applause" (10.441-506). In a parallel scene in the *Iliad*, Achilles vaunts over and despoils the body of Hector, calling for songs of triumph from the Greeks.[14] Ironically, both these triumphs show the victors at their moral nadirs. Yet Achilles' actions are those of a man driven by grief and rage into desperate, aberrant behavior, whereas Satan reaches the logical end-point of his debased heroic course in this display of exultant self-congratulation and sheer egomania. Achilles' triumph inspires tragic terror. Satan's inspires reprehension, leading us to take satisfaction in the divine punishment that turns this epic triumph into abject humiliation as the vaunting conqueror becomes a grovelling serpent.

HEROIC TRAGEDY

Superimposed upon but extending beyond the Satanic epic of wrath is a Satanic version of heroic tragedy. For this generic paradigm we are directed first to Aeschylus' *Prometheus Bound* and then to a succession of less noble models, reflecting the course of Satan's decline. Throughout Book One, Satan's situation, attitude, and language recall Prometheus' defiant refusal to submit to Zeus, and his consequent endurance of overwhelming suffering and catastrophe. Indeed, Satan presents himself as the noble and indomitable victim of a God far more implacable, irrational, tyrannical, and wrathful than Zeus: a God who tempted the angels' revolt by hiding "The force of those dire Arms"; who drove the vanquished angels to hell by "Thunder / Wing'd with red Lightning and impetuous rage"; and who continues to wreak vengeance upon them with unending torments (1.93-94, 174-75). Against all this, and against the sheer odds of power which alone (Satan claims) differentiates God from the angels, Satan pits his endurance, constancy, and will. He will not "repent or change, / Though

chang'd in outward luster"; he claims the "courage never to
submit or yield"; and he asserts the power of his own mind
to dominate and transform his surroundings: "The mind is its
own place, and in itself / Can make a Heav'n of Hell, a Hell
of Heav'n" (1.94-109, 254-55).

But even as we are moved by this language so reminiscent
of Prometheus,[15] we are prompted to distinguish between the
noble courage of Aeschylus' hero who suffers unjustly at the
hands of a tyrannical Zeus for actions that benefit humankind,
and the self-regarding pride that motivates Satan to plot to
ruin the human race in order to revenge himself upon God.
Satan is a debased Prometheus, and as such a parodic exem-
plar of that "better fortitude / Of Patience and Heroic Mar-
tyrdom" which the Bard holds forth as the highest heroism.

In Books Four and Nine, Satan's use of a characteristic for-
mal element from Elizabethan tragedy, the soliloquy, directs
us to other tragic paradigms. In his five great soliloquies Satan
is associated successively, and on a descending scale of moral
worthiness, with various kinds of Elizabethan tragic heroes,
villain-heroes, and tragic antagonists.

Satan is a Faustian hero in his great soliloquy on Mount
Niphates (4.32-113)—his paradigmatic scene of suffering, as
John Steadman notes.[16] Yet even as we respond to Satan's
anguish with the appropriate tragic emotions, pity and fear,
we recognize that he has declined from a resolute, indomita-
ble, long-suffering Promethean hero into a Faustian one, voic-
ing the spiritual agonies of the damned soul. Satan now re-
sembles Doctor Faustus in his last hour, or Claudius in *Hamlet*
striving unsuccessfully to pray. Like them he is forced to ac-
knowledge his guilt and his own responsibility for his plight;
like them he is tormented by remorse but unable to repent.[17]
The Faustian comparison is made explicit when Satan restates
Mephistopheles' terrible perception of hell's ubiquity, "Which
way I fly is hell; myself am Hell," and echoes Faustus in his
agonized but ineffectual wish to repent, "O then at last relent:
is there no place / Left for Repentance, none for Pardon left?"[18]

As this soliloquy proceeds, however, we watch Satan de-
cline from Faustian hero to villain-hero driven by ambition.

From a despairing Faustus he becomes a tormented Macbeth, prodded by "Ambition" and "dread of shame" to maintain his rule whatever the cost. In the final lines, as he makes the deliberate, horrendous choice, "Evil be thou my Good," he declines yet further: now like Richard III he embraces evil as his means to power (to share "Divided Empire" with God), and delights in it for its own sake. In his next soliloquy (4.358-92) he combines the villain-hero of ambition with the revenge hero (a Richard III with a Barabbas), appealing to "Honor and Empire with revenge enlarg'd" as justification for the utter villany of destroying the innocent.[19] In his third soliloquy (4.505-35) he has fallen lower still: no longer a hero of evil grandeur like Macbeth or Richard III or even Barabbas, he now becomes the devious, ignoble antagonist of Adam and Eve. In this passage he displays the sheer malignity of an Iago— wracked with jealousy as he witnesses marital happiness he cannot share, lurking to spy out information, devising plots, and exulting in his evil plans: "O fair foundation laid whereon to build / Thir ruin."

In Book Nine, as Satan prepares to enter the serpent he becomes a parodic tragic hero. In the classic paradigm of tragedy the hero seeks to soar above humanity and is felled by fate or fortune or his own *hamartia*. But Satan, in full awareness that he is enacting a reversal of that pattern, now chooses to "imbrute" himself and so literally sinks below humanity:

> O foul descent! that I who erst contended
> With Gods to sit the highest, am now constrain'd
> Into a Beast, and mixt with bestial slime,
> This essence to incarnate and imbrute,
> That to the highth of Deity aspir'd;
> But what will not Ambition and Revenge
> Descend to? who aspires must down as low
> As high he soar'd, obnoxious first or last
> To basest things.
>
> (9.163-71)

At this point we realize that Satan has moved outside and below both the classical and the Elizabethan paradigms for tragedy. Both paradigms involve a fall from happiness into misery, resulting in grievous loss and waste but leading ultimately to release, catharsis. By contrast, Satan's course is now a continuous and progressive fall, which produces no catharsis. There is no insight or new integrity gained through suffering, as with Adam or Othello or Lear; no exhaustion of evil as with Macbeth; no final relief in action as with Hamlet; not even the release of meeting the worst at last, as with Faustus.

In Book Ten, then, when God punishes Satan and the fallen angels by turning them into serpents, this last "fall" is entirely outside the domain of tragedy. It pertains, rather, to the realm of Dante's *Commedia*, where the evil are fixed eternally and grotesquely in the natures they themselves have chosen. The fallen angels' punishment is rather like that of the thieves in *Inferno* 24-25, who enact their malice, deceit, and craft by being changed continuously into serpents and then restored to human shape.[20] From a debased Prometheus, still noble and indomitable in his tragic suffering, Satan becomes at last the butt of scorn and derision in this grotesque black comedy of God's devising.

QUEST EPIC AND ROMANCE

Intersecting with the epic of wrath and the several paradigms of tragedy is an Odyssean quest epic—which also includes romance in several forms. This link is sanctioned by Renaissance critical theory, notably by Giraldi Cinthio who observed that "in makeup the Romances are much more like Homer's *Odyssey* than the *Iliad*."[21] The *Odyssey* is a quest epic that is also an epic of return. Though the end is long delayed, and though Odysseus will wander again, the epic is given strong closure by the hero's homecoming, his total victory over the suitors, and his reunion with the long-besieged, faithful Penelope. Romance is the quintessential quest form: quests characterize romance as a genre (the medieval romances), and also as a mode interacting with the heroic mode in many Renaissance epics. As Patricia Parker notes, the action of romance is located in the place of wandering, of trial and error, where the final object of the quest is continually postponed.[22]

Milton incorporates in *Paradise Lost* a complete mini-*Odyssey*. Satan in this "epic" is the subtle fiend who has turned from force to fraud, and he is measured against the crafty Odysseus, "man of many ways."[23] As the Council in Hell concludes, Beelzebub points out that the agent sent to earth will need Odysseus-like qualities:

> what strength, what art can then
> Suffice, or what evasion bear him safe
> Through the strict Senteries and Stations thick
> Of Angels watching round? Here he had need
> All circumspection.
>
> (2.410-14)

Moreover, the Bard directs us to the continuing parallels between Satan's adventures and those of Odysseus by two explicit references to Odysseus' encounter with Scylla and Charybdis, the ultimate sources for Sin and Death.[24]

The Odyssean narrative pattern begins as Satan sets forth on his journey to earth in Book Two, and ends with his return to hell in Book Ten, after a victory which liberates his daughter-wife, Sin, and his Son, Death, from captivity in hell. Structurally, Satan's journey through Chaos recalls Odysseus' entire sea voyage, but especially the three days he is buffeted by storms before being cast upon Alkinoös land.[25] Like Odysseus with Circe, the Cyclops, Nausikaa, and others, Satan shows himself to be a skilled rhetorician, a master of persuasion, and at times a liar. He talks his way with flattering words past Sin, Death, and the Anarch, Chaos, defusing present dangers and eliciting help; and he misrepresents to Gabriel his motives for coming to Eden. Like Odysseus also, Satan is a master of disguises, often ignoble ones. Odysseus blinds Polyphemos and escapes hidden beneath a ram's belly; Satan disguised as a stripling Cherub figuratively blinds Uriel, the sharp-eyed guardian of the Sun—and both heroes subsequently reveal themselves by a display of passion.[26] Odysseus disguises himself as a tattered beggar to observe and test the members of his household; Satan reconnoiters and tempts in Eden as cormorant, lion, tiger, toad, and snake. Finally, as Odysseus caused the Fall of Troy by a deception about the Trojan horse, so Satan causes the Fall of Adam and Eve by a deception about the apple.[27]

But the striking contrasts between the two heroes make Satan's *Odyssey* parodic. Odysseus' ruses and deceptions were undertaken in the cause of survival and homecoming, with the aid of the goddess of wisdom; Satan's for revenge against God. Odysseus triumphed in Ithaca by a combination of deception and martial prowess; Satan relied on fraud alone. Most important, whereas Odysseus through all his trials and adventures strove for eventual reunion with his chaste and faithful wife, Penelope, and his worthy son, Telemachus, Satan at the very beginning of his quest is reunited with but does not recognize his reprehensible daughter-wife, Sin, and the hideous offspring of their incestuous union, Death. At Odysseus' homecoming Penelope and Telemachus honor him for his decisive victory over the suitors, and at Satan's return to hell Sin and Death honor him for his conquest in Eden—but that honor turns to ignominy as Satan's followers (transformed to snakes) greet his victory speech with a universal hiss.

Incorporated within the Satanic mini-*Odyssey* are Satanic analogues to the romance mode in general, and to the major romantic epics. We first encounter Satan's perversion of the basic narrative paradigm of romance—the continual questing of knights-errant. In romance, medieval and Renaissance, ultimate goals or principal quests tend to be postponed almost indefinitely, or to be only partly attained, or to fall outside the confines of an incomplete text, while the emphasis falls upon the wanderings and adventures of knights-errant who fight whatever monsters present themselves and take on whatever quests are offered them. Knights-errant normally undertake to serve and defend virtue, though they are often deceived or swayed by passion or deflected from greater goods by lesser—mirroring in this the fallen human condition.

In Satan and the rebel angels this wandering propensity becomes an absolute. Waiting for Satan's return from earth, some fallen angels explore the hardest philosophical questions—"Fixt Fate, Free will, Foreknowledge absolute"—but find "no end, in wand'ring mazes lost." Some others explore the physical landscape, wandering "O'er many a Frozen, many a Fiery Alp, / Rocks, Caves, Lakes, Fens, Bogs, Dens, and shades of death" but find "No rest" (2.557-65, 614-28). Satan's own flight through Chaos magnifies beyond measure the erratic flights of Charlemagne's knights pursuing Angelica, or Ruggiero unable to control the Hippogriff, or Godfrey's knights pursuing Armida—though Satan is "transported" by rage rather than erotic passion (3.80-81). And instead of a wandering wood or labyrinthine landscape or tumultuous sea, Satan traverses "a dark / Illimitable Ocean without bound, / Without dimension" (2.891-93), with no control whatever over his own motions and directions. He "swims or sinks, or wades, or creeps, or flies" as he can (2.950), subjected entirely to the winds of chance—a physical manifestation of the fact that he recognizes chance rather than God as Final Cause.

The Bard then associates Satan with romantic epics of various sorts, and with specific episodes in those works. He turns first to the *Faerie Queene* to find models for Sin, Death, and the Anarch Chaos. As readers have long recognized,[28] these figures are distinctively Spenserian in appearance and in the development of their allegorical significance. Like Fradubio's tale which reveals the moral complexity of a doubting nature through its wealth of narrative detail,[29] Sin's account of her generation (2.747-810) reveals what sin is in its complex and deceptive essence. The allegory serves as a reference point for subsequent scenes of sin in action, and links the entire chain of proliferating evils to Satan as their progenitor. Sin is first a depravity of the intellect (she is born from Satan's head, in parody of Athena's birth as goddess of widsom from Zeus' head, and of the Son's generation from the Father as his Word and Wisdom). Sin is at first alarming to the tempted, but then becomes alluring and pleasing to them. It is perverted self-

68

love (Satan loves Sin as his own image, and incestuously begets Death upon her). It is self-destructive (Sin is hideously disfigured in giving birth to Death, and then is raped by him). It constantly proliferates (Sin's hellhound brood continually reenter her womb, feed upon her, and are reborn).

The iconography of Sin owes something to Spenser's Serpent Errour, the first evil the Red Cross Knight must conquer in his quest for true holiness, and much more to Duessa, beautiful at first as she deceives Red Cross into alliance with her, but unmasked at length as a vile hag. These Spenserian analogues present Satan as a parodic Red Cross who pursues evil rather than holiness, who instead of destroying the evil monsters he meets embraces them as his own progeny, and who instead of promoting virtue and civilized order allies himself with the monsters' purposes—the spread of disorder, destruction, and death.

We observe Satan's perversion of another romance role in the Paradise of Fools, long recognized as a darker version of Astolfo's journey to the Limbo of Vanities in the *Orlando Furioso*.[30] Astolfo is a gentle ironist who has learned the folly of love and chivalric endeavor, a magician-poet who uses his horn, book, horse, and lance to understand and control his world. Parodying Dante, Astolfo descends a very short distance into hell, and then climbs to the earthly paradise, from whence (with St. John as guide) he visits the Limbo of Vanities in the moon to bring back Orlando's lost wits.[31] The vanities in Ariosto's Limbo are for the most part follies endemic to the human condition—all that on earth is lost "by fault, by time, by fortune"[32]—and the wits held there (including some of Astolfo's wits) were chiefly lost for love. By contrast, Satan's Paradise of Fools does not lie in a pleasant valley of the unspotted moon but on the outside shell of the universe, "Dark, waste, and wild, under the frown of Night" (3.424). As a parodic Astolfo, Satan is utterly devoid of self-irony, he has no saintly poet-prophet as guide, and he is not here on a rescue mission but because he is himself the source of all the vanities that will later be housed in this place. Moreover, the inhabitants of the Satanic Paradise of Fools obtain their places not by eros but by self-regard or self-deception: they are glory-seekers, false zealots, the credulous, the superstitious.[33]

Next, Satan's encounter with Uriel, the Regent of the Sun, leads us to associate Satan with the pilgrim Dante and his wholly spiritual quest. Satan's inquiries to Uriel about God's creation of the world recall Dante's persistent questions to and instructions from the saints he encounters in the various heavenly planets—notably the great doctors and teachers of the Church who inhabit the Sun.[34] But Satan is a parodic Dante: since he only pretends to be a Cherub seeking knowledge of God's ways, he cannot receive spiritual knowledge and illumination as Dante did. This analogue also leads us to recognize Satan's journey in its entirety as a recapitulation and parody of Dante's: he first views and responds to the landscape of hell, then makes his way with great difficulty through a middle region (for him Chaos rather than Purgatory), and finally voyages among the celestial planets. But Satan only reaches the Sun, source of the physical light of the universe, whereas Dante (and the Miltonic Bard) find the celestial light of God.

When Satan makes his way into the Edenic garden, he again parodies a major topos of the romance mode—the hero's adventure in a Garden of Love. Some knights enter such gardens to win a lady's love (The Lover in the *Romance of the Rose*, Scudamore in the Garden of Adonis); some are offered the delights of such gardens as respite, refreshment, or reward (Lope da Vega and his men in the *Lusiads*); some are temporarily seduced by an enchantress to seek sensual ease and wanton pleasure in such gardens (Ruggiero in Alcina's Garden, Rinaldo in Armida's Garden); some come to rescue enchanted knights and destroy sinful gardens (Guyon in the Bower of Bliss).[35] Satan, however, can only pervert all these familiar romance roles. As his own words make clear, he cannot win love in Eden, or find sensual delight, or enjoy sensuous refreshment; instead, he here sees "undelighted all delight" and

70

feels more intensely than before the agony of his own loneliness, lovelessness, and unsatisfied desire:

> Sight hateful, sight tormenting! thus these two
> Imparadis't in one another's arms
> The happier *Eden*, shall enjoy thir fill
> Of bliss on bliss, while I to Hell am thrust,
> Where neither joy nor love, but fierce desire,
> Among our other torments not the least,
> Still unfulfill'd with pain of longing pines.
>   (4.505-11)

Incapable of love, Satan violates the fundamental ethos of the romance hero, though he engages in many of the conventional activities of the knightly lover in a Garden of Love. He woos Eve with a nocturnal serenade; he flaunts and preens before her in his snake disguise; and he pays her hyperbolic Petrarchan compliments—"sovran Mistress," "sole Wonder," "A Goddess among Gods," "Celestial Beauty" (9.532-48). At length, he seduces her to sin—but not, ironically, through love. A perverse Guyon, Satan detroys in Eden not a wantonly sinful but a joyously innocent Bower of Bliss and Love.

In the final scene in hell the romance paradigm, like the others, finds its fitting resolution. Satan, who began by claiming the monsters he encounters as his own progeny, and winning them as allies, now completes the pattern by becoming a monstrous snake himself. A truly perverse Red Cross Knight (St. George), he does not slay but turns into the Dragon.

METAMORPHOSES

Another heroic kind associated with Satan is Ovid's *Metamorphoses*.[36] Ovid claimed epic status for the poem with an epic proposition and invocations, several heroic episodes, and a concluding prophecy that his grand opus would gain for him immortal fame; and modern criticism is now recovering the classical and Renaissance tradition which recognized the *Metamorphoses* as epic.[37] Since Ovid's poem is the single major

71

exemplar of its epic type, the generic paradigm for the epic of metamorphoses in *Paradise Lost* is wholly derived from the narrative and allusive patterns in that work.

Milton draws heavily upon Ovidian themes and episodes to contrast the divine processes of creation and change with their Satanic perversions. Ovid's great theme is mutability, continual vicissitude—"There's nothing permanent; all ebbe and flow: ... / What was before, is not, what was not, is: / All in a moment change from that to this"[38]—a theme arising from the jarring seeds and continuous warring elements in Ovid's Chaos. Together with Hesiod, Ovid supplies many features of Milton's Chaos—where the four elements in their pregnant causes strive for mastery, where atoms adhere temporarily and then promptly separate, where Chaos sits umpire, and under him "*Chance* governs all" (2.907-10).[39] For both Ovid and Milton, Chaos is the primordial matter from which a god forms the cosmos, the earth, and all being; it is the substratum of all created things, all subsequent making. For both, accordingly, change is a basic principle of nature, the ground of all creation and creativity.

As we shall see, Milton draws upon several Ovidian passages to describe Creation as a vital, organic, generative process that the Father begins by making the Earth and all the creatures continuously prolific. And for the diabolic invention which is the counterpart to the divine creative process Milton calls upon other Ovidian descriptions, notably of the Iron Age inventors who continually violate nature as they rend the earth's "secret entrailes" to bring forth the instruments of vice and bloody warfare—"Curst Steele, more cursed Gold."[40] Milton identifies the fallen angels as the originals of these fabricators. Mammon first prompted men to rifle "the bowels of thir mother Earth / For Treasures better hid." Before that he led his own crew to open in hell's soil "a spacious wound" and dig out "ribs of Gold" (1.684-90), which they used to build Pandaemonium in all its opulence and showy magnificence. Still earlier, during the War in Heaven, Satan directed the fallen angels to rifle the celestial soil, where they discovered the minerals and stone from which to make cannon and gunpowder. These diabolic mining and engineering feats culminate in the bridge over Chaos—a parody of the divine creation in which Death, Gorgon-like, uses his "Mace petrific" (10.292-324) to turn chaotic matter, which is instinct with energy and life, into stone.

Milton also uses Ovid to point up the contrast between divine metamorphosis which operates as a natural law in the universe of the poem, and its Satanic perversions. In Ovid the idea of continual mutability and change in nature is developed chiefly through tales of virtually instantaneous metamorphosis, usually imposed by external agency—a curse, the jealousy of a god or goddess, a magic potion or object. But in *Paradise Lost* the divine processes of change operate gradually rather than instantaneously, and physical changes are seen to reflect and to depend upon moral changes and choices. Raphael explains to Adam and Eve that all created beings "if not deprav'd from good" will undergo gradual refinement, "Till body up to spirit work, in bounds / Proportion'd to each kind" (5.469-79), while the Father explains that those depraved will experience a gradual but continuous degradation: "hard be hard'n'd, blind be blinded more" (3.200). All of *Paradise Lost* is an epic of divine creativity and metamorphosis, within which Satan sponsors a debased version of Ovidian instant metamorphosis.

The contrast is underscored in the portrayal of Sin, modelled upon Ovid's story of Scylla. In Ovid, a magic potion placed by Circe in Scylla's bath changed her instantly from a beautiful nymph to a monster, transformed from the waist down into a mass of barking dogs; soon thereafter, "powerful Fate" again changed her—instantaneously—into a rock.[41] Milton's Sin tells her own story in much the same way, as a series of sudden, inexplicable, surprising transformations: she sprang from Satan's head as a beautiful armed goddess; her body was deformed and distorted in giving birth to Death; raped by Death she hourly gives birth to yelling monsters who further deform her (2.746-814).

Satan and Sin offer no interpretation of these transforma-
tions: their version of Ovid is quite literal. But the Bard's
readers are expected to know how to allegorize Ovid in phys-
iological or philosophical or theological terms, guided by tra-
ditional medieval and Renaissance interpretations.[42] For ex-
ample, George Sandys reads Scylla's story as an allegory of a
licentious woman who is at last hardened in her sins.[43] This
intrepretative tradition leads us to recognize, as Sin does not,
that her metamorphosis presents an allegory based on James
1:15, of the gradual but inevitable manifestation of the nature
and effects of sin: "Then when lust hath conceived, it bringeth
forth sin; and sin, when it is finished, bringeth forth death."

Beyond this, we should now recognize the central signifi-
cance of the allegorical mode in *Paradise Lost*, to which Ad-
dison and Dr. Johnson objected so strongly.[44] By portraying
Sin and Death as allegorical characters Milton emphasizes their
ontological status as concepts, lacking the reality of living beings.
By contrast with God's begetting of a Son ontologically dis-
tinct from himself, and God's prolific generation of separate
and sexually active creatures along the entire chain of being,
the allegorical progeny of Satan emphasize his essential steril-
ity. He can only produce from his head incestuous images of
himself. As Maureen Quilligan has observed, "Sin is Satan's
fiction," ironically unrecognized even by her author.[45]

The contrast between divine and diabolic concepts of met-
amorphosis is manifested in Satan and the rebel angels. We
note from the beginning of the poem that they are undergo-
ing a gradual metamorphosis in which physical changes mir-
ror moral change. Satan is startled to see the alteration in his
lieutenent Beelzebub immediately after the fall into Hell—"If
thou beest hee; But O how fall'n! how chang'd" (1.84)—though
he attempts to discount any such process in himself. At first
Satan is simply an "Arch-Angel ruin'd" who has not lost all
his original brightness, and he assumes he will remain sub-
stantially unchanged: "What matter where, if I be still the
same, / And what I should be?" (1.591-94, 256-57). In Eden,
however, he is forced to take account of his inevitable decline
when his proud taunt to the angelic guard, "Know ye not

74

mee?" is answered by reference to his changed appearance:
"Think not, revolted Spirit, thy shape the same, / Or undi-
minisht brightness, to be known / As when thou stood'st in
Heav'n upright and pure; / . . . thou resembl'st now / Thy sin
and place of doom obscure and foul" (4.827-50). We are shown
the beginning of the fallen angels' moral and physical deteri-
oration in the Battle in Heaven, when they first experience
pain. We are also shown, in prospect, a much later stage in
their decline. The epic catalogue of Book One (376-522) de-
scribes the fallen angelic leaders not as the heroic warriors
they still are, but as the ignoble, bestial, vicious, and degen-
erate idols they are to become in human history.

Satan and his cohorts prefer, however, their own literal ver-
sion of Ovid. They often change their shapes deliberately, like
Ovid's Proteus or Jove, though unlike the Ovidian shape-shifters
the shapes they choose inevitably reflect their moral and phys-
ical decline. Just before the Grand Consult the angelic masses
reduce themselves to the size of dwarfs or faery elves so as to
fit into Pandaemonium. Later, Satan turns himself from ti-
tanic Seraph into, successively, stripling Cherub, cormorant,
lion, tiger, snake. And the several allusions relating Satan's
serpentine transformation to that of Ovid's Aesculapius re-
mind us that Aesculapius assumed serpent form in order to
save Rome from plague (for Sandys he is a type of Christ, the
brazen serpent), whereas Satan did so in order to bring a plague
of death and sin upon all humankind.[46]

At length Satan himself takes on the role of perverse Ovid,
inventing for his temptation of Eve a story of literal, instant
magical transformation. He claims to have been an ordinary
serpent who, upon eating magical fruit, was immediately en-
abled to speak and think as a man, and he invites Eve to ex-
pect an analogous instant transformation from that same fruit:
"That ye should be as Gods, since I as Man, / Internal Man,
is but proportion meet, / . . . And what are Gods that Man
may not become / As they, participating God-like food?" (9.710-
17). He tempts Eve, that is, to substitute a literalistic Ovidian
concept of metamorphosis for the divine metamorphic plan.

Appropriately, then, Satan and the fallen angels are made

to undergo (lke Ovid's Cadmus) a transformation into serpents, instantly and by direct divine agency.[47] But this transformation is only a temporary punishment, recurring periodically but then reversed so as to permit the divinely ordained, natural process of gradual moral and physical decline to continue. As the Bard's Ovidian *Metamorphoses* reaches a climax in this episode, we have again been led by generic paradigms and specific references to discriminate among epic values— Ovid literalized and Ovid moralized, Satanic and divine processes of metamorphosis.

EPIC OF EXODUS

Yet another heroic kind associated with the fallen angels is the biblical Exodus "epic," recorded in the Books of Exodus and Deuteronomy.[48] According to patristic and Renaissance tradition, the biblical story itself is epiclike, narrating the wonderful deeds God wrought through Moses in delivering the Israelites from Egyptian bondage: the plagues; the miraculous Red Sea crossing; the drowning of Pharoah's forces; the desert trials and wanderings; the crossing of Jordan into the Promised Land. Also, the Mosaic hymn summarizing and celebrating these wonderful acts (Exod. 15:1-21) was thought to have been written in hexameter, and several Renaissance literary works present the Exodus story as epic.[49] The Exodus is present in Milton's poem not as a generic paradigm but as a narrative pattern alluding to the single work that comprises this subgenre of biblical epic. It overlays the classical paradigms and patterns traced, testing Satan against a higher, Old Testament standard.

The Exodus pattern in *Paradise Lost* begins with an epic simile comparing the rebel angels, just fallen from heaven and scattered over the Red Sea of hell, to the Egyptian forces whose "floating Carcasses / And broken Chariot Wheels" were strewn over the Red Sea (1.305-12). The simile indicates that the fallen angels are archetypes for Egyptian tyranny and its overthrow by divine power, rather than for Mosaic deliverance to freedom.[50] Also, the catalogue describing the fallen angels as the idols they are to become—the "Gods ador'd / Among the Nations"—identifies Satan as the source of all the idolatry that is to surround, seduce, and threaten Israel.

Subsequently, this pattern develops as parody, with Satan as a perverse Moses attempting but miserably failing to deliver his followers from bondage in hell. This parody is more shocking than others we have traced, since Moses is a type of the true deliverer, Christ, and an exemplar of the biblical higher heroism of service to God. An epic simile (1.338-43) compares Satan arousing his troops from the fiery sea to Moses calling up a plague of locusts with his rod—and we realize that Satan's followers will not be delivered by, but will themselves become, a plague of locust upon the earth. As the pattern continues, Satan traverses his Jordan (Chaos) though no path opens before him, and the Eden he enters is no promised land for him since he is unable to enjoy any of its abundant blessings. Finally, in parody of the miraculous path through Jordan, Sin and Death construct a bridge over Chaos to facilitate the destruction, not the settlement, of a land flowing with milk and honey and all good things.

This pattern also finds resolution in Book Ten, with the transformation of the rebel angels to serpents. Whereas Moses erected a brazen serpent to cure his followers of the snakebites suffered enroute to Canaan (a type of Christ curing mankind of sin), Satan causes his followers to become snakes, imaging their role as dispensers of the venom of sin. As we trace out the Exodus epic pattern, we are to recognize that Satan, as perverse Moses, is forever incapable of delivering himself or his followers from bondage, or of leading them to any version of Canaan. He can only cause them to become the instruments, the emblems, the incarnations of plague, bondage, and tyranny.

THE BARD presents Satan and the fallen angels with reference to a wide range of generic paradigms and also specific patterns derived from major works in the heroic mode. Interweaving them, and at the same time ordering them so as to display Satan's decline, he defines a complex attitude toward the heroic in the literary tradition. We come to see that Satan and his crew pervert all the heroic values set forth in the greatest epics, romances, and tragedies we know. However, the fact that Satan is Achillean, or Promethean, or Odyssean, or Ovidian, does not mean that Achilles, or Prometheus, or Odysseus, or Ovid, or the various romance heroes are Satanic. Those heroes, those values, those genres, and those works are not in themselves debased by the Satanic association. Rather, it is by measuring Satan against the heroic standards embodied in those works that we come to recognize how far Satan has perverted what in him was (and in some measure remains) magnificent.

Yet by the same process we become conscious of the inadequacy and fragility of all the heroic virtues celebrated in literature, of the susceptibility of them all to demonic perversion. The Bard's generic strategy leads us by stages to refine our concept of the heroic, pointing us at last toward the divine heroic model, which subsumes what is best in the various literary formulations of human heroism—and perfects it.

FOUR

"Semblance of Worth, not Substance":
The Discursive and Lyric
Genres of the Damned

MANY ASPECTS of Satan and his infernal society are revealed through the genres of speech and song associated with them: epic and dialogic exchanges, tragic soliloquies, rhetorical speeches, a very few lyrics. Whereas the various epic and dramatic genres are incorported in *Paradise Lost* through their paradigms and topoi, these smaller kinds are usually embedded in the narrative, set off by specific genre conventions and indicators of commencement and closure.

Certain genres of discourse and lyric were common in epic, given Homeric precedent and the perception of Homer as source of all the arts and all the literary forms.[1] Among the topoi of epic are several kinds of set speeches—exhortations to the troops, taunts, praises, battlefield conferences, debates in council about war and peace. In addition, all three kinds of rhetoric were associated with epic, especially deliberative oratory.[2] Pointing to Homer as "a model and an inspiration for every department of eloquence," Quintilian asked: "do not the ninth book [of the *Iliad*] containing the embassy to Achilles, the first describing the quarrel between the chiefs, or the speeches delivered by the counsellors in the second, display all the rules of art to be followed in forensic or deliberative oratory?"[3] There is also epic precedent for including many lyric genres—chiefly hymns, prayers, laments, funeral dirges, love complaints, encomia, and invitations to love.

Milton calls upon these traditions in selective and complex ways as he identifies some genres of discourse and lyric (but not others) with Satan and his followers. The dominant speech forms for them are deliberative rhetoric and soliloquy: true lyrics are outside their repertoire; and other kinds such as dialogue and lament take on the characteristics of the dominant genres. Milton has, moreover, transformed their conventional epic speeches into substantive comments on ethics, politics, history, and theology. With these generic strategies he begins the poem-long process of educating the reader to make complex discriminations about the uses and perversions of language.

He continues that educative process by inviting us to measure the speech and song of hell against the norms and best models of such language from classical times onward. Some such reference points are the notable Homeric and Virgilian models of epic speech and the great tragic soliloquies of the Elizabethan stage. Others are the norms and prescriptions for rhetoric as defined by Plato, Aristotle, Cicero, Quintilian, and others, as well as the political speeches attributed to various historical personages by the great classical historians, Herodotus, Thucydides, Sallust, and Livy. Such comparisons indicate that the eloquent speech of the fallen angels, magnificent as it is, debases those noble precepts and models, pointing us at last toward celestial norms and models of speech and song.

Epic Exchange and Dialogue

The Satanic forces engage in several kinds of epic exchanges—challenges, taunts, consultations on battle tactics—which are transformed by rhetorical pressures or deformed by malevolent irony from the Homeric and Virgilian standard. Some of these exchanges are dialogues in form though not in substance: the fallen angels do not exchange views, or explore a topic together, or pursue truth through some process of dialectic. Instead, infernal dialogue usually takes on the character of manipulative rhetoric.

Satan's dialogue with his "nearest Mate" Beelzebub (1.84-282) recalls several epic scenes in which a heroic leader holds an open-ended discussion with friends and associates about some notable crisis, inviting and often accepting their advice.

An example is the Patroklos-Achilles dialogue occasioned by the desperate danger to the Greek ships, which concludes with Achilles agreeing to Patroklos' proposal to lead the Myrmidons in to battle clad in Achilles' armor (*Iliad* 16.1-100).[4] By contrast, in the Satan-Beelzebub exchanges Satan initiates all the topics, inviting nothing and receiving nothing from his companion. Rather than engaging in dialogue, Satan sometimes muses about his situation as if in soliloquy, sometimes addresses deliberative discourse in the high style to his audience of one.

His opening words appear to invite dialogue by emphasizing the shared interests and conditions of the two angels—their "mutual league, / United thoughts and counsels, equal hope, / . . . equal ruin" (1.87-91). We soon perceive, however, that the assertion of equality is not a statement of fact but simply a rhetorical gesture to engage the good will of the audience. Satan's high-sounding proclamations of "fixt mind," "unconquerable Will," and "courage never to submit or yield" show him working out a new self-image, but also serve as ethical proof, demonstrating that he is a worthy leader still: firm, courageous, indomitable. Then, to help insure Beelzebub's continued loyalty and service he promulgates a fallacious view of politics, causality, and recent history through a series of assertions and rhetorical questions: No one could have known that "He with his Thunder" would prove stronger. The outcome of the war was long in doubt. The cause was and is good—a mass rebellion by innumerable spirits who chose Satan's leadership over the "Tyranny of Heav'n." The present situation is not hopeless since the rebels' strength is undiminished and they can learn from past experience how to wage future wars.[5] Beelzebub's hesitant speculation that God may allow them their strength for his own purposes is met with the dismissive retort that that strength will always be used to promote evil.

The dialogue resumes after the two angels move, at Satan's initiative, from burning lake to dreary plain. Satan at once lays formal claim to hell—"Receive thy new Possessor." Then, speaking almost as if in soliloquy, he seeks to persuade both

81

himself and his comrade that his mind can remain unchanged and can transform the environment. At length he proclaims in stirring rhetoric the political foundations of his new society: freedom from a divine tyranny that is based solely on force, and rightful equality. As he does so, however, a revealing shift of pronouns (*we* to *my*) and an aphorism borrowed from Julius Caesar ironically reveal his absolutist intentions:

> Here at least
> We shall be free;
> . . . .
> Here *we* may reign secure, and in *my* choice
> To reign is worth ambition though in Hell:
> Better to reign in Hell, than serve in Heav'n.
> (1.259-64)[6]

This first infernal dialogue provides the pattern for others. Satan's dialogue with his daughter-wife Sin at hell's gate (2.727-870) parallels and parodies the dialogue in heaven between God and the Son. Ironically, however, Satan does not here engage another person in a dialogue but only an extension of himself, since Sin is an allegorical quality or power derived from him. In this exchange also other kinds of speech largely overwhelm the dialogic elements: Sin's long autobiographical narrative,[7] and Satan's manipulative rhetoric promising his newfound family liberation and scavaging rights to all the earth. As Sin agrees to open hell's gate to him, she spins fantasies about the future which are the direct effect of Satan's promises:

> Thou art my Father, thou my Author, thou
> My being gav'st me; whom should I obey
> But thee, whom follow? thou wilt bring me soon
> To that new world of light and bliss, among
> The Gods who live at ease, where I shall Reign
> At thy right hand voluptuous, as beseems
> Thy daughter and thy darling, without end.
> (2.864-70)

These fantasies echo but stand in sharp contrast to the Son's prophecy of his death, resurrection, and ascension, prompted only by his faith in God (3.243-65).

Another epic dialogue, the battlefield conference after the first day's battle in heaven (6.406-97), is concerned with tactics and immediate dangers rather than large political issues. We are invited to recall, and contrast, the scene from the *Iliad* (14.27-134) in which four wounded Greek leaders—Nestor, Odysseus, Diomedes, and Agamemnon—discuss their plight. Taking seriously Nestor's comment that "A man cannot fight on when he is wounded," they agree to avoid hand-to-hand combat when they return to the field.[8] Satan, however, meets his problem of wounds and enemy advantage by manipulation. Discounting as trivial the new experience of pain that dismays his troops, Satan assures them that having sustained one day's battle against supposed omnipotence they can do so for "Eternal days," and invites them to discuss better weaponry. And when Nisroch raises Nestor's objection Satan deflects it by the revelation that he has himself discovered the new weapons needed, cannon and gunpowder.

The scoffing, punning dialogue of Satan and Belial as they display their cannon and discharge it against the loyal angels is a deeper degradation of epic speech (6.555-634). These ambiguous ripostes are a version of the battle taunt directed to the enemy—traditionally a ritual public contest of words preceding the contest of arms. Here, however, epic taunts become petty and malicious in-jokes at the enemies' expense, as the rebel leaders allude to their violent new weapons of war in wholly misleading euphemisms. More shocking still, these exchanges purport to be a consultation about proposing terms of peace to the enemy:

> O Friends, why come not on these Victors proud?
> Erewhile they fierce were coming, and when wee,
> To entertain them fair with open Front
> And Breast, (what could we more?) propounded terms
> Of composition, straight they chang'd thir minds,

83

Flew off, and into strange vagaries fell,
As they would dance, yet for a dance they seem'd
Somewhat extravagant and wild, perhaps
For joy of offer'd peace . . .
(6.609-17)[9]

The Satanic forces debase even the rhetoric of ridicule, derision, and irony as they enact a prototype of the doublespeak about war and weaponry which observers throughout history, from Thucydides to Orwell, have noted.[10]

DELIBERATIVE RHETORIC

For Satan and the fallen angels, the dominant discursive genre is deliberative or political rhetoric—that addressed to a political assembly or ruler to persuade them to some course of action on some public issue. Their speeches constantly evoke notable classical analogues; and their arguments concerning war and peace, the public good, and the foundations of political power invite evaluation according to the highest classical ideal of deliberative rhetoric—principled statesmanship grounded upon true philosophy. Plato proclaimed that ideal in its loftiest form (though he had little hope of its realization): for him the orator must be a philosopher who knows "the truth about all the particular things of which he speaks and writes," especially about virtue and justice, and who is himself a good and just man.[11] Cicero and Quintilian (who thought the ideal can be and has been realized) called more generally and more pragmatically for the orator to be a good man with broad and deep knowledge of logic, ethics, metaphysics, natural philosophy, civil law, politics, history, human psychology, and more.[12]

In this tradition the purpose of deliberative rhetoric is to promote virtue and the common good. Plato insisted that it be used "for this one purpose always, of pointing to what is just."[13] Cicero emphasized the orator's role in promoting civilization, a virtuous social order, and "the safety of countless

84

individuals and of the entire state," ascribing great power to his eloquence:

> His duty too it is to arouse a listless nation, and to curb its unbridled impetuosity. By one and the same power of eloquence the deceitful among mankind are brought to destruction, and the righteous to deliverance. Who more passionately than the orator can encourage to virtuous conduct, or more zealously than he reclaim from vicious courses? Who can more austerely censure the wicked, or more gracefully praise men of worth? Whose invective can more forciby subdue the power of lawless desire? Whose comfortable words can sooth grief more tenderly?[14]

Milton's description of the poet's public role in *The Reason of Church Government*—"to imbreed and cherish in a great people the seeds of virtu, and publick civility, to allay the perturbations of the mind, and set the affections in right tune"[15]— derives directly from the exalted Ciceronian ideal of the orator as statesman.

Judged against this ideal the fallen angels are worse than the Sophists Plato excoriated: they are not only ignorant of truth, justice, and moral goodness, but they consider power and *raison d'état* to be the common good and the ends of political rhetoric.[16] In technical terms, however, they are brilliant orators who follow the best classical prescriptions for deliberative rhetoric. As Aristotle recommended, they address themselves primarily to the issue of expediency.[17] Quintilian names as topics of expediency "whether a thing is easy, great, pleasant or free from danger"; and the author of the *Rhetorica ad Herennium* proposes the general topics of might and craft— the latter including promises, dissimulation, and deception.[18] The diabolic orators also appeal to honor—for Cicero and Quintilian the primary argument in political oratory—though without referring it to moral virtue. They consider possibility, since what is thought to be either impossible or absolutely necessary is not subject to debate.[19] They make impressive use of pathetic proof, in line with Quintilian's prescriptions about swaying the audience through anger, fear, ambition, hatred, or other emotions, and glossing over apparent evils when addressing unworthy audiences.[20] Also, Satan gives special attention to ethical proof, finding his own perverse equivalents for the moral criteria Quintilian held forth as establishing the speaker's authority: "he, who would have all men trust his judgment as to what is expedient and honourable, should both possess and be regarded as possessing genuine wisdom and excellence of character."[21]

The first of the two major varieties of deliberative rhetoric associated with Satan and his crew is the formal Council of State—The Grand Consult in Pandaemonium (2.1-505). Here the epic topos of the war council becomes a full-scale deliberation by political leaders as to how—or whether—to continue a war. A vehement call for war is followed by two distinct and elaborate arguments for peace, after which the council hears and accepts a plan for a new kind of warfare (by fraud) carried on by proxy, in another place.

The chief epic parallel is probably the lengthy sequence in the *Iliad* (2.50-397) in which Agamemnon's plan to test the Argives' resolution almost miscarries and sends them rushing homeward. Agamemnon's own ambivalence is revealed in his eloquent, despairing speech urging an immediate return to Greece; Thersites the epic malcontent casts discredit on the war and the leadership; Odysseus with great difficulty stems the rush to the ships by denouncing the Argives' cowardice and vacillation; Nestor suggests ways to promote unity and responsibility among the several armies; and at last Agamemnon is able to deliver a call to arms that meets with resounding applause. In *Paradise Lost* Satan's directive to the council setting the terms of their debate—whether to conduct open or covert war against God—is intended to prevent such disunity. But this council almost takes a wrong turning as well, as Belial and Mammon play Thersites' role in urging abandonment of the war. Beelzebub takes on the roles of Odysseus and Nestor in recalling the rebels to their war commitment. But unlike

the Greek heroes, who think and act for themselves, Beelze-
bub is simply a front man for his leader, manipulating the
council so as to make Satan's plan prevail.

Virgil provides another parallel for the Council in Hell, and
especially for Moloch. In *Aeneid* 11.234-468—in some ways
a reprise of the Homeric council just discussed—King Latinus
proposes to offer peace and friendship to the Trojans, sec-
onded by the aged Drances (a more honorable Thersites) who
expatiates eloquently on the hopelessness of war. In furious
response, Turnus denounces speeches and councils, sounding
an insistent call to arms: "Plenteous indeed, Drances, ever is
thy stream of speech in the hour when battle calls for hands
. . . Why lingerest? . . . Nay Citizens . . . convene a council
and sit praising peace; yonder they rush upon the realm in
arms" (11.377-461).[22] The echoes in Moloch's speech are un-
mistakable:

> My sentence is for open War: Of Wiles,
> More unexpert, I boast not: them let those
> Contrive who need, or when they need, not now.
> For while they sit contriving, shall the rest,
> Millions that stand in Arms, and longing wait
> The Signal to ascend, sit ling'ring here . . .
> (2.51-56)

Yet Turnus, however mistakenly, still hopes for victory, while
Moloch seeks only perpetual war.

Even more important as reference points for the speeches
in the Grand Consult are certain political orations in the great
classical histories. Satan's throne of "*Barbaric* Pearl and Gold"
befitting a despot of the "gorgeous East" points us to Herod-
otus' account of the Persian King Xerxes undertaking war
against Athens for revenge and glory. Yet unlike Satan, Xerxes
explains his plans openly to his council and invites discussion:
"to show that I am not self-willed in this matter, I lay the
business before you, and give you full leave to speak your
minds upon it openly."[23] Mardonius, a better Moloch, sup-
ports the war but urges careful, realistic preparations, while

Artabanus, a nobler Belial, counsels peace—motivated not by sloth or sensual ease or procrastination but by fear of tempting the gods through hubris or covetousness. Accepting Artabanus' advice, Xerxes calls off his war plans, returning to them only because directed to do so in a dream he takes to be divine.[24]

In more general terms, the Grand Consult recalls other famous debates over issues of war and peace: Thucydides' account of the Lacedaemonians and their allies debating war with Athens, and of Pericles' several speeches to the Athenians promoting war with Sparta; Livy's report of the several debates in the Roman Senate about the Punic Wars; and Demosthenes' several speeches urging the Athenians to resist Philip of Macedon. The diabolic speakers employ the statesmanlike tone, the formal rhetorical structure, and the specific rhetorical topics (expediency, honor, justice, possibility) characteristic of those orations,[25] though to baser purpose. The Satanic orators also build upon classical assumptions about fate,[26] human nature, and history, and each employs the level of style (grand, middle, low) appropriate to his own ethos, or to the ethical proof he wishes to present.

Among its other functions, Satan's initial charge to the Grand Consult (2.11-42) is manifestly effective as ethical proof. Satan intends to be perceived as a calm, statesmanlike leader laying before his counselors the essential aspects of a complex situation in a direct, analytic, plain style. But this ethos masks a hidden political and rhetorical agenda. Addressing his followers by one after another of their glorious titles—"Powers and Dominions," "Deities of Heav'n," "Celestial Virtues"— Satan insinuates that the recovery of heaven will follow easily and inevitably from the angelic nature these titles manifest. Then he reviews the grounds for his sovereignty, appealing to all the bases recognized in ancient and modern political thought: the "fixt Laws" of heaven; the "free choice" of the angels; and his own "merit" in war and council. Finally, speaking to the topic of possibility, he touts his infernal state as more secure and united than heaven and entirely safe from envy and ambition, since preeminence here brings greatest pain. He concludes from all this that the rebels now are "Surer to prosper than prosperity / Could have assur'd us." These arguments are so obviously strained and their optimism so evidently misplaced that their rhetorical motivation is patent: to secure Satan's reign, and commit his followers to the plan he has already proposed to Beelzebub. All this, of course, conditions the apparent openness of his final invitation: "who can advise, may speak."

The ethos presented by Moloch's speech (2.51-105) conforms to his true nature: a bold and bluff soldier impatient with deliberations and wholly governed by wrath and love of war. Uninterested in the polity of hell or heaven, he sees God simply as a "Torturer"—the projection of his own violence. His is a grand, almost bombastic style characterized by vehemence, urgency, violent imagery, and powerful emotional appeals. All Moloch's arguments urge the possibility and expediency of continuing the war. Hell's soldiers number millions and they can use hell's flames and torments as weapons. Return to heaven will be easy because consonant with angelic nature—"in our proper motion we ascend." They cannot be in worse plight since annihilation (if even possible for angelic natures) would bring release from pain. Moloch evidently believes his own arguments but his fury undermines their logic and consistency. As Belial soon points out, Moloch's hopeful war plans are belied by his argument about annihilation, grounded in despair. Also, Moloch's prediction of victories in which God's throne will be "Mixt with *Tartarean* Sulphur, and strange fire," soon gives way to the sharply revised claim that the rebels can "Alarm, / Though inaccessible, his fatal Throne: / Which if not Victory is yet Revenge."

Belial projects the ethos of a graceful, humane, rational, and dispassionate statesman who gives careful consideration to all the options. Only by degrees do we perceive the nature the narrator describes—a sophist who "could make the worse appear / The better reason," and a skillful but perverse rhetorician whose sweet middle style and "persuasive accent" please

the ear but cloud the mind. His long, carefully structured or-
ation (2.119-25), with its exordium to win audience good
will, its trenchant refutation of Moloch's case, and its telling
arguments from necessity, builds to the apparently inevitable
conclusion that the fallen angels should attempt no action
whatsoever.

The refutation of Moloch is based on experience. Military
revenge is impossible since heaven is impregnable and the di-
vine throne has been proved incorruptible. And worse punish-
ment is indeed possible—the burning lake was worse and the
entire loss of being in annihilation would be worse still (as-
suming that God could or would give it). Belial then moves
the debate beyond the terms set by Satan, arguing that the
only realistic course is submission to and endurance of what-
ever conditions the victor imposes. But Belial reveals the il-
logic and sheer wishful thinking beneath this seeming reason-
ableness when he suggests that if they do nothing at all things
are likely to get better by themselves. In time God may "much
remit" his punishment. Future days may bring new chances
and changes. And angelic nature may at length overcome, or
become inured to, or be changed and conformed to the ele-
ments of hell. Belial's easy acceptance of that degradation of
angelic nature—inconceivable to Satan or Moloch and hardly
consistent with his declared unwillingness to "lose, / Though
full of pain, this intellectual being, / Those thoughts that wan-
der through Eternity"—reveals more clearly than anything else
the slothful sensuality that is Belial's true ethos.

Mammon's speech (2.229-83) has no direct prototype. A
materialist projector, empire-builder, pragmatist, and would-
be real-estate developer, he measures all action by its success
and all good by wealth and splendor. His brisk, no-nonsense
plain style with its pointed antitheses, crisp statements, and
direct rhetorical questions, is calculated to present him (by
way of ethical proof) as one who will neither give way to
passion like Moloch nor bandy words about like Belial, and
whose good sense can accordingly be trusted. At length, how-
ever, we realize that the low style is precisely suited to the low

thoughts of this "least erected Spirit that fell / From Heav'n" (1.679-80). Quickly dismissing the other proposals as doomed to failure—God cannot be dislodged from a throne secured by fate, and utter submission is both unacceptable and unlikely to win readmission to heaven—he urges instead that the fallen angels seek "Our own good from ourselves, and from our own / Live to ourselves . . . / Free, and to none accountable" (2.254-56).

Denouncing the "splendid vassalage," forced halleluiahs, and servile praise demanded in heaven, he assumes the stance of a Roman Stoic denouncing the corruptions of degenerate courts and empires. His speech echoes Horace's "Epistle 1.18," praising simple country contentment far from dependence on the great.[27] Ironically, however, Mammon is proposing to create a rich and magnificent empire, rivalling heaven. Also, Mammon's rallying cry of "Hard liberty before the easy yoke / Of servile Pomp" (2.257-58) echoes the exhortations of Roman republicans such as Lepidus, urging the Roman citizenry to take up arms against tyrants.[28] But Mammon, ironically, is calling for the renunciation of war so as to get on with producing gems and gold and splendid buildings. And Mammon's notion that ostentatious wealth *is* the public good places him at the farthest remove from the Athenian ideal defined by Pericles: "we are lovers of the beautiful, yet simple in our tastes . . . Wealth we employ, not for talk and ostentation, but where there is a real use for it."[29] These comparisons underscore the baseness of Mammon's materialism, which can make no distinction between golden magnificence and true beauty (to say nothing of celestial light) and which can anticipate with equanimity the entire transformation of angelic spirit into hellish matter: "Our torments also may in length of time / Become our Elements . . . our temper chang'd / Into their temper" (2.274-77).

Beelzebub is portrayed as a "Pillar of State," whose appearance reflects his nature: "deep on his Front engraven / Deliberation sat and public care; / And Princely counsel in his face yet shone, / . . . With *Atlantean* shoulders fit to bear / The weight of mightiest Monarchies" (2.302-307). His two speeches

(2.310-78, 390-416) also manifest this ethos, with their grand style, *gravitas*, dignity, weighty parallelisms, and trenchant irony. Using that irony to dampen the general enthusiasm stirred up by Mammon's speech, he ridicules by turns Mammon's projection of a rival empire, Belial's fantasy of peace through inaction, and Moloch's reckless war plans. At length he appeals to the topic of necessity—"War hath determin'd us"—and returns the debate to the terms Satan had set, presenting Satan's own plan as the only option not yet discredited: warfare by fraud, directed against the new creation.

As a statesman seeking to persuade a populace that has opted for peace, ease, and wealth to sustain a posture of war, Beelzebub invites comparison with the greatest Greek orator-statesmen, Pericles and Demosthenes. He echoes many of the latter's arguments in calling for war preparations against Philip of Macedon: peace is no longer possible; to fail to resist is to accept slavery; it would be better to carry on the war in a third country rather than in our own.[30] Yet Demosthenes was urging preparations for defense and the heroic engagement of the whole populace, who must at last realize they cannot fight by proxy,[31] whereas Beelzebub is proposing an offensive against a peaceful earth with Satan acting as proxy for all.

Beelzebub also lacks the moral independence and integrity that characterize the great Greek and Roman advisors to the state.[32] Though no sycophant, he is the instrument of his prince: he is to Satan what Wolsey and Cromwell were to Henry VIII—a highly intelligent and imaginative minister of state who explains, expands upon, wins assent for, and executes the policy of his leader. After he wins a favorable vote for Satan's project his second speech heightens its desirability: perhaps earth can be a staging place for reentry to heaven; perhaps their scars will be healed by the heavenly light shining upon earth. And by his graphic portrayal of the dangers attending the mission, Beelzebub insures that his call for volunteers will be met with silence, so that Satan's offer will have maximum political effect.

In making that offer (2.430-66), Satan cites his readiness to undertake the perilous mission as evidence of his right to sovereignty. He directs the others to improve and safeguard hell while he (anticipating in parody the Son's role as redeemer) seeks deliverance for all. Without discounting Satan's courage, we are to recognize that he has staged a masterful scenario of political manipulation, aided by the oratory and strategy of his chief minister.[33] When the council concludes, he has won his immediate goal of continuing the war on his terms and has also greatly strenghened his rule, as the assembly pays him the "awful reverence prone" due to a god.

Satan himself most often employs a second kind of deliberative oratory—the advisory speech urging citizens or magistrates to resist oppression and win their proper liberty and rights. In Book One we see Satan transforming the epic exhortation—the general's address rallying his troops before a major battle or reviving them after a defeat—into such a speech. By way of preparation, he rebukes them for their "abject posture" in the burning lake and calls them forth: "Awake, arise, or be for ever fall'n" (1.315-30).[34] But the unconscious irony reverberates as we realize that they will be forever fallen whatever they now do. As they assemble he glories in their vast numbers and loyalty, and weeps bitter tears for the loss and pain they suffer—even as Xerxes wept over the inevitable mortality of his massed followers, and Agamemnon wept before his assembled troops alarmed by the Trojan threat to the Greek ships.[35] But unlike Agamemnon Satan has no impulse to give over the struggle, and unlike Xerxes he bears responsibility for the very existence of Death, physical and spiritual.

As an address to a defeated populace in desperate circumstances, Satan's oration (1.622-62) invites comparison with Pericles' speech to the Athenians after the second Peloponnesian invasion and the onset of the plague. Seeking to force his countrymen to face the hard choice of fighting for freedom and empire or submitting to the loss of both, Pericles openly confronted their anger and despondency: "I was expecting this outburst of indignation; the causes of it are not unknown to me."[36] By contrast, Satan's rhetoric of flattery and insinuation is designed to defuse his followers' resentment against his failed war policy, and to circumvent choice. Insisting that their defeat was wholly unpredictable, and denying that "counsels different, or danger shunn'd / By me, have lost our hopes," he treats the continuation of the war as a matter beyond question, proposing a debate only about means. Unlike Pericles, Satan appears to offer choices while in fact closing them off, and the comparison invites us to discriminate between honorable political rhetoric and demagogic manipulation.

Satan evidently intended his address proposing rebellion to his assembled cohort in heaven (5.772-907) as another such speech. Immediately after God's proclamation of his Son, Satan began a campaign of deceit and innuendo, again using Beelzebub as instrument.[37] Ostensibly proposing to consult about the reception of the new King in his Progress, he suggests instead that "better counsels" might "teach us to cast off this Yoke." His republican rhetoric recalls Cicero urging the Roman citizens to defend their liberties against Mark Antony,[38] but it hardly accords with the podium Satan chooses for his speech—a throne on a mountaintop closely imitating that from which God proclaimed his son King. He evidently intended to incite his followers to declare a revolution by acclamation:

> Will ye submit your necks, and choose to bend
> The supple knee? ye will not, if I trust
> To know ye right, or if ye know yourselves
> . . . .
> Who can in reason then or right assume
> Monarchy over such as live by right
> His equals, . . .
> . . . .
> And look for adoration to th' abuse
> Of those Imperial Titles which assert
> Our being ordain'd to govern, not to serve?
> (5.786-802)

However, Abdiel's outraged interruption at this point turns the occasion into a formal debate about politics, history, ethics, and causality, forcing the angels to consider alternative arguments and so to make their choices consciously and freely.

94

Abdiel thereby counters the Satanic debasement of delibera-
tive oratory with a truly heroic, indeed heavenly, model.

When tempting Eve, Satan delivers another such oration
(9.670-732), this time uninterrupted, and adapted to the sit-
uation of the solitary female auditor. Adam, who might have
played the part of an Abdiel, is absent. At the start, Satan
employs fulsome compliments and invents a false autobiog-
raphy to win Eve's favor and induce her to follow him to the
supposedly miraculous tree. But when she defines God's pro-
hibition on the fruit as a positive law, standing outside the
Law of Reason (and hence not to be understood through
rational argument), Satan dazzles her with a finished, formal
oration calculated to blur that sharp distinction. Milton invites
us to compare Satan with the great orators who advised the
governing assemblies of democratic Athens and the republic
of Rome on high issues of war and peace and public safety: a
Demosthenes warning against Philip of Macedon, a Pericles
advising of dangers from Sparta, a Cicero fulminating against
Cataline or Marc Antony. Like them, Satan now,

> New part puts on, and as to passion mov'd,
> Fluctuates disturb'd, yet comely, and in act
> Rais'd, as of some great matter to begin.
> As when of old some Orator renown'd
> In *Athens* or free *Rome*, where Eloquence
> Flourish'd, since mute, to some great cause addrest.
>
> (9.668-72)

We are meant to recognize the disproportion, as a splendid
snake brings all this to bear upon a solitary, nymphlike Eve in
a pastoral garden. But on a larger view we should recognize
that the heroic rhetoric is decorous: Eve is queen of the earth
and upon her decision rests the fate, not of a single nation
but of the entire human race. In essence, however, Satan per-
verts the noble political advice of a Demosthenes or a Cicero.
We might rather compare him with Curio in Lucan's epic,
goading Caesar to revolt by enumerating the rightful honors
enviously denied him by the Senate and by pandering to his
ambition: "You can have the whole world for yourself."[39] In

95

this vein Satan addresses Eve as "Queen of this Universe," suggests that God or the gods have enviously deprived her of her due, and stimulates her ambition for godlike knowledge.

Satan's speech puts to brilliant use the technical advice of the rhetorical treatises. His gestures and motions engage his audience and establish ethical proof even before he begins to speak, intimating his "Zeal and Love / To Man, and indignation at his wrong." His prefatory apostrophe to the tree, delivered in the "highth" of the impassioned grand style, provides further ethical proof as he affects to have gained from the tree the powers that make him a wise and authoritative counselor for Eve: "O Sacred, Wise, and Wisdom-giving Plant, / Mother of Science, Now I feel thy Power / Within me clear, not only to discern / Things in thir Causes, but to trace the ways / Of highest Agents, deem'd however wise."[40] His management of pathetic proof is masterly throughout, as he arouses in Eve, by turns, wonder at the marvelous tree, pleasure in the admiration of the serpent, a nagging sense of inadequacy, a vague resentment of wrongs at the hands of God, and ambitious desire for godhead.

After the apostrophe Satan's style becomes terse, emphatic, and plain, as he confronts Eve with a barrage of definitions, examples, false syllogisms, and rhetorical questions, subtly complimenting those rational powers wherein she knows herself inferior to Adam. His strategy is to force her to think very quickly about many complex ideas, to confront in rapid succession a host of difficult questions and his answers to them, and to reel before the shifting meaning he ascribes to such terms as God, the gods, death, knowledge, good and evil. By such means he leads her to analyze the prohibition she once knew to be outside the province of reason, as if it were some obscure oracle requiring elaborate critical interpretation. Death, Satan suggests, cannot really mean death: God could not justly punish Eve for such a petty trespass but will rather praise her for daring to seek a higher life. Death must in fact mean transmutation to higher status: "So ye shall die perhaps, by putting off / Human, to put on Gods, death to be wisht." Knowledge of good and evil he defines as the special characteristic of the gods, but also as the magical property of certain apples, which whoso eats "forthwith attains / Wisdom."

He further confuses Eve by playing upon the terms "God" and "gods." First, he devises a false syllogism based on God's attributes to prove that God could not punish Eve for seeking knowledge of good and evil:

> Of good, how just? of evil, if what is evil
> Be real, why not known, since easier shunn'd?
> God therefore cannot hurt ye, and be just;
> Not just, not God; not fear'd then, nor obey'd:
> Your fear itself of Death removes the fear.
> (9.698-702)

Later, his query as to whether "the gods" are the origins of all things and so possess by right the tree and its knowledge implicitly denies any real distinction between God the Creator and the angels—the position argued explicitly by Satan in his debate with Abdiel. By such wordplay Satan intimates that it is not clear from whom the prohibition comes or whether it has any basis other than the malice and envy which he attributes to the gods and/or to God. His final salutation to Eve as "Goddess humane" proclaims her rightful place in this ambiguous company.

As political or deliberative orators, then, Satan and the fallen angels exhibit all the technical skills taught by the rhetorical theorists and in this regard match or surpass the greatest orators of epic and history. But they fail utterly to meet the standard of Plato, Cicero, and Quintilian for the political orator—that he make the citizenry better. Satanic rhetoric always seeks to make its audiences worse—in heaven, in hell, and on earth.

TRAGIC UTTERANCE: SOLILOQUY AND LAMENT

Soliloquy is the other kind of discourse characteristic of the damned, and elegiac lament mixed with complaint is their major lyric genre. Both are normally tragic in mode: the soliloquy is closely identified with the great Elizabethan tragic heroes; and the lament is especially prominent in Homer's tragic epic, the *Iliad*. As Satan uses them, these forms are very much mixed. The classification of elegy as a lyric kind is itself highly ambiguous in the Renaissance,[41] and in any case Satan's brief, passionate outbursts of grief and pain soon modulate to argument, analysis, and soliloquy, as if the damned consciousness cannot long sustain lyric expression of such personal emotion. Also, the privateness of soliloquy as meditative speech or self-analysis is continually subverted by the admixture of public, rhetorical elements—suggesting that the damned consciousness cannot long sustain a direct confrontation with the self in any genre.

Satan's five soliloquies associate him with the great tragic protagonists of the Elizabethan stage—flawed heroes, revengers, villains—all of whom give vent to their passions, work out their plans, and lock themselves into their fatal choices in soliloquies.[42] Satan's soliloquies manifest what the hell within really means: terrible psychological isolation, spiritual suffering, and "the hateful siege / Of contraries" (9.121-22), which destroy all vestiges of the heaven or the paradise within. He begins each soliloquy by responding to the beauty, goodness, and joy of God's Creation, but then finds that he cannot because he will not act on these good impulses. His damned nature can develop only according to its own psychological laws—"hard be hard'n'd, blind be blinded more." Accordingly, each soliloquy ends with plots and sneers, transforming the pity and fear we first feel for Satan into revulsion. At their noblest, Elizabethan tragic soliloquies are honest, painful, probing self-analyses leading to insight. Satan's soliloquies turn into rationalizations for ever-more-reprehensible actions.

Satan's laments, mixed with complaint, are not centrally concerned with major elegiac subjects, death and love, but address other recognized topics: exile, defeats in battle, loss of honor or goods, desolation of cities and countries.[43] Love elegies and funeral elegies flourished in the Renaissance, the latter usually displaying a tripartite structure of praise, lamentation for loss, consolation.[44] Laments are also common in epic, especially in the *Iliad* where they promote pathos and intensify the tragic tone. Valedictions and elegies for the dead and those fated to die echo throughout that poem, and dirges, choral and monodic, are chanted over the bodies of Patroklos and Hector.[45] In the related genre of complaint, prominent in romantic epics, the speaker blames his love miseries or other unhappiness on a lover, or fortune, or some other cause, and pleads for a remedy. Often enough the two forms are combined: Dido's several outbursts when Aeneas leaves Troy supply a precedent for Satan in their mixture of grieving lament with bitter complaint.[46] Significantly, Satan often begins but cannot sustain laments, so they do not provide that partial cure of grief Puttenham ascribed to the kind.[47] Yet truncated and self-involved as they are, these poignant tragic utterances evoke, at least briefly, our pity.

Several speeches in Book One begin with apostrophes of lament, which soon modulate to analytic discourse. Satan's first words to Beelzebub—"If thou beest hee; But O how fall'n! how chang'd"—recall epic laments or epicedes for dead heroes in the *Iliad* and the *Aeneid*. But Satan's lament, evoked by the signs of spiritual death on his companion's countenance, quickly gives way to analysis of his own situation.[48] Soon after, he begins an *apobaterion*—a valedictory lament for familiar places and joys upon going into exile: "Farewell happy Fields / Where Joy for ever dwells: Hail horrors, hail / Infernal world, and thou profoundest Hell / Receive thy new Possessor."[49] But again, lament gives way almost immediately to claims and plans regarding the new land.

On Mount Niphates Satan delivers his first great soliloquy, which incorporates elements of lament and judicial oration (4.32-113). In its essence, it resembles Faustus' anguished soliloquy during his last hour on earth, and Claudius' desperate attempt to pray after Hamlet's mousetrap is sprung. Satan here admits his entire responsibility for his fall, and makes an ineffectual gesture toward repentance—"O then at last relent: is there no place / Left for Repentance, none for Pardon left?" However, he does not, like Faustus, give way utterly to anguish and terror, nor does he, like Claudius, indulge himself in false hopes of grace and pardon.[50] In them the impulse to repentance is subverted by despair and unwillingness to amend life; in Satan, as he himself declares, it is also blocked by more vicious passions—envious ingratitude, deadly hate, proud disdain.

Contained within this soliloquy is a truncated lament whose topics—praise, lamentation and complaint for losses, consolation—are briefly voiced but not developed. After a hate-filled dispraise of the Sun as "the God / Of this new World," Satan briefly enumerates and praises what he has lost: his glory above the Sun's sphere, his creation "in that bright eminence," the easy service of heaven's "matchless King." Later, he breaks into despairing lamentation as he realizes that his mind is indeed its own place, and that place always hell:

> Me miserable! which way shall I fly
> Infinite wrath, and infinite despair?
> Which way I fly is Hell; myself am Hell;
> And in the lowest deep a lower deep
> Still threat'ning to devour me opens wide,
> To which the Hell I suffer seems a Heav'n.
> O then at last relent: is there no place
> Left for Repentance, none for Pardon left?
> (4.73-80)

The phonetic echo of the opening of Psalm 51—"Me miserable," "Miserere me"—calls attention to the biblical model for lament which Satan here explicitly rejects as he refuses to sue for mercy. As the soliloquy concludes, a second brief *apobaterion* bids a final farewell to every vestige of the inner paradise: "So farewell Hope, and with Hope farewell Fear, / Farewell Remorse: all Good to me is lost." It is followed by a brief and terrible parody of consolation in which Satan commits himself yet more entirely to evil—"Evil be thou my Good"— thinking thereby to share empire with God.

100

In essence, however, Satan's speech is soliloquy, not elegy—
a soliloquy that takes on some tonalities of public rhetoric and
some features of the judicial oration. As Satan argues his case
before the court of his own conscience, we are invited to com-
pare the very different judicial oration in which God argues
the case against mankind in a public forum, the court of Heaven
(3.80-134).[51] Technically, Satan's oration is of the equitable
kind, concerned with whether an action is right or wrong; it
addresses an "assumptive" issue (he admits guilt but tries to
develop some defense from extraneous circumstances); and it
shifts continually between topics pertaining to defense and to
accusation.[52]

His exordium portrays the opponent as haughty, cruel, and
malicious, in accordance with a recommended exordium topic:
it intimates that the Sun, God's emblem, deliberately dimin-
ishes the light of other stars, and intensifies Satan's own pain.[53]
His brief narration describes his actions and motives in such
a way as to suggest that he was the hapless object of abstract
forces: "Pride and worse Ambition threw me down / Warring
in Heav'n against Heav'n's matchless King." In the *confirmatio*
he takes on the role of prosecutor, proving the case against
himself from the topic of "persons"[54] as he contrasts God's
goodness to him with his own ambition and ingratitude. Then,
as defendant, he attempts to shift some responsibility for his
fall to his exalted station,[55] but finds himself refuted by the
case of the loyal inferior angels, and by his own experience of
free will. He closes the case for the defense by cursing "Heav'ns
free Love" as the cause of his plight, but then calls for judg-
ment against himself: "Nay curs'd be thou; since against his
thy will / Chose freely what it now so justly rues." His per-
oration includes the poignant lament already discussed, which
develops topics of pathos proper for a guilty defendant[56] but
eschews the expected plea for mercy. Instead, he shifts to top-
ics appropriate to a prosecutor's peroration, arguing against a
pardon on the grounds of his own hardened nature and the
certainty that he would again revolt.[57] The peroration ends
with proud defiance of God, a parody of Cicero's recommen-

dation that the accused show himself "lofty, noble, patient of misfortune."[58]

In his second soliloquy—"O Hell! what do mine eyes with grief behold" (4.358-92)—Satan finds himself attracted to the manifold graces and the divine resemblance shining in Adam and Eve, but his good impulse to admire, love, and pity them is vitiated from the outset by envy. Again he turns to rhetoric, presenting much of his soliloquy as if it were an ironic ceremonial address from a head of state to magistrates of another state, offering them league, friendship, hospitality, refuge from imminent danger, and assimilation into a larger empire:

> this high seat your Heav'n
> Ill fenc't for Heav'n to keep out such a foe
> As now is enter'd; yet no purpos'd foe
> To you whom I could pity thus forlorn
> Though I unpitied: League with you I seek,
> And mutual amity so strait, so close,
> That I with you must dwell, or you with me
> Henceforth; my dwelling haply may not please
> Like this fair Paradise, your sense, yet such
> Accept your Maker's work; he gave it me,
> Which I as freely give; Hell shall unfold,
> To entertain you two, her widest Gates,
> And send forth all her Kings; there will be room,
> Not like these narrow limits, to receive
> Your numerous offspring.
> (4.371-85)

He then voices the politics of a Machiavellian Prince, citing "public reason," honor, empire, and revenge as requiring the else abhorrent destruction of these innocents. Such necessity, the narrator reminds us, is always the tyrant's plea.

Satan's third soliloquy—"Sight hateful, sight tormenting!" (4.505-35)—recalls Richard III blaming his malice upon the deformity that isolates him from all love and pleasure, and especially Iago working out his plot against Othello with malicious glee.[59] Again Satan is momentarily attracted to good—

102

here, marital bliss. But his brief epithalamic praise of Adam and Eve "Imparadis't in one another's arms" is spoken with "jealous leer malign"; and it promptly gives way to analysis of his own sexual jealousy and envy, his "fierce desire . . . unfulfill'd," and his "pain of longing." From self-analysis he soon turns to rhetoric again, trying out, as it were, his temptation strategy on a sympathetic audience:

> Knowledge forbidd'n?
> Suspicious, reasonless. Why should thir Lord
> Envy them that? can it be sin to know,
> Can it be death? and do they only stand
> By Ignorance, is that thir happy state,
> The proof of thir obedience and thir faith?
> O fair foundation laid whereon to build
> Thir ruin!
>
> (4.515-22)

The tone of malign delight continues as Satan predicts success for the several arguments he will build on this foundation.

When Satan returns to Eden a week after his ignominious expulsion by Gabriel he delivers a long complaint-lament which modulates to soliloquy (9.99-178). Milton clearly identifies the first genre (ll. 97-114) as he describes Satan pouring forth his "inward grief" and his "bursting passion" into "plaints." This most complete Satanic lyric occurs just after the Bard has changed his notes to tragic, and it is, appropriately, the first in a series of laments and complaints for the lost paradise which echo through the fallen world in Books Nine to Twelve. For Satan Paradise is already lost: his inner hell prevents him from finding joy or ease in any of the Edenic beauties and delights.

The complaint-lament begins with a long, eloquent praise of the earth and of man, the only unalloyed praise Satan speaks in the poem. But even here Satan reveals failures in perception and discrimination, valuing earth's beauties over those of heaven and assuming (as Raphael did not) that earth is the center of a Ptolemaic universe:

O Earth, how like to Heav'n, if not preferr'd
More justly, Seat worthier of Gods, as built
With second thoughts, reforming what was old!
For what God after better worse would build?
Terrestrial Heav'n, danc't round by other Heav'ns

. . . .
                    so thou
Centring receiv'st from all those Orbs; in thee,
Not in themselves, all thir known virtue appears
Productive in Herb, Plant, and nobler birth
Of Creatures animate with gradual life
Of Growth, Sense, Reason, all summ'd up in Man.
With what delight could I have walkt thee round,
If I could joy in aught, sweet interchange
Of Hill and Valley, Rivers, Woods and Plains.

                                        (9.99-116)

Then, lamenting his loss of all these goods, he complains that
he can find no "place or refuge" on earth and that the Edenic
delights only intensify the "hateful siege of contraries" in him.
The lyric ends with a truncated, perverse, parodic consolation
as Satan declares, "only in destroying I find ease," and then
slides into analytic speech, soliloquy.

The soliloquy segment (ll. 135-78) reviews the other base
motives for Satan's intended crime against Adam and Eve:
glory from his cohort, jealousy and envy of man, revenge and
spite against God. Drawing once again upon the judicial or-
ation, Satan also attempts a "retort of the charge"[60]—justify-
ing or partly excusing an act on the ground of wrongful prov-
ocation. His claim is that God spitefully affronted the angels
by enduing humans (created from base earth) with angels'
spoils and subjecting "Angel wings" to their service. Then, as
he prepares to imbrute himself in the serpent, he again breaks
out in anguished complaints, recognizing in this self-chosen
degradation the loss of his very essence:

O foul descent! that I who erst contended
With Gods to sit the highest, am now constrain'd

104

Into a Beast, and mixt with bestial slime,
This essence to incarnate and imbrute,
That to the highth of Deity aspir'd.
(9.163-67)

After this Satan has no more lyric moments, though he does attain a moment of moral clarity as he voices the paradox that ambition will stoop to any baseness in order to climb, and the fact that revenge inevitably recoils upon itself. But he pulls back at once, and his last words project his own spite upon creature and Creator alike: "this Man of Clay, Son of despite, / Whom us the more to spite his Maker rais'd / From dust: spite then with spite is best repaid" (9.176-78).

His brief soliloquy just before embarking on the temptation of Eve—"Thoughts, whither have ye led me" (9.473-93)—follows upon a powerful attraction to the beauty and innocence of Eve. An elegant epic simile compares him to a jaded city dweller suddenly placed in a pastoral *locus amoenus* inhabited by a nymph. For the nonce he is struck "Stupidly good, of enmity disarm'd, / Of guile, of hate, of envy, of revenge" (9.445-66). He uses the soliloquy to recall himself to his purpose, and to argue the need to seize the occasion offered by Eve's solitary situation. He now admits that the hell within has so debased and enfeebled him that he hesitates to confront Adam's intellect, courage, and strength. He also admits the "terror" he has experienced from the love, grace, and beauty attendant upon Eve, but concludes with some confidence that his hatred, masked as love, will prove stronger. His plot now underway, he has no further need for soliloquy.

LYRIC AND RHETORIC OF PRAISE

Though Milton's hell is preeminently a society of speech, some music and song are heard there. "Dulcet Symphonies," apparently spontaneous and accompanied by "voices sweet," resound when Pandaemonium rises out of the ground (1.712): even diabolic artistic creativity, it seems, evokes such harmonies. As Plato recommended, music in the Dorian mood by "Flutes and soft Recorders" accompanies the martial pageant of the Satanic armies in hell (1.549-53).[61] Also, some of the fallen sing epic songs—not about other heroes (as did Achilles and Demodocus),[62] but songs of themselves, of "Thir own Heroic deeds and hapless fall" (2.546-55). But they cannot sustain the impulses characteristic of lyric—praise, love, or even (as we have seen) unalloyed grief.

Occasionally Satan inverts or parodies a strain or two of the songs which continually resound thoughout heaven and Eden. Of course he sings no hymns (the highest lyric genre), but his first soliloquy in Book Four begins with a parody of the Bard's hymnic praise of the Celestial Light in the proem to Book Three. The opening lines are a perverse invocatory "hymn" of hate and dispraise to the Sun, as emblem of God in the world:

> O thou that with surpassing Glory crown'd,
> Look'st from thy sole Dominion like the God
> Of this new World; at whose sight all the Stars
> Hide thir diminisht heads; to thee I call,
> But with no friendly voice, and add thy name
> O Sun, to tell thee how I hate thy beams.
>
> (4.32-37)

Similarly, Satan's third soliloquy begins with an epithalamic strain, but he greets the marriage of Adam and Eve with envy rather than celebration.[63] And his praise of the earth in Book Nine is elegiac in tone rather than odelike, in consonance with its function as part of a complaint-lament.

Satan voices two love lyrics as part of his temptation of Eve—graceful in form but suspect in theme and tone. The charming serenade which Eve reports at second hand as part of her Satan-inspired dream evokes the courtly love ethos of starved lovers, elegant seductions, and nocturnal trysts:

> Why sleep'st thou *Eve*? now is the pleasant time,
> The cool, the silent, save where silence yields
> To the night-warbling Bird, that now awake

Tunes sweetest his love-labor'd song; now reigns
Full Orb'd the Moon, and with more pleasing light
Shadowy sets off the face of things; in vain,
If none regard; Heav'n wakes with all his eyes,
Whom to behold but thee, Nature's desire,
In whose sight all things joy, with ravishment
Attracted by thy beauty still to gaze.
(5.38-47)

The sensuous imagery, conventional romantic diction, and hyperbole in this nocturne are evident when we make the intended comparison with Adam's lovely *aubade* and its source in Canticles 2:10.[64] In Book Nine, Satan initiates his temptation of Eve with a Petrarchan sonnetlike poem of praise (9.532-48) which is a pastiche of the phrases and conventions of the kind: "sovran Mistress," "sole Wonder," "arm / Thy looks, the Heav'n of mildness, with disdain," "awful brow," "Fairest resemblance of thy Maker fair," "Celestial Beauty," "A Goddess among Gods," and more. For this poem, the standard of judgment is Eve's own lovely, tender, and eloquently simple love sonnet in praise of Adam (4.641-56). Still more important, Satan's love songs violate the essential nature of lyric: they do not express but falsify his emotions, sentiments, and purposes.

Satan's return to hell after his success on earth is presented as a travesty of a Roman Triumph, with appropriate demonstrative rhetoric. Also, the ceremonies and speeches of praise often echo and parody the celestial honors accorded the Son at the Creation—there, in exalted hymns, not speeches. As Satan returns from earth over the bridge spanning Chaos, Sin formally presents that bridge to him as a "Trophy" of his victory and as a surrogate triumphal arch (10.354-83).[65] Like a Roman magistrate awarding a Triumph, Sin proclaims Satan's vast and definitive conquests and benefits to the state. Appealing to the most honorable of the three topics commonly proposed for epideixis, the goods of character involving noble deeds and great virtues,[66] Sin represents Satan's treachery

107

in Eden as a victory of *virtus* and *sapientia* over God's brute
force:

> O Parent, these are thy magnific deeds,
> Thy Trophies, which thou view'st as not thine own,
> Thou art thir Author and prime Architect:
> . . . .
> Thine now is all this World, thy virtue hath won
> What thy hands builded not, thy Wisdom gain'd
> With odds what War hath lost, and fully aveng'd
> Our foil in Heav'n.
> (10.354-75)

Going far beyond the godlike honors accorded the Roman
imperator (who was reminded of his mortality even while rid-
ing in his triumphal chariot garbed as Jupiter[67]) Sin proclaims
that Satan now divides the monarchy of the universe with
God. And Satan's response (10.384-409) parodies the impe-
rator's customary praises of his soldiers for their part in the
victory, for by lauding Sin and Death as progeny worthy of
their ancestry and describing their glorious deeds as responses
to his own, he arrogates all honor to himself.[68]

Satan's subsequent address to the "great consulting Peers"
in Pandaemonium (10.460-503) is the highest flight of Sa-
tanic demonstrative rhetoric—a panegyric to himself that is
also designed for maximum political effect.[69] In tone and
manner it reminds us of a Roman emperor proclaiming a
Triumph for himself, but also demonstrating that his victory
meets the more noble and stringent criteria required during
the Republic for the award of a Triumph to a victorious gen-
eral. Those criteria were: that he win with his own troops a
major and decisive battle against a foreign enemy, that he kill
at least five thousand of the enemy while sustaining few losses,
and that his victory extend the boundaries of the state.[70] Satan
claims he has won an amazing victory single-handed by the
remarkable strategem of the apple, bringing death to all man-
kind and extending the rebels' dominion over all the earth.
But the comparison Satan's language invites reminds us that

Roman Triumphs were awarded for glorious military victories, not strategems perpetrated by fraud. And his scoffing allusion to God's judgment upon him—"A World who would not purchase with a bruise, / Or much more grievous pain?"—reminds us that Satan's victory is not decisive, that the final victory belongs to the Woman's Seed.

Finally, Satan would reverse the course of a Roman triumphal procession in which the imperator was solemnly led from outside the walls into the city,[71] when he proposes to lead his forces "Triumphant out of this infernal Pit" and *to* a conquered land which they would "possess, / As Lords" (10.463-67). The reversal underscores the ironic fact that the fallen angels have lost forever their true heavenly city, and that no conquest can restore them to it. And Satan's concluding invitation—"up and enter now into full bliss"—points forward ironically to the true apocalyptic triumph in which the Son will lead his redeemed from exile in hell into the "full bliss" of heaven.

These Satanic flights of high epideictic rhetoric are followed immediately by bathos, contrived by the divine Satirist. Satan's would-be triumphal celebration turns into a ceremony of grotesque humiliation. Instead of applause and songs of triumph he hears "A dismal universal hiss" from his followers transformed to snakes. And instead of putting on God-like splendor, he assumes the form of a "monstrous Serpent" writhing in the dust.

Milton's fallen angels are masters of several kinds of deliberative, epic, dialogic, and epideictic speech as well as of tragic soliloquy—though all of these kinds are perverted from their ideal uses and noblest models. The tendency of these several genres to take on the characteristics of deliberative rhetoric, as well as the virtual absence of lyric in the infernal society, testify to the imaginative and emotional poverty of the damned. Hell's generic repertoire stands in sharp contrast to the wide variety and constant mixture of genres and modes in Milton's heavenly and human societies.

FIVE

"Other Excellence": Generic Multiplicity and Milton's Literary God

IT IS A commonplace of criticism that the most difficult problem Milton faced in *Paradise Lost* involved the portrayal of God. Milton indeed undertook to "justify the ways of God to men," but the problem for many readers—from his day to ours—has been to justify Milton's ways with God. Early to late, readers have questioned the theological appropriateness and literary success of Milton's anthropomorphic presentation of God as epic character. For Addison he is simply dull, a school divine delivering long sermons; for Shelley and Empson a cruel torturer and tyrant; for A.J.A. Waldock a divine egotist; for Douglas Bush an "almighty cat watching a human mouse."[1]

Recent theological approaches offer somewhat more positive interpretations: C. A. Patrides' examination of Milton's theology of Accommodation; Michael Lieb's attention to the poem's evocation of the numinous; Dennis Danielson's study of the poem as a literary theodicy; Georgia Christopher's analysis of Milton's God in Reformation terms, as a powerful dramatic and noetic voice challenging characters and readers alike.[2] And newer critical methods have redefined the problem in other terms. Stanley Fish emphasizes the fallen reader's inappropriate responses to a "determinedly non-affective" God; William Kerrigan analyzes the God of the poem in terms of the Oedipal psychic history of the poet; and Andrew Milner's Marxist analysis finds in *Paradise Lost* an unfortunate hybrid of the anthropomorphic God of Genesis and the God of Milton's true belief—the abstract principle of Reason.[3]

In my view, interpretation should start from the fact that

110

God and the Son in *Paradise Lost* are literary portraits. As Bard, Milton had to imagine the divine beings poetically, and also to accommodate that apprehension to his readers in terms suited to his poetic and educative purposes. To these ends he employed generic multiplicity, calling upon an even wider range of literary forms than he used in presenting Satan. They include generic paradigms, conventions, and topoi from epic, romance, drama, dialogue, judicial oratory, and more; as well as models and analogues from Homer and Virgil, from Hesiod and Ovid, from Plato and Lucretius, from Genesis and Exodus, and other texts.

The several paradigms do not carry through the poem to be resolved in a scene of closure (as with Satan), but are provided as interpretative frames for particular scenes and episodes in which specific aspects of God are presented. Such complex layering and fusion of genres in individual scenes provide multiple perspectives upon God, suggesting the divine totality and transcendence, and at the same time pointing up how partial, inadequate, and incomplete is any single frame— even the biblical one. An analysis of the literary means by which both Bard and reader imagine the God of the poem may not dispel all our resistance to that figure, but it should indicate that Milton finds a more daring and more satisfactory resolution to his poetic problem than we have realized.

This poetic strategy is, moreover, entirely consonant with the theological principles Milton outlined in the *De Doctrina Christiana* as guidelines for all conceptions of or imaginations of God—and so by definition those of a poet intending to write a great and true epic of the human condition. The first principle, wholly commonplace, is that God "as he really is" is utterly beyond human conception or imagination.[4] The second principle, also a commonplace among Protestants but potentially radical in its forthright repudiation of metaphysics, is that our idea or image of God should correspond precisely to the way he is presented in the Bible—not because the biblical image is literally true (it cannot be) but because that is how God wishes to be understood by us, the way in which he has accommodated himself to our capacities:

111

It is safest for us to form an image of God in our minds which corresponds to his representation and description of himself in the sacred writings. Admittedly, God is always described or outlined not as he really is but in such a way as will make him conceivable to us. Nevertheless, we ought to form just such a mental image of him as he, in bringing himself within the limits of our understanding, wishes us to form. Indeed he has brought himself down to our level expressly to prevent our being carried beyond the range of human comprehension, and outside the written authority of scripture, into vague subtleties of speculation. . . . We should form our ideas with scripture as a model, for that is the way in which he has offered himself to our contemplation.[5]

The third principle, yet more radical as Milton interprets it, is that *all aspects* of the biblical portrayal of God are intended by him to figure in our conception, so that we should not try to explain away passages that seem to us "unworthy" of God, or that present him anthropomorphically:

On the question of what is or what is not suitable for God, let us ask no more dependable authority than God himself. If *Jehovah repented that he had created man*, Gen. vi.6, *and repented because of their groanings*, Judges ii.18, let us believe that he did repent. . . . If it is said that God, after working for six days, *rested and was refreshed*, Exod. xxxi.17, and if he *feared his enemy's displeasure*, Deut. xxxii.27, let us believe that it is not beneath God to feel what grief he does feel, to be refreshed by what refreshes him, to fear what he does fear. . . . In short, God either is or is not really like he says he is. If he really is like this, why should we think otherwise? If he is not really like this, on what authority do we contradict God? If, at any rate, he wants us to imagine him in this way, why does our imagination go off on some other tack?[6]

112

One implication of this radically metaphoric but yet insistently biblical imagination of God is that it gives Milton full warrant as poet to portray God as an epic character who can and does feel a range of emotions (fear, wrath, scorn, dismay, love), who makes himself visible and audible to his creatures in various ways, who engages in dialogue with his Son, with the angels, and (through the Son) with man and woman. Moreover, though the portrayal of God and the Son in *Paradise Lost* draws heavily upon biblical language and imagery,[7] the fact that, for Milton, the Bible itself offers only accommodated images of God evidently sanctions for him the use of other literary accommodations that accord with and help to expand the biblical images. In addition, since Milton sees that the biblical portrayal is by no means univocal, that God is variously conceived and represented by the various biblical writers through a panoply of literary forms—folk tale, history, law, prophecy, allegory, epic story, drama, psalm, and proverb, among others—he has warrant for his similar generic strategy in *Paradise Lost*.

Milton does not, then, attempt to make the incomprehensible God a unified, fully realized character in *Paradise Lost*, or, always, an attractive one by human standards. I think he would have considered such an undertaking presumptuous and absurd. Rather, following the biblical model, he employs a mix of generic patterns and references to suggest the manifold qualities and aspects associated with the Deity in the Old and New Testament, as well as in Christian theology and Western literature. The Son is presented often but by no means exclusively in terms of heroic patterns transformed. And the Father is presented at times with reference to various Old Testament theophanies, but also with reference to the activities of Zeus in Homer and Hesiod, and of Jove in Ovid. This method accommodates God and the Son to us as figures in a kaleidoscope, presenting different images as the generic perspective shifts,[8] and requiring from us a strenuous process of comparison, contrast, and judgment. The analogues in themselves help to image the divine attributes and acts, but also to refine our conceptions as we recognize that they are exceeded in an infinite scale by the nature and deeds of God and the Son. The final effect is to suggest God's transcendence of any and all biblical or literary accommodations—including that offered in *Paradise Lost*.

THE DIALOGUE IN HEAVEN: LOVE DIVINE

The Dialogue in Heaven (3.56-343) offers the most complex layering and mixture of genres in the entire poem. Introducing the scene, the Miltonic Bard provides some guide to its interpretation. He portrays God "High Thron'd above all highth," with his eye encompassing all time, past, present, and future, and regarding "His own works and their works at once"—the "Sanctities of Heaven," the "radiant image of his Glory," "Our two first Parents," "Hell and the Gulf between, and *Satan*." This striking description identifies God as the origin and final cause of all these creatures and their actions, while at the same time indicating that his creatures also shape themselves by their own choices and works.

Also, the inclusion of the Son among the "works" of God prepares us for Milton's presentation of him in the ensuing Dialogue and throughout the poem in a manner consistent with the antitrinitarianism of the *De Doctrina*. That tract argues that the Father is the supreme and only self-existent God; that he generated the Son "within the bounds of time" as the "firstborn of the creatures," by an act of will (not natural necessity); and that he imparted to the Son only "as much as he wished of the divine nature and attributes."[9] As we will see, the poem also accords with the theology of the tract in portraying the Son as the Father's Image; as the agent or instrument of the Father's creation, vengeance, judgment, regeneration, and providential government; and as an independent moral agent, taking on these roles freely, in obedience and by choice.[10]

The Dialogue in Heaven scene emphasizes the aspect of divine love. The Father indicates the centrality of this issue as he poses his challenge to the heavenly assembly:

> Say Heav'nly Powers, where shall we find such love,
> Which of ye will be mortal to redeem
> Man's mortal crime, and just th' unjust to save,
> Dwells in all Heaven charity so dear?
> (3.213-16)

Later, the Father declares that the Son's voluntary offer to die for humankind proves him "By Merit more than Birthright Son of God," because in him "Love hath abounded more than Glory abounds" (3.309-12). The suggestion is that heroic love, freely tendered, is the core of the Son's goodness and merit, and is the quality wherein he most closely resembles the Father as image of divine love.

Milton imagines and presents the Dialogue in Heaven through many generic frames and with reference to several specific models, developing true and transcendent norms to supplant Satan's debased or perverted ones. First of all, the scene is a species of epic *Concilia Deorum*.[11] The Father's self-justification is intended to remind us of the Council of the Gods in the *Odyssey*, in which Zeus and Athena discuss Zeus' ways toward Odysseus, and Zeus defends himself by pointing to humankind's own responsibility for the evils they suffer:

> O for shame, how the mortals put the blame upon us
> gods, for they say evils come from us, but it is they,
>   rather,
> who by their own recklessness win sorrow beyond what is
>   given.[12]

Zeus applies this precept to the punishment of Aigisthos, who despite the gods' warnings persisted in his design to kill Agamemnon, and now has paid for it. Milton's God offers a more elaborate theological defense, but in much the same aggrieved tones and terms:

115

They therefore as to right belong'd,
So were created, nor can justly accuse
Thir maker, or thir making, or thir Fate;
As if Predestination over-rul'd
Thir will, dispos'd by absolute Decree
Or high foreknowledge; they themselves decreed
Thir own revolt, not I.
                                        (3.111-17)

This analogue intimates that the problem of God's justice
is perennial and the particular solutions always partial. But
further comparison underscores the profound difference be-
tween the two epics in the relation of God and man. In the
Odyssey, Athena, goddess of wisdom, plays the suasory role in
the Council of the Gods. Appealing to the same principles of
justice that rightly condemned Aigisthos, she bespeaks pity
and aid for beleaguered Odysseus, who is agreed to be wise
and worthy. By contrast, the Son's pleas for fallen man (hardly
wise and worthy) are appeals for mercy, not justice; and
Athena's advice and assistance to Odysseus pale before the aid
the Son provides to humankind at the cost of his own life.

The Son's offer to die for fallen man also recalls another
generic topic from epic and romance—deeds of bravery and
self-sacrifice inspired by erotic love and noble friendship. The
specific frame is Nisus' offer (*Aeneid* 9.427-28) to exchange
his life for that of his captured friend, Euryalus: "me, me,
adsum, qui feci, in me convertite ferrum, / o Rutuli! mea fraus
omnis." ("On me—on me—here am I who did the deed—on
me turn your steel, O Rutulians! Mine is all the guilt.")[13] The
Son directly echoes Nisus: "Behold mee then, mee for him,
life for life / I offer, on mee let thine anger fall" (3.236-37).
Pursuing the indicated comparison, we recognize that, unlike
Nisus, the Son had no share whatever in the guilt for which
he offers to die, and that his love extends beyond the individ-
ual friend or beloved to all humankind.[14]

This comparision points up how the Son's heroic love tran-
scends and transvalues the heroic virtues and actions central

116

to epic and romance. By willingly embracing suffering and death for love of mankind, he provides the true pattern for the "better fortitude / Of Patience and heroic Martyrdom" which the Bard exalts and which Satan perverts in his brave but prideful endurance of loss and pain in hell. By saving, not a tribe or a country but an entire creation, he utterly transforms the concept of epic action. He also revises the paradigm of the romance quest as, like a knight at Arthur's court, he undertakes to win man's salvation, but projects for that quest an absolute closure foreign to the romance mode: the return of all creation to union with the Father, so that "God shall be All in All" (3.335-41).

Yet another analogue and reference point, indicated by broad structural patterns and specific allusions, is the dialogue between Apollo and Phaethon in Ovid's *Metamorphoses* (2.1-152). In both scenes a son undertakes, in colloquy with his father, an enterprise that causes his death. Milton's description of God on his throne echoes Ovid's description of Apollo on his radiant throne in the Palace of the Sun.[15] Also, God's proclamation that the Son has shown himself "By Merit more than Birthright Son of God" (3.309) is a rather surprising echo of Apollo's declaration that Phaethon is indeed his son and worthy of the name: "nec tu meus esse negari / dignus es, et Clymene veros." In Sandys' 1632 version this is rendered, "By merit, as by birth, to thee is due / That name."[16]

These allusions point up how entirely the Father-Son dialogue in Milton reverses that in Ovid. In the *Metamorphoses* Phaethon initiates the dialogue with Apollo to seek confirmation of his sonship, and Apollo immediately testifies to that sonship and to Phaethon's merit; in *Paradise Lost* the Son's relation to the Father is never in doubt, but God testifies to the Son's merit only after that merit has been demonstrated in the dialogue itself. In Ovid Apollo rashly offers Phaethon any boon he wishes, and Phaethon (still seeking to prove his sonship) rashly asks to drive Apollo's chariot despite Apollo's lengthy and urgent efforts to dissuade him. In *Paradise Lost* the Son undertakes his passion and death after full and reasoned discussion, and with the high praise of the Father. Phaethon, a mortal who takes on through hubris a divine role he cannot perform, wreaks fiery havoc upon heaven, earth, and mankind and is himself destroyed. The Son, a God humbling himself to human estate to save mankind, succeeds in his undertaking and makes possible a re-creation after apocalyptic fire: "The World shall burn, and from her ashes spring / New Heav'n and Earth, wherein the just shall dwell" (3.334-35). By such reversals, and by the incarnation that links divine nature with human nature, the Son transcends the Ovidian metamorphic patterns and their Satanic perversions, promoting a divine metamorphosis:

> Therefore thy Humiliation shall exalt
> With thee thy Manhood also to this Throne;
> Here shalt thou sit incarnate, here shalt Reign
> Both God and Man, Son both of God and Man.
> (3.313-16)

The Bard also imagines and presents this scene in relation to a dramatic model, the allegorical "Parliament of Heaven" scene which figured prominently in medieval mystery and morality plays and in Milton's own outline for a drama on the topic of the Fall.[17] The basis of the episode was Psalm 85:10, a text prominent in the Christmas liturgy: "Mercy and truth are met together; righteousness and peace have kissed each other." The "Parliament" usually took the form of a debate among these four qualities (called daughters) of God over the issue of Adam's or mankind's sin and its punishment, with Truth and Righteousness ranged against Mercy and Peace. The issue was ultimately resolved—often after a thorough search of heaven and earth for volunteers to substitute for man—by the offer of the Son of God (sometimes called Heavenly Love or Sapience).

Milton's Dialogue in Heaven alludes to this dramatic tradition by the issues raised in the theological discourse, by the Son's response to a call throughout heaven for a volunteer, and quite specifically by language in the four speeches focusing, in turn, upon the four qualities. Here, however, instead of allegorical personifications stating fixed and apparently exclusive positions, the two speakers are dramatic characters, each of whom responds to and incorporates the argument of the other.[18]

God's first speech (3.80-134) sets forth the *truth* of things—Satan's escape, his impending success in the temptation, man's Fall, the doctrines of free will, sufficient grace, and personal responsibility for choice—but concludes with an affirmation of other qualities: "In Mercy and Justice both, / Through Heav'n and Earth, so shall my glory excel, / But Mercy first and last shall brightest shine." Responding to that statement, the Son (3.144-66) pleads the case for *mercy* to mankind, but appeals also to God's justice to prevent the triumph of Satanic evil: "That far be from thee, Father, who art Judge / Of all things made, and judgest only right." The Father's next speech (3.168-216) pronounces the stern demands of *justice*—"Die hee or Justice must"—but it begins with a restatement of his purpose to renew and save mankind, and it ends with a call to all the heavenly powers for "charity." The Son's response (3.227-65) emphasizes the "*peace* assured, / And reconcilement" he will achieve for man, but affirms as well that he will satisfy God's justice by his death and so allow the divine mercy to flow to man. The Father's concluding speech (3.274-343) celebrates the Son for reconciling all these elements in love: "So Heav'nly love shall outdo Hellish hate."

In mode this scene is tragicomic: it begins in wrath, strife, and loss, and we are made aware throughout of the potential for a tragic outcome, but it ends in joyful resolution and celebration. God's words seem to proclaim the Fall an irreversible tragic event—until the Son elicits God's plan for redemptive grace. And the dilemma God poses in regard to man's guilt—"Die hee or Justice must"—seems an insoluble tragic dilemma until the Son breaks through that impasse by agreeing to "pay / The rigid satisfaction, death for death." The love and patient endurance with which he offers to endure suffering and death so as to fulfill divine justice holds forth to us

119

the paradigm and norm for Christian tragedy.[19] It transcends the Promethean norm of defiant endurance of a divine tyrant's unjust tortures, and comments on the debased, Satanic parody of Promethean tragedy. In this scene we see the Son embrace the tragedy of the human fallen condition. But the scene as a whole provides an emblem of the final resolution of that human tragedy within God's all-embracing divine comedy.

Several discursive genres, chiefly varieties of dialogue, also provide frames of reference for this scene. Though the Father sometimes makes formal, solemn proclamations, as when he proclaims his Son Vice-gerent (5.600-15), his speech most often permits or invites an auditor to make a genuine verbal contribution to the interpretation or implementation of the divine purposes. Even as the Father's commission to Raphael and Michael allowed them great freedom to shape their discourse as they judged best, so here God's speech is designed to promote a dialogue that engages the Son to share in and assume responsibility for the full elaboration and realization of God's will.

God's first speech is not couched in the unrhetorical, passionless style of his proclamations.[20] Rather, it begins as informal dialogue—"Only begotten Son, seest thou what rage / Transports our adversary" (3.80-81)—and then takes on the character of a forensic or judicial oration before the heavenly court, accusing Satan and the human pair for the crime about to occur. It conforms closely to the norms laid down by Cicero and others for a prosecutor's speech of the equitable kind, concerned with "the nature of justice and the right or the reasonableness of reward and punishment"; and it presumes a defense based upon a *remotio criminis* issue, that is, an attempt to shift the guilt or responsibility from the accused to another.[21] Remarkably, Milton presents God arguing his own case publicly and submitting it, as it were, to the bar of angelic and human judgment. (Satan's comparable speech on Mount Niphates, we will recall, fuses the judicial oration with the private genre of soliloquy, subverting both kinds.)

The opening lines serve as exordium, inviting abhorrence

of Satan by showing him "transported" by rage and bent on desperate revenge. Then a brief narration describes the crime, and the motives and attitudes of those involved:[22] Satan's "false guile" and "glozing lies"; man's faithless transgression of God's sole command. The *confirmatio* or argument proving the guilt of the accused follows Cicero's recommendation to begin this kind of case by defending the one to whom the responsibility might be shifted.[23] Accordingly, God offers a long and passionately reasoned defense of his ways—"Ingrate, he had of mee / All he could have; I made him just and right, / Sufficient to have stood, though free to fall"—concluding that fallen men and fallen angels alike must take full responsibility for their actions: "they themselves ordain'd thir fall" (3.96-128). At this point, however, he distinguishes between the accused parties: the angels fell "self-deprav'd" but Adam and Eve were deceived by Satan and so have some basis for a *remotio criminis* plea against him. The Father's conclusion is delivered not as prosecutor but as a judge, taking all this into account and pronouncing sentence in decisive if somewhat ambiguous terms: "Man therefore shall find grace, / The other none: in Mercy and Justice both, . . . shall my glory excel, / But Mercy first and last shall brightest shine" (3.131-34).

The Son's plea for mercy breaks through and transforms the rigid structure of forensic debate. As sentence has already been passed, this is not a speech for the defense, intended to answer charges, or mitigate guilt, or stir up pathos. Rather, the Son challenges his Father to explain the ambiguities of the sentence, calling attention to his own continued vulnerability before the court of opinion if his enemy should wreck his creation: "So should thy goodness and thy greatness both / Be question'd and blasphem'd without defense" (3.165-66). The exchange between God and the Son transforms the forensic debate of adversaries into a dialogue, during which the divine litigants agree to a unique *remotio criminis*, assigning full responsibility and guilt to Satan and humankind but shifting the punishment from man to his divine advocate.

The Father's final speech proclaims a new judgment revising

the first sentence, as the harsh logic of judicial oratory gives
way to gracious prophecy of mankind's salvation. Beginning
with a fervent, loving apostrophe, this speech is formally a
demonstrative oration praising the Son for his nature, his vir-
tue, his worthy deeds and their glorious consequences:

> O thou in Heav'n and Earth the only peace
> Found out for mankind under wrath, O thou
> My sole complacence!
> . . . .
> Because thou hast, though Thron'd in highest bliss
> Equal to God, and equally enjoying
> God-like fruition, quitted all to save
> A world from utter loss, and hast been found
> By Merit more than Birthright Son of God,
> Found worthiest to be so by being Good,
> Far more than Great or High; because in thee
> Love hast abounded more than Glory abounds,
> . . . .
> All knees to thee shall bow.
>   (3.274-322)

Another frame is provided by several Old Testament dia-
logues of mediation in which a prophet strives with God on
behalf of his erring people. Verbal echoes recall Moses plead-
ing for the rebellious Israelites who seek to return to bondage
in Egypt, and Abraham begging God to save Sodom and Go-
morrah for the sake of even ten righteous who might be found
in those cities. Abraham argues (Gen. 18:25), "That be far
from thee to do after this manner, to slay the righteous with
the wicked: and that the righteous should be as the wicked,
that be far from thee: Shall not the Judge of all the earth do
right?"[24] The Son echoes this argument:

> For should Man finally be lost, should Man
> Thy creature late so lov'd, thy youngest Son
> Fall circumvented thus by fraud, though join'd
> With his own folly? that be from thee far,

That far be from thee, Father, who art Judge
Of all things made, and judgest only right.
(3.150-55)

But the Son cannot ground his plea for mankind on right-
eousness, until he himself agrees to become the one just man
for whom humankind (unlike Sodom and Gomorrah) will be
spared. By such associations we are led to recognize the Son
as the original and antitype of all the Old Testament media-
tors, and the Dialogue in Heaven as the paradigm for all sub-
sequent biblical dialogues of mediation.

Again, and especially in retrospect, we are led to view the
exchanges between God and the Son as a species of Socratic
dialogue. In them the Father deliberately refrains from reveal-
ing his providential plan for man's salvation, so as to challenge
the Son to discover, through dialogue, how the divine good-
ness can overcome the evils of the Fall, how God's design for
man can yet be realized, and just what a heroic love embracing
both justice and mercy must be—and do. Like Socrates, whose
judicial oration at his trial included an example of the dialec-
tical method denounced as dangerous by his accusers, Mil-
ton's God justifies his ways in part by his use of dialogue, a
genre which promotes in the Son the freedom of choice that
is the very ground of the divine justification.[25]

The later dialogue between God and Adam (8.357-450)
also has a Socratic dimension. There, Adam prays to be given
a mate and God seems to oppose his request, forcing Adam
through dialogue to achieve and manifest self-knowledge. As
he meets God's counterarguments, Adam is led to define for
himself what it is to be human: that it is not to find company
with beasts, or to be perfect in himself as God, but to seek
completion, help, and solace in human companionship and
human love.

On both occasions God uses dialogue to achieve the essen-
tial Socratic purpose, education in self-knowledge. However,
he departs from Socrates' structured dialectical method of
leading his interlocutors by a chain of successive questions to

123

affirm or deny a series of propositions, or to choose between alternative statements. Instead, he promotes the growth of his divine and his human sons by a somewhat more open—and more gracious—method: he challenges them with an apparent dilemma, casts full responsibility upon them to work out its terms in dialogue with him, and then honors them highly for doing so. He commends Adam for knowing himself rightly and reasoning well, rewarding him with the mate he desires; and he commends the Son for having realized his own nature, showing himself in his abounding love to be "By Merit more than Birthright Son of God."

EPIC OF WRATH, EPIC OF CREATION: POWER DIVINE

In the Battle in Heaven and the Creation the Bard emphasizes the divine power. These episodes have been discussed above as Raphael's "epics" but, of course, the encompassing narrative voice and purpose are those of the Miltonic Bard. In both sequences he employs a complex weave of epic and discursive genre patterns, less dense than in the Dialogue in Heaven episode but of great interpretive importance. The Son's victory in the Battle in Heaven as bearer of God's omnipotence transforms the Homeric epic of wrath and strife into a "brief epic" of divine power exercising divine vengeance. And God's creation of the world through the Son's agency transforms the classical or hexaemeral Creation poem into a second "brief epic" celebrating the power of God as exuberant vitality and creativity.

During the Battle in Heaven sequence God's speeches are transformations of various kinds of epic speech. God's decree proclaiming the Son vice-gerent and pronouncing doom to all who disobey him recalls Zeus' proclamation in the *Iliad* restraining the gods from battle and threatening assorted dire punishments to the recalcitrant.[26] But the tone of God's decree is profoundly different. A mélange of psalmic and biblical echoes, it is majestic, awesome, unconditional—the voice of Omnipotence declaring the divine will:

Hear all ye Angels, Progeny of Light,
Thrones, Dominations, Princedoms, Virtues, Powers,
Hear my Decree, which unrevok't shall stand.
This day I have begot whom I declare
My only Son, and on this holy Hill
Him have anointed, whom ye now behold
At my right hand; your Head I him appoint;
And by my Self have sworn to him shall bow
All knees in Heav'n, and shall confess him Lord:
Under his great Vice-gerent Reign abide
United as one individual Soul
For ever happy: him who disobeys
Mee disobeys, breaks union, and that day
Cast out from God and blessed vision, falls
Into utter darkness, deep ingulft, his place
Ordain'd without redemption, without end.
                    (5.600-15)[27]

At the other extreme in manner and tone, the dialogue be-
tween Father and Son at the first stirrings of the revolt (5.719-
42) is an ironic council of war. The Father's irony—"Son . . .
/ Nearly it now concerns us to be sure / Of our Omnipotence
/ . . . and all imploy / In our defense, lest unawares we lose /
This our high place, our Sanctuary, our Hill"—is correctly
interpreted by the Son, who responds "with calm aspect and
clear": "Mighty Father, thou thy foes / Justly hast in derision,
and secure / Laugh'st at thir vain designs and tumults vain."
The ostensible war council is here redefined in the light of
Psalm 2:4: "He that sitteth in the heavens shall laugh: the
Lord shall have them in derision." And the divine irony—
private, deft, appropriate to the circumstances—affords a
standard by which to measure the utter degradation of irony
in the cannon episode, as Satan and Belial deliver malicious
battle taunts in the language of an ostensible peace parlay.[28]
    God delivers other speeches as an epic battle leader, the
Lord of Hosts. He rouses his forces with an epic exhortation
to battle, charging his generals (Michael and Gabriel) to "lead

forth to Battle these my Sons / Invincible, lead forth my armed
Saints" and drive the enemy forth "Into thir place of punish-
ment" (6.29-55). However, God again transforms the kind.
The speech begins with a formal praise of Abdiel, a passage
of demonstrative rhetoric exalting that angel for winning a far
better victory in a very different kind of battle from that which
will now be fought:

> Servant of God, well done, well hast thou fought
> The better fight, who single hast maintain'd
> Against revolted multitudes the Cause
> Of Truth, in word mightier than they in Arms;
> And for the testimony of Truth hast borne
> Universal reproach, far worse to bear
> Than violence.

Moreover, the stirring exhortation is not really designed to
spur the angels on to victory, since God knows full well they
cannot fulfill the charge given them. Rather, he challenges
them to imitate Abdiel's loyalty and obedience in their own
spheres of duty.

In another exhortation to battle, God invests the Son with
his power and charges him to win the decisive victory (6.681-
718). The speech recalls Achilles investing Patroklos with his
armor and charging him to lead the Myrmidons into battle in
his stead (*Iliad* 16.49-100). But while Achilles dwells on the
glory of warfare the Father comments on its chaos and futil-
ity: "War wearied hath performed what War can do / And to
disorder'd rage let loose the reins."[29] Also, while Patroklos
bears only the trappings of Achilles' power and is fated to
meet death, the Son is invested with divine omnipotence itself[30]
and so is able to win total victory:

> Into thee such Virtue and Grace
> Immense I have transfus'd . . .
>
> . . . .
>
> To manifest thee worthiest to be Heir
> Of all things, to be Heir and to be King

Go then thou Mightiest in thy Father's might,
Ascend my Chariot, guide the rapid Wheels
That shake Heav'n's basis, bring forth all my War,
My Bow and Thunder, my Almighty Arms
Gird on.

(6.703-14)

This epic exhortation modulates to dialogue as the Son formally accepts the charge—"I . . . can put on / Thy terrors, as I put thy mildness on, / Image of thee in all things." The dialogue concludes with further revision of the epic ethos as the Son anticipates his greater joy in resigning the scepter to his Father, "when in the end/ Thou shalt be All in All" (6.723-45).

Finally, in his call to the angelic hosts to cease fighting (6.801-24) the Son revises the epic hero's conventional offer to decide a battle by single combat, alluding to the biblical precept, "Vengeance is mine, I will repay, saith the Lord."[31] Accordingly, he issues no epic challenge but simply proclaims himself minister of God's vengeance: "Vengeance is his or whose he sole appoints; / . . . stand only and behold / God's indignation on these Godless pour'd / By mee" (6.808-12).

For the Battle in Heaven as a whole the Bard employs several generic frames, of which the *Iliad* is primary. Through that frame we see that the Son's heroic role is defined by, but wholly transcends, the Homeric ethos. He exhibits martial prowess and attains battle glory beyond anything imaginable in Achilles. If Achilles' strength was greater than that of all others, and his acts more violent, the Son is the bearer of omnipotence itself.[32] If Achilles prevented the Achaians from casting their spears at Hector so that he might defeat him in single combat,[33] the Son restrains the angels from battle and engages the entire Satanic force in single combat. And if Achilles—like Hector, Diomedes, and many others—values above all things the winning of glory, the Son obtains surpassing glory when he rides in his mystic, triumphal chariot to and from the battle; when the angelic choirs celebrate his triumph by singing and waving palms; and when the Father receives him "into Glory."

He does not, however, ascribe value to or seek glory from his martial deeds, observing ironically that he will engage the rebels on these terms "since by strength / They measure all, of other excellence, / Not emulous, nor care who them excels" (6.820-22).[34] And before he does so, his restoration of heaven's lovely pastoral landscape offers the multitudes on both sides the opportunity to recognize the truly glorious, creative uses of power:

> Before him Power Divine his way prepar'd;
> At his command the uprooted Hills retir'd
> Each to his place, they heard his voice and went
> Obsequious, Heav'n his wonted face renew'd,
> And with fresh Flow'rets Hill and Valley smil'd.
> This saw his hapless Foes, but stood obdur'd.
>
> (6.780-85)

In the Battle in Heaven the Son bears God's power, exercises God's vengeance, and seeks God's glory, not his own, as hero of a transcendent epic of wrath.

Other generic frames draw our attention to God as source of the power and vengeance the Son images. When the angels turn to hill-hurling and the battle reaches an impasse in which heaven's destruction is threatened, the frame is clearly Hesiod's *Theogony*. In Hesiod, "wide Heaven was shaken and groaned, and high Olympus reeled from its foundation" when the giants, whom Zeus engaged as his allies in the war against the Titans, began hurling huge rocks.[35] At this point Zeus' heart was "filled with fury and he showed forth all his strength," joining with the giants to hurl the Titans to Tartarus.[36] By contrast, in *Paradise Lost* the Son of God defeated the rebels without any assistance at all, even though he checked "his Thunder in mid-Volley" (6.855) and withheld half his divine power.[37] By such transformations of Hesiod, the Bard em-

128

phasizes the incalculable distance between Zeus, strongest of the gods, and divine omnipotence.

Yet another frame from the Old Testament Exodus "epic" overlays the Hesiodic pattern, presenting the divine omnipotence in terms of the awesome theophanies of God to his people, and the terrible destruction that "The Lord Mighty in Battle" wreaks on his and Israel's enemies.[38] As the Father dispatches the angels to battle, the imagery of clouds, flames, smoke, and sounding trumpets points us to the Sinai theophany before God delivered the Decalogue to Moses.[39] And a direct allusion establishes the Lord's destruction of Pharoah and his forces as frame for the final rout of the rebel angels. Moses' charge to the Israelites on the shores of the Red Sea— "Fear ye not, stand still, and see the salvation of the Lord, which he will shew to you to day" (Exod. 14:13)—echoes in the Son's command to the angels: "Stand still in bright array ye Saints, here stand / . . . stand only and behold / God's indignation on these Godless pour'd" (6.801-11).[40] Still other allusions frame this episode in terms of the "epic" visions of apocalyptic wrath and terror in the Book of Revelation.[41]

As the Son goes forth to battle, the remarkable fusion of classical and biblical images and emblems of power suggests the absolute difference between Satanic military might and divine omnipotence, which defeats the rebels by its awful manifestation more than by its exercise. Carrying the Jovian "Bow / And Quiver with three-bolted Thunder," and clad in armor made of the "radiant *Urim*" of Aaron's breastplate of judgment, the Son rides with Winged Victory beside him, in a marvellous war chariot appropriated from Ezekiel's vision.[42] The effect is wonderfully evocative:

> Full soon
> Among them he arriv'd; in his right hand
> Grasping ten thousand Thunders, which he sent
> Before them, such as in thir Souls infix'd
> Plagues.
> . . . .

129

Nor less on either side tempestuous fell
His arrows, from the fourfold-visag'd Four,
Distinct with eyes, and from the living Wheels,
Distinct alike with multitude of eyes;
One Spirit in them rul'd, and every eye
Glar'd lightning, and shot forth pernicious fire
Among th' accurst, that wither'd all thir strength,
And of thir wonted vigor left them drain'd,
Exhausted, spiritless, afflicted, fall'n.
                    (6.835-52)

The psychological effect upon the rebel angels recalls the Ho-
meric scene in which Apollo "drove terror" upon the Greeks
by shaking before them the aegis of Zeus: "the spirit inside
them was mazed . . . they forgot their furious valour . . . [and]
fled so in their weakness and terror" like a herd of sheep. It
also recalls the Gadarene swine possessed by devils that Christ
had expelled, who flung themselves from a steep precipice into
the sea.[43] So the rebels, terrified of Chaos but yet more terri-
fied of the divine power manifested to them, threw themselves
"headlong . . . / Down from the verge of Heav'n" like a herd
of goats. By such means, the Miltonic Bard approaches as
close as literary accommodation can come to the apprehension
of God's awesome power in the dimension of wrath and
vengeance.

In a very different vein, the brief epic of Creation is de-
signed to emphasize divine creativity as the primary manifes-
tation of God's power. To end the Battle in Heaven the Fa-
ther "transfus'd" his power into the Son, that he might
demonstrate his worthiness "to be Heir and to be King" (6.704-
708); by contrast, at the Creation the Son is portrayed as the
instrument by which God creates.[44] As God's Creating Word
the Son here images all the divine qualities: not only is he
"Girt with Omnipotence" as in the Battle in Heaven, but also
"with Radiance crown'd / Of Majesty Divine, Sapience and
Love / Immense" (7.194-96). Also, the angels' hymns ascribe
greatest glory to the act of creation: "Thee that day / Thy

Thunders magnifi'd; but to create / Is greater than created to destroy" (7.606-608).

Divine speech in this episode is occasionally dialogue, but chiefly formal proclamation and fiat. The Creation episode begins with God's address to his Son (7.139-73), commenting on the rebels' defeat, the multitudes that remain faithful, and his purpose to fill up the places of those lost by creating a new race of men to dwell on earth, "till by degrees of merit rais'd / They open to themselves at length the way / Up hither, under long obedience tri'd." As he sets these conditions and delegates the Son to speak the words of creation, his speech modulates from informal discourse to solemn proclamation:

> And thou my Word, begotten Son, by thee
> This I perform, speak thou, and be it done:
> My overshadowing Spirit and might with thee
> I send along, ride forth, and bid the Deep
> Within appointed bounds be Heav'n and Earth,
> Boundless the Deep, because I am who fill
> Infinitude, nor vacuous the space.
> Though I uncircumscrib'd myself retire,
> And put not forth my goodness, which is free
> To act or not, Necessity and Chance
> Approach not mee, and what I will is Fate.
>   (7.163-73)

This proclamation and the narrator's comment (7.174-79) identifies God's "immediate" decree as the essential creating act, which the Son executes by speech and which is accommodated to human ears as a six-day "process." However, the Bard finds warrant in Genesis 1:26 to portray man's creation by another method, as the direct and audible decree of the Father himself, spoken to rather than through the Son: "therefore th'Omnipotent / Eternal Father (For where is not hee / Present) thus to his Son audibly spake. / Let us make now Man in our image, Man / In our similitude" (7.516-20).

The actual creation decrees remain very close indeed to Genesis,[45] but the Creating Word also echoes other biblical language to convey other aspects of God's creativity. In calming the raging seas of Chaos he repeats the words Christ used to calm the Sea of Galilee—"Peace, be still" (Mark 4:39)—implying that omnipotence performs both acts with equal ease: "Silence, ye troubl'd waves, and thou Deep, peace" (7.216). Also, he marks off the boundaries of Creation from Chaos—"Thus far extend, thus far thy bounds, / This be thy just Circumference, O World" (7.230-31)—with golden geometer's compasses from the Creation account in Proverbs 8:27,[46] emphasizing thereby the ordering aspect of divine creativity, the giving of form to the protean matter of Chaos.

Milton's Creation epic has Genesis paraphrase and hexaemeral epic as its primary generic frames. As we have seen, at one level Raphael "invents" the genre of hexaemeral epic, the prototype, as it were, of Du Bartas and Tasso,[47] to accommodate the Creation story to Adam and Eve even as the Miltonic Bard accommodates it to us. Comparison with those analogues reveals that the Bard's poem is governed by a unified and powerful conception of divine creativity as vitality and generative potency, and he expands upon all elements in the biblical text that afford some color for that imaginative vision. The Hebraic metaphor of the Spirit of God "brooding" upon the face of the deep (Gen. 1:1) is elaborated to present the divine creating power under the aspect of procreative, generative force, both male and female: "on the wat'ry calm / His brooding wings the Spirit of God outspread, / And vital virtue infus'd, and vital warmth / Throughout the fluid Mass" (7.234-37).[48] As the narrative proceeds, each day's work is introduced by a close paraphrase of the creating words ascribed to God in Genesis, but Milton renders the creatures' responses very freely, highlighting by vibrant descriptive terms and dynamic verbs the vitality evoked from all things by the source of that vitality, God. The creation of light is typical. God's fiat is quoted directly from Genesis: "Let there be Light, said God." But the Bard then elaborates the biblical phrase, "And there was light," into a vivid account of how light *sprung* from the deep, *journeyed* through the airy gloom, and *so-journed* in a tabernacle.[49]

Another generic frame is supplied by a classical poem of origin, the *De Rerum Natura* of Lucretius.[50] Milton directs us to Lucretius by the terms of Adam's near-presumptuous query to Raphael broaching the creation topic: "what cause / Mov'd the Creator in his holy Rest / Through all Eternity so late to build / In *Chaos*" (7.90-94).[51] Lucretius asks an analogous question, but ironically, intimating that the gods could have had nothing to do with Creation: "What novelty could so long after entice those [Immortal Gods] who were tranquil before to desire a change in their former life?"[52]

The Bard lays Lucretius under contribution especially in presenting the work of the third, fifth, and sixth days, to develop the implications of the phrase in Genesis 1:12, "And the earth brought forth." Lucretius portrays the earth as a marvellously fecund and prolific *magna mater* who gives birth to and nurtures all creatures: she is "our fostering mother earth" who receives liquid drops of water from heaven, "and then teeming brings forth bright corn and luxuriant trees and the races of mankind, [and] . . . all the generations of wild beasts."[53] Milton heightens the metaphor, presenting earth first as an embyro brought to birth in the cosmic waters, and then herself the fertile womb within which the seeds of all life were conceived:

> The Earth was form'd, but in the Womb as yet
> Of Waters, Embryon immature involv'd,
> Appear'd not: over all the face of Earth
> Main Ocean flow'd, not idle, but with warm
> Prolific humor soft'ning all her Globe,
> Fermented the great Mother to conceive,
> Satiate with genial moisture.
> (7.276-82)

Milton also draws upon Lucretius' account of the flora of the earth springing to life:

With new birth-throes . . . the earth gave forth the dif-
ferent kinds of herbage and bright verdure about the hills
and all over the plains, and the flowering meadows shone
with the colour of green; then to the various kinds of
trees came a mighty struggle, as they raced at full speed
to grow up into the air. As feathers and hair and bristles
first grow on the frame of four-footed creatures or the
body of strong-winged birds, so then the new-born earth
put forth herbage and saplings first . . .[54]

Milton's representation of the analogous event is much more
vigorous and sensuous:

> He scarce had said, when the bare Earth, till then
> Desert and bare, unsightly, unadorn'd,
> Brought forth the tender Grass, whose verdure clad
> Her Universal Face with pleasant green,
> Then Herbs of every leaf, that sudden flow'r'd
> Op'ning thir various colors, and made gay
> Her bosom smelling sweet: and these scarce blown,
> Forth flourish'd thick the clust'ring Vine, forth crept
> The swelling Gourd, up stood the corny Reed
> Embattl'd in her field: and th' humble Shrub,
> And Bush with frizzl'd hair implicit: last
> Rose as in Dance the stately Trees.
>   (7.313-24)

And while Lucretius' portrayal of the earth generating crea-
tures and pouring them forth from several wombs[55] probably
stands behind Milton's striking description of the animals
emerging from the earth as at a birth, Milton's lines are, again,
more graphic:

> The Earth obey'd, and straight
> Op'ning her fertile Womb teem'd at a Birth
> Innumerous living Creatures, perfet forms,
> Limb'd and full grown: out of the ground up rose
> As from his Lair the wild Beast . . .
> . . . .

The grassy Clods now Calv'd, now half appear'd
The Tawny Lion, pawing to get free
His hinder parts, then springs as broke from Bonds,
And Rampant shakes his Brinded mane; the Ounce,
The Libbard, and the Tiger, as the Mole
Rising, the crumbl'd Earth above them threw
In Hillocks; the swift Stag from under ground
Bore up his branching head.
                    (7.453-70)

These several generic frames assist our apprehension of the divine creativity through a process of comparison and contrast. We are intended to see that the marvelous processes of creation in Lucretius are begun and continued by the random motion of atoms, whereas the yet more marvelous processes the Miltonic Bard describes emanate from the prodigious vitality of a divine Father, who makes his creatures vigorous, active, and potent, and sustains them in continuous processes of growth and generation. By his several generic frames and brilliantly evocative imagery, Milton presents the Creation to us as the epic act of God himself, the ground of all other action,[56] evoking from us the quintessential epic response, wonder.

The Synods of God: Divine Judgment

In Books Ten and Eleven of *Paradise Lost* three scenes are presented in which God dispenses judgments upon fallen mankind and the fallen world. All are public assemblies—or synods, as the third and most formal of them is called, appropriately suggesting an ecclesiastical court. Language in them is often close to biblical paraphrase—sometimes formal proclamation, sometimes harsh invective, and at times dialogue. In them the Son enacts the roles, first of appointed judge, then of mediatorial priest.

Important generic frames for these scenes are biblical paraphrase and hexaemeral epic, which supply many of the topics

135

though few formal elements.[57] For the narrative sequence as a whole, the primary literary paradigm and reference point is Ovid's account of the universal flood in the *Metamorphoses*.[58] In Ovid's story, Jove summons the gods to a council (which Sandys translates by Milton's word, synod)[59] to declare his determination to destroy the race of mankind, whose all-pervasive wickedness he observed at first hand when he visited earth in human form. The gods approve Jove's design, though "they all grieved over the threatened loss of the human race,"[60] even as Milton's angels respond to the news of the Fall with "dim sadness . . . mixt / With pity" (10.23-25). Jove proceeds then to inundate the earth with flood waters, and only Deucalion and his wife Pyrrha survive. Milton directs us to Ovid by an explicit comparison of Adam and Eve's repentant prayer to the petitions of Deucalion and Pyrrha: "nor important less / Seem'd thir Petition, than when th' ancient Pair / In Fables old, less ancient yet than these, / *Deucalion* and chaste *Pyrrha* to restore / The Race of Mankind drown'd, before the Shrine / Of *Themis* stood devout" (11.9-14). But Milton uses the Ovidian paradigm chiefly to highlight how different God's judgments are from Jove's judgments.

The first synod (10.17-84) seems in many respects a completion of the Dialogue in Heaven, with the qualities of mercy and justice now fully harmonized in both Father and Son. It begins as God reassures the distressed angel guard of Eden that they could not have prevented the Fall, summarizing what he foretold to them at the earlier heavenly council. Then, transferring all power of judgment in earth, heaven, and hell to the "Vicegerent Son," he notes that his purposed union of mercy with justice is achieved by sending "Man's Friend, his Mediator, his design'd / Both Ransom and Redeemer voluntary, / And destin'd Man himself to judge Man fall'n" (10.55-63). Responding in dialogue to God's decree (10.68-84) the Son accepts its terms, promising that his judgment will "temper so / Justice with Mercy, as may illustrate most / Them fully satisfied, and thee appease." But he yet claims his right as mediator to "mitigate thir doom / On me deriv'd." All this is a far cry from Jove's sweeping condemnations, and also from the furious punishments he meted out to the wicked when he visited earth in human form.[61] The contrast is further emphasized at the arraignment of Adam and Eve in the Garden, conducted in language very close to Genesis. Here the Son restores dialogue with the human pair through a series of pointed questions, links their sentence with the promise of redemption, and clothes their bodies as a symbol of the regeneration that will cover their spiritual nakedness.

The second synod (10.613-706), during which the Father visits punishments upon the earth, bears some resemblance to the scene in Du Bartas in which God sends the apocalyptic evils, famine, war, and sickness, to wreak havoc upon the earth after the Fall.[62] In *Paradise Lost*, by contrast, the "wasteful Furies" Sin and Death are not sent from God but are admitted to the world by the Fall itself. God, however, finds a role in his providential design for them: to lick up the "draff and filth" of man's polluting sin and thus keep the moral ecosystem in better balance. God's denunciation of these hellhounds is the harshest and most contemptuous invective in the entire poem: "cramm'd and gorg'd, nigh burst / With suckt and glutted offal" they will at last be utterly destroyed by the Son and sent to choke up the mouth of hell forever (10.616-37). At the end of this synod, recalling the scene in Ovid in which Jove unleashed the south winds and all the rains of heaven to cause the Flood,[63] the Father dispatches his angels to change the earth's axis (or the Sun's course) so as to produce extremes of seasonal temperatures, storms, droughts, and other such "Outrage from lifeless things" (10.707). But the point, again, is the difference. God's cosmological adjustments are not arbitrary punishments (like Jove's) but a manifestation of the fundamental principle of creation and metamorphosis in the universe the poem portrays, whereby the physical conditions of every place are framed so as to conform to the moral condition of its inhabitants. The harsh extremes of climate and the reduced fertility of soil that result from the planetary adjustments accord with the nature of sin-hardened, intemperate man as he now is.[64]

The third and more formal synod pronounces man's expulsion from Eden (11.67-125). It is preceded by a colloquy in which the Son acts formally as priest and advocate, offering Adam and Eve's repentant prayer to God and pleading for alleviation of their punishment (11.20-66). Developing from biblical images an elaborate metaphor of husbandry, the Son attributes the "first fruits" of repentance in man's heart to the "seeds" sown and the grace "implanted" there by God. He also proposes that all man's works be "ingrafted" upon him, so that God may receive thereby "The smell of peace toward Mankind."[65] The Son here evokes a divine georgic mode, in which the processes of justification and regeneration are the georgic labor of Father and Son. In his response, God declares himself the source both of Adam and Eve's regeneration and of the Son's mediation: "all thy request was my Decree" (11.47).

God now summons the angels with solemn trumpets, relating this synod to other solemn scenes of judgment convened by trumpets—the delivery of the Law to Moses, and the "general Doom" at the end of the time (11.73-82). He opens the synod with a close paraphrase of Genesis 3:22-23:

> O Sons, like one of us Man is become
> To know both Good and Evil . . .
> . . . but let him boast
> His knowledge of Good lost, and Evil got,
>
> . . . .
> Lest therefore his now bolder hand
> Reach also of the Tree of Life, and eat,
> And live for ever, dream at least to live
> For ever, to remove him I decree.
> (11. 84-96)[66]

This somewhat elliptical language is interpreted and its harshness mitigated by the colloquy that precedes it, and also by the Ovidian frame which is designed to render God's decrees more comprehensible and acceptable to us. Unlike Ovid's Jove,

God does not begin a new human race from stones, but begins new life in stony hearts hardened by sin. And unlike Jove who acted chiefly to preserve what is pure from man's corruption,[67] Milton's God expels man from Eden in part for his own good, since the immortality the Garden nourishes would now simply "eternize woe" (11.60). Nor is the expulsion an arbitrary act: articulating the natural law of the Miltonic universe that links metamorphic processes to moral states, God observes that the "pure immortal Elements" in the garden would themselves "Eject" those tainted by sin, and that Adam, no longer fit for Paradise, should now "Till / The Ground whence he was taken, fitter Soil." The synod concludes with God commissioning Michael to expel Adam and Eve from Eden, but only after instructing them about the covenant of grace so that they may depart "sorrowing, yet in peace" (11.111-17).

MILTON'S METHOD in presenting God and the Son involves the use of many generic paradigms and specific texts as frames for the several scenes in which the divine characters appear. These literary accommodations lead us to make constant comparisons and contrasts, and thereby to apprehend something of Milton's literary God in the aspects of his justice and mercy, his omnipotence and creativity, his judgments and his love. By design we are presented with multiple reflections—at times uncongenial as well as attractive—of a God who cannot be seen whole. But for all that, Milton emphasizes certain of the divine qualities—by the dense layering of generic frames in some passages, by surprising departures from indicated models, by poetic language of special brilliance. Those dominant and peculiarly Miltonic aspects are surely the heroic love the Son manifests in the Dialogue in Heaven; the vibrant, exuberant creativity that the Father infuses into and nurtures in all his creatures; and the dialogic processes by which God as Socratic educator promotes reason, self-knowledge, and freedom of choice in all his sons.

SIX

"Our Happy State":
Literary Forms for Angelic Wholeness

MILTON PORTRAYS angelic society in *Paradise Lost* through a mix of literary modes—pastoral, georgic, and heroic. He also associates with these modes several kinds of discourse and lyric, which render other aspects of the heavenly community. The angels' discourse is most often prophetic dialogue, though they also use invective, rebuke, debate, and other speech genres as specific situations require. And they are highly accomplished lyric poets, singing hymns of several kinds and enacting elaborate ceremonies to celebrate all the great events of the poem—the Dialogue in Heaven, the Son's victory over Satan in the Battle in Heaven, the Creation, and even the divine judgments pronounced upon man and the earth after the Fall. Through this mixture of modes and genres the Miltonic Bard imagines the angelic realm—otherwise "invisible to mortal sight"—as an embodiment of wholeness and human possibility, and accommodates that ideal to us with appropriate tact and great attractiveness.

MIXED MODES AND THE "VITA BEATA" OF HEAVEN

The mixture of literary modes in the several scenes depicting angelic activities displays the angels' ready and continuous access to the entire spectrum of feelings and values the several literary modes embody. The angels enjoy the *otium* of pastoral without its limitation to rustic things. They take on the constant cares and responsibilities of georgic with none of the drudgery of tending farm or garden or bees. And they engage in martial pageantry and in battle, manifesting the valor, military prowess, and magnificence of the heroic, without its concomitant ambition, emphasis on personal *aristeia*, or glorification of warfare. The harmony, integrity, and variety of angelic existence are gifts of the Creator to these exalted creatures. But at the same time, the angels themselves must infuse their pastoral-georgic-heroic natures and lives with that virtue which alone can preserve and further perfect their happy state, the free and continuous and loving choice to serve God. As Raphael explains to Adam, "freely we serve, / Because we freely love, as in our will / To love or not; in this we stand or fall"(5.538-40).

The comprehensiveness of the angelic life is intimated by the mix of topoi and images describing heaven and the heavenly landscape. Leland Ryken has pointed to the prominent imagery of jewels, gold, and gleaming surfaces, derived from or modelled upon the Book of Revelation[1] and suggestive of permanence and courtly magnificence: "Opal Tow'rs and Battlements adorn'd / Of living Sapphire" (2.1049-50); a "Kingly Palace Gate / With Frontispiece of Diamond and Gold / Imbellisht; thick with sparkling orient Gems" (3.505-507); a "Glassy Sea" and a pavement "whose dust is Gold" (7.577, 619). But as John Knott has shown, the pastoral imagery of fruits, flowers, and harvests is equally characteristic of heaven:[2] its trees bear "ambrosial fruitage," the vines yield nectar, the boughs are covered each morning with "mellifluous Dews" and the ground with "pearly grain" (5.426-30). This mixture of topoi and the literary modes they signal present heaven to us as a place where permanence and magnificence are not emblems of stasis but of organic life and growth.

The angelic pastoral is most prominent in Raphael's description of the day God proclaimed his Son Vice-gerent (5.583-657). From the phrase, "That day, as other solemn days" (5.618), and from the morning-to-night organization of the account, Milton intends his readers to recognize it as a transmutation of the familiar "ideal day" topos of pastoral. We are invited to recall Theocritus' Idyl 7, "The Harvest-home," in which Lycidas sings of an imagined perfect day to be spent

141

reclining and drinking wine, wearing chaplets of snowflakes and rosebuds, and listening to pipers' songs—all within the framework of an actual ideal day he and Simichidus are passing in fellowship and song as they journey to the harvest festival and banquet that climax the evening.[3] We might think also of the pastoral idyl in Virgil's second *Georgic* which presents the rural labors and pastimes of day and evening and concludes with a holiday celebrating Bacchus, and of many other classical and Renaissance examples.[4] Normally, the delights of the pastoral ideal day were directly opposed to the activities of court and forum. But the celestial ideal day unites these supposed opposites, testifying to the integrity and inclusiveness of the heavenly life and giving the lie to Satan's description of it as fawning subservience to a tyrant.

The day opens with martial ceremonies appropriate to the heroic mode, as the angelic hosts are gathered by "Imperial summons" under their hierarchs, with ensigns, standards, and gonfalons waving, But the angels' standards are emblazoned with "Holy Memorials, acts of Zeal and Love" (5.593), rather than emblems of war. After God's solemn proclamations of the Vice-gerent Son, these martial legions turn court masquers, singing and dancing about the "State" (God's Throne).[5] However, the angels' dance figures find analogy in the cosmic choreography of the planets, not the artifice and ostentation of an Inigo Jones production. The angels present,

> about the sacred Hill,
> Mystical dance, which yonder starry Sphere
> Of Planets and of fixt in all her Wheels
> Resembles nearest, mazes intricate,
> Eccentric, intervolv'd, yet regular
> Then most, when most irregular they seem:
> And in thir motions harmony Divine
> So smooths her charming tones, that God's own ear
> Listens delighted.
>   (5.619-27)

On the celestial ideal day, as on the pastoral, evening is the time for feasting: food, nectar—and love-making also, we later learn from Raphael[6]—are among the angelic pleasures. Epitomizing the mix of modes in heaven, angels drink and eat from magnificent vessels of jewels and gold while reclining on pastoral flowers:

> all in Circles as they stood,
> Tables are set, and on a sudden pil'd
> With Angels' Food, and rubied Nectar flows:
> In Pearl, in Diamond, and massy Gold,
> Fruit of delicious Vines, the growth of Heav'n.
> On flow'rs repos'd, and with fresh flow'rets crown'd,
> They eat, they drink, and in communion sweet
> Quaff immortality and joy, secure
> Of surfeit where full measure only bounds
> Excess, before th' all bounteous King, who show'r'd
> With copious hand, rejoicing in thir joy.
>   (5.631-41)

The topoi recall Zeus' daylong feast for the gods in the *Iliad*, where nectar flows freely and the Muses sing; and also Virgil's Elysian Fields where some heroes and bards "trip it in the dance and chant songs," while others feast "per herbam" within a fragrant laurel grove. Yet the emphasis on the nectar as heaven's own produce also has pastoral associations, recalling Theocritus' harvest feast.[7] The image of these angelic feasters, sated with delights but without languor or any excess, must remind Milton's fallen readers of all those literary banquets of sense and pleasure that contrast so sharply with this perfection: Circe's banquet, the Lotus Eaters, Tasso's Garden of Armida, Spenser's Bower of Bliss, and many more.[8]

At nightfall, the angels do not return to pastoral cottages, but to their "heroic" formations; they are "Disperst in Bands and Files" into a camp with "Pavilions numberless." Yet that camp is situated in a pastoral landscape—"By living Streams among the Trees of Life." These pastoral features derive from Revelation 22:1-2, but the scene is enhanced by other elements drawn from the common storehouse of pastoral topoi. The angelic squadrons take their rest in a "grateful Twilight" where they are lulled to sleep by "roseate Dews," "cool Winds," and "Melodious Hymns" (5.650-57).

The angelic georgic is presented through various scenes of care and responsibility for God's Garden of Eden and its inhabitants, and through the mixture of georgic topoi with heroic and pastoral motifs. At the gates of Eden the angel guardians of that pastoral place—the "unarmed Youth of Heav'n"—exercise in heroic games, though their magnificent arms seem rather for display than use: "Celestial Armory, Shields, Helms, and Spears / Hung high with Diamond flaming, and with Gold" (4.550-54). These angels keep "night watches in warlike Parade" (4.780), but their confrontation with the disguised Satan is described by a simile from husbandry, intimating their georgic care to guard God's human harvest. They encircle Satan "With ported Spears, as thick as when a field / Of *Ceres* ripe for harvest waving bends / Her bearded Grove of ears, which way the wind / Sways them; the careful Plowman doubting stands / Lest on the threshing floor his hopeful sheaves / Prove chaff" (4.980-85).

Similarly, Raphael's visit to Eden has a georgic as well as an epic aspect. It is an epic mission of warning, compared explicitly as well as through structural and verbal parallels to the mission of Mercury to Aeneas.[9] But whereas Mercury delivers an abrupt and terrifying message from Jove warning Aeneas to flee from Dido's embraces so as to fulfill his destiny as founder of Rome, Raphael undertakes to teach Adam how to fulfill his very different divine charge—to live happily and obediently within his love bower. In georgic terms, Raphael seeks to "cultivate" the minds of Adam and Eve through discourse, planting and fostering in them attitudes that alone can enable them to act upon his warning against disobedience. He comes to teach them how to cultivate both their garden and themselves.

After the Fall, the angelic georgic takes on, briefly, a tragic dimension, as the caretakers hasten to heaven, "mute and sad" because they were not able to prevent Satan's entry to Eden. But they are commended by God for carrying out their charge with "sincerest care"—always the true measure of georgic virtue (10.17-37). Then Michael is sent to Eden on a much harsher georgic mission, to cultivate the stony soil of fallen human nature so as to prepare man and woman for the difficult task of bringing forth fruits from the now resistant earth and the sinful self. Clearly, the angelic georgic can sound darker tones than those normally heard in the georgics of Virgil and Horace.

The angelic heroic mode is chiefly in evidence during the Battle in Heaven, presented by Raphael to Adam and Eve as a brief epic prototype of Homer and Hesiod, but by the Bard to the literate reader in a more complex generic perspective. The angels manifest "Heroic Ardor" and perform "advent'rous deeds" (6.66), not for personal glory but in obedience to God's charge to them to expel his enemies from heaven. God sends them forth as an "Invincible" host of "armed Saints / By Thousands and by Millions rang'd for fight" (6.47-48), though in the event their military prowess cannot win this battle and they cannot fulfill their charge. As Stella Revard has shown, Milton's Battle in Heaven (like no other Renaissance treatment of the subject) severely tests the angels' faith as they are forced to give over their expectation of winning a clear and decisive victory.[10] Nevertheless, they are highly honored by the Son for a heroism of duty and responsibility, for their faithful and fearless warfare according to their powers: "as ye have receiv'd, so have ye done / Invincibly" (6.805-806). This emphasis upon duty and this willing acceptance of limitation are georgic elements in the angelic heroic.

Moreover, the angels affirm values that reach beyond the heroic, directly challenging the Satanic claim that warfare is a "strife of Glory" (6.290). Refusing to play the role of compliance assigned to the angels in Satan's rigged council of war, Abdiel resists demagoguery, war-mongering, and mob rule as he stands alone amid universal scorn and hostility: "unmov'd, / Unshak'n, unseduc'd, unterrifi'd / His Loyalty he kept, his Love, his Zeal" (5.898-900). God pays highest tribute to Abdiel's bold witness to "the Cause / Of Truth, in word mightier than they in Arms" (6.31-32). And Abdiel himself, before he engages with Satan in the first skirmish of the battle, pronounces the impending contest of arms "brutish . . . and foul, / When Reason hath to deal with force" (6.124-25). Even Michael, prince of the celestial armies and foremost in "Military prowess" (6.45), disparages warfare and exalts the goods of peace. As he confronts Satan before their single combat, he praises "Holy Rest" and the "bliss" of heaven which "Brooks not the works of violence and War" (6.271-74). Both Abdiel and Michael win their single combats, but not decisively—and they have to learn from this that only God's power, not the force of arms, can finally make truth and reason prevail, and heavenly bliss endure.

In the battle itself the loyal angels and the Satanic forces exhibit the same martial prowess and battle courage, and are described by the same Homeric topoi. Both forces ride in brazen chariots, wave fiery swords, wear massy armor, carry adamantine shields, discharge fiery arrows, parry taunts and vaunts, engage in single combats and grand melees. Both sides do "deeds of eternal fame," and each angel fights as if "only in his arm the moment lay / Of victory" (6.238-41).[11] Nevertheless, the angelic legions of God display even in their battle formation the unity and integrity of heaven, as they march to war with something of the harmony that characterized their dances on the "solemn day":

> in mighty Quadrate join'd
> Of Union irresistible, mov'd on
> In silence thir bright Legions, to the sound
> Of instrumental Harmony that breath'd
> Heroic Ardor to advent'rous deeds
> Under thir God-like Leaders, in the Cause
> Of God and his *Messiah*. On they move
> Indissolubly firm; nor obvious Hill,
> Nor straitening Vale, nor Wood, nor Stream divides
> Thir perfet ranks; for high above the ground
> Thir march was, and the passive Air upbore

Thir nimble tread; as when the total kind
Of Birds in orderly array on wing
Came summon'd over *Eden* to receive
Thir names of thee.
(6.62-76)

The comparison of the marching legions to birds alludes to famous Homeric and Virgilian similes,[12] and also serves Raphael's need to accommodate an unfamiliar martial subject to Adam's pastoral experience. It has the further important function of underscoring the integrity of the heavenly life, in which pastoral is wedded to heroic (and georgic) in perfect harmony.

But the combat with Satan cannot be sustained at this exalted level. As the Satanic forces turn from the conventions of Homeric battle to invent the cannon and gunpowder of modern warfare, they debase the conflict beneath heroic, as Milton indicates by employing at this point the topoi of mock-epic.[13] We are invited to recognize how the rebels (and modern warriors after them) have debased an activity regarded by the loyal angels as foul and brutish at its Homeric best. The Satanic forces become "gamesome" and their language ignoble as they exchange outrageous puns and scoff at their enemies in "ambiguous words." And as Michael Lieb notes, Milton describes their "devilish Enginry" in flagrantly scatological imagery:[14]

Immediate in a flame,
But soon obscur'd with smoke, all Heav'n appear'd,
From those deep-throated Engines belcht, whose roar
Embowell'd with outrageous noise the Air,
And all her entrails tore, disgorging foul
Thir devilish glut, chain'd Thunderbolts and Hail
Of Iron Globes, which on the Victor Host
Levell'd.

(6.584-91)

The loyal angels do not escape involvement in this mock-heroic bathos, though they do not glorify war, Homeric or

147

modern. We are led to smile at the ridiculous spectacle they present as the cannon tumbles them about—all the more easily for their bright armor and marvelous battle formations:

> None on thir feet might stand,
> Though standing else as Rocks, but down they fell
> By thousands, Angel on Arch-Angel roll'd;
> The sooner for thir Arms; unarm'd they might
> Have easily as Spirits evaded swift
> By quick contraction or remove; but now
> Foul dissipation follow'd and forc't rout.
> (6.592-98)

The scorn and ignominy these angels endure is at once a trial of their fidelity—not unlike that faced by Abdiel—and also an object lesson against trusting to arms in the battle against evil. The episode illustrates as well the enduring plight of the good, whose very instincts for civility place them at a disadvantage before the technology of violence.

The loyal angels respond to this diabolic debasement of warfare by changing its form yet again, to a primitive, pre-Homeric mode. Temporarily at a loss, and moved (for the first time) by "rage," they cast away their arms, and, like the giants in Hesiod's *Theogony* who bury the Titans under huge rocks, they uproot the hills of heaven to hurl at their enemies.[15] Though they are without guilt, the angels here face the tragic dilemma of the good in any war,[16] driven by its mad inner logic of mounting devastation to destroy what they value even as they seek to save it—here, heaven's lovely landscape, and the blissful, integrated life it nourishes: "They pluckt the seated Hills with all thir load, / Rocks, Waters, Woods, and by the shaggy tops / Uplifting bore them in thir hands" (6.644-46). This escalation calls forth an escalation in kind from the rebels, until annihilation seems imminent:

> So Hills amid the Air encounter'd Hills
> Hurl'd to and fro with jaculation dire,
> That under ground they fought in dismal shade:

Infernal noise; War seem'd a civil Game
To this uproar; horrid confusion heapt
Upon confusion rose: and now all Heav'n
Had gone to wrack, with ruin overspread . . .
(6.664-70)

As he sends forth the Son to avert this potential tragedy by his decisive victory over Satan, God comments on war in terms that the loyal angels (and the Bard's audience) will now understand. Those terms suggest that warfare, however good the cause, however heroic the warriors, however divinely authorized and necessary as a response to blatant evil, is in its essence and its effects tragic, not glorious:

In perpetual fight they needs must last
Endless, and no solution will be found:
War wearied hath perform'd what War can do,
And to disorder'd rage let loose the reins,
With Mountains as with Weapons arm'd, which makes
Wild work in Heav'n, and dangerous to the main.
(6.693-98)

As exemplars of the wholeness of heavenly life, and as archetypes of the Miltonic higher heroism, the angels here experience, however briefly and reversably, the tragic costs that inevitably attend warfare. They must accept and fulfill their responsibility to fight against evil at God's command, and at the same time recognize that their own strength is insufficient to extirpate that evil. For a decisive victory, the angels (like humankind later) must depend upon the divine power manifested in the Son. In all this, the Battle in Heaven foreshadows the struggle of good and evil throughout human history, as portrayed in Books Eleven and Twelve of the poem. And the magnificent victory of the Son witnessed by all the angels foreshadows (as William Madsen has noted) the apocalyptic victory of Christ over Satan, to be witnessed by all the Saints.[17] But foreshadowed is not quite the term: what we are shown rather is a continuum, presenting the struggle against evil as, in its essence, everywhere the same—in heaven, in Eden, and in the postlapsarian world.

ANGELIC DISCOURSE: DIALOGUE AND PROPHETIC TESTIMONY

Milton imagines the angels as "a nation of prophets," embodying the Mosaic ideal which he himself urged so fervently upon the English nation.[18] Accordingly, their speech is imbued with prophetic zeal in searching for and testifying to truth. In conformity with the central Protestant tradition Milton identified prophecy with Christ's "PROPHETIC function . . . TO EDUCATE HIS CHURCH IN HEAVENLY TRUTH AND TO TEACH THE WHOLE WILL OF HIS FATHER," a function exercised not only by the visionaries and oracular prophets of the Old and New Testament but "under the gospel" by all those with "the simple gift of teaching, especially of public teaching."[19] The distinct kinds of discourse Milton's angels hold with their various audiences—other loyal angels, unfallen Adam and Eve, fallen but redeemed Adam and Eve, reprobate angels—find analogues in the specific kinds of prophetic teaching Milton identifies in his *Apology* for Smectymnuus as appropriate for audiences of different character:

> Our Saviour who had all gifts in him was Lord to expresse his indoctrinating power in what sort him best seem'd; sometimes by a milde and familiar converse, sometimes with plaine and impartiall home-speaking. . . . otherwhiles with bitter and irefull rebukes if not teaching yet leaving excuselesse those his wilfull impugners. What was all in him, was divided among many others the teachers of his Church; some to be severe and of a sad gravity that they may win such, & check sometimes those who be of nature over-confident and jocond; others were sent more cheerefull, free, and still as it were at large, in the midst of an untrespassing honesty; . . . Some also were indu'd with a staid moderation, and soundnesse of argu-

150

ment to teach and convince the rationall and sober-
minded; . . . in times of opposition . . . then Zeale . . .
ascends his fiery Chariot . . . to expresse power, high au-
thority and indignation . . . [or] to cast derision and scorne
upon perverse and fraudulent seducers; . . . Thus did the
true Prophets of old combat with the false . . . [with] a
sanctifi'd bitternesse.[20]

When the angels in *Paradise Lost* speak among themselves
or with unfallen man their characteristic speech is dialogue,
and the tone is that of "milde and familiar converse." Nor-
mally, they do not speak in soliloquy or use deliberative rhet-
oric—though Abdiel employs both as special circumstances
warrant. Their dialogic speech no doubt has its source in God's
own penchant for dialogue,[21] but unlike God they do not
normally proceed by posing apparent dilemmas or ambiguous
counter arguments. With unfallen respondents the angels en-
gage in a species of Platonic dialogue, employing that "skill in
asking and answering questions," and that concern to refer
particular issues to first principles of truth, knowledge, and
virtue which the Platonic Socrates exemplified and wished to
nurture in the philosopher-guardians of his *Republic*.[22] In form,
however, the angelic exchanges more closely resemble Boe-
thian dialogue, in that the superior intelligence develops the
understanding of an inferior by commenting on and answer-
ing his questions at some length, as well as by propounding
his own probing questions.[23]

In these dialogues, the hierarchical inferior (angel or man)
normally seeks knowledge by posing a question, and the su-
perior responds with a critique of that question as regards its
conformity with God's design—the guiding principle for all
intellectual discourse. The critique might consider: whether
the questioner is properly motivated; whether the question is
properly formulated; whether the questioner is seeking
knowledge proper to his condition and needs; whether the
respondent can in fact answer the question asked; and, if so,

how he can best impart that knowledge to this audience. Only after such a critique is the question itself engaged.

This process is evident in the dialogue between the great archangel of the Sun, Uriel—the "sharpest-sighted Spirit of all in Heav'n"—and the seeming cherub who (unknown to Uriel) is Satan in disguise (3.634-739). Satan looks and acts his role to perfection: he is youthful, graceful, charming, with flowing hair and brightly colored wings. He approaches his superior with "decent steps," asking his question with due deference and a proper explanation of his motives, so that Uriel has no suspicions whatsoever. The "Cherub" claims (echoing Psalm 8) that he desires to see God's new creation at first hand, and asks direction to man's abode,

> That I may find him, and with secret gaze,
> Or open admiration him behold
> On whom the great Creator hath bestow'd
> Worlds, and on whom hath all these graces pour'd;
> That both in him and all things, as is meet,
> The Universal Maker we may praise.
> (3.671-76)[24]

Uriel's critique of the question determines that the supposed cherub's curiosity "leads to no excess / That reaches blame, but rather merits praise / The more it seems excess," since it is directed to the knowledge and praise of God's works. Then, echoing psalm verses and Wisdom's creation account in Proverbs 8:27, Uriel praises the creation and claims eyewitness knowledge of it, focusing on the planetary system (rather than the earth or man) as the feature most significant for angels.[25] Only when his critique is completed does Uriel answer the cherub's specific question by offering clear directions: "Look downward on that Globe . . . / That place is Earth the seat of Man . . . / That spot to which I point is *Paradise*, / *Adam's* abode" (3.722-34).

The long dialogue between Raphael (clad as winged Seraph) and unfallen, majestic Adam, has the same general characteristics, though (as we have seen) Raphael incorporates

152

within this dialogic frame various literary genres to accommodate the several kinds of knowledge Adam asks him to impart.[26] The tone is again "milde and familiar converse." And here also the hierarchical inferior, Adam, initiates the various topics while the angel prefaces each response with a critique of Adam's requests or queries, referring them to first principles.

Adam's first question emerges from his role as host: he queries whether the fruit he offers is "unsavory food perhaps / To spiritual Natures," but adds immediately, "only this I know, / That one Celestial Father gives to all" (5.401-403). In response, Raphael observes at the outset that Adam has properly stated the first principle upon which resolution of this issue depends, the universal fatherhood of God as creator of all. Then he sets forth several ontological concepts which flow from that principle: the similarity of angelic and human natures, the common need of all created beings for sustenance, the common material substratum of all being, and the processes of choice and change in the universe. But his answer quite ignores Adam's subsidiary and irrelevant question as to how angelic and human food compare.

When Adam, responding to a casual allusion by Raphael, asks for the full story of the angels' revolt, Raphael begins as before, by analyzing the implications of the request: he notes his own limitations as narrator; the problem of accommodating such high matter to this audience; and the fact that he has dispensation to reveal these possibly forbidden "secrets of another world" for Adam's good. When Raphael completes the narrative of the Battle in Heaven Adam requests account of the world's creation, affirming the usefulness of such knowledge and worthiness of his motive: "wee, not to explore the secrets ask / Of his Eternal Empire, but the more / To magnify his works, the more we know" (7.86-97). However, because Adam asks his question in potentially blasphemous form—"what cause / Mov'd the Creator in his holy Rest / Through all Eternity so late to build / In *Chaos*"[27]—Raphael begins with an especially careful critique. He commends Adam's good motives, warns him against probing into God's secrets, reaffirms that the knowledge he seeks should be appropriate to human capacity and human needs, and proclaims that temperance should control the appetite for knowledge as for food.

Adam's next query—about the cosmos—is posed without his usual caution and without linking the question and request to a desire to praise God; he seeks only to resolve some "doubt" concerning what he thinks to be disproportions in Nature's (and by implication God's) design. Raphael's usual preliminary analysis of this question highlights two basic principles: that questions about the cosmos are not in themselves blameworthy if primarily motivated by desire to know and praise God; and that God's secret reasons for disposing as he does in the cosmos are not to be scanned by men or angels. Then he designs his entire discourse as a critique of Adam's faulty assumptions, demonstrating that "whether Heav'n move or Earth" does not finally matter to human life and human good. The angel's success in teaching through dialogue and literary invention is confirmed after this discourse, as Adam declares himself freed from perplexing thoughts and ready to take the lead himself in speaking of "things at hand / Useful"—his own history and his feelings of passion for Eve (8.179-205).

Michael's dialogue with fallen but redeemed Adam and Eve is also designed to educate, and also incorporates several genres. However, Michael's firm direction rather than Adam's requests and questions propels this dialogue, whose subject is a divine given: the proclamation of banishment, together with the revelation of what is to come in future times. That the Fall has greatly increased the distance separating man and angel is evident from the severity with which this prophetic teacher reproves and corrects Adam's now-constant errors.

In Book Eleven, Michael begins the dialogue by pointing out to Adam several emblematic Old Testament scenes, offering little or no comment about them. Adam responds to each with faulty interpretations and questions. Michael then supplies corrections and clarifications which lead Adam by stages to sounder notions about God's justice, the nature of sin and death, and the deceits of pleasure. As this book ends, Adam for the first time correctly interprets an emblem—the rainbow—as a manifestation of God's covenant with man, and Michael responds with approval: "Dext'rously thou aim'st" (11.884).

At the beginning of Book Twelve Michael pauses to see "If *Adam* aught perhaps might interpose," and hearing nothing, explains that the failure of mortal sight dictates a shift in his role and Adam's: "Henceforth what is to come I will relate, / Thou therefore give due audience, and attend" (12.11-12). The dialogic process is maintained, however, as Adam often interrupts Michael's narrative of biblical history with comments and questions, and Michael often pauses to correct Adam's erroneous or imperfect interpretations of political tyranny, the Law, and the protoevangelion. The dialogue appears to end as Adam "last repli'd" with a statement of faith, recognizing Christ as exemplar of the new heroism of obedience and suffering, and acknowledging him as "My Redeemer ever blest." But Michael has still to complete what Adam has omitted: "th' Angel last repli'd" by advising Adam to add virtuous deeds to his new knowledge (12.552-87).

The loyal angels' discourse with Satan and his followers cannot proceed as dialogue, since they do not agree on first principles or share a common commitment to education and to truth. Such discourse retains some features of dialogue, notably the disposition to press for answers to probing questions. It also incorporates some elements of deliberative or political rhetoric, notably arguments concerning heaven's polity and God's sovereignty. But to such audiences the loyal angels usually speak to convict rather than to persuade: their prophetic speech testifies zealously to the truth and refutes Satanic lies with scorn and indignation.

When the angelic guard of Eden surprise Satan at Eve's ear, their questions transform the epic battle taunt into prophetic testimony. Satan's scornful question, "Know ye not mee? . . . / Not to know mee argues yourselves unknown," elicits a "grave

rebuke" from the youthful cherubs, testifying to Satan's al-
tered appearance and its cause (4.827-846). When Satan is
brought before Gabriel, that angel assumes the role of judicial
examiner, sharply questioning Satan's motives and purposes
in Eden and subjecting his answers to penetrating analysis,
thereby forcing him from one unlikely explanation to another.
Posing further questions as he summarizes, Gabriel convicts
Satan of constant shifts and lies, and testifies eloquently to the
truths Satan would deny or pervert:

> To say and straight unsay, pretending first
> Wise to fly pain, professing next the Spy,
> Argues no Leader, but a liar trac't,
> *Satan*, and couldst thou faithful add? O name,
> O sacred name of faithfulness profan'd!
> . . . .
> And thou sly hypocrite, who now wouldst seem
> Patron of liberty, who more than thou
> Once fawn'd, and cring'd, and servilely ador'd
> Heav'n's awful Monarch? wherefore but in hope
> To dispossess him, and thyself to reign?
> (4.947-61)

Gabriel concludes by interpreting to Satan the divine sign of
his defeat in the heavenly scales, compelling him to recognize
the entire dependence of his power upon God's will.

Abdiel's debate with Satan in Book Five is a more complex
kind of prophetic discourse, in part because for a time there
is some question about the moral character of the audience.
In this scene Abdiel, impelled by zeal for truth and love of
God, transforms Satan's intended incitement to revolt into an
open, formal debate on the divine polity. Abdiel speaks in a
vehement high style, but like the prophet Micah the power of
his speech does not come from rhetorical strategies but from
the ethos of the speaker, the strength of his feelings, and the
force of truth. Through his zealous testimony to truth Abdiel
also undertakes to persuade and move his erstwhile comrades

to a better course, thereby providing a paradigm for a new heroic rhetoric transformed by the spirit of prophecy.

Two parallel scenes of provocation to revolt afford points of reference, indicating how the Satanic rhetoric was intended to work absent Abdiel's prophetic testimony. One is Cataline's exhortation to his greedy and dissolute soldiers, as reported by Sallust. As a cloak for his own ambition, Cataline appealed to the ancient rights and liberties of Romans and the need to resist tyrants: "Awake, then! Lo, here, here before your eyes, is the freedom for which you have yearned, and with it riches, honour, and glory. . . . Unless haply I delude myself and you are content to be slaves rather than to rule."[28] The other is Caesar's speech upon crossing the Rubicon, as reported by Lucan. Playing masterfully upon his army's emotions, Caesar elaborated upon the injustices and ingratitude they have suffered from the Senate, and the threat of tyranny from Pompey: "we are but dislodging a tyrant from a state prepared to bow the knee."[29] Caesar's men wavered until Laelius, the chief centurian, proclaimed his willingness to perform any monstrosity at Caesar's command, after which the army gave its assent with a deafening shout.

These scenes illuminate Satan's rhetorical strategies, and the challenge presented to him when in place of a Laelius he meets with an Abdiel. Addressing the assembled angels by their titles—"Thrones, Dominations, Princedoms, Virtues, Powers"—Satan intimates that their newly appointed King, the Son, intends to eclipse those titles and powers. He then asks, rhetorically, "what if better counsels might erect / Our minds and teach us to cast off this Yoke?" (5.722-86). Offering such counsel himself, he sets aside as inappropriate to angels the Aristotelian precepts that monarchy is properly the office of the worthiest and that there is need for one to give laws to the community. Rather, he defines their condition in terms of other Aristotelian principles: since angels are equal in freedom if not in nature and are perfectly good without law, they are ordained "to govern, not to serve" (5.787-802).[30] Like Cataline and Caesar, he here misapplies precepts concerning the rights of a free citizenry—and also Milton's own arguments about the basis of human government and political liberty in the *Tenure*.[31]

Abdiel breaks in at this point, moved to furious denunciation—"O argument blasphémous, false and proud!" (5.809-48). Dialogue-fashion, he poses a series of insistent, probing questions that point to their proper answers, forcing into the open the suppressed terms of Satan's argument. Those questions underscore the folly of extending to the Creator of all things the political laws that pertain to his creatures: "Shalt thou give Law to God, shalt thou dispute / With him the points of liberty, who made / Thee what thou art, and form'd the Pow'rs of Heav'n / Such as he pleas'd, and circumscrib'd thir being?" Then, setting aside the charge of divine tyranny by appealing to the angels' common experience of divine goodness, he launches another barrage of questions to show the entire irrelevance of the argument from equality in reference to God's own begotten Son, "by whom / As by his Word the mighty Father made / All things." He concludes by interpreting the elevation of the Son as a kind of "incarnation" honoring the angels, as the Son "One of our number thus reduc't becomes."

Abdiel's probing questions, if answered truthfully, would convict Satan of falsehood and correct his political theory in the light of heaven's special circumstances. Accordingly, his speech offers the assembled angels—thus far entirely passive and possibly deceived—an opportunity to reverse course even at this late moment. The speech ends with a direct rhetorical appeal to them and to Satan: "Cease then this impious rage, / And tempt not these; but hast'n to appease / Th' incensed Father, and th' incensed Son, / While Pardon may be found in time besought." The clear and rather surprising suggestion is that mistakes about heavenly polity, however egregious, are not necessarily damnable if the errant seek pardon.

Satan's rebuttal (5.853-71) turns from politics to theology, since he can answer Abdiel's defense of divine kingship grounded upon creation only by denying that creation. Unleashing his own barrage of questions in the interests of confusing rather than clarifying the issue, he appeals to the angels' experience and memory: "who saw / When this creation was? remember'st thou / Thy making, while the Maker gave thee being? / We know no time when we were not as now." Refusing to admit that such ignorance must be the common condition of creatures—"for who himself beginning knew?" Adam later asks (8.251)—Satan concludes with manifest illogic that this very ignorance argues the angels "self-begot, self-rais'd / By our own quick'ning power." His speech ends with an appeal to might as the measure of equality: "our own right hand / Shall . . . try / Who is our equal."

The resounding applause that greets this speech marks the moment of choice for the rebel angels, as, with the options now clearly before them, they commit themselves to the Satanic atheism and monomania. At this point Abdiel properly gives over the argument, finding no ground for further debate with those who have denied their derivation from the source of being. In ringing, prophetic terms he denounces Satan as reprobate: "O alienate from God, O Spirit accurst, / Forsak'n of all good; I see thy fall / Determin'd . . . other Decrees / Against thee are gone forth without recall" (5.877-95).

Abdiel continues his debate with Satan on the battlefield, transforming the epic battle taunt with its characteristic *ad hominem* tirades and vaunts of self-praise into a vehicle for political argument and prophetic testimony (6.114-88). He first explores in a brief soliloquy[32] the relation of reason and physical strength, indicating his expectation with God's aid to defeat Satan in arms, "whose Reason I have tri'd / Unsound and false." Challenging Satan—not now to convince but to convict him—Abdiel underscores the folly of taking arms "Against th' Omnipotent" and of supposing that numbers determine truth and wisdom: "I alone / Seem'd in thy World erroneous to dissent / From all: my Sect thou seest, now learn too late / How few sometimes may know, when thousands err." In his turn Satan extols his forces for their "Vigor Divine" and love of liberty, disparaging the loyal angels as creatures enervated by long servility, feast and song—"the Minstrelsy of Heav'n."

Abdiel then challenges Satan's high rhetoric about freedom in terms of the Platonic tradition which locates freedom quintessentially in the soul rather than the state. He distinguishes sharply between service properly due "When he who rules is worthiest," and servitude that emanates from inner slavery: "This is servitude, / To serve th' unwise, or him who hath rebell'd / Against his worthier, as thine now serve thee, / Thyself not free, but to thyself enthrall'd." Abdiel is permitted a fully satisfactory closure to this debate as he finds the strength of his argument reflected in the strength of his spear, forcing to his knees the rebel who refused knee tribute to God. In heaven right makes might: how Milton must have wished it had been so in England.

Angelic Hymns and Ceremonies

The lyric genre characteristic of the angels is, not surprisingly, the hymn—by definition a praise of God or the gods. Milton has devised for the angels a large repertoire of hymns, differentiated by subject, kind, and model, influenced by both biblical and classical traditions, and usually located within elaborate ceremonies of praise—pageants, masque dances, triumphs.[33] These hymns are sometimes summarized, sometimes quoted as embedded forms within the narrative.

In their influential theoretical treatises, Menander and Scaliger distinguished several kinds of classical "literary" hymns— invocatory, valedictory, natural (celebrating the numen of a god or some divine force), mythical (narrating myths about a god), genealogical (describing a god's ancestors, birth, and descendants), and fictional (inventing new myths or adding to received ones).[34] Christian poets and theorists, notably Scaliger, provided precepts and models for adapting some of these kinds to Christian purposes—by addressing one or another of the three divine persons, or focusing upon one or more of the divine attributes.[35] While classical literary hymns in hexameters and their Christian progeny comprise a tradition distinct from that of lyric and congregational hymns (classical and Christian[36]), this distinction was often blurred in Christian theory because the major biblical exemplars of hymn, the Psalms, were associated with both kinds. In their lofty eloquence and art they were likened to the "Homeric" and Callimachan hymns, while also serving as liturgical hymns for congregational worship.[37] Puttenham offers a useful summary of Renaissance views:

> The Gods of the Gentiles were honoured by their Poetes in hymnes, which is an extraordinarie and divine praise, extolling and magnifying them for their great powers and excellencie of nature in the highest degree of laude. . . . And these hymnes to the gods were the first forme of Poesie and the highest & the stateliest, & they were song by the Poets as priests, and by the people or whole congregation as we sing in our Churchs the Psalmes of *David*.[38]

Throughout the English Renaissance the Psalms and the Book of Revelation were widely recognized as sources and models for Christian hymns. Psalms 8, 19, 66, 103, 104, the Alleluia Psalms (113-18), the Gradual Psalms or Songs of Degree (120-35), as well as most of the final fifteen were usually identified as hymns. George Wither specified several varieties among them:

> *Hymnes* were Songs, in which were the praises of God onely, and that with joy and triumph; . . . those that are intituled *Halleluiah* are *Hymns* also, mentioning particularly the praises of God for benefits received. . . . When he [the Psalmist] intends either to set forth the wondrous works of the eternall God, or the glorious magnificence of our Redeemers Empire, then his divine *Muse* mounts the heights of Heroicall *Poesie*.[39]

Most of the Psalmic hymns are thanksgivings for benefits received; for the hymns of triumph, and the praises of God's great glory, models were also found in the Mosaic hymn (Exodus 15) celebrating victory over Pharoah, and in the angelic hymns described in the Book of Revelation.[40] In *Paradise Lost* the angels' hymns draw upon all these kinds—psalms, classical and Christianized literary hymns, and especially the exalted hymns and ceremonies recorded in the Book of Revelation.

Brief references throughout the epic indicate that heaven and Eden are continually suffused with angelic harmonies and music, hymnic in purpose though not always in form.[41] But on several occasions hymns and ceremonies are rendered in considerable detail, sometimes through description, sometimes as embedded lyrics. An extended passage describes the Son's conquest over the rebel angels as a Triumph:

> Sole Victor from th' expulsion of his Foes
> *Messiah* his triumphal Chariot turn'd:
> To meet him all his Saints, who silent stood
> Eye-witnesses of his Almighty Acts,
> With Jubilee advanc'd; and as they went,
> Shaded with branching Palm, each order bright,
> Sung Triumph, and him sung Victorious King,
> Son, Heir, and Lord, to him Dominion giv'n,
> Worthiest to Reign: he celebrated rode
> Triumphant through mid Heav'n, into the Courts
> And Temple of his mighty Father Thron'd
> On high; who into Glory him receiv'd.
> (6.880-91)

The description evokes the palm-waving saints in John's Apocalypse (7:9, 12:10) proclaiming the Son's worthiness to reign, and the multitudes proclaiming Christ's kingship at his entrance into Jerusalem (Matt. 21:8-9). It especially recalls Roman Triumphs, in which the victorious general was led in solemn procession into the city and then on to the Senate and the Temple of Jupiter, preceded by the armies shouting "Io Triumphe." However, the Son's Triumph is portrayed as more glorious than that of any imperator, and it is set in sharp contrast to Satan's perverse and aborted Triumph in Book

162

Ten.[42] Nevertheless, we are given only the theme for the angels' triumphal hymn, without development.[43]

By the same token, in a ceremony suggested by Revelation 19:6,[44] the angels laud God's justice when he proclaims the use he will make of Sin and Death in executing and mitigating the curse upon the earth. But Milton renders their hymn only by a brief statement of its themes, without elaboration. Appropriately, one theme is derived from the hymn text proclaimed at the opening of the seals (Rev. 16:5,7), "Thou art righteous, O Lord, which art, and wast, and shall be, because thou hast judged thus / . . . Even so, Lord God Almighty, true and righteous are thy judgments." The second theme praises the Son as restorer of heaven and earth:

> He ended, and the heav'nly Audience loud
> Sung *Halleluiah*, as the sound of Seas,
> Through multitude that sung: Just are thy ways,
> Righteous are thy Decrees on all thy Works;
> Who can extenuate thee? Next, to the Son,
> Destin'd restorer of Mankind, by whom
> New Heav'n and Earth shall to the Ages rise,
> Or down from Heav'n descend. Such was thir song.
> (10.641-48)

Other occasions, however, call forth much more elaborate and impressive angelic ceremonies and hymns. The Dialogue in Heaven is followed by a solemn, masquelike ceremony which draws upon many elements in Revelation 4-5—the jasper, emerald, and "sea of glass like unto crystal"; the white raiment, golden crowns, and harps of the elders; the multitudes of angels singing. The sequence of events in this ceremony also follows that in Revelation 4-5.[45] After the shouts of jubilee and loud hosannas comes a ceremony in which the angels cast off and take up again their crowns—golden and floral at once, in keeping with the paradoxical fusion of courtly splendor and pastoral delight in Milton's heaven:

>   lowly reverent
> Towards either Throne they bow, and to the ground
> With solemn adoration down they cast
> Thir Crowns inwove with Amarant and Gold,
> . . . .
> And where the river of Bliss through midst of Heav'n
> Rolls o'er *Elysian* Flow'rs her Amber stream;
> With these that never fade the Spirits elect
> Bind thir resplendent locks inwreath'd with beams,
> Now in loose Garlands thick thrown off, the bright
> Pavement that like a Sea of Jasper shone
> Impurpl'd with Celestial Roses smil'd.
> Then Crown'd again thir gold'n Harps they took . . .
>   (3.349-65)

With those harps they then played a "Preamble sweet" to the two polyphonic hymns that follow, in which all voices join "Melodious part": the first praises God for his ineffable glory, the second praises the Son for his heroic love. These hymns are incorporated in the text, though we are not sure with either of them exactly where summary ends and direct quotation begins.

The themes of the "Hymn to God the Father," though not its language, may derive from the praises shouted by the elders (Rev. 4:11) as they cast down their crowns, a passage described by the commentators as a celebration of God's attributes: "the praising which the Elders use . . . celebrates the *holinesse, Dominion, omnipotency*, and truth of God."[46] In its form the hymn recalls brief Homeric hymns hailing the god and enumerating his chief attributes, often in a series of epithets:[47]

> Thee Father first they sung Omnipotent,
> Immutable, Immortal, Infinite,
> Eternal King; thee Author of all being,
> Fountain of Light, thyself invisible
> Amidst the glorious brightness where thou sit'st
> Thron'd inaccessible, but when thou shad'st

164

The full blaze of thy beams, and through a cloud
Drawn round about thee like a radiant Shrine,
Dark with excessive bright thy skirts appear,
Yet dazzle Heav'n, that brightest Seraphim
Approach not, but with both wings veil thir eyes.
                                                (3.372-82)

The "Hymn to the Son" takes its thematic import from the "new Song" of Revelation 5:9-14, "Worthy is the Lamb that was slain to receive power, and riches, and wisdom, and strength, and honour, and glory, and blessing."[48] Heinrich Bullinger explained that the "new song" of Revelation celebrates man's redemption and Christ's exaltation through his passion and death: "And in the Hymne they singe, that al thyngs are subjecte to Christ . . . that he humbled him selfe to the deathe, and was therefore exalted above all things."[49] The Miltonic hymn also recalls the "Hymn to Hercules" (*Aeneid* 8.293-302), incorporated within Evander's Arcadian festival for the god.[50]

In form, the hymn's classical, three-part structure resembles that of the longer Homeric or Callimachan literary hymns.[51] Milton's version of the exordium, often a series of epithets pointing to the god's qualities, is a praise of the Son's dominant attribute as Image and reflection of God:

Thee next they sang of all Creation first,
Begotten Son, Divine Similitude,
In whose conspicuous count'nance, without cloud
Made visible, th' Almighty Father shines,
Whom else no Creature can behold; on thee
Impresst th' effulgence of his Glory abides,
Transfus'd on thee his ample Spirit rests.
                                                (3.383-89)

The middle, expected to develop one of these qualities or recount a myth or myths associated with the god, recounts the Son's great deeds: his role in the Creation and in the destruction of the rebel hosts, and especially the act of "unexampl'd love" he has just performed in offering to die for man. Finally, the peroration contains the expected hymnic "Hail," and the traditional promise to continue the god's praises forever:

> Hail Son of God, Savior of Men, thy Name
> Shall be the copious matter of my Song
> Henceforth, and never shall my Harp thy praise
> Forget, nor from thy Father's praise disjoin.
>   (3.412-15)[52]

The mix of hymnic kinds in these first embedded angelic hymns seems intended to suggest and accommodate the perfection of angelic hymnody. They combine the highest hymnic models we know—their substance chiefly biblical, their form classical. The classical models offer useful conventions—the string of epithets, and the metaphoric expansion of a single attribute (here, light)—which allow Milton to use the resonances of lyric suggestiveness to render divine qualities he cannot portray in dialogue and action. Also, by mixing hymnic kinds and creating some deliberate ambiguity as to what is summary and what is quotation, he intimates that the hymns he presents are approximations only, and cannot be otherwise. We are certain of the shift to quotation only with the peroration of the second hymn, "Hail Son of God." At this point, the Miltonic Bard suddenly and brilliantly exploits the ambiguity as he associates his own praises with those of the angelic choir, claiming their hymn as "my song."

God's creation of the universe (Book Seven) gives rise to a very extensive series of angelic hymns and ceremonies. They are warranted by the usual interpretation of Job 38:7—"When the morning stars sang together, and all the sons of God shouted for joy"—as a reference to angelic song at the Creation. The Miltonic creation hymns are descants on or adaptations of biblical hymn texts, preserving the decorum of the hexaemeron Raphael devises to accommodate the Creation to Adam. But whereas in Book Three the Miltonic Bard maintained some decorous ambiguity as to the exact language of the angelic hymns he reported, Raphael designates the creation hymns with clear markers ("So sung they") and often quotes them at considerable length. Though still accommodated, these hymns derive authority from the Angel Bard and from the citation of biblical texts as themes. Milton's use of predominantly biblical hymnody for the celebration of what he took to be the most glorious of all heavenly deeds, the Creation, accords with his belief that the hymns of the Bible surpass classical hymns, "not in their divine argument alone, but in the very critical art of composition."[53]

The first hymn is a song of "triumph and rejoicing," celebrating the Father's decree of Creation as an act far more glorious than the military victory over the rebel angels, since it brings good out of their evil. The hymn text, "Glory to God in the highest, and on earth peace, good will toward men" (Luke 2:14), is the angels' hymn for Christ's nativity, transposed here to celebrate the nativity of the universe.[54]

> Glory they sung to the most High, good will
> To future men, and in thir dwellings peace:
> Glory to him whose just avenging ire
> Had driven out th' ungodly from his sight
> And th' habitations of the just; to him
> Glory and praise, whose wisdom had ordain'd
> Good out of evil to create, instead
> Of Spirits malign a better Race to bring
> Into their vacant room, and thence diffuse
> His good to Worlds and Ages infinite.
> So sang the Hierarchies.
> (7.182-92)[55]

The hymn is followed by a triumphal Progress, with Psalm 24:7 as its reference point, in which the Son rides forth in the Chariot of Paternal Deity to execute God's Creation decree.[56]

The First Day's work, the creation of light, ends with angelic hymns which are not quoted but described as descants on the hymn text, "God the Creator":

Thus was the first Day Ev'n and Morn:
Nor pass'd uncelebrated, nor unsung
By the Celestial Choirs, when Orient Light
Exhaling first from Darkness they beheld;
Birth-day of Heav'n and Earth; with joy and shout
The hollow Universal Orb they fill'd,
And touch'd thir Golden Harps, and hymning prais'd
God and his works, Creator him they sung,
Both when first Ev'ning was, and when first Morn.
                                            (7.252-60)

This interpretation and expansion of the Genesis refrain—"And
the evening and the morning were the __ day"—indicates that
such hymns and ceremonies were repeated on each successive
day, though the narrator is not always explicit: "So Ev'n / And
Morning *Chorus* sung the second Day" (7.274-75); "So Ev'n
and Morn recorded the Third Day" (7.338); "Glad Ev'ning
and glad Morn crown'd the fourth day" (7.386); "Ev'ning
and Morn solémnized the Fift day" (7.448).

The Sixth Day begins "With Ev'ning Harps and Matin"
(7.450) and concludes with a hymn of triumph embedded in
the text and quoted at length as the chariot of God returns to
heaven in a solemn Triumph. The hymn is an elaborate des-
cant on Psalm 24:7-8: "Lift up your heads, O ye gates; and
be ye lift up, ye everlasting doors; and the King of glory shall
come in. / Who is this King of glory? The Lord strong and
mighty, the Lord mighty in battle." Since this text was also a
point of reference when the Son rode forth to begin his cre-
ating work, its elaboration as theme for this hymn provides
fitting closure. Milton's rather surprising choice of this Psalm
text, originally intended to extol the martial victories of the
Lord of Hosts over his enemies, identifies the Creation as the
true triumph of divine power. However, the Son's triumphal
procession on this occasion far surpasses those accorded any
military conqueror, including the Son himself after the Battle
in Heaven:

Up he rode
Follow'd with acclamation and the sound
Symphonious of ten thousand Harps that tun'd
Angelic harmonies: the Earth, the Air
Resounded, (thou remember'st, for thou heard'st)
The Heav'ns and all the Constellations rung,
The Planets in thir station list'ning stood,
While the bright Pomp ascended jubilant.
Open, ye everlasting Gates, they sung,
Open, ye Heav'ns, your living doors; let in
The great Creator from his work return'd
Magnificent, his Six days' work, a World;
Open, and henceforth oft; for God will deign
To visit oft the dwellings of just Men
Delighted, and with frequent intercourse
Thither will send his winged Messengers
On errands of supernal Grace. So sung
The glorious Train ascending.
(7.557-74)

An even more elaborate celebration of the Creation occurs on the first sabbath, with music, song, incense, and a long hymn (quoted in its entirety) which revises both biblical and classical hymn models. Heaven's orchestra on this occasion includes a full range of stringed and wind instruments—harp, pipe, dulcimer, "all Organs of sweet stop, / All sounds on Fret by String or Golden Wire"—and the heavenly choir sings variously, "with Voice / Choral or Unison" (7.592-99). The sabbath hymn takes its text from the saints' hymn celebrating the victory over the Beast in Revelation (Rev. 15:3-4):

And they sing the song of Moses the servant of God, and the song of the Lamb, saying, Great and marvellous are thy works, Lord God Almighty: just and true are thy ways, thou King of saints.
Who shall not fear thee, O Lord, and glorify thy name?

for thou only art holy: for all nations shall come and worship before thee; for thy judgments are made manifest.

The first segment of the angels' sabbath hymn is a descant on these verses. As the biblical text authorizes, it also incorporates elements of the Song of Moses (Exod. 15), which celebrates the Lord's victory over Pharoah's troops drowned in the Red Sea.[57] However, the Miltonic angels discount the martial triumph central to both biblical songs as they again glorify the Creation as God's greatest victory:

> Creation and the Six days' acts they sung:
> Great are thy works, *Jehovah*, infinite
> Thy power; what thought can measure thee or tongue
> Relate thee; greater now in thy return
> Than from the Giant Angels; thee that day
> Thy Thunders magnifi'd; but to create
> Is greater than created to destroy.
> Who can impair thee, mighty King, or bound
> Thy Empire? easily the proud attempt
> Of Spirits apostate and thir Counsels vain
> Thou hast repell'd, while impiously they thought
> Thee to diminish, and from thee withdraw
> The number of thy worshippers. Who seeks
> To lessen thee, against his purpose serves
> To manifest the more thy might: his evil
> Thou usest, and from thence creat'st more good.
> Witness this new-made World, another Heav'n
> From Heaven Gate not far, founded in view
> On the clear *Hyaline*, the Glassy Sea;
> Of amplitude almost immense, with Stars
> Numerous, and every Star perhaps a World
> Of destin'd habitation; but thou know'st
> Thir seasons: among these the seat of men,
> Earth with her nether Ocean circumfus'd,
> Thir pleasant dwelling-place.
> (7.601-25).

The last segment of the angels' hymn celebrates the greatest of God's creations, man. In substance it echoes Genesis 1:26 and Psalm 8:6, exalting man as image of God with dominion over all his works.[58] It also recalls Virgil's apostrophelike celebration of the husbandman's blessed lot (*Georgics* 2.458-60): "O happy husbandmen! too happy should they come to know their blessings! for whom, far from the clash of arms, most righteous Earth, unbidden, pours forth from her soil an easy sustenance."[59] But whereas Virgil implies that his husbandmen cannot know how happy they are and why, Milton's angels insist that Eden's gardeners can only retain their blessed state *if* they have full knowledge of their happiness and the conditions upon which they hold it:

> Thrice happy men,
> And sons of men, whom God hath thus advanc't,
> Created in his Image, there to dwell
> And worship him, and in reward to rule
> Over his Works, on Earth, in Sea, or Air,
> And multiply a Race of Worshippers
> Holy and just: thrice happy if they know
> Thir happiness, and persevere upright.
> (7.625-32)

Imagining and presenting angels and their celestial life in an epic poem poses a daunting authorial problem, but Milton finds a brilliant solution to it through the mixture of literary modes and the creation of a distinctive angelic discourse and hymnody. The discourse is comprised of dialogue, heroic rhetoric, and prophetic testimony. The hymnody mixes the highest hymnic kinds and transmutes their values, as the angels rise to their highest flights of praise in celebrating the divine love manifested in the Dialogue in Heaven, and the glorious creativity of the Father. The effect of Milton's literary strategies is to make these beings at once familiar to us, and yet (in their completeness) appropriately distant.

These strategies also allow Milton to use his portrait of angelic life to comment upon other orders of being in the epic.

The perversion of the celestial ideal by Satan's followers is obvious enough. In addition, all that the angels are and do reflects and helps define the nature of Milton's multifaceted God, who created their nature and established the conditions of their various and happy life. More important still, the angelic wholeness projects, at a higher level of integration and excellence, the Miltonic ideal for *human* life—an ideal involving process not stasis, complexity not simplicity, and the continuous and active choice of good rather than the absence of evil.

SEVEN

"A Happy Rural Seat of
Various View": Pastoral Idyl and
the Genres of Edenic Innocence

PASTORAL IS THE dominant mode for the portrayal of Eden
and the life of prelapsarian Adam and Eve.[1] Though our first
parents are gardeners rather than shepherds or herdsmen, their
life in Eden exhibits the essential qualities of Golden Age or
Arcadian pastoral: freedom and leisure; the perfect harmony
of man and nature; an abundance of natural goods satisfying
all human needs; a range of activities consisting primarily of
love, song, and pleasant conversation; and pastoral *otium*—a
state of tranquillity and contentment which, as Thomas Ro-
senmeyer notes, also includes "liveliness and play."[2]

Edenic pastoral has little relation to the prominent Renais-
sance idea of pastoral as the most humble of the genres, re-
quiring simple, rustic characters, base matter, and low style.[3]
It derives instead from the alternative theory linking pastoral
to epic and to the Golden Age. That conception is reflected
in Minturno's division of epic poetry into three categories,
heroic, philosophical, and bucolic; in the mixture of the two
modes in Sidney's *Arcadia*; and in the inclusion of pastoral
episodes or sequences within heroic poems (e.g., the Erminia
episode in Tasso or the Pastorella episode in Spenser).[4] Also,
many Renaissance critics view pastoral as a species of allegory,
treating great subjects in humble guise.[5] Others emphasize the
dignity and nobility of pastoral in the Golden Age and in the
Bible, where men of rank, prophets, and even kings were
shepherds.[6] In 1659 René Rapin went so far as to exalt pas-
toral poetry above heroic:

173

A God fed Sheep in *Thessaly*. . . . *Hercules* the Prince of
Heroes . . . graz'd on mount *Aventine* . . . Jacob, Esaw,
Moses, Joseph, and David were shepherds. . . . Pastoral
is . . . a perfect image of the state of Innocence, of that
golden Age, that blessed time, when Sincerity, Inno-
cence, Peace, Ease, and Plenty inhabited the Plains. . . .
[As much as] the Golden Age is to be preferr'd before
the Heroick, so much *Pastoral* must excell *Heroick* Poems.[7]

As the literary embodiment of the Golden World, and by
that standard more ancient and more excellent than heroic
poetry, pastoral is clearly the appropriate mode for rendering
prelapsarian Eden. But Milton's Edenic pastoral undergoes
continuing redefinition as it is made to incorporate values per-
taining to other genres. There are, from the outset, georgic
and romance concerns in Eden. Husbandry, though unlabo-
rious, is necessary to the maintenance of the Garden. The love
between Adam and Eve is not cool and casual (as in pastoral)
but passionate. The divine prohibition on the Tree of Life
constitutes one all-important restriction on pastoral freedom.
And the Edenic world is not self-contained (as is usual in
pastoral) but is penetrated constantly by supernatural pow-
ers—God and the angels. In this redefined Edenic pastoral
Adam and Eve are intended to enjoy the pastoral pleasures of
sensory delight and natural beauty, but they are also expected
to develop intellectually, to learn to know themselves, their
world, and God, better and better.

Indeed, the central issue for Adam and Eve can be framed
in terms of literary mode. How are they to integrate the georgic
and even heroic challenges that arise from their work, their
complex love relationship, their intellectual curiosity, their in-
dividual responsibilities in a hierarchical universe, and their
duty to resist and conquer evil into the pastoral mode that
defines their lives? Beginning from a pastoral version of hu-
man life, they are expected to attain something approaching
the integrity and wholeness of angelic life.

As readers have long recognized, the Edenic passages are

the most allusive in the poem. They incorporate echoes and motifs drawn from Arcadian fields, groves, and forests; from romance gardens and love bowers; from the gardens and *loci amoeni* of classical myth and poetry; from Golden Age landscapes; and from hexaemeral, exegetical, and literary portraits of Eden. In this case, however, Milton does not intend us to focus upon specific comparisons but rather to respond to the cumulative effect, which intimates that Eden is beyond all compare. The syntax of several epic similes makes that point explicitly: "Not that fair field / of *Enna* . . . / nor that sweet Grove / Of *Daphne* . . . / nor that *Nyseian* Isle / . . . Nor . . . Mount *Amara*" can compare with "this Paradise / Of *Eden* (4.268-81).

To portray the Edenic life, Milton again uses genre choices and transformations as vehicles of poetic apprehension, accommodation, and education. For this segment of the poem, however, his generic strategy is to proceed sequentially from simpler to more complex pastoral genres—notably, from a set-piece topographia describing a *locus amoenus* in Book Four to a fully developed Symposium or Dialogue of Love in Book Eight. That strategy provides a mimesis of Adam and Eve's development within their pastoral world, from simpler to more complex kinds of knowledge, awareness, and experience. Even more clearly, this strategy provides the reader with expanding perspectives on the Edenic life, leading him to revise his stereotypes of the state of innocence as stasis, childlikeness, ignorance of evil, sexual abstinence, and the like, and to recognize it instead as a condition of continuous growth and change.[8]

Specifically, Book Four presents a pastoral idyl with descriptive, lyric, and eclogic parts, whereas Books Five to Eight present scenes and dialogues in the georgic and comedic modes. That genre progression is consonant with Scaliger's view that the earliest poetry, pastoral, reflected the earliest manner of life, and that comedy evolved next.[9] It is consonant also with Northrop Frye's representation of Platonic dialogue as the extreme limit of social comedy, reaching toward myth.[10]

The pastoral idyl of Book Four is wholly enclosed by heroic

episodes: the book begins with Satan's romancelike journey to and penetration of the Garden, and it ends with his capture and expulsion by the angelic guard. Satan's unhampered movement within Eden, his soliloquies responding to the place and its people, and his easy invasion of its most private places (the marital bower and the recesses of Eve's subconscious) keep us constantly and painfully aware of his damned consciousness as one register of interpretation. Another register, defined at the outset of Book Four, is the Miltonic Bard in the role of a John of Patmos, certain of impending catastrophe but unable to forestall it: "O for that warning voice, which he who saw / Th'*Apocalypse*, heard cry in Heav'n aloud, / Then when the Dragon, put to second rout, / Came furious down to be reveng'd on men, / *Woe to the inhabitants on Earth!*"

The passage describing Satan's approach to and entrance into Eden (4.131-94) invites us first to see the Eden sequence as romance,[11] and in the terms of that genre to anticipate Satan's success in the Edenic adventure. Satan's lengthy and difficult journey up the steep, heavily wooded mountain "With thicket overgrown, grotesque and wild" will recall similar journeys by romance heroes and heroines to find and rescue knights trapped by temptresses in enclosed gardens of love. Normally such journeys are tortuous and fraught with danger: Guyon must make his way past many temptations to reach Acrasia's Bower of Bliss; Armida's palace and pleasure gardens lie (like Eden) atop a forested mountain made difficult of access by crags and cliffs and savage animals.[12] Satan's stage-by-stage incursion into the Garden invites comparison with the structure of such romance episodes: we first observe the difficult approach, then the delights of the Garden itself, then the inhabitants and their activities; and finally the secret bower where the love-making takes place. But in Satan's romance journey the values are precisely reversed; he comes not to rescue the virtuous from an immoral and enervating romance garden, but to pollute and destroy a pastoral garden of love that is entirely pure and good.

In the main, however, the Bard invites us in Book Four to

respond to Eden as pastoral idyl, from the vantage point of our human and fallen condition—with delight, nostalgia, and a sense of aching loss. The pastoral perspective emphasizes Eden's fragility and vulnerability. In literary tradition pastoral places are often destroyed by invaders embodying the values of court or city or savage nature: war, deception, ambition, brute force. We might think of Meliboeus, his lands confiscated, bidding sad farewell to Tityrus and the happy rural life in Virgil's "Eclogue I," and of the near-destruction of Arcadia by moral deterioration, rebellion, and warfare in Sidney's prose romance. We may also recall the utter annihilation of the pastoral enclave in Spenser's *Faerie Queene* (6:10-11), when brigands murdered good old Meliboe and his wife, and captured Pastorella. We know of course that Eden will also be destroyed, but the fragility emphasized in Book Four serves not only to foreshadow that eventuality but also to prepare us for the incorporation of hardier georgic and comedic elements into Edenic pastoral. If successful, that generic transformation could allow the Edenic pastoral world (in theory at least) to withstand the onslaughts of evil, since comedy is a mode in which difficulties can be met and happily resolved, in which growth and change are nurtured and privileged, and in which self-knowledge and social harmony are advanced by dialogue.

From the Miltonic Bard's—and our—perspective, the Edenic segments of Book Four constitute a unified pastoral idyl to which Satan's romance journey serves as prelude and continuing threat. Though the idyl is not a genre with distinct formal qualities and a clear literary tradition, seventeenth-century commentators described poems so titled as "little pictures" of rural life and love—simple, delicate, and often suggesting the fragility of human life.[13] The normative examples were Theocritus' several sketches of simple country life. Milton's idyl in Book Four presents a sketch of Edenic life in late afternoon—by convention the most tranquil time of the pastoral day as the shepherds wend their way homeward to rest or to enjoy some rural feast. At this time, in this genre, the *otium* of Edenic life is most clearly displayed.

The Edenic idyl is created through the juxtaposition of several small pastoral genres. The Bard's several topographia describing Eden as *locus amoenus* are followed by iconic portraits, or blasons, of Adam and Eve on their way home after their day's gardening. They rest on a flowery bank to enjoy the frolic of their herd (the animals of Eden), to take their supper fruits, and to engage in eclogic dialogue—which includes a narrative of pastoral courtship happily concluded and an exquisite love song. Then they continue homeward, and upon arrival offer a psalmic night prayer drawn from the biblical pastoral tradition before they enter their nuptial bower to unite in love. Strong closure is provided for this idyl as we find we have moved from the savage underbrush outside the Garden to its most secluded and artfully ornamented enclave, and that the love whose first beginnings we heard about in Eve's story of her first awakening is now celebrated as a perfect marital union by the Bard's rapturous pastoral epithalamium.

Landscape, "Locus Amoenus," and Pastoral Blason

Eden is first presented in static terms, through set-piece descriptions of the place and its inhabitants. The first extended description is a prospect from outside and below, presenting Eden as an enclosed garden atop a high mountain (4.131-71); we are invited to recall Dante's Eden atop Mount Purgatory, or the Mount of Venus in Spenser's Garden of Adonis, or the pleasance where the Graces dance for Colin Clout atop Mount Acidale. In terms of genre, this description transforms the rhetorical figure topographia into a landscape (as James Turner has noted and as Milton's term "lantskip" precisely indicates), which presents a unified, awe-inspiring prospect from a given vantage point, as in contemporary landscape painting.[14] For this landscape our vantage point, like Satan's, is from the "savage thicket" at the base of the mountain; and as C. S. Lewis perceptively observed, we experience an almost kinesthetic sense of straining to look higher and higher so as to take in the full view.[15]

We first observe the "champaign head / Of a steep wilderness." Then, "overhead," we see the several varieties of trees ascending in their rows to "Insuperable highth of loftiest shade," forming a "woody Theatre / Of stateliest view." Looking "Yet higher than thir tops," we see the "verdurous wall of Paradise" from which (we are told) Adam has a general prospect upon all his empire below. "And higher than that Wall" we see a "circling row" of fruit trees, which signify their Edenic essence by bearing "Blossoms and Fruits at once" (a fusion of spring and summer), and by their "golden hue" and "gay enamell'd colors" (a fusion of nature and art). As part of this landscape we also respond (with Satan) to the pure air and odiferous winds wafting down from Eden. This first landscape description is abruptly terminated when Satan, forced by the thick undergrowth to give over his "pensive and slow" climb up the mountains, makes a sudden, effortless leap over the wall, like a wolf invading God's sheepfold.

Eden is then portrayed from within as a *locus amoenus* (4.205-85). The set-piece description has all the elements Ernst Curtius associated with that topos in classical and medieval literary texts: a beautiful, shaded site, trees, meadows, a spring or brook, birdsong, flowers, gentle breezes.[16] But as several readers have noted, Milton's *locus amoenus* differs from its nearest literary analogues—Dante's Eden, Sidney's Arcadia, Spenser's Garden of Adonis, Ovid's field of Enna—in that it is not simply a catalogue of delights but, again, a landscape with spatial depth presented from a single angle of vision.[17] The perspective again is Satan's, now sitting like a cormorant atop the Tree of Life and viewing with "new wonder . . . In narrow room Nature's whole wealth." But while Satan here "Saw undelighted all delight" the Bard is the register of consciousness for us, as he records in living detail all the delights Eden affords to human sense. Milton's descriptive technique owes something to those landscapes in epic which combine spaciousness and prospect, such as Odysseus' first view of Alki-

179

noös' estate from the door of the house, or Aeneas' vision of the Elysian fields first from the entrance and then from a mountain ridge.[18] It owes something also, as recent critics have noted, to seventeenth-century Italian and English styles in landscape gardens,[19] as well as to contemporary landscape paintings by Titian, Georgione, Jan Bruegel the Elder, and especially Poussin.[20]

Milton's *locus amoenus* first distinguishes those features, at once natural and symbolic, which arrest the eye as it sweeps over the entire scene. They include "all Trees of noblest kind," and prominent among them the Tree of Life "blooming Ambrosial Fruit / Of vegetable Gold." There are also flowers in abundance, not arranged in beds or "curious Knots" as in formal gardens but "Pour'd forth profuse on Hill and Dale and Plain." Also, a river rises through the mountain as a "Sapphire Fount," and its several rills meander over "Orient Pearl and sands of Gold / With mazy error" to water the Garden.

Describing this landscape as "A happy rural seat of various view," the Bard then focuses on particular areas that recall and surpass all the chief kinds of *loci amoeni* in the literary tradition. There are several groves of trees, some of gums and spice, some of fruit "burnisht with Golden Rind"—said to be far superior to the grove of Daphne with its Castalian spring, the Garden of the Hesperides with its golden fruit, and the gardens of Solomon with their spice trees and cedars of Lebanon.[21] Between these groves are "Lawns, or level Downs, and Flocks / Grazing the tender herb"—recalling the pastoral landscape of Sicily and Arcadia. Interspersed are flowery valleys, lovelier than the field of Enna where Ovid's Proserpine gathered flowers[22] and distinguished by that quintessentially Edenic feature, the thornless rose. There are also "umbrageous Grots and Caves" with grapevines creeping over them and a murmuring waterfall, somewhat resembling Calypso's island with its caves, vines, and fountains.[23] The passage concludes with a lovely evocation of Ovid's myth of Flora and the birth of Spring, and the depiction of that myth in Botticelli's *Primavera:*[24]

The Birds thir choir apply; airs, vernal airs,
Breathing the smell of field and grove, attune
The trembling leaves, while Universal *Pan*
Knit with the *Graces* and the *Hours* in dance
Led on th' Eternal Spring.
(4.264-68)

Milton's *locus amoenus* description establishes the idyllic
quality of Eden, but also intimates the movement of Edenic
life beyond pastoral. The description of Eden as Adam's es-
tate, his "happy rural *seat*," prepares us to discover the struc-
tural patterns of the country-house poem within the Edenic
idyl.[25] We are led through Eden much as we are led through
Penshurst or Appleton House in the poems so titled: we first
view the savage nature outside the wall; then make a circuit
of the grounds noting their abundant flora and fauna; then
observe the inhabitants and their activities, and the tribute
paid to them by all nature. At length we focus on the house
itself (here the nuptial bower), observing that its simplicity
and beauty perfectly accord with the inhabitants' nature and
needs, and that their virtuous love is consummated here, giv-
ing promise of permanence through progeny. This pattern ac-
commodates Eden to us by reference to its nearest postlapsar-
ian analogue—those islands of regenerate society (like
Penshurst) where the lord "dwells" at the center and sustains
the whole through his virtue.[26] Within the description of Eden
as idyllic pastoral *locus amoenus*, this pattern foreshadows its
public and social dimension as the future capital "seat" of a
flourishing society.

We are next presented with icons of Adam and Eve, set-
piece descriptions of them as motionless figures in the land-
scape suddenly brought into close-up focus (4.288-311). Put-
tenham defines the rhetorical figure *Icon* as a "resemblance by
imagerie or pourtrait," which likens a human person and his
or her parts or qualities to any other living creature or natural
thing, "alluding to the painters terme, who yeldeth to th' eye
a visible representation of the thing he describes and painteth

181

in his table."[27] The Miltonic portraits of Adam and Eve are reminiscent of the famous paintings of that subject by Cranach and especially Dürer, and also of the iconic, tapistrylike descriptions of Red Cross, Una, and the Dwarf with which Spenser begins his *Faerie Queene*.[28]

In terms of genre, the descriptions of Adam and Eve are also related to the blason, the French epigramlike poem describing and celebrating a single object—usually, some part or parts of the female anatomy.[29] In pastoral blasons a shepherd swain normally describes and praises the elements of his shepherdess's beauty and grace.[30] In *Paradise Lost*, however, the Miltonic Bard blazons both figures, and in terms that extend beyond pastoral. He could find precedent for adapting the genre to exalted personages in the numerous pastoral blasons of Queen Elizabeth,[31] and for blasons of both Bridegroom-lover and Bride in the Song of Songs—which Milton like many of his contemporaries viewed as a pastoral drama. The conventional identification of the Bridegroom of Canticles with Christ led to emblematic and symbolic interpretation of the Canticles blasons.[32]

The icons or blasons in *Paradise Lost* describe Adam and Eve together, then separately, interpreting their physical features as emblems of nature and character. The blason of their pair together (4.288-95) focuses upon their "Godlike erect" stature and their "looks Divine," as emblems of the "true autority" and the "Truth, Wisdom, Sanctitude severe and pure" both exhibit as images of God. Two striking oxymorons—"native Honor" and "naked Majesty"—emphasize the fusion in them of unfallen courtly virtues and ideal pastoral simplicity. Pastoral characters customarily wear simple, rustic garb instead of rich or elegant clothing, but Adam and Eve are majestic in complete nakedness, emblem of their innocence and their entire freedom from sexual shame. And while postlapsarian pastoral figures eschew rank, place, and public honor, this pair enjoys the highest place and honor by nature, as images of God and lords of all creation.

The individual blasons highlight the inequality of the pair, in part by use of nature similes (4.295-311). Adam's "fair large Front and Eye sublime" betoken that he is made for contemplation and "Absolute rule"; and his clustering, shoulder-length "Hyacinthine Locks" relate him both to pastoral nature and to the epic hero Odysseus.[33] Eve's long golden tresses waving "Dishevell'd . . . in wanton ringlets . . . / As the Vine curls her tendrils" are an emblem of her "subjection," softness, and "sweet attractive Grace" and also of the "coy submission, modest pride, / And sweet reluctant amorous delay" with which she yields to love. In this blason Eve is identified with the pastoral world more closely than Adam was. But she is separated completely from the bevy of proud and coy shepherdesses refusing love, since her sweet delay intends only and serves only to enhance pleasure.

ECLOGUE AND EPITHALAMIUM

At this point the figures in the landscape begin to move—"So pass'd they naked on"—and to take part in a pastoral eclogue. Adam and Eve's casual conversation in Book Four treats the usual topics of eclogue—the pleasant conditions of pastoral life, personal experience in love, praise of the loved one, the daily round—and include as well a personal narrative and a love song (4.319-688). But from the outset their dialogues also include several nonpastoral topics: duty, responsibilities, prohibitions, testimonies of relationship to God, speculation about the cosmic order. Also, their exalted speech and their high style of epic address to one another indicate that they are pastoral characters of a most extraordinary kind. Such mixtures of conventions, together with the two soliloquies of Satan that break in upon the pastoral scene, underscore the tenuousness and limitations of pastoral idyl, indicating that more complex generic paradigms will be needed to meet the challenges of this happy garden.

Setting his scene (3.319-55), the Miltonic Bard describes the "endearing smiles" and "youthful dalliance" of the young lovers, at times reminding us of romances, pastoral and heroic, as Bartlett Giamatti suggests.[34] But the comparison serves only to highlight the differences: there is no hint here of the lasciviousness and ennui that infect Rinaldo in Armida's Garden; nor of the titillating sexual ignorance displayed by Daphnis and Chloe in their various encounters in caves and fields; nor of the ungovernable passions that mar the elopement tryst of Pamela and Musiodorus in a lovely pleasance.[35] Though Adam and Eve enjoy the sensual delights of their joyful nuptial league, their speech and actions maintain the coolness, the *otium*, the serenity and repose of pastoral.

This first dialogue takes place in a conventional eclogic setting. Typically in pastoral eclogue shepherds or other herdsmen rest from their occupations and the heat of noon on some shady bank or in some arbor or bower, as their flocks graze about them; in such a place they have a modest repast and amuse themselves with conversation and poetic activities such as singing matches and love laments.[36] So here, with the difference that Adam and Eve are enjoying supper fruits rather than a noontime repast, and their "flocks" are all the Edenic animals disporting themselves for the couple's pleasure:

> Under a tuft of shade that on a green
> Stood whispering soft, by a fresh Fountain side
> They sat them down, and after no more toil
> Of thir sweet Gard'ning labor than suffic'd
> To recommend cool *Zephyr*, and made ease
> More easy, wholesome thirst and appetite
> More grateful, to thir Supper Fruits they fell,
> Nectarine Fruits which the compliant boughs
> Yielded them, side-long as they sat recline
> On the soft downy Bank damaskt with flow'rs:
> . . . .
> About them frisking play'd
> All Beasts of th' Earth, since wild, and of all chase
> In Wood or Wilderness, Forest or Den;
> Sporting the Lion ramp'd, and in his paw
> Dandl'd the Kid; Bears, Tigers, Ounces, Pards

Gamboll'd before them, th' unwieldy Elephant
To make them mirth us'd all his might, and wreath'd
His Lithe Proboscis.
(4.325-47)

In this conversation (4.411-502) both express delight with their life in Eden and their relationship. Adam begins by addressing Eve in terms which are both loving and honorific— "Sole partner and sole part of all these joys, / Dearer thyself than all." He then infers the goodness of God from his bountiful gifts to them, describes the single "easy prohibition" of the fruit as the only earnest of their obedience, and mentions the threatened punishment of death without much comprehension—"whate'er Death is, / Some dreadful thing no doubt." He concludes by affirming the joys of praising God and tending the garden—"Which were it toilsome, yet with thee were sweet" (4.439). In response, Eve proclaims by an elaborate apostrophe her full understanding of and delight in her hierarchical position of subordination to Adam.

Eve then proceeds to "invent" the genre of autobiography to relate her earliest experiences (4.449-91). The Miltonic Bard presents her story as a self-contained narrative, manifesting a high order of literary creativity. She recounts, as an event "oft remembered," how she woke to life on a flowery bank; how she responded first to the murmur of waters and then to her own reflected watery image; how she was led to Adam by God's voice; how she turned from him at first, thinking him "Less winning soft, less amiably mild, / Than that smooth wat'ry image"; and finally how Adam's urgent pleas based upon derivation, love, and natural law convinced her to accept him as her mate. We are of course to recognize what Eve's version of the Narcissus myth implies with regard to her potential for self-love.[37] But the point of the story she tells with such obvious relish is that she did *not* remain fixed forever staring at her image. Rather, she was led first by God, then by Adam, to choose her proper human role: sharing love and companionship with the one whose image she is, and preparing to

generate living images, "Multitudes like thyself." Eve's auto-
biography is in fact the antithesis of the Narcissus myth, and
also of those narrations common in Renaissance eclogues in
which a shepherd complains of his nymph's coyness, or a nymph
of her lover's unfaithfulness.[38] Eve, by contrast, artlessly re-
joices that her lover's ardent persuasion to love overcame her
hesitations and led her to choose rightly. In the Edenic ec-
logue love, so often the source of grief and pain in fallen pas-
toral, is mutual, contented, fulfilled, blissful.

Indeed, Eve offers her tale not simply as autobiography or
pastoral *narratio*, but as exemplum, a moralized life designed
to emphasize what she has learned from the first events of her
life—that "beauty is excell'd by manly grace / And wisdom,
which alone is truly fair."[39] However, Satan's hate-filled solil-
oquy and the activities of the angelic guard follow hard upon
this exchange, indicating that the stasis and closure Eve voices
in these final lines can only be temporary. We are to recognize
that the pastoral idyl of Eden can only endure if it proves able
(like the angelic model of *genera mixta*) to appropriate and
integrate values appropriate to other literary modes and kinds.

Following the Satanic interruption Adam and Eve's eclogue
resumes (4.610-88), again graced by the use of honorific ti-
tles: "Fair Consort," "My Author and Disposer," "Daughter
of God and Man, accomplisht *Eve.*" As night approaches, Adam
observes that humankind's daily round is in perfect harmony
with the courses of pastoral nature—"Labor and rest, as day
and night to men / Successive." He indicates also that georgic
concerns are properly a part of Edenic pastoral. The "daily
work of body or mind" is both an emblem of human dignity
and a vital necessity in a garden whose condition is not stasis
but burgeoning growth:[40]

> With first approach of light, we must be ris'n,
> And at our pleasant labor, to reform
> Yon flow'ry Arbors, yonder Alleys green,
> Our walk at noon, with branches overgrown,
> That mock our scant manuring, and require

More hands than ours to lop thir wanton growth:
Those Blossoms also, and those dropping Gums,
That lie bestrown unsightly and unsmooth,
Ask riddance, if we mean to tread with ease.
(4.624-32)

We are to recognize as well that the constant though pleasant georgic labor required to order, prune, and restrain the growth or the Garden is an emblem of the labor required to order the self—pruning unwarranted impulses and ordering the burgeoning growth of human possibilities.[41] Eve's autobiography has already provided an example of such growth and its proper direction as, led by God and then by Adam, she corrected her first impulse to infantile solipsism and self-love, choosing instead adult human love and familial responsibilities.

In her response, Eve proclaims Adam the epitome of the Edenic condition for her, and the mediator through whom she understands and obeys God's Law. She then invents the first love song we hear in Eden, a rhetorically elaborate lyric of eighteen lines, containing one vast sixteen-line epanalepsis ("Sweet . . . is sweet"). That figure incorporates elaborate patterns of repetition and circularity which build to the extreme periodicity of lines 650-56, as the meaning of the entire passage finds completion in the final half-line:

With thee conversing I forget all time,
All seasons and thir change, all please alike.
Sweet is the breath of morn, her rising sweet,
With charm of earliest Birds; pleasant the Sun
When first on this delightful Land he spreads
His orient Beams, on herb, tree, fruit, and flow'r,
Glist'ring with dew; fragrant the fertile earth
After soft showers; and sweet the coming on
Of grateful Ev'ning mild, then silent Night
With this her solemn Bird and this fair Moon,
And these the Gems of Heav'n, her starry train:
But neither breath of Morn when she ascends
With charm of earliest Birds, nor rising Sun

187

On this delightful land, nor herb, fruit, flow'r,
Glist'ring with dew, nor fragrance after showers,
Nor grateful Ev'ning mild, nor silent Night
With this her solemn Bird, nor walk by Moon,
Or glittering Star-light without thee is sweet.
                                        (4.639-56)

This embedded lyric has been discussed as a submerged sonnet or sonnet-like poem,[42] and indeed the penetrating analysis of personal emotion, the rhetorical complexity, and the *volta* at line 649 give it a subject, structure, and texture akin to those aspects of the Petrarchan sonnet. In further confirmation of its genre, Eve's love poem echoes (but far surpasses in poetic merit) a sonnet by Milton's earlier contemporary, William Drummond:[43]

The *Sunne* is faire when he with crimson Crowne
And flamming Rubies leaves his Easterne bed,
Faire is *Thaumantias* in her Christall gowne
When clowds engemm'd hang azure, greene and Red.
To Westerne Worlds when wearied Day goes downe,
And from Heavens windowes each *Starre* showes her Hed,
Earths silent daughter *Night* is faire though browne,
Faire is the *Moone* though in *Loves* liverie clad.
The *Spring* is faire when it doth paint Aprile,
Faire are the *Meads*, the *Woods*, the *Flouds* are faire
Faire looketh *Ceres* with her yellow haire,
And *Apples*-Queene when *Rose*-cheekt Shee doth smile.
    That Heaven, and Earth, and Seas are faire is true,
    Yet true that all not please so much as you.

Some motifs in Eve's poem also recall various pastoral eclogues and lyrics that praise the "sweetness" of nature or music or love, Theocritus' First Idyl, for example:

Thrysis: Something sweet is the whisper of the pine that makes her music by yonder springs, and sweet no less, master Goatherd, the melody of your pipe . . .

188

Goatherd: As sweetly, good Shepherd, falls your music
as the resounding water that gushes down from the top
o' yonder rock.[44]

Eve invents, then, a pastoral love sonnet of delicate beauty
and delightfulness, drawing upon the pastoral *locus amoenus*
of Eden and its serene natural order for her comparisons, and
eschewing any hint of the frustrations and anxieties that are
the staple of the postlapsarian Petrarchan sonnet. It is worth
noting that Eve's actual and freely proclaimed hierarchic in-
feriority to Adam is in some degree counterbalanced by Mil-
ton's generic strategy, as he portrays Eve sharing in all the
georgic responsibilities and duties of the Garden as well as in
all the arts of speech and song and dialogue that pertain to
humankind. In this scene she "invents," and anticipates Adam
in using, such literary forms as the autobiographical narrative
and the love sonnet.[45]

Eve also makes the first foray into the realm of astronomical
speculation when, immediately following her lyric, she poses
a question about the stars: "But wherefore all night long shine
these, for whom / This glorious sight, when sleep hath shut
all eyes?" The question unintentionally implies possible waste-
fulness in the divine cosmic arrangements, and Adam's several
suggested answers speak to that implication: starlight holds
the reign of darkness at bay, nourishes the earth by night, and
affords light to "Millions of spiritual Creatures" who walk the
earth unseen. Still characterized by the serenity of pastoral,
and still celebrating the harmony between nature and human
nature, Adam and Eve's dialogue here ventures upon cosmic
matters far beyond the pastoral realm. As their eclogue ends,
we recognize that they have employed that genre of pastoral
dialogue in quite unusual ways, as a means of integrating fully
and harmoniously into the pastoral mode the several georgic
aspects of their lives: work, law, duty to God, natural hier-
archy, familial responsibility, intellectual exercise and growth,
and the maintenance of order.

The pastoral idyl of Book Four concludes with an extended

epithalamic passage (689-775) celebrating the marital union of Adam and Eve as the epitome of their paradisal state. It has three parts: the description of Adam and Eve's "blissful Bower" (their nuptial chamber and couch); the couple's evening prayer at the entrance to that bower; and the Bard's embedded lyric epithalamium praising "wedded Love." This passage provides a climax for epithalamic topoi introduced earlier in Book Four and also a point of reference for later passages incorporating such topoi elsewhere in the poem: Adam's description to Raphael of his wedding day; the postlapsarian love-making of Adam and Eve; and the degenerate marriages between the sons of God and the daughters of Cain presented and described in Michael's prophetic visions.[46]

In Book Four, the Miltonic Bard signals his genre shift from eclogue to epithalamium as he directs attention to the unfallen couple about to enter their "blissful Bower" for love-making and sleep (4.689-90). His epithalamium conforms thereby to the definition indicated by the genre's name, *epi thalamou*, a song sung at the bridal chamber door. As Puttenham explains, such songs were "song very sweetely by Musitians at the chamber dore of the Bridegroome and Bride . . . and they were called *Epithalamies* as much to say as ballades at the bedding of the bride."[47] However, as Adam and Eve's marriage occurred some days (or weeks) earlier,[48] the Bard's epithalamium does not celebrate the wedding day but marriage itself.

To this special purpose, Milton uses, adapts, and alters topics and conventions developed throughout the entire history of the genre.[49] Catullus' lyric epithalamium, #61—perhaps the most widely imitated model for Renaissance poets—introduced the basic features: the poet himself as choragus or master of ceremonies; invocations to Hymen; a hymnic celebration of the god's matchless powers and the great social benefits he brings; description of the bride's conflicting emotions; narration of the events of the day (wedding feast, fescennine jests, bedding the bride); promises of offspring; and realistic advice to the couple about making love (*allocatio sponsalis*).[50]

The Miltonic Bard, like other Renaissance epithalamists, also drew upon the Greek rhetorician Menander for the elaboration of suitable topics. Menander recommended a passage on Hymen and on marriage itself (*peri gamou*), an encomium on the bridal couple, and a "description of the bridal chamber and alcoves" with reference to the promise of offspring. The *peri gamou* should urge the benefits of marriage—the union of heaven and earth, the ordering of the universe, all human goods—showing "how it is due to Marriage that the sea is sailed, the land is farmed, philosophy and knowledge of heavenly things exist, as well as laws and civil governments."[51] Scaliger's extended discussion of the genre supplied additional topics.[52]

For the use of pastoral settings and topics in epithalamia there was classical precedent in Theocritus #18, "The Epithalamy of Helen," and in Catullus #62; influential English examples were Sidney's epithalamium for Lalus and Kala in the *Arcadia* and Spenser's *Epithalamion*.[53] Also, the characterization of the Song of Songs as a pastoral epithalamium for King Solomon and his bride supplied biblical warrant for the use of exalted, even regal personages in this genre, and for exalting human marriage as a figure of Christ's union with the Church and with the regenerate soul.[54]

Some other models provide a basis for Milton's use of the genre in epic. Catullus #64 celebrates marriage itself rather than a particular wedding, and Renaissance imitators readily transformed such praises of Hymen for the goods of marriage into praises of marriage as the glorious ordinance of God. Catullus #64 is an epyllion which includes a lyric epithalamion, and the epics of Virgil and Spenser also include epithalamic passages.[55] For some elements of theme and language in Adam and Eve's prayer (4.724-35) and in Adam's brief epithalamium in Book Eight (ll. 510-20) Milton draws upon Spenser's magnificent *Epithalamion*, which the bridegroom-poet sings his own marriage song fusing classical, Neoplatonic, and Canticles' elements, and in which all nature pays tribute to a particular marriage as emblem of the social and cosmic significance of marriage itself. Also, for the themes and structure (though not the language and tone) of the Miltonic Bard's lyric epithalamium (4.749-75), there are analogues in Du Bartas' embedded epithalamium for Adam and Eve, which apostrophizes and praises the institution of marriage and denounces its pollution in the postlapsarian world.[56]

Formally taking on the role of choragus, the Miltonic Bard develops his epithalamic passage in Book Four with careful attention to the special circumstance—an occasion other than the wedding day. The first segment adapts the topic of the bridal chamber and couch to the description of the "sacred and sequester'd" place which is at once Adam and Eve's love bower and their domestic abode (4.690-719).[57] Milton presents their bower as a third *locus amoenus* passage, paralleling the prospect of Eden from outside its walls, and the view of the "happy rural seat" from within. In the bower nature and art are perfectly fused. All nature's beauties of flower and vine are placed here for human delight by God "the sovran Planter," some of them set forth as an intricate mosaic: "*Iris* all hues, Roses and Jessamin / Rear'd high thir flourisht heads between, and wrought / Mosaic; underfoot the Violet, / Crocus, and Hyacinth with rich inlay / Broider'd the ground, more color'd than with stone / Of costliest Emblem" (4.698-703).

Milton marks this description as an epithalamic topos by appending to it an account of Adam and Eve's wedding night. On that night a "genial Angel" took the part of Genius or Hymen in bringing Eve to Adam "in naked beauty," while the heavenly choirs sung "the Hymenaean." Then Eve (not having the usual virgins and matrons to do the office) "first" decked her own marriage bed with "Flowers, Garlands, and sweet-smelling Herbs." The time reference implies that she continues to do so, reviving the nuptial ceremonies nightly and continuing to enhance nature by art in imitation of the divine Artist who designed the bower. Then, reversing the terms of the epithalamic topos whereby a particular marriage is compared to the unions of the gods, the Miltonic Bard declares that this bower is more sacred and sequestered than those of Pan, Silvanus, or Faunus, and that Eve presented to Adam was lovelier than Pandora presented to Epimetheus. But he exclaims proleptically, "and O too like / In sad event."

The second segment is an embedded lyric, Adam and Eve's "unanimous" prayer just before entering their bower. This prelapsarian prayer is psalmic, a paraphrase and elaboration of Psalm 74:16—"The day is thine, the night also is thine: thou hast prepared the light and the sun." The choice is decorous, since the Psalms were often described as pastoral poems devised by the shepherd David, and as perfect models for all kinds of prayer and praise, suited to all occasions, needs, and states of soul.[58] But the topoi used for amplification in this prayer are epithalamic: like Spenser, Adam and Eve here celebrate their own marriage. They thank God for the mutual help and love which they along with Milton evidently take to be the prime end of marriage; and they joyfully anticipate the offspring promised by God:

> Thou also mad'st the Night,
> Maker Omnipotent, and thou the Day,
> Which we in our appointed work imploy'd
> Have finisht happy in our mutual help
> And mutual love, the Crown of all our bliss
> Ordain'd by thee, and this delicious place
> For us too large, where thy abundance wants
> Partakers, and uncropt falls to the ground.
> But thou hast promis'd from us two a Race
> To fill the Earth, who shall with us extol
> Thy goodness infinite, both when we wake,
> And when we seek, as now, thy gift of sleep.
> (4.724-35)

That final request reverses the customary topic advising the newly wedded couple to remain wakeful throughout the night to beget children, but the Miltonic Bard's commentary makes clear that this couple does not avoid or refuse "the Rites / Mysterious of connubial Love." The point is that love-making and sleep are equally appropriate and innocent blessings of the night in Eden, both of them integrated with perfect harmony and without conflict into the daily round.

Now the Miltonic Bard delivers his lyric epithalamium at the chamber door. It is a self-contained ode praising marriage—"Hail wedded Love" (4.750-75)—which is devised almost entirely from Menander's topic, *peri gamou*. Though this is not a hymn to Hymen or God, it begins with epithets that partly personify the abstraction "wedded Love" through its qualities: "mysterious Law, true source / Of human offspring, sole propriety / In Paradise." The Bard next celebrates its powers and benefits: it expels adulterous lust from humankind; it is the perpetual fountain of all "Domestic sweets"; and it is the ground of all social relations—"all the Charities / Of Father, Son, and Brother." At length, implying a sharp contrast to Petrarch's "Triumph of Love" and Spenser's Masque of Cupid in the House of Busirane, the Bard insists that marriage is the true field for the higher Cupid: where his shafts are golden, not iron-tipped or flaming; where he bears (Hymen-like) a constant and not a flickering lamp or torch; where he truly "Reigns . . . and revels."[59]

This implied contrast leads the Miltonic Bard to his second topic, the dispraise of false love in its several kinds:[60] "the bought smile / Of Harlots"; the frivolity and licentiousness of "Court Amours, / Mixt Dance, or wanton Mask, or Midnight Ball"; and Petrarchan idolatry in which an ever-frustrated "starv'd Lover" sings to and serves his "proud fair." Over against all these he sets the blissful image of Adam and Eve sleeping, with the beauties of nature enhancing the joys of their innocent, fulfilled love. He concludes with a passionate *allocutio sponsalis*, enjoining them not only to physical rest, but also to spiritual content:

> These lull'd by Nightingales imbracing slept,
> And on thir naked limbs the flow'ry roof
> Show'r'd Roses, which the Morn repair'd. Sleep on,
> Blest pair; and O yet happiest if ye seek
> No happier state, and know to know no more.
>   (4.771-75)

As he concludes this epithalamium, the Miltonic Bard indulges himself (and us) for a time in the nostalgic wish to fix time here, in this vision of Eden at its most idyllic. Yet for all that, he does not warn Adam and Eve against *any* further knowledge or happiness, but against the fraudulent offers of both which the impending temptation will urge. Throughout the pastoral idyl of Book Four, which presents Eden at its most tranquil and static, Milton has imported elements that point beyond pastoral to the values of other modes and genres. In Book Five he shifts at once to those other literary forms, forcing himself and his readers to move beyond nostalgia as they contemplate the course of human development within the state of innocence.

EIGHT

"Our Pleasant Labor":
Georgic and Comedic Modes
and Genres in Eden

WITH THE COMING of morning in Eden, at the beginning of Book Five, we are no longer in the realm of pastoral idyl. The change is highlighted but not caused by Eve's disturbing, Satan-inspired dream: according to the natural rhythm of life in Eden, the peace and rest of evening give way to the activities and responsibilities of the day. As we have seen, in Book Four the idyllic and cyclic qualities of pastoral are emphasized; in Books Five to Eight pastoral gives way to the georgic and the comedic modes, which together inform the several genres we now encounter. Dialogue is here the dominant rhetorical form, the vehicle for a georgic of the mind and for the resolution of difficulties in comedy.

The georgic mode presents Adam and Eve growing in perfection through the pleasant labor of body and mind, in accordance with the Father's decree that they be tried "under long obedience" until "by degrees of merit rais'd / They open to themselves at length the way / Up hither" (7.157-59). Though Adam and Eve earlier discussed their ordained and necessary task of ordering the Garden (4.623-33), we now see them engaged in those georgic labors, pruning "where any row / Of Fruit-trees overwoody reach'd too far / Thir pamper'd boughs, and needed hands to check / Fruitless imbraces," or leading "the Vine / To wed her Elm" (5.212-16). These labors are analogous to the pruning and direction required to keep their own souls and their marital relationship in order, as we see in the dialogue occasioned by Eve's dream, and at much greater length in the dialogues of Adam and Raphael.

The great model for Golden Age georgic (as distinct from Golden Age pastoral) is the magnificent paean in Virgil's *Georgics* (2.458-542) celebrating the happy husbandman's life as "the life golden Saturn lived on earth."[1] In marked contrast to Virgil's usual emphasis upon the cares and responsibilities of the georgic life this passage parallels the joys of the philosopher and poet with those of the husbandman:

O happy husbandmen! too happy, should they come to know their blessings! for whom, far from the clash of arms, most righteous Earth, unbidden, pours forth from her soil an easy sustenance . . .

But as for me—first above all, may the sweet Muses whose holy emblems, under the spell of a mighty love, I bear, take me to themselves, and show me heaven's pathways. . . . But if the chill blood about my heart bar me from reaching those realms of nature, let my delight be in the country, and the running streams amid the dells.
. . .

Blessed is he who has been able to win knowledge of the causes of things, and has cast beneath his feet all fear and unyielding Fate, and the howls of hungry Acheron! Happy, too, is he who knows the woodland gods. . . . He plucks the fruits which his boughs, which his ready fields, of their own free will, have borne.[2]

But whereas Virgil presents the georgic labors of mind and body as alternatives, in Eden they are necessary complements defining the perfect human life. Both Adam and Eve are to engage continuously in both kinds of cultivation, as their common work in the Garden and their common attendance upon Raphael's discourses indicates. Nor does Eve eschew the cultivation of the mind for that of the Garden when she goes forth to tend her flowers while Adam discusses astronomy with Raphael, for the Miltonic Bard makes clear that she will pursue the astronomy lesson later, with Adam.[3] We are to recognize that Adam and Eve, unlike Virgil's happy husband-men, can preserve their happiness only *if* they attain a full and conscious understanding of their condition.

The comedic mode in Eden has its basis in the inclusive formula of the ancient grammarians, that comedies begin in troubles and end in peace and happiness[4]—though in Eden before the Fall dangers are only potential, not real, and the troubles actually experienced are slight. A more important paradigm is supplied by theorists such as Demetrius of Pha-lareum, Tasso, and Sidney, who distinguish comedy which evokes delight from that classical and neoclassical kind which evokes scornful laughter.[5] Prelapsarian Adam and Eve defy all the canons of that latter kind: they cannot be objects of de-risory laughter since they are immeasurably more noble than we, are of kingly as well as private station, are threatened by serious dangers, and are possessed of no real follies or vices.[6] Rather, their life in Eden is presented in terms of the alter-native tradition, embodied in such Renaissance kinds as pas-toral interlude, entertainment, masque, and romantic comedy and usually characterized by noble characters, wonderful ac-tions, and graceful style.[7] As Sidney intimated, the delight evoked in such comedies is a species of Neoplatonic wonder or *admiratio*:

> The whole tract of a Comedie should be full of delight, as the Tragidie should bee still maintained in a well raised admiration. . . . For delight wee scarcely doo, but in thinges that have a conveniencie to our selves, or to the generall nature: Laughter almost ever commeth of thinges moste disproportioned to our selves, and nature. Delight hath a joy in it either permanent or present. Laughter hath onely a scornfull tickling. For example, wee are ravished with delight to see a faire woman, and yet are farre from beeing mooved to laughter . . . We delight in good chaunces, wee laugh at mischaunces.[8]

For the comedic mode of Books Five to Eight, Milton draws upon the tradition associating comedy with delight and wonder. He may also have recalled Sidney's intimation that only such comedy might mix decorously with tragedy and epic.[9]

In addition, the Adam-Raphael dialogues in these books are set forth as a species of Platonic symposium or philosophical comedy, widely recognized as a subgenre of comedy. Both Cicero and Northrop Frye point to Socrates as type of the comic *eiron*, and Frye locates the symposium at "the extreme limit of Social Comedy."[10] Extending that concept, the Renaissance critic Girolamo Zoppio places Dante's *Commedia* and the Platonic dialogues in the same genre, "Poesia Epica Comica d'attione Philosophica."[11] Whether or not Milton had heard of, or read, Zoppio on Dante, he could certainly reach the similar conclusion that in the *Commedia* as in Plato dialogue is the means by which moral and intellectual difficulties are focused, analyzed, and then resolved, and that this process has affinities to the movement of comedy. Books Five to Eight of *Paradise Lost* highlight the primary role of dialogue in resolving difficulties, and represent life in Eden as comedic—a mode that can render human development and growth within the state of innocence.

Enfolded within the pervasive georgic and comedic modes are several specific genres. Adam and Eve voice lyrics of several kinds, Adam narrates a lengthy autobiography, and, as we have seen, Raphael "invents" a variety of literary genres to accommodate various subjects to Adam and Eve. Also, the action of these books is disposed into three distinct kinds of comedy, in an ascending scale of dialogic and generic complexity: first a Moral Interlude, then an Entertainment, and finally a Neoplatonic Dialogue of Love.

MORAL INTERLUDE

The scene and dialogue centering upon Eve's dream (5.1-219) constitute a brief moral interlude which begins and ends with lyrics of surpassing beauty. At the outset of this scene Adam finds his lyric voice, as he undertakes to rouse Eve from her unquiet slumber with a dawn song in the tradition of the

medieval *alba* and *aubade*. Central to the *alba* are complaints
that dawn comes so soon to separate lovers who have enjoyed
a night of clandestine, adulterous love; the assumption is that
night is the good time for lovers and day is evil.[12] The *aubade*
is a lover's song to awaken his mistress—usually sung at her
door or window: it welcomes day, implying that the love
meeting has yet to take place.[13] Adam's lyric is the perfect
original of both faulty kinds. He greets the day joyously,
awakening his beloved who is also his wife with affirmations
that the work and activities of the day will unite them as closely
as their nocturnal love-making has done. We should also rec-
ognize that Adam's dawn song and Satan's serenade are coun-
tergenres: the one praises day, the other night; the one voices
mutual and fulfilled love, the other courtly service and wor-
ship of a lady; the one celebrates the joys and contentment of
married love, the other solicits clandestine encounters and for-
bidden acts.

Adam's *aubade* echoes Canticles 2:10: "Rise up, my love,
my fair one, and come away. / For, lo, the winter is past, the
rain is over and gone; / The flowers appear on the earth; the
time of the singing of birds is come, and the voice of the turtle
is heard in our land." But it adapts that *reverde* or spring song
to the manifestations of nature in the Edenic daily round, which
are without seasonal change:

> Awake
> My fairest, my espous'd, my latest found,
> Heav'n's last best gift, my ever new delight,
> Awake, the morning shines, and the fresh field
> Calls us; we lose the prime, to mark how spring
> Our tended Plants, how blows the Citron Grove,
> What drops the Myrrh, and what the balmy Reed,
> How Nature paints her colors, how the Bee
> Sits on the Bloom extracting liquid sweet.
> (5.17-25)

We are, I think, to recognize Adam's *aubade* as a more excel-
lent love lyric than was Eve's exquisite, rhetorically complex

love sonnet in Book Four, by reason of its freer form, its
vibrant imagery, its more intense feeling, and its highly hon-
ored biblical model. The Bridegroom's song to the Bride in
Canticles was regularly described in the commentaries as the
most beautiful of scriptural songs, vastly superior to all secular
love poems.[14]

The fact that Adam's *aubade* and the parody of it in Satan's
serenade so obviously echo the Canticles' song directs us to
that biblical book as paradigm for the entire scene. Though
the Song of Songs was often considered to be an epithala-
mium or a sequence of wedding songs, many commentators
followed Origen in emphasizing its dramatic elements, some-
times terming it an "interlude," in evident reference to its brevity
and comedic form.[15] Making the comedic designation explicit,
Cornelius à Lapide described Canticles as "an allegory written
in comic and bucolic style," and Milton evidently intended the
same emphasis when he contrasted the "divine pastoral Drama"
of Canticles with the "high and stately Tragedy" of Revela-
tion.[16] Moreover, Protestant exegetes often interpreted the al-
legory in terms of a comedic plot: the soul (Bride) awakens
to grace and spiritual advancement at Christ's (the Bride-
groom's) call; then during his absence she falls into diffidence,
distraction, and sin; and at length she is brought by grace to
repentance and joyful reunion with him.[17]

That plot is replicated with Adam and his spouse in this
scene, though all that pertains to sin and fault is here matter
of dream rather than fact, and the movement is toward co-
medic resolution of difficulties through dialogue. Awakened
by her bridegroom, Eve is startled and discomposed rather
than joyous. She begins the dialogue with a full account of
her troubled dream: a voice (Satan's) which she mistook for
that of her husband called her forth with a serenade and led
her to the tree. There she saw an angel-like figure who ate of
the fruit, enticed her to taste of it, and then seemed to fly with
her to the heavens. She concludes with exclamations of heart-
felt relief "To find this but a dream"(5.93).

Adam, knowledgeable about faculty psychology but igno-

201

rant of Satan's agency, explains the dream as the product of Eve's fancy. Yet even though he cannot account for the "addition strange" of evil, the happy resolution of this dialogue and this difficulty does not require knowledge of all such circumstances. Adam need only understand and articulate (as he does) the essential fact that without the will's consent there can be no sin: "Evil into the mind of God or Man / May come and go, so unapprov'd, and leave / No spot or blame behind" (5.117-19). Building upon that perception, Adam also declares his hope that the dream experience itself, a virtual experience of evil and its aftermath in remorse and trouble, will deter Eve from the actual deed: "what in sleep thou didst abhor to dream, / Waking thou never wilt consent to do" (5.120-21). Reassured, Eve exhibits the signs of repentance—tears of "sweet remorse / And pious awe, that fear'd to have offended" (5.134-35)—and Adam kisses those tears in joyful reaffirmation of their union.

We are of course to see in this interlude the adumbration of the Fall tragedy and its aftermath, as well as the foreshadowing of the Canticles comedy of sin and repentance in the regenerate. But we are also to recognize this episode itself as a comedic interlude: it presents Adam and Eve employing dialogue properly to reach a happy resolution of their slight trouble, after which "all was clear'd" (5.136).

The interlude concludes, as it began, with a lyric—Adam and Eve's magnificent morning hymn of praise (5.160-208), which is their most eloquent and complex lyric in the entire epic. They are the creators (on earth) of the hymn genre, identified in Renaissance criticism as the noblest kind of lyric and perhaps the greatest of all literary genres.[18] This hymn is the composition of them both, sung *a capella* with sublime beauty and ease: "such prompt eloquence / Flow'd from thir lips, in Prose or numerous Verse, / More tuneable than needed Lute or Harp / To add more sweetness" (5.149-52). They sing, moreover, with a "holy rapture" which marks them as true poets, but does not (like the Platonic divine afflatus) take over and obliterate their rational powers.[19] Moreover, the fact that they create this sublime hymn just after the troubling experi-

202

ence of Eve's dream indicates that their innocence is in no way compromised. Indeed, the successful resolution of that difficulty has elicited their highest achievement in art and divine praise.

Adam and Eve's hymn is presented as the archetype of human hymnody, containing elements of all the subgenres of hymn presumed to have evolved from it.[20] The Bard's introduction points to the hymn's complexity and comprehensiveness. It combines prayer ("orisons") and praise. The verses are "Unmeditated," yet sung by Adam and Eve together with "prompt eloquence"—thereby combining, as Joseph Summers has happily observed, "all the richness of ritual joined with all the freedom and variety of spontaneity."[21] And the hymn's "various style / . . . in fit strains pronounct or sung / . . . in Prose or numerous Verse" encompasses many kinds: classical narrative or literary hymns in "proselike" hexameters; chanted biblical psalms with their patterns of rhythmic repetition; classical lyric hymns (choral or monodic) used in public worship; and Christian hymns and anthems, both liturgical and vernacular. This complexity and comprehensiveness is at once a means of accommodation to us, suggesting the perfection of unfallen hymnody through a fusion of the most exalted hymnic forms we know, and also a testimony to the sublime artfulness of Adam and Eve's poetic accomplishment.

Formally, the hymn has the three-part structure of a Callimachan literary hymn. The exordium consists of an apostrophe to God with the expected catalogue of epithets—"Parent of good," "Almighty," "Unspeakable" "wondrous." The body of the hymn expands upon all these epithets by calling upon all the works of God, whose beauty and power reflect his glory, to praise him.[22] The peroration contains the formulaic "Hail" customary in the close of the Homeric and Callimachan hymns, along with a petition that also recalls those sources:

> Hail universal Lord, be bounteous still
> To give us only good; and if the night

Have gather'd aught of evil or conceal'd,
Disperse it, as now light dispels the dark.
(5.205-208)[23]

In its substance the hymn combines several of the kinds of
classical literary hymns enumerated by Menander and Scaliger:
invocatory (in invocations to God and to all God's works);
precatory (in the prayers); physical (in the praises of God
through his manifestations in the natural world); and geneal-
ogical (in the celebration of God as true source of all those
entities—sun, moon, earth, wind, etc.—which were identified
as deities in classical myths of origin.[24]

The verse form, however, identifies Adam and Eve's com-
position as a lyric hymn, archetype of those classical hymns
which Scaliger associated with the public worship of "the gods
at their altars."[25] The irregular stanzas or strophes pointed up
in Summers' fine analysis are somewhat suggestive of the Pin-
daric ode form, but the closest classical lyric model may well
be Horace's *Carmen Seculare*, in which Apollo and Diana are
each invoked in their various aspects and asked to shed grace
and favor upon Rome.[26] Adam and Eve's unfallen hymn re-
vises and reverses Horace, invoking the sun, moon, and other
elements of nature as manifestations of God's glory, and urg-
ing them to praise their Creator.

Even more obviously, Adam and Eve's hymn incorporates
elements of those psalms of praise and thanksgiving which
Reformation commentary identified as the great models for
Christian hymnody—notably Psalms 8, 19, 66, 113-18, 120-
35, and 146-50.[27] As several readers have noted, the body of
this hymn is a descant on Psalm 148[28] (with echoes also of
Psalms 8 and 19). In Psalm 148 the speaker addresses angels,
sun and moon, stars, waters, and all the creatures of earth,
exhorting them to praise God; according to David Dickson,
the psalm shows "how the world is full of Gods glory [and]
. . . pointeth at matter of his praise," but it focuses upon man
as the "chief, both matter and instrument of Gods praise."[29]
Adam and Eve's hymn addresses by name a larger roster of
God's creatures, and also expands upon the role of humankind

as choir director for all the creatures praising God. Indeed, Adam and Eve are shown here as creators of an archetypal psalmic hymn of praise, of which Psalm 148 is an abbreviated version.

Beyond that, their hymn also has features of the metrical psalms or vernacular Christian hymns which were based upon or modelled upon the Psalms and which were enormously popular in the wake of the Reformation.[30] Those features include the loose stanzaic pattern and the refrain. As John Hollander perceptively notes, Adam and Eve's hymn transcends "the anaphora and catalogue of its precursor Psalm 148 by seeming to generate its refrain—indeed the very idea of refrain—during the course of its unfolding."[31] Accordingly, the repetitions in the early verses—"praise him in thy Sphere," "sound his praise," "resound / His praise"—in later verses fall into position at the ends of lines, marking stanza-like segments with a recurrent refrain: "still new praise," "advance his praise," "tune his praise," "notes his praise," "taught his praise."

Adam and Eve have obviously sung hymns before this one. We are surely to understand that the morning hymn before work is a regular feature of their day. But it is nonetheless significant that this magnificent hymn is presented to us at the close of this comedic episode, and that its complexity and exaltation contrast sharply with the comparative simplicity of the nocturnal prayer in Book Four. The effect is part of the Bard's generic strategy throughout Books Five to Eight, leading us to revise our conception of the state of innocence as we watch the development of Adam and Eve from the simplicity and stasis of pastoral to the activity, complexity, and higher perfection of the georgic and comedic life.

ENTERTAINMENT

A second comedic genre, the entertainment, structures most of the long sequence presenting the visit of Raphael (5.219-8.178), which encompasses several dialogues, narratives, and lyrics. The occasion for the typical Elizabethan and Jacobean entertainment was the visit of a monarch—on a Progress through the countryside with great retinue and state—to a nobleman's castle or an important city. Such entertainments usually involved ceremonial greetings by the host, magnificent feasts, and elaborate, masquelike shows employing mythological and often pastoral conceits. Notable examples were Leicester's entertainment for Elizabeth at Kenilworth (1575), or the Lord Mayor of London's entertainment for King James (1604).[32] However, the archetypal Edenic entertainment is conformed to a biblical model and contrasts sharply with the extravagant and ostentatious royal entertainments of the fallen world.

Raphael's journey to Eden is of course a version of the "Descent from Heaven" epic topos, and the explicit comparison of the angel to *"Maia's* son" points to its primary source in Mercury's visit to Aeneas (*Aeneid* 4.238-78).[33] But it is also a kind of Progress. Raphael passed first through the midst of heaven where the angelic choirs part to speed him down "th' Empyreal road"; then through the "glittering Tents" of the angelic watch in Eden where the bands "to his state, / And to his message high in honor rise"; and then through the "Groves of Myrrh" and "spicy Forest" of Eden. Adam greets him ceremonially, as the lord of one great province welcoming an even more exalted prince. Yet he does so with a primitive simplicity explicitly contrasted to courtly pomp:

> Meanwhile our Primitive great Sire, to meet
> His god-like Guest, walks forth, without more train
> Accompanied than with his own complete
> Perfections; in himself was all his state,
> More solemn than the tedious pomp that waits
> On Princes, when thir rich Retinue long
> Of Horses led, and Grooms besmear'd with Gold
> Dazzles the crowd, and sets them all agape.
> (5.350-57)

The entertainment Adam and Eve offer is pastoral in fact and not merely in conceit. In a pastoral bower that affords shade from the "meridian heat" they set forth a simple repast of Eden's fruits artfully mingled to enhance their natural goodness. And the pleasures of that banquet are further enhanced by the hospitable ministrations of Eve clad only in her innocent beauty and grace.

As Jason Rosenblatt has observed, numerous parallels and verbal echoes direct us to the biblical model for this simple and decorous Edenic banquet, graciously offered and graciously received—Abraham's entertainment of three angels in his tent at Mamre (Gen. 18:1-11).[34] Parallels include the settings of both banquets in a place of shelter from the noontime heat, the deference of both Abraham and Adam in offering hospitality to angels; the human hosts' concern with preparing food for the feast; and the angels' promise of a blessed issue to the women (Sarah and Eve). The verbal echoes emphasize Abraham's and Adam's haste to make preparation for the angels' visit. Abraham "ran to meet them from the tent door"; then "hasted into the tent unto Sarah, and said, Make ready quickly three measures of fine meal"; then "ran unto the herd, and fetcht a calf tender and good" which he gave to a servant who "hasted to dress it." Similarly, at Raphael's approach Adam summons Eve urgently—"Haste hither *Eve*"— and directs her to "go with speed" to bring forth food from her stores. Eve, observing that stores are of little use in Eden declares that she will instead "haste" to pluck fruit from the trees, and sets off to do so "with dispatchful looks in haste." By such echoes the entertainment in Eden is identified as the archetype of Abraham's at Mamre.

As Thomas Kranidas notes, there is some gentle humor in this scene as Adam and Eve scramble a bit to bring off their pastoral luncheon-cum-state occasion.[35] But this is clearly the comedy of delight, with no vestige of ridicule in it: we smile with pleasure as this pastoral couple meet the challenge of entertaining an angel, and provide an appropriate setting for the more important feast of the intellect which is to be supplied by conversation.

In another reversal of court practice, it is not the host in Eden but the exalted guest who supplies the magnificent shows

(The War in Heaven, The Creation). The angel himself is a masquer of sorts, having sailed to Eden like a phoenix and then donned six pair of wings "with downy Gold / And colors dipt in Heav'n" for his visit. But Raphael has no need for the masque machinery of an Inigo Jones: he evokes surpassing awe and wonder in his audience by his own natural powers and by his poetic narratives and descriptions which act directly upon Adam and Eve's imaginations.

For all that, Adam as host retains ultimate responsibility for the entertainment in Eden in that each topic treated is initiated by his explicit questions. As we have seen,[36] the angel accommodates his several subjects to Adam and Eve by using a variety of literary genres, and he conducts the frame dialogues in such a way as to clarify principles that Adam imperfectly understands or to correct attitudes that are potentially dangerous. At the conclusion of each discourse Adam proclaims his gratitude for the new knowledge gained, and demonstrates what he has learned from Raphael's dialogic critiques and literary creations.

The educative thrust and method of these dialogues is broadly Platonic, and their mode is georgic and comedic: they exercise Adam and Eve in the "gardening" their own natures constantly require—pruning to remove excessive or unsightly growth, direction of overreaching tendencies, propping of possible weaknesses, correcting initial misjudgments or mistakes, and thereby learning how to learn. Edenic innocence, these dialogues make clear, is a matter not of stasis in perfection but of continual growth toward greater perfection.[37] Keenly intelligent, Adam and Eve have named (and thus understood) the natures of all the creatures beneath them in the scale of being, but they have much yet to learn—by speculation, revelation, and experience—about the cosmos, about God and the angels, and about the complexities of marital and social interaction. The Adam-Raphael dialogues provide models for seeking such knowledge and ordering such growth. They also provide models for resolving intellectual and practical difficulties in comedic rather than tragic terms, through dialogues which advance self-knowledge and insight.

Adam's offer of the banquet to Raphael gives rise to their first dialogue. Adam's expressed fear that human food may be "unsavory" to angels indicates that he does not clearly understand the relation of human and angelic nature. Raphael explains, and by eating the fruit demonstrates, that those natures differ only in degree, not kind. But Raphael pointedly ignores the specific thrust of Adam's next, merely curious, question inviting him to compare earthly and heavenly banquets. He develops instead a topic of fundamental importance to Adam and Eve—the common substratum of all being and the dynamic hierarchical system within which all natures not depraved are by degrees refined and ascend toward God. Adam then voices his delight with Raphael's philosophical poem "On the Nature of Things," and shows himself ready to apply the principles he has learned to the attainment of further knowledge: "Well hast thou taught the way that might direct / Our knowledge . . . whereon / In contemplation of created things / By steps we may ascend to God" (5.508-12).

The second exchange arises from the angel's warning against disobedience and allusion to the revolt in heaven, evoking Adam's comment that he finds such concepts wholly unimaginable. Accordingly, Raphael's epic narrative of the War in Heaven is designed specifically to develop Adam and Eve's imagination of evil through literary mimesis, affording them a vicarious experience of Satanic rhetoric, of the subtlety of temptation, and of the catastrophe wrought by sin. The story fills Adam and Eve "With admiration, and deep muse," and dispels Adam's earlier doubts (7.51-60).

Next, Adam poses a question about the Creation of the world in unintentionally blasphemous terms, querying why God disturbed his sacred rest to create, and why he built "so late" in Chaos. Such terms cry out for the correction Raphael's careful analysis provides, and for Raphael's explicit warning to eschew "Things not reveal'd, which th' invisible King, / Only Omniscient, hath supprest in Night" (7.122-24). More-

209

over, the angel's creation story is set forth as a poetic hexa-
emeron, a literary form designed to demonstrate that all re-
vealed knowledge must be mediated and accommodated to
humankind. At its conclusion Adam declares himself filled with
wonder, gratitude, and delight that the angel "thus largely
hast allay'd / The thirst I had of knowledge" (8.7-8).

Adam's final query implies in its formulation the ineptitude
of God or nature in designing an apparently irrational and
inefficient Ptolemaic cosmos. Raphael responds with a "Dia-
logue of the Two World Systems" which pointedly declines
to decide the issue between Ptolemy and Copernicus, offering
instead a critique of human presumption and a demonstration
of the reverence and the humanistic emphases that ought to
control scientific inquiry. Again Adam announces himself sat-
isfied, relieved of perplexity and anxiety and able to make a
general application of Raphael's specific lesson:

> But apt the Mind or Fancy is to rove
> Uncheckt, and of her roving is no end;
> Till warn'd, or by experience taught, she learn
> That not to know at large of things remote
> From use, obscure and subtle, but to know
> That which before us lies in daily life,
> Is the prime Wisdom.
> (8.188-94)

Such satisfying resolutions of perplexing intellectual issues
and problems prepare Adam and Eve for a continuing life in
Edenic innocence, even as they display tendencies that fore-
shadow the Fall. The dialogues with Raphael serve not so
much to provide Adam and Eve with knowledge absolutely
necessary to their lives, as to exercise them in the right way
of meeting intellectual and moral challenges and difficulties.
As Eve's hierarchical superior Adam has already assumed with
Eve after her dream the role Raphael here plays in relation to
him, and Eve there took on Adam's role—questioning, seek-
ing, learning, and allowing herself to be corrected when she
formulates wrongly. Presumably, both would have played these

roles regularly had the Fall not occurred, resolving difficulties in comedic terms, with delight and satisfaction. (In the event, however, they badly mismanage their next dialogue, with tragic consequences.)

At this point Adam takes over completely the host's customary responsibility to provide the entertainment, supplying not only the topics for discourse but the subject matter as well—his own life story. His proposal affirms the Socratic precept that self-knowledge is the highest wisdom, thereby demonstrating his growth in understanding under the angel's tutelage: "Therefore from this high pitch let us descend / A lower flight, and speak of things at hand, / Useful . . . now hear mee relate / My Story" (8.198-205).

Adam's autobiography consists of a personal narrative centered upon his creation and the first hours of his life, which compliments Eve's similar narrative in Book Four (ll. 449-91). Eve, however, employed the genre of moral exemplum to relate a brief autobiographical episode, upon which she had often meditated and from which she drew the appropriate lessons.[38] Adam, by contrast, presents a long spiritual autobiography (8.250-523), analyzing all the events of his life to date, as shaped by God's actions and his own responses. As he did with the love lyric, Adam again brings to higher perfection a literary kind created by Eve: here he develops the prototype of Augustine's *Confessions*, Bunyan's *Grace Abounding*, and other such works.[39] Adam offers his spiritual autobiography with modest disclaimers but Raphael graciously attributes to it both instruction and delight, anticipating that it will supplement his own knowledge of God's works, and display Adam's own very considerable literary skills: "Nor are thy lips ungraceful, Sire of men, / Nor tongue ineloquent . . . I attend, / Pleas'd with thy words no less than thou with mine" (8.218-48).

Adam recognizes the difficulties of autobiography, with its conventional expectation that the narrative begin with an account of origins and earliest influences: "For Man to tell how human Life began / Is hard; for who himself beginning knew?" (8.251-52). Like Eve, he solves his problem by focusing upon his earliest observations and sensations, and his delight in discovering and using his faculties. By contrast with Eve, however, Adam glanced toward heaven immediately upon awakening; then sprang upright "By quick instinctive motion"; then quickly surveyed the landscape, the creatures, and himself; then spoke and named all he saw. At this point (like a good scholastic) he deduced the existence of a good Creator from the evidence of the natural world, the creatures. With lively pace and fine descriptive detail Adam then recounts subsequent events: his aimless wandering and straying; his dream of God leading him to the Garden; his first impressions of Eden and hunger for its fruits; God's charge to him to keep the Garden and avoid the Tree of Knowledge; his dialogue with God requesting a mate; Eve's creation from his side during a waking dream; his instant love for her and dismay when she disappears for a time; and finally their joyous nuptials. He ends his account with those nuptials as happy climax: "Thus I have told thee all my State, and brought / My Story to the sum of earthly bliss / Which I enjoy" (8.521-23). But this apparent strong closure is in fact weak, for Adam at once opens a new dialogue to explore the problem he sees as the concomitant of his bliss—the force of his passionate love for Eve.

Adam's autobiography, then, is more comprehensive, analytic, open-ended, and concerned with intellectual development than was Eve's. Adam also incorporates other genres within it—reports of two lyrics and a dialogue—perhaps in imitation of Raphael's generic strategies. The first lyric is Adam's eloquent invocation to the sun and the earth immediately after his creation—presumably spoken then just as he here reports it to Raphael. We are expected to recall classical hymns invoking the deities of the sun, moon, earth, and other aspects of nature, as well as the Renaissance commonplace that such hymns were "the first forme of Poesie and the highest and stateliest."[40] Ascribing those earliest hymns to Orpheus, Musaeus, and Amphion, humanist critics often declared them to be in fact praises of the true God in allegory.[41] But comparison points up the difference. Adam's lyric is not an invocatory *hymn* in the strict sense of the term, for he unambiguously invokes the elements of nature as creatures, not deities, begging them to reveal to him the Maker of them all:

> Thou Sun, said I, fair Light,
> And thou enlight'n'd Earth, so fresh and gay,
> Ye Hills and Dales, ye Rivers, Woods, and Plains
> And ye that live and move, fair Creatures, tell,
> Tell, if ye saw, how came I thus, how here?
> Not of myself; by some great Maker then,
> In goodness and in power preeminent;
> Tell me, how may I know him, how adore,
> From whom I have that thus I move and live,
> And feel that I am happier than I know.
>
> (8.273-82)

The first lyric Adam attributes to himself, then, is a prelapsarian version of that hymnic kind often taken to be the earliest form of human literary expression.

Adam's second lyric is the epithalamic passage with which his autobiography concludes. He here takes over the role of choragus performed by the narrator in Book Four, and—like Spenser in his "Epithalamion" or the Bridegroom in the Song of Songs—celebrates his own wedding:

> To the Nuptial Bow'r
> I led her blushing like the Morn: all Heav'n,
> And happy Constellations on that hour
> Shed thir selectest influence; the Earth
> Gave sign of gratulation, and each Hill;
> Joyous the Birds; fresh Gales and gentle Airs
> Whisper'd it to the Woods, and from thir wings
> Flung Rose, flung Odors from the spicy Shrub,
> Disporting, till the amorous Bird of Night
> Sung Spousal, and bid haste the Ev'ning Star
> On his Hill top, to light the bridal Lamp.
>
> (8.510-20)

Epithalamia are usually couched in the present tense, describing the joyous events of the wedding day as if it is in progress, and concluding with prayers that the day's happiness will endure. Adam celebrates his wedding as an event recently past, but he testifies in doing so that the bliss of his nuptial day has in fact endured, that that day has brought him to "the sum of earthly bliss."

However, Adam presents as the centerpiece of his spiritual autobiography his dialogue with God on the first day of his life. In that dialogue, as we have seen, God played the role of ironic Socratic educator, concerned to exercise and advance Adam's self-knowledge.[42] Prodded by God's apparent resistance to his request for a mate, Adam properly defined the human condition: he is neither beast nor god, and can therefore find completion only in human love and human companionship. Adam's performance in this dialogue was highly commended by God: "Thus far to try thee, *Adam*, I was pleas'd, / And find thee knowing not of Beasts alone, / Which thou hast rightly nam'd, but of thyself" (8.437-39). And his successful engagement with God in dialogue was then rewarded with a mate "exactly to thy heart's desire" (8.451).

The dialogues with Raphael thus reinforce what Adam's first direct encounter with God taught him: that dialogue is the means to the happy resolution of difficulties, and that God himself honors human argument based upon right reason and true self-knowledge. The emphasis Adam places upon this dialogue in his autobiography indicates that he understands the importance of dialogue for the georgic and comedic life of Eden.

THE DIALOGUE OF LOVE

Concluding his story, and the entertainment proper, with his epithalamion, Adam shifts to dialogue again as he introduces the problem of his passion for Eve. But now he does not simply ask questions of the angel. Instead, he plays a major role as interlocutor, even as he did in the dialogue with God. Milton presents this dialogue (8.523-51) as a third comedic kind, a dialogue of love whose generic models are Plato's *Symposium* and several Neoplatonic versions and imitations of it—

by Ficino, Leone Ebreo, and especially Castiglione.[43] Such dialogues present competing conceptions of love, privileging one without denying all validity to the others.

In the Miltonic version Adam seems to play the role of the young lover still caught up in the life of the seasons, while Raphael is the strict Neoplatonist (like Bembo in *The Courtier*) who points Adam to that ladder of love by which he may transcend sensual love and rise by stages to the pure love of God.[44] But the Neoplatonic ladder of love based on the dichotomy of matter and spirit must necessarily take quite another form in a Milton's monistic universe. Accordingly, this dialogue of love revises Castiglione. At the outset, as before, Raphael corrects Adam's faulty assumptions. But Adam then takes on the role of comic protagonist, posing judicious questions and drawing sound inferences which lead to more adequate statements about human and angelic love.

As Adam expands upon the "passion . . . Commotion strange" stirred up in him by the experience of sex and by the "charm of Beauty's powerful glance" (3.530-33), he makes yet another erroneous assumption. Like many critics of the poem he supposes that he should not be having these feelings and that their presence indicates some defect in human nature: either he has been made too weak, or Eve has been given "Too much of Ornament," since in her presence he can hardly maintain, or even believe in, his own superior wisdom, knowledge, authority, and reason. Raphael however does *not* assume that the "Commotion strange" is an anomaly, that tension and difficulty are out of place in Eden. Scoring the notion that such feelings argue defects in Adam or Eve (or in the divine plan) he insists rather that Adam must learn not to give way before those feelings: "take heed lest Passion sway / Thy Judgment to do aught, which else free Will / Would not admit" (8.635-37). To this end, Adam should strengthen his proper self-knowledge and self-esteem by contemplating the true superiority of his qualities to the outside loveliness of Eve.

Raphael began his first speech with "contracted brow," and

215

he ends it by taking what seems to be a harsh line on the pleasures of sex. He appears indeed to go well beyond Bembo in contrasting sensual and rational love. Disdaining the pleasures of touch as sensations "voutsaft / To Cattle and each Beast," he urges love of Eve for her higher qualities—"Attractive, human, rational"—explaining that such love "refines / The thoughts, and heart enlarges, hath his seat / In Reason, and is judicious, is the scale / By which to heav'nly Love thou may'st ascend" (8.589-92). Raphael has evidently concluded (not surprisingly but not entirely correctly) that Adam's love of Eve is based chiefly upon beauty and sex, and that his passion for her is indeed overwhelming; and he obviously feels called upon to reprove Adam sharply for his readiness to blame God or nature for his problems rather than himself. But that rhetorical situation leads Raphael to overstate his case: the ladder of love he describes seems to involve an entire transcendence of physical desire.

Sensing that he has been misunderstood, Adam tries "half abash't" to do better justice to himself. He insists that he does indeed value more highly than beauty or sex "those graceful acts, / Those thousand decencies that daily flow / From all her words and actions, mixt with Love" (8.600-602); that these subject not; and that he was describing inward sensations rather than any actual surrender to passion. While Adam's assertion that he has himself firmly under control is too facile, revealing some deficiency in self-knowledge, it does indicate that he has understood Raphael's lesson: he is expected to control his passions in the future as he has in the past—"yet still free / Approve the best, and follow what I approve" (8.610-11).

Nor does Adam accept Raphael's virtual identification of human sexual love with animal copulation. Adam's own experience in his nuptial bower has been rather different, and it has been confirmed for us by the Bard's sublime testimony to the great human good of marital love in his epithalamion to Adam and Eve. And so, though Adam accepts the scale defined by Raphael (and by Milton in the divorce tracts), ranking companionship and social intercourse as higher and more essential human goods than sexual intercourse, he also enters his opinion that the relations of the "genial Bed" are "higher . . . by far" than animal copulation, and worthy of "mysterious reverence" (8.598-99). Mindful that he was highly approved when he disputed with his Creator in defense of his own right judgment, Adam proposes a qualification of Raphael's position on the same basis of reason and his own experience of the human condition.

Adam's question about angelic love is part of this qualification, not mere curiosity or an effort to avoid his own problem.[45] Having been urged to ascend in the scale of love to something like the angelic condition, he is properly interested in that final state. And he finds it hard to imagine, given his own experience of the "genial Bed" and Raphael's recent demonstration that angels continue to require and to enjoy food, that love in heaven can be so entirely without physical desire and expression as Raphael has seemed to imply. And so he asks, humbly enough but yet conscious that he is making a worthy argument, "Bear with me then, if lawful what I ask; / Love not the heav'nly Spirits, and how thir Love / Express they" (8.614-16).

Raphael's answer also asks interpretation in relation to the generic paradigm of the dialogue of love. He responds "with a smile that glow'd / Celestial rosy red, Love's proper hue" (8.618-19)—and we are expected to recall that those angels who most fully embody the quality of love, the Seraphim, are traditionally portrayed as fiery red and flamelike.[46] Adam is not here prying into angelic bedrooms, nor does Raphael blush like a Victorian schoolgirl because sex has been mentioned, and hurry away after a mumbled answer.[47] Rather, Adam is seeking confirmation of his intuition about angelic sex, and Raphael concedes and clarifies that point. Even as angelic food is more highly refined and delightful than human food, so is angelic sex more highly refined and more delightful than the human counterpart: "Union of Pure with Pure / Desiring" without any obstacle of "membrane, joint, or limb." The angel's rosy smile is evidence of his own love and friendship for Adam, and his gracious answer testifies to his pleasure in his pupil's right understanding of the scale of nature and the scale of love, enabling him to infer points omitted in the angelic account. Raphael's response is the counterpart of God's delight when Adam so soundly argued his need for a mate against God himself.

This dialogue of love shows Adam's potential weakness and propensity to passion, but shows at the same time his intellectual strength. His skill in dialogue is now very highly developed. He can accept and profit from corrections, he is able to endure discomfiture when his errors are revealed, and he can urge his own true inferences and qualifications even to angels. It is precisely such skill in working though mistakes and misunderstandings that Adam has required and will continue to require in order to maintain life in Eden as comedy. As the dialogue of love concludes, its issues are happily resolved on the theoretical level. But we recognize clearly enough the considerable practical challenge Adam and Eve will face on a daily basis as they seek to resolve continuing difficulties and meet new problems through appropriate dialogues.

THE SEVERAL GENRES of Books Five to Eight—an interlude, an entertainment, and a dialogue of love—present the development of Adam and Eve from the stasis of pastoral to the activity of the georgic and comedic modes. Through these modes and genres Milton presents the life in innocence as an exaltation of humanism, maturity, and civilization in happiest conjunction with vitality, change, and growth. That growth is also underscored by Adam's lyric poems and spiritual autobiography, works more complex and elaborate than Eve's comparable literary creations in Book Four.

The reason for this is not only that Adam is a finer artist than Eve. Nor is it simply that Adam raises to higher perfection the several literary forms Eve invents. Rather, in Milton's universe we see that each individual is stimulated to intellectual and literary expression in relationship to and in conference with a superior. Eve is stimulated in this way by Adam,

218

and Adam by Raphael. Beyond this, the more complex lyric and narrative genres of Books Five to Eight are consonant with the greater perfection of the georgic and comedic modes as compared to pastoral. That Eve fully shares in that complexity and that greater perfection is evidenced by the most elaborate and eloquent literary creation of all, the magnificent morning hymn (5.160-208) which is ascribed to Adam and Eve together.

These literary strategies do not obliterate our ominous forebodings of the tragic future, nor are they intended to do so. But they allow us first to experience the state of innocence as comedy, as a condition in which humankind might have developed—without suffering, violence, despair, and death though not in the least without tension and trial—the rich resources and large potentialities of the human spirit.

NINE

"I Now Must Change Those Notes to Tragic": The Fall and the Tragic Genres

IN HIS PROEM to Book Nine the Miltonic Bard announces quite explicitly his shift in mode—from the pastoral scene of "rural repast" and the comedic symposium of "venial discourse" to the tragic matter of revolt and disobedience, anger and judgment, misery and death. As we have seen, this proem is a verse epistle on poetics,[1] answering in advance Addison's objection that a tragic plot in which the protagonist falls "from some eminent Pitch of honour and prosperity into Misery" is "not so proper for an Heroick Poem."[2] Citing Homeric and Virgilian precedent for a tragic argument or subplot in epic, the Miltonic Bard claims that his subject is both more tragic and more heroic than that of any other epic, classical or contemporary. His statement points to the two modes that govern the remaining books: tragic in Books Nine and Ten, heroic (a Christian heroic redefined through the fusion of several genres and modes) in Books Eleven and Twelve.

The verse epistle indicates not only that the mode of Books Nine and Ten is tragic, but also that those books are designed with reference to the paradigms and conventions of tragedy as genre. As many readers have recognized, the sequence of scenes presenting the Fall and its aftermath is intensely dramatic—filled with conflict, character development, colloquial dialogue, and a striking peripeteia and discovery.[3] Indeed, while critics have erred in judging these scenes by purely dramatic criteria,[4] in some respects Books Nine and Ten constitute an embedded tragedy within the epic, presented first in Aristotelian, then in Christian terms. This sequence also incorporates the tragic lyric genres of lament, complaint, and elegy, and its several dialogues build toward tragic complication and catastrophe, rather than comedic resolution.

ARISTOTELIAN AND CHRISTIAN PARADIGMS OF TRAGEDY

Walter Raleigh spoke for the majority of critics when he identified the eating of the fruit as the dramatic climax in *Paradise Lost*, toward which and from which everything moves.[5] Some others, however, recognize a progressive "fall" taking place through most of Books Nine and Ten—from the marital dispute to the eating of the fruit, to the ever more terrible effects of sin—and identify the reconciliation of Adam and Eve (10.914-65) as the true climax or turning point.[6] This reading has implications for genre, in that it interprets this sequence as tragicomedy rather than tragedy. The point at issue is whether the scenes of reconciliation and spiritual restoration instigated by God's grace constitute a comedic reversal.

In fact, the action of Books Nine and Ten seems to fall well outside Renaissance norms for tragicomedy, as those evolved in the debate over the prime exemplar of that form, Guarini's *Il Pastor Fido*. Guarini explained that the mixed form ought properly to be created by removing the extremes of both tragedy and comedy—the "terrible and the atrocious" from tragedy, the "dissolute laughter" from comedy. Illustrous persons are brought into some danger of death or misfortune, but all real unpleasantness is avoided, and the happy ending is made even more delightful by the earlier anxieties.[7] John Fletcher defined the form more simply: "A tragie-comedie is not so called in respect of mirth and killing, but in respect it wants deaths, which is inough to make it no tragedie, yet brings some neere it, which is inough to make it no comedie."[8] These definitions describe *Il Pastor Fido*, Fletcher's *Faithful Shepherdess*, and Beaumont and Fletcher's *Philaster* well enough: in these plays the good characters experience some danger and mental anguish from which they are almost miraculously delivered,

221

as all appearances of wrongdoing or infidelity are proved erroneous, all disgrace is obliterated, and all reports of harm or death are proved false. But this clearly is not the paradigm Milton calls upon to present the Fall and the "world of woe" it produces for Adam and Eve and all mankind. Neither is the Fall sequence a tragicomedy according to the familiar modern formula—an ironic portrayal of the disparity between what man would be and what he is.[9]

Nor is the Fall presented as a tragedy with a "plot of double issue" in which calamities and misfortunes redound to the wicked and happiness to the good—a formula for tragedy which Aristotle noted but disapproved of.[10] Some Renaissance writers (e.g., Gascoigne) defined tragicomedy by this formula, but Giraldi Cinthio termed such dramas "mixed tragedy" in that "the spectators are suspended between horror and compassion until the end, which, with a happy outcome, should leave everyone consoled."[11] Such a conception evidently led Theodore Beza to label as tragedy his *Abraham Sacrifiant*, described in his preface as "partly tragical and partly comicall," but holding more of one than of the other.[12] We do indeed feel horror and compassion for Abraham's terrible predicament until the last moment when the sacrifice of Isaac is averted by the angel. But the tragic catastrophe of the Fall and its terrible consequences are not averted from Adam and Eve and all mankind even though, by the end of Book Ten and still more by the end of the poem, they and we have been consoled by the prophecy of the final "happy end" at the millennium.

I suggest, rather, that Milton presents the Fall in Book Nine as an Aristotelian tragedy, but in Book Ten looks instead to the paradigm for Christian tragedy.[13] In Christian tragedy catastrophes are not usually averted: Adam falls and brings upon himself and his progeny the ravages of sin and death; Christ is crucified and dies; the faithful suffer trials, sicknesses, catastrophes, deaths, martyrdoms in this life. Christian tragedy looks forward, indeed, to the final reversal of fortunes at the Last Judgment, termed by Tertullian the apocalyptic catastrophe of the universal providential drama.[14] But it is only at the end of history that the long series of particular tragedies comprising that history will be experienced as episodes in a divine comedy.

For Christians generally, as for Milton, the Fall of Man is the archetypal tragedy and a primary reference point for the genre's basic structure. Such compendia as Boccaccio's *De Casibus virorum illustrirum* and Chaucer's *Monk's Tale* begin with the Fall of Adam as origin and model for all subsequent tragic falls of illustrious men from high estate. Similarly, the native English mystery cycles begin with the triple falls of Lucifer, Adam, and Cain, which serve as paradigms for many other biblical tragedies.[15] The cycles present the entire course of providential history, leading to Christ's redemption and culminating in the Last Judgment; and Renaissance neoclassical tragedies on the Fall of Adam and Eve normally make at least brief reference to that providential design.[16]

However, many biblical tragedies by Reformation Protestants looked instead to another model, the Book of Revelation, understood as the tragic history of the suffering saints culminating in the Apocalypse.[17] In these plays the label "tragedy" sometimes means little more than that they differ from comedies in having exalted characters and an action evoking wonder.[18] Often, however, the label is used with some generic precision, to identify dramas in which the ultimate comic reversal bringing happiness to the just is foreseen but not achieved in the dramatic action. An example is Thomas Kirchmeyer's *Pammachius*, a "tragœdia nova" which presents in four acts and alternating scenes the tragic sufferings of the elect and the jubilation of the papal Antichrist and his followers. The play ends abruptly with the Reformation, as Kirchmeyer explains that he has written no fifth act because Christ will provide his own catastrophe in which the damned will be punished and the elect victorious.[19] A similar pattern obtains in John Bale's *Kynge Johan*, Nicholas Grimald's *Archipropheta*, and several others. Christian tragedy in sixteenth-century England seems in essence to involve the endurance of sin and suffering, pain and loss, while waiting in faith and hope for God's providential design to be brought to its final comedic resolution.[20]

Milton had, then, both dramatic and exegetical precedent when he pointed (twice) to the Book of Revelation as a model for tragedy. In *The Reason of Church Government* (1642) he termed it "the majestick image of a high and stately Tragedy,"[21] and almost thirty years later he cited it in the Preface to *Samson Agonistes* among the precedents for his own biblical tragedy. David Pareus, the "grave authority" Milton refers to on both occasions, was one of many exegetes who described the Book of Revelation as a tragedy by reason of its form (a series of dramatic scenes or shows or acts separated by choral songs and presented as in a theater), and also by reason of its matter, the sufferings and agons of the faithful, defiled by sin but redeemed by grace.[22]

In Book Nine of *Paradise Lost* Milton presents the Fall itself as a tragedy, according to a somewhat modified version of the Aristotelian paradigm. In Book Ten he presents the aftermath of the Fall according to the norms for Christian tragedy, and then extends that paradigm into Books Eleven and Twelve, where it becomes a prominent element in the mixed mode of the Christian heroic. But first, Milton underscores the Satanic perversion of both those paradigms.

At the beginning of Book Nine Satan pours forth in "plaints" his tragic emotions—"inward grief" and "bursting passion," "Torment within," and the "hateful seige / Of contraries"— and then sets his revenge plot in motion. He now sees himself as hero of his own revenge tragedy, but in fact his story combines two kinds of plots Aristotle identified as essentially untragic: that in which an evil protagonist falls from happiness into misery, and that in which an evil protagonist passes from misery to happiness[23]—in this case, the happiness of succeeding in his revenge. As a revenge hero he also perverts the usual Elizabethan paradigm.[24] He has not been wronged by anyone; he can cause no harm to his true enemy, God; and the human beings he ravages are not his enemies, save insofar as their happy state provokes his envy. Having fallen from heaven as a result of his proud revolt against God, Satan now undertakes, deliberately, a further "foul descent," imbruting himself in the serpent to implement a revenge which he knows to be self-destructive: "Revenge, at first though sweet, / Bitter ere long back on itself recoils" (9.163-72). In Book Ten, Satan's parodic tragedy concludes with a further debasement as he suffers an involuntary and punitive metamorphosis into a serpent, and the divine Author thereby rewrites the Satanic revenge tragedy as black comedy.

By contrast with Satan's parodic tragedy, Milton devised the Fall of Adam and Eve to conform to Aristotle's prescriptions for the best kind of tragedy. The plot presents a change in the fortunes of the protagonists from happiness to misery, as Adam's outcry—"O miserable of happy" (10.720)—precisely articulates. As Aristotle recommended, those protagonists are persons better than ourselves, though Milton's fable prevented his choice of intermediate personages "not preeminently virtuous and just":[25] prelapsarian Adam and Eve are, of course, superlatively virtuous and intelligent, indeed perfect. Nevertheless, as we have seen, Milton portrays that prelapsarian perfection as fully consistent with mutability, inexperience, learning by trial and error, and qualities of mind and temperament requiring constant direction and control. In consequence, we recognize Adam and Eve as our first parents indeed, so like us that we readily feel the Aristotelian pity and terror on their account—and our own.

Milton's tragic hero and heroine fall through *hamartia*. Aristotle's term means "some error of judgment," but it is glossed by many Renaissance commentators to mean also some sin or crime.[26] The sin that is the donnée of Milton's fable, the eating of the forbidden fruit, cannot in itself evoke the intrinsic horror that attends the deeds of Oedipus or Orestes, but the poet also associates that primal disobedience with hubris and ingratitude—especially in Eve as she reaches beyond the human condition, aspiring to Godhead. Milton also makes Adam and Eve's *hamartia* an entirely deliberate sin, not simply a tendency to passion. Eve's earlier impulses to vanity and Adam's to uxoriousness were not heretofore sinful because they were controlled. We now see that control greatly weakened during the marital dispute, rendering both protagonists especially vulnerable to temptation and self-delusion. Nonetheless, both have a moment of choice when they are "yet sinless" and when they see the issues clearly, so that their decision to disobey God's command is free and deliberate.

Adam and Eve's *hamartia* also involves errors in judgment, but these errors are culpable as their earlier errors were not, because now the errors are deliberately indulged. Though Eve does not recognize the serpent as Satan, and though she lets herself be deceived by his arguments, she shows a clear understanding of the issues involved when she first arrives at the tree. Restating the prohibition, she describes it as the "Sole Daughter" of the voice of God, outside the Law of Reason which governs humankind in all else (9.653). This perception makes her a party to her own deception when she then gives respectful attention to Satan as he reasons about the fruit.

Similarly, Adam recognizes Eve's fallen state the moment she appears before him—"How art thou lost, how on a sudden lost, / Defac't, deflow'r'd, and now to Death devote?" (9.900-901); and he is not deceived by her argument repeating the Satanic promises. He sees his situation as a tragic dilemma: either he must lose Eve whom he loves as his own flesh and whose "sweet Converse and Love" he cannot forgo, or he must also eat the fruit and share her fate. (Eve had earlier posed to herself a parallel problem which is a parody of Adam's tragic dilemma: either to share the fruit with Adam and so lose the supposed advantage of superiority, or keep it for herself and so risk death and loss of Adam to "another Eve.") Adam's immediate and entirely deliberate decision to fall with Eve is based upon an unquestioned assumption that his situation is utterly hopeless. He gives no thought at all to alternatives which his experience of God's goodness might have suggested to him—an appeal to God to forgive Eve, or even (had he been able to imagine true Christian heroism) an offer to die for her. His haste and lack of faith make him culpable in misjudging his situation.

Aristotle preferred a complex to a simple tragic plot, and Milton's tragic plot is complex, with reversal of fortune (*peripeteia*) and recognition (*anagnorisis*). The reversal, according to Aristotle, should arise from "the probable or necessary sequence of events."[27] Milton follows this dictim, but in a manner consonant with the centrality of free will and moral choice in his theology and poetic argument. As we have seen, by using comedic genres in Books Four to Eight to present Edenic life Milton underscores the fact that the Fall is not a necessary outcome of Adam and Eve's story. In Book Nine, however, the marital dispute begins a sequence of complications that culminate in the tragic reversal. In that dispute we watch Adam and Eve lock themselves into attitudes and set themselves upon a course that leads directly to their catastrophic fall from happiness into sin and misery. There is still no question of necessity, since both have their moment of choice with the issues sharply defined. But the sequence of events in Book Nine is devised to make the Fall seem ever more probable. And the Bard's anguished outcries intensify our sense of tragic inevitability by reminding us that we know the sad conclusion: "O much deceiv'd, much failing, hapless *Eve*, / Of thy presumed return! event perverse!" (9.404-405).

Milton's *peripeteia* also involves reversals of expectation, with attendant tragic ironies. Eve, setting out alone after the marital dispute, hardly imagines that "A Foe so proud will first the weaker seek," though she expects to come off gloriously if he does so (9.383-84). As it happens, she does not even recognize the serpent as Satan, and she is easily overwhelmed by his dazzling rhetoric. Eating the fruit, Eve has "expectation high / Of knowledge, nor was God-head from her thought"— but later sees that she was "eating Death" (9.790-92). For his part, Adam expects Eve's gratitude and love for his decision to fall with her, but meets with a very different response: "Is this the Love, is this the recompense / Of mine to thee, ingrateful *Eve*, . . . / And am I now upbraided, as the cause / Of thy transgressing?" (9.1163-69).

The Miltonic tragedy of the Fall also involves discovery or recognition (*anagnorisis*), the second element of Aristotle's complex plot: "A Discovery is, as the very word implies, a change from ignorance to knowledge, and thus to either love or hate, in the personages marked for ignorance or knowledge."[28] The *peripeteia* of Book Nine is at first attended with false discoveries, heavy with tragic irony. Immediately after eating the fruit Eve believes she has gained divine knowledge: "opener mine Eyes, / Dim erst, dilated Spirits, ampler Heart, / And growing up to Godhead" (9.875-77). Adam at first believes that the fruit has greatly enhanced sensual and sexual pleasure—"Much pleasure we have lost, while we abstain'd / From this delightful Fruit, nor known till now"—and blinded by lust he thinks Eve "fairer now / Than ever, bounty of this virtuous Tree" (9.1022-33). However, the true recognition comes when Adam and Eve awaken from their lust-induced sleep, as they realize that they have gained nothing and lost all they had:

> our Eyes
> Op'n'd we find indeed, and find we know
> Both Good and Evil, Good lost, and Evil got,
> Bad Fruit of Knowledge, if this be to know,
> Which leaves us naked thus, of Honor void,
> Of Innocence, of Faith, of Purity,
> Our wonted Ornaments.
> (9.1070-76)

As John Steadman notes, this recognition is accompanied by the "hate" called for in Aristotle's definition: the pair engage in vicious recriminations, "And of thir vain contést appear'd no end."[29]

The kinds of plot and characters Aristotle recommends are those he thinks will best evoke the tragic emotions, pity and terror, pity being occasioned by "undeserved misfortune," terror by the misfortune of "one like ourselves."[30] As we have

228

seen, though prelapsarian Adam and Eve are vastly better than ourselves, Milton's portrayal of them as very like us enhances the terror we feel for them, and for ourselves. Also, though their deliberate sin precludes our viewing their Fall as undeserved misfortune, we pity Adam and Eve because Milton makes them so attractive and so very human in their propensity to err and to give way to passion under great pressure. Milton further reinforces the Aristotelian pity and terror by presenting several characters moved to like emotions by the tragic event. Satan himself declares that he "could pity" Adam and Eve "thus forlorn"; the narrator cries out in pity as Eve departs from Adam "O much deceiv'd, much failing, hapless *Eve*"; the angels' visages exhibit "dim sadness . . . mixt / With pity" when they learn of the Fall.[31] Those closest to and most affected by the event are wracked by both tragic emotions. At his first sight of fallen Eve, Adam "Astonied stood and Blank, while horror chill / Ran through his veins," and his first words underscore the pathos of the situation: "O fairest of Creation . . . / How art thou lost, how on a sudden lost, / Defac't, deflow'r'd, and now to Death devote?" (9.890-901). Nature herself responded to Eve's sin with sighs and "signs of woe, / That all was lost"; and when Adam completed the "mortal Sin / Original" she wept and groaned and "trembl'd from her entrails" (9.783-84, 1000).

In Aristotle's paradigm the third element of the tragic plot is pathos, or the scene of suffering: "an action of a destructive or painful nature, such as murders on the stage, tortures, woundings, and the like."[32] Steadman points out that Renaissance commentators, notably Tasso, understood this definition to include lamentations and mental torment as well as physical suffering,[33] and that this concept is of primary importance in Milton's concept of tragedy. Indeed, in the Preface to *Samson Agonistes* Milton identifies the passions of pity and fear as the object of imitation—a highly significant departure from the Aristotelian definition of tragedy as the imitation of an "*action* serious, complete, and of a certain magnitude."[34] Milton's definition links that imitation of passions directly to the tragic catharsis:

> "Tragedy, as it was anciently compos'd, hath been ever held the gravest, moralest, and most profitable of all other Poems: therefore said by *Aristotle* to be of power by raising pity and fear, or terror, to purge the mind of those and such like passions, that is to temper and reduce them to just measure with a kind of delight, stirr'd up by reading or seeing those passions well imitated."

Samson Agonistes itself might be aptly described as one long scene of suffering in which the hero continually laments his afflictions but also struggles toward regeneration.[35]

Adam and Eve enter upon a comparable scene of suffering after the Fall as they lament and cry out against the new conditions of their life: shame, guilt, remorse, passion, torments of conscience, spiritual and mental damage, isolation, physical decline, destruction of the Edenic world, and the prospect of death. Adam's long complaint in Book Ten, "O miserable of happy" presents this suffering at its most intense, as Adam, like Satan before him on Mount Niphates, is forced to recognize what he has lost, and forced also to admit his own entire responsibility for that loss. Yet while Satan forges from such suffering the renewed commitment to evil which leads him to become a parodic revenge hero, Adam is paralyzed by despair and can find no escape from the abyss, "from deep to deeper plung'd!" At this point however, the Aristotelian paradigm gives way to the paradigm of Christian tragedy from the Book of Revelation, as Adam and Eve begin to respond to the grace of regeneration. Like Samson they now repent, struggle to understand God's prophecies, learn to endure suffering with patience, and prepare to wait with faith and hope for the working out of God's providential design.

Milton's presentation of the aftermath of the Fall as Christian tragedy involves the transformation of the Aristotelian plot elements into their Christian counterparts. This metamorphosis of genre is the literary manifestation of the action of

230

divine grace, won for man by the sacrifice of the Son. In counterpoise to the *peripeteia* wrought by the Fall, God now works his own *peripeteia*, mitigating and reversing those changes. This process begins to be manifest at the opening of Book Ten, when the Son judges Adam and Eve and at the same time clothes their physical and spiritual nakedness. Then, because prevenient grace has already removed "The stony from thir hearts, and made new flesh / Regenerate grow instead" (11.3-5), Eve is able to break off the exchange of mutual accusations and recriminations by humbly repenting and begging forgiveness of Adam. By this act she turns Adam from the paralysis of despair to love and reconciliation, after which both repent, confess their fault, and are reconciled to God.

The regeneration and restoration inaugurated by the divine *peripeteia* continue throughout history. They are accompanied by a divine *anagnorisis* in which prophetic illumination counters Satan's false promises of knowledge and the blindness of the intellect produced by sin. This process begins with the protoevangelion pronounced at the judgment, and continues throughout history as progressive revelations are offered to man by God. Michael's revelations of providential history encapsulate this process, whose import Adam recognizes when he apostophizes the angel as "True opener of mine eyes," and "Seer blest." The divine transformations and revelations change the character of the scene of suffering as well: while the pain, loss, and death attendant upon the Fall are not much mitigated, the mental anguish is, transforming despair into patient endurance in expectation of the Apocalypse.

These changes also transform the catharsis of Christian tragedy. The Preface to *Samson Agonistes* explains that the tragic terror and pity are to be tempered and reduced through dramatic imitation of those passions, and the chorus experiences such a catharsis as they partly perceive how Samson's suffering may be subsumed within the divine plan. In *Paradise Lost* God's description of the emotional state Michael's account of providential history is to induce in Adam and Eve precisely defines the catharsis intended, as the Aristotelian tragedy of the Fall gives way to Christian tragedy. Adam and Eve are to go forth from the Garden, and we from the poem, "not disconsolate," "sorrowing, yet in peace" (11.113-17).

TRAGIC SPEECH

As we have seen, speech in unfallen Eden (as in heaven) is primarily dialogue, promoting and resulting in greater understanding, the meeting of minds, the resolution of problems. By contrast, Satanic speech is most often soliloquy or rhetorical persuasion, forms that preclude any genuine interchange. In the Fall sequences of *Paradise Lost* we watch the transformation of comedic dialogue into a debased instrument, exacerbating misunderstandings, exaggerating difficulties, and promoting catastrophe.

The Fall scenes in *Paradise Lost* develop motifs intimated in the Genesis account and common to Renaissance neo-Latin, Italian, and Dutch tragedies on the Fall by Hugo Grotius, Giambattista Andreini, Serafino della Salandra, and Joost van den Vondel.[36] William Lauder's charges that such resemblances amount to plagiarism on Milton's part[37] have been universally and deservedly ridiculed, but they have perhaps kept us from attending as carefully as we might to Milton's deliberate uses of such echoes to set his tragic sequence within the generic tradition of "Fall" tragedies. Typically, Milton develops these common motifs (and invents others) so as to heighten tragic effect, emphasize the progressive deterioration of dialogue, and provide his own profoundly moving and psychologically acute interpretation of these human events.

Although all dramatizations of the Fall have to account in some way for the separation of Adam and Eve in order to provide occasion for Satan's temptation, the marital dispute scene that Milton invents (9.205-386) is entirely without precedent. Grotius has Eve simply wander off while Adam seeks her throughout the Garden; Salandra's Adam hears a mysterious voice (Echo) calling him and goes in persuit; Vondel's Adam, ironically, turns away from Eve to offer thanks to God for her companionship.[38] But in Milton's brilliant scene the separation is not simply accidental. It results from a badly conducted dialogue in which (for the first time in Eden) Adam and Eve enmesh themselves in ever-greater misunderstandings, culminating in a false and dangerous resolution of the issues raised. Yet while Adam and Eve display their weaknesses in this dialogue they do not sin, because they do not here make deliberate choice of evil.

Eve's well-meaning but misguided proposal for temporary separation seeks to address a genuine problem—the tendency of the Garden to "wanton growth." She speaks tentatively, with appropriate deference to Adam's leadership role: "Thou therefore now advise / Or hear what to my mind first thoughts present" (9.212-13). To be sure, Eve exaggerates both the seriousness of the problem and the value of efficiency when she proposes (like a good capitalist) that they improve their gardening productivity by removing the distraction of loving conversation—which is a higher good. And she entirely ignores the threat posed by Satan. Yet Adam's similar misapprehensions in his dialogues with Raphael, as well as the continued use of honorific epithets throughout the marital dispute—"Sole *Eve*, Associate sole"; "Offspring of Heav'n and Earth, and all Earth's Lord"; "Daughter of God and Man, immortal *Eve*"—suggest that for this dialogue also a comedic resolution might conceivably be found.

Adam's "mild answer" begins very well. Complimenting Eve on studying "household good" and seeking to promote good works in her husband, he lovingly corrects her overvaluation of work in Eden. He urges also that the legitimate pleasure of occasional solitude is outweighed by the dangerous opportunity it offers to a foe. And he points out, as Puritan marriage treatises often did, the importance of mutual help in spiritual dangers, so that "each / To other speedy aid might lend at need."[39] Had Adam stopped here, the archetypal marital dispute might have concluded happily, but (as his progeny will so often do in similar cases) he talks on until he unintentionally affronts his spouse. With woeful lack of tact he states the hierarchical principle of Eden in a pompous platitude, emphasizing Eve's weakness rather than (as before) the need of both for mutual help and reinforcement in danger: "The Wife, where danger or dishonor lurks, / Safest and seemliest by her Husband stays, / Who guards her, or with her the worst endures."

Hurt and offended, Eve overreacts to the slight, "as one who loves, and some unkindness meets." Speaking "with sweet austere composure" she voices surprise and dismay that Adam should suppose her so infirm. This response throws Adam so far off balance that his strong logical powers desert him. "With healing words" he assures Eve of his trust, but he then claims that he seeks to shield her from the aspersion of dishonor which a temptation in itself would bring. He ends by reiterating the promising theme of mutual need for mutual help: "I from the influence of thy looks receive / Access in every Virtue, in thy sight / More wise, more watchful, stronger . . . / Why shouldst not thou like sense within thee feel / When I am present, and thy trial choose / With me, best witness of thy Virtue tri'd."

But Eve seizes upon Adam's illogical statements. She knows perfectly well that temptation itself is no dishonor: "his foul esteem / Sticks no dishonor on our Front, but turns / Foul on himself; then wherefore shunn'd or fear'd / By us? who rather double honor gain / From his surmise prov'd false." Adam's resort to irrational argument evidently reinforces Eve's sense of being slighted, and she now seems more concerned to win her case than to understand her situation: no doubt she enjoys having the better of the argument for once. She is right to insist that in their "happy State" of innocence each of them is able to resist temptation alone. But she is quite wrong to infer from this that "exterior help" (divine or human) is to be shunned, or that reasonable precautions in the presence of danger violate Edenic happiness. As we have seen, angelic society and prelapsarian human society are alike based on loving interdependence and are alike open to evil. Eve sounds rather like a romance heroine eager to prove her prowess and gain honor in victorious single combat with the enemy. She means

well, but we hear a distant echo of the Satanic claims to ab-
solute autonomy in her statement of heroic self-sufficiency:
"And what is Faith, Love, Virtue unassay'd / Alone, without
exterior help sustain'd?"

Adam replies "fervently," developing at last an argument
that meets both the logical and the psychological issues. He
agrees that neither of them is left "imperfet or deficient" by
the Creator, and that both are secure from outward force. But
he underscores the genuine and ever-present danger that their
reason (not keeping strictest watch) might be deceived by some
"fair appearing good" and so mislead the will into sin. He
concludes with an explanation of his motives and an eloquent
appeal to Eve in just the right terms: "Not then mistrust, but
tender love enjoins, / That I should mind thee oft, and mind
thou me." Urging Eve not to seek out a temptation which is
certain to come unsought, he points out that in fact she can
only satisfy her desire to win honor and praise if she meets
her trial in his presence: "Not seeing thee attempted, who
attest?"

If Adam had stopped at this point he would almost cer-
tainly have won Eve's agreement and brought the dialogue to
happy resolution. He has now offered her a clear and free
choice: she can either defy him and go off alone anyway (highly
unlikely), or she can admit (perhaps a bit reluctantly) that she
is convinced by his good arguments and solaced by his loving
sentiments. But Adam again talks too much, exhibiting his
admitted tendency to attribute more wisdom to Eve than is
warranted by her nature. In so doing he gives away his case.
He offers Eve a better reason for going than those she has
thought of herself. And his repeated imperatives—"Go," "Go,"
"rely," "do"—produce unintended but intense psychological
pressure, making it virtually impossible for Eve now to decide
to stay without seeming to back down ignominiously:

> But if thou think, trial unsought may find
> Us both securer than thus warn'd thou seem'st,
> Go; for thy stay, not free, absents thee more;

Go in thy native innocence, rely
On what thou hast of virtue, summon all,
For God towards thee hath done his part, do thine.
(9.370-75)

It was not Adam's place in prelapsarian Eden to command
Eve to stay and so to control her free choice, but neither was
it his place to help her choose such a dangerous course of
action. How completely Adam has now given over his proper
leadership role is evident when we compare his wooing of Eve
in Book Four: he did not conclude his fervent appeal on that
occasion by saying, "If you really think it best to go back and
stare at yourself in that pool for awhile, perhaps you are right.
Go ahead." As she takes her leave, Eve refers explicitly to Ad-
am's formal permission and the force of his "last reasoning
words."

Neither Adam nor Eve has sinned in this dialogue: Eve has
not disobeyed and Adam has intended to act for the best. But
their emotions, imperfectly controlled, have sabotaged the
dialogic exchange. For the first time in Eden, dialogue has
resulted in a false accord, clouding rather than clearing the
issues.

In the major Renaissance tragedies of the Fall the scene of
Eve's temptation is intensely dramatic, with the serpent en-
gaging Eve in a fast-paced colloquy and employing a great
variety of arguments to meet her objections and questions. In
Paradise Lost, by contrast, the scene especially emphasizes Sa-
tan's subversion of dialogue. At the outset Eve speaks directly
and ingenuously to the serpent, posing questions and seeking
information, whereas Satan largely avoids dialogic inter-
change, substituting other forms of communication.

Satan first attracts Eve's attention by mute display—the beauty
and almost balletic movements of the serpent disporting him-
self before her. He follows this with a hyperbolic encomium
of Eve in the tones and language of a courtly lover. Naturally
enough, Eve responds first to the marvel of serpentine speech
rather than to the words spoken, and asks for an explanation.

236

In answer, the Satanic serpent devises a false autobiography—
parodying the autobiographies recounted by Eve to Adam and
by Adam to Raphael—in which he describes how he gained
speech and reason by eating apples from one of the trees of
Paradise (9.568-612). Though Eve recognizes hyperbole when
she hears it in Satan's inappropriate compliments—"Serpent,
thy overpraising leaves in doubt / The virtue of that Fruit, in
thee first prov'd" (9.615-16)—the pleasure she takes in these
compliments displaces the wariness they ought to evoke. Sus-
pecting nothing, Eve asks the location of this tree, and accepts
the serpent's offer to lead her to it.

In all the major Renaissance Fall tragedies, as in Genesis,
Eve restates the divine prohibition,[40] but Milton gives very
special emphasis to that speech. As soon as Milton's Eve reaches
the forbidden tree she not only declares the prohibition but
also distinguishes the ground for it (God's direct command)
from the Law of Reason which governs all other human be-
havior:

> Serpent, we might have spar'd our coming hither,
> Fruitless to mee, though Fruit be here to excess,
> The credit of whose virtue rest with thee,
> Wondrous indeed, if cause of such effects.
> But of this Tree we may not taste nor touch;
> God so commanded, and left that Command
> Sole Daughter of his voice; the rest, we live
> Law to ourselves, our Reason is our Law.
>   (9.647-54)

Hooker himself could not have stated more precisely the dis-
tinction between positive and natural law. Though evidently
disappointed, Eve certainly merits the narrator's description
of her as "yet sinless"; this speech demonstrates her clear un-
derstanding of the matter at issue and therefore her full re-
sponsibility for her choices. She, as well as Adam, is "Suffi-
cient to have stood, though free to fall." She need only hold
firmly to the principle she has stated, that the divine prohibi-
tion is outside the domain of reason, to be proof against the

barrage of rational arguments Satan adduces. But his eloquence, in the posture of "some Orator renown'd / In *Athens* or free *Rome*," succeeds in confusing that issue for her and she is dazzled by his persuasive words, "impregn'd / With Reason, to her seeming, and with Truth."

After concluding this oration, Satan does not speak again in this scene. But Eve does not act immediately and impulsively. Instead, she turns from dialogue to soliloquy (9.745-79). In several Renaissance tragedies on the Fall Eve also soliloquizes at this juncture: Grotius shows her arguing both sides of the case as she considers what to do, and Vondel portrays her torn between fear and desire.[41] But Milton invests Eve's soliloquy with special significance, as the formal means by which she takes full responsibility for her act. Her first words suggest that even before she begins to speak she is probably already guilty of what Milton terms the first degree or mode of sin, "evil desire, or the will to do evil."[42] But then, "Pausing a while," she reviews Satan's arguments carefully and makes them her own: the tree will bring knowledge and wisdom, God is unjust or envious in forbidding it to man, and therefore "such prohibitions bind not." She finds especially persuasive Satan's false analogy between her prospects and the serpent's supposed experience: the serpent apparently attained higher status (human reason and language) by eating the fruit; he was not punished by death or in any other way; and his friendliness to man in sharing the fruit contrasts markedly with the divine malice in withholding it.[43] In the course of this soliloquy Eve rationalizes her desire, deals with the only constraint she yet recognizes, the threat of death, and so brings herself to enact the fatal sin.

After eating the fruit and experiencing sensations of intoxication, Eve voices a hymn of praise to the tree as to a god. Then, turning again to soliloquy, she poses a question to herself which reveals a new concern with role-playing, with seeming: "But to *Adam* in what sort / Shall I *appear*" (9.816-17).[44] She thinks first of keeping her act secret, reserving to herself the supposed superiority of knowledge. Adopting Satan's view of hierarchy now, she asks his rhetorical question, "For inferior who is free?" (9.825).[45] But then, weighing the possibility of her own death and Adam's remarriage, she quickly resolves that "*Adam* shall share with me in bliss or woe"—and her moral obtuseness is such that she terms this jealous calculation an evidence of her dear love for him.

The scene in which Eve offers the fruit to Adam is also intensely dramatic in the major Renaissance tragedies of the Fall. Typically, Adam voices his shock at Eve's deed and is quite reluctant to eat the fruit himself, while Eve wears down his resistance by argument, blandishments, and loving appeals.[46] Milton handles the scene very differently, as a dialogue in which communication is entirely undermined by role-playing and disguise (9.849-1011). Eve comes with fruit in hand, offering apologies for being late and a brief account of her experiences with the serpent and the tree. She then describes the divinizing effects of the fruit upon herself, falsely claiming that she sought Godhead chiefly for him and urging Adam to eat also so that her new elevation may not separate them. Adam on his side wholly disguises his true thoughts and feelings from Eve. In a poignant interior lament he bewails her ruin and decides instantaneously to die with her, so distraught at the thought of life without her that he cannot even consider whether he has any other alternatives. He speaks to Eve "in calm mood," arguing at some length the likelihood that they will not be punished by death and proclaiming his determination to share her lot whatever it may be. Praising this "glorious trial of exceeding Love," Eve probably half-believes the lie she reiterates, that she is giving Adam the fruit only because she expects no evil to result, and because she wants to share divinity with him.

With Adam's fall human speech degenerates further, taking on other Satanic qualities. Adam becomes flippant, referring to Eve's "judicious" palate as evidence of her sapience, and mocking the divine prohibition: "if such pleasure be / In things to us forbidden, it might be wish'd / For this one Tree had been forbidden ten" (9.1024-26). Love-language is now trivialized, shorn of its former reverence, mutuality, and beauty. As he urges Eve to "play," Adam, impelled by lust, speaks only of his *own* desires, his "inflamed" senses, and his "ardor to enjoy" her. After the love-making, the seal of their mutual guilt, Adam and Eve are "strick'n mute" when they wake to shame, darkened minds, and an awareness of lost innocence. Adam breaks this silence with a harsh etymological pun—"O *Eve*, in evil hour thou didst give ear / To that false Worm"— and then underscores the bitter irony of their *anagnorisis*: "our Eyes / Op'n'd we find indeed, and find we know / Both Good and Evil, Good lost, and Evil got, / Bad Fruit of Knowledge" (9.1067-73). They are now only too ready to reveal their bitter thoughts to each other, though shame moves them to hide their bodies with fig-leaves.

At the end of Book Nine, Adam and Eve can only exchange bitter and continuous mutual accusations marked by "Anger, Hate, / Mistrust, Suspicion, Discord" (9.1123-24). With "alter'd style" Adam throws up to Eve her refusal to listen to him, her "strange / Desire of wand'ring," and her folly in seeking to prove her faith. Eve responds with excuses—the Fall might equally well have occurred with Adam present, and in any case she could hardly remain by his side forever like "a lifeless Rib." She then counterattacks, ascribing the Fall to Adam's weakness in giving way to her:

> Being as I am, why didst not thou the Head
> Command me absolutely not to go,
> Going into such danger as thou said'st?
> Too facile then thou didst not much gainsay,
> Nay, didst permit, approve, and fair dismiss.
> Hadst thou been firm and fixt in thy dissent,
> Neither had I transgress'd, nor thou with mee.
> (9.1155-61)

This, understandably, is more than Adam can bear. "Incenst," he denounces Eve's ingratitude in blaming his very mildness toward her for the Fall, even as she ignores the sacrifice he has made to share her fate. Adam is right to protest that "force

240

upon free Will hath here no place," but wrong to deny his own share of responsibility for the failure of the marital dialogue. He takes refuge at last in blatant misogyny, denouncing womankind's determination to follow her own will, and readiness to blame man's "weak indulgence" if evil ensues.

At the beginning of Book Ten, in the Judgment scene, the Son begins the transformation of classical into Christian tragedy with the restoration of dialogue (10.92-223). Of course the easy exchanges of the prelapsarian state which led to comfortable, comedic resolutions of simple problems can never be restored. Christian tragic dialogue is presented as painful and difficult communication, requiring men and women to face, accept, and engage with the harsh realities of fallen human nature and a fallen world.

In judging them, the Son forces that kind of dialogue upon Adam and Eve as he calls them forth from their hiding places, and strips away their excuses. Adam invites and receives the harsher reproof. With fine psychological acuteness Milton portrays Adam's inability to sustain under such duress the noble posture of a romance lover ready to die with his lady. Now he is eager to blame her (and her Maker) for everything:

> This Woman whom thou mad'st to be my help,
> And gav'st me as thy perfet gift, so good,
> So fit, so acceptable, so Divine,
> That from her hand I could suspect no ill,
> And what she did, whatever in itself,
> Her doing seem'd to justify the deed;
> Shee gave me of the Tree, and I did eat.
> (10.137-43)

The Son, however, gives short shrift to these self-serving and querulous complaints, and demands that Adam face the true situation: "Was shee thy God, that her thou didst obey / Before his voice, or was shee made thy guide, / Superior, or but equal, that to her / Thou didst resign thy Manhood, and the Place / Wherein God set thee" (10.145-50). By contrast, Eve is now "nigh overwhelm'd" with shame and guilt, and she answers her Judge simply, directly, and without excuse: "The Serpent me beguil'd, and I did eat" (10.162). With this answer, which is followed by the Son's curse on the serpent and proclamation of the messianic promise in the woman's seed, Eve begins to enact a redemptive role as type of Mary, agent of God's grace to man. That role is first manifested in the restoration of human communication and so of human society.

The first effects in Eden of the invasion by Sin and Death, and of the alterations God makes in the cosmos evoke from Adam a loud and long lament. At times this lament modulates to soliloquy as Adam (like Satan on Mount Niphates) blames God for his predicament, but is then forced "after all Disputes" to absolve him. Challenging God's justice he demands, "Did I request thee, Maker, from my Clay / To mould me Man?" Soon, however, he admits that no father can solicit consent from a son prior to giving him life, and that by failing to object to God's conditions earlier he gave his implicit consent. He then questions the goodness of a God who would make death deathless and woes endless "For anger's sake," but soon perceives that both he and death may be by nature eternal. At length he impugns God's justice again, for condemning all mankind for one man's fault, but then admits that any progeny he would produce must necessarily be corrupt and so deserve damnation. While Satan's soliloquizing ended in defiance, Adam's ends in despair as he plunges even deeper into an "Abyss of fears / And horrors." Solitary, hopeless, crying out for death as he lies "Outstretcht . . . on the cold ground," he is unable to lessen his calamities or to alleviate his misery in the slightest degree.

At this point Eve tries to solace him with "Soft words," but Adam, wild with pain and loss, answers with a fierce invective castigating her and all womankind:

> Out of my sight, thou Serpent, that name best
> Befits thee with him leagu'd, thyself as false

And hateful; nothing wants, but that thy shape,
Like his, and color Serpentine may show
Thy inward fraud, to warn all Creatures from thee
Henceforth; lest that too heav'nly form, pretended
To hellish falsehood, snare them. But for thee
I had persisted happy.
. . . .
                       O why did God,
Creator wise, that peopl'd highest Heav'n
With Spirits Masculine, create at last
This novelty on Earth, this fair defect
Of Nature, and not fill the World at once
With Men as Angels without Feminine,
Or find some other way to generate
Mankind? this mischief had not then befall'n,
And more that shall befall, innumerable
Disturbances on Earth through Female snares.
                    (10.867-97)

Adam has forgotten the stern reproof such blame-shifting and
misogyny elicited from the Son at the Judgment. But Eve,
responding as she did then with a simple confession of guilt,
meets this rebuke with a poignant plea to Adam for forgive-
ness and a proposal (echoing the Son's language in the Dia-
logue in Heaven) to take upon herself the whole of God's
wrath.

This confession of guilt breaks through the impasse of charge
and countercharge, and restores dialogue. Adam now accepts
his own guilt toward "Thy frailty and infirmer Sex . . . / To
me committed and by me expos'd," and looks to the future,
raising the question of how they can "light'n / Each other's
burden in our share of woe." Eve responds with some diffi-
dence as she recalls her former errors, but she takes up again
the responsibilities of dialogue: "from thee I will not hide /
What thoughts in my unquiet breast are ris'n, / Tending to
some relief of our extremes, / Or end" (10.974-77). Again she
plays the initiatory role which seems to be properly hers—

advancing notions which Adam can then consider, revise, or set aside in favor of better plans. Her recourse is to Stoicism: to refrain from sexual intercourse and so remain childless, or if that prove too difficult, to seek death immediately, in suicide. Rejecting these proposals as counsels of despair, Adam reasons that such actions would thwart the divine promises proclaimed in the protoevangelion. Reviewing the punishments pronounced, he finds them less than terrible: Eve's pain in childbearing will be recompensed with joy for the child born, and their work, however arduous, will be better than idleness. Finally, recalling the Judge's mercy in clothing their nakedness, Adam infers that he will also, if asked, teach them how to "pass commodiously this life, sustain'd / By him with many comforts." He proposes that they pray for forgiveness, and Book Ten ends with such a prayer, indicating that dialogue is now restored not only between man and woman, but also between humankind and God.

TRAGIC LYRIC

Books Nine and Ten contain a series of laments, complaints, and elegiac passages, resembling the kinds of poems often designated as tragic lyrics in Renaissance criticism.[47] The Bard's elegiac laments for and descriptions of the lost (or soon to be lost) pastoral world, and the laments and complaints of Adam and Eve after the Fall evoke pathos, and contribute markedly to the tragic effect of these books. We first hear Satan's passionate complaint (9.99-123) which begins with odelike praise of the Earth's loveliness—"O Earth, how like to Heav'n." That praise has an poignant, elegiac quality, since Satan can no longer enjoy the loveliness he describes and the reader knows it will be marred all too soon. Like all Satan's lyrics, these elegiac praises and complaints soon modulate to soliloquy—to argument and scheming.[48] By contrast, Adam and Eve's sustained laments and complaints throughout Book Nine strengthen our identification with them and intensify our pity and fear for them. In Book Ten they turn to a lyric kind appropriate to Christian tragedy, repentant prayer.

The Miltonic Bard's apostrophes, laments, and elegiac pastoral descriptions mourn the loss of the innocent pastoral life in Eden. His apostrophe to Eve as she sets out to garden alone anticipates that catastrophe:

> O much deceiv'd, much failing, hapless *Eve*,
> Of thy presum'd return! event perverse!
> Thou never from that hour in Paradise
> Found'st either sweet repast, or sound repose;
> Such ambush hid among sweet Flow'rs and Shades
> Waited with hellish rancor imminent
> To intercept thy way, or send thee back
> Despoil'd of Innocence, of Faith, of Bliss.
> (9.404-11)

A few lines later he again interrupts his narrative with a poignantly lovely pastoral description of Eve amidst her flowers, elegiac in its intimations of imminent violation by Satan:

> *Eve* separate he spies,
> Veil'd in a Cloud of Fragrance, where she stood,
> Half spi'd, so thick the Roses bushing round
> About her glow'd, oft stooping to support
> Each Flow'r of slender stalk, whose head though gay
> Carnation, Purple, Azure, or speckt with Gold,
> Hung drooping unsustain'd, them she upstays
> Gently with Myrtle band, mindless the while,
> Herself, though fairest unsupported Flow'r,
> From her best prop so far, and storm so nigh.
> (9.424-33)

The pastoral elegiac strain is continued in an epic simile comparing Satan to a city sophisticate enjoying a day's outing in the country and taking delight in all the rural sights and sounds—"The smell of Grain, or tedded Grass, or Kine, / Or Dairy"—and especially in the all-too-vulnerable pastoral nymph, Eve (9.445-57).

The Bard's descriptions of pastoral nature's reaction to the Fall are not pathetic fallacy as in later elegy, but nature's appropriate response to her own ruin. At Eve's Fall, "Earth felt the wound, and Nature from her seat / Sighing through all her Works gave signs of woe, / That all was lost" (9.782-84). At fallen Eve's first encounter with yet unfallen Adam, the floral wreath Adam wove for her dropped from his "slack hand . . . and all the faded Roses shed" (9.838-42, 892-93). And at Adam's Fall, "Earth trembl'd from her entrails, as again / In pangs, and Nature gave a second groan, / Sky low'r'd, and muttering Thunder, some sad drops / Wept at completing of the mortal Sin / Original" (9.1000-1004). But when "fierce antipathy" and death enter Eden, the Bard gives over elegy, and describes with harsh realism pastoral nature in the process of destroying itself: "Beast now with Beast gan war, and Fowl with Fowl, / And Fish with Fish; to graze the Herb all leaving, / Devour'd each other; nor stood much in awe / Of Man, but fled him, or with count'nance grim / Glar'd on him passing" (10.710-15).

Eve's first tragic lyric is her idolatrous hymn praising the forbidden tree just after she eats its fruit and does "low reverence" to the magical power she supposes to dwell within it:

> O Sovran, virtuous, precious of all Trees
> In Paradise, of operation blest
> To Sapience, hitherto obscur'd, infam'd,
> And thy fair Fruit let hang, as to no end
> Created; but henceforth my early care,
> Not without Song, each Morning, and due praise
> Shall tend thee, and the fertile burden ease
> Of thy full branches offer'd free to all;
> Till dieted by thee I grow mature
> In knowledge, as the Gods who all things know.
> (9.795-804)

Eve is still disposed to worship some higher power and so, unlike Satan on Niphates, she completes her perverse hymn before turning to soliloquy, to rationalize sharing the fruit with Adam.

Adam's tragic lyrics are laments for what is lost. His immediate response upon seeing Eve fallen is an anguished interior lament for her ruin and for the bleakness of life without her. He does not argue or weigh options in soliloquy, but simply states his decision in the course of his lament:

> O fairest of Creation, last and best
> Of all God's Works, Creature in whom excell'd
> Whatever can to sight or thought be form'd,
> Holy, divine, good, amiable, or sweet!
> How art thou lost, how on a sudden lost,
> Defac't, deflow'r'd, and now to Death devote?
> Rather how hast thou yielded to transgress
> The strict forbiddance, how to violate
> The sacred Fruit forbidd'n! some cursed fraud
> Of Enemy hath beguil'd thee, yet unknown,
> And mee with thee hath ruin'd, for with thee
> Certain my resolution is to Die;
> How can I live without thee, how forgo
> Thy sweet Converse and Love so dearly join'd,
> To live again in these wild Woods forlorn?
> Should God create another *Eve*, and I
> Another Rib afford, yet loss of thee
> Would never from my heart.
> (9.896-913)

Adam's speech of *anagnorisis* after he arises from sex and sleep in guilty shame contains another lament for the enormity of his loss:

> How shall I behold the face
> Henceforth of God or Angel, erst with joy
> And rapture so oft beheld? those heav'nly shapes
> Will dazzle now this earthly, with thir blaze
> Insufferably bright. O might I here
> In solitude live savage, in some glade

247

> Obscur'd, where highest Woods impenetrable
> To Star or Sun-light, spread thir umbrage broad,
> And brown as Evening: Cover me ye Pines,
> Ye Cedars, with innumerable boughs
> Hide me, where I may never see them more.
>   (9.1080-90)

As the effects of the Fall become ever more apparent, Adam turns from simple lament to complaint: characteristically, a speaker in that genre laments his miseries but also pleads desperately for some remedy or some relief for his anguish.[49] Milton introduces Adam's longest lyric outburst (10.720-844) with an explicit genre identification: Adam "in a troubl'd Sea of passion tost, / Thus to disburd'n sought with sad complaint." As we have seen, this complaint slides at times into soliloquy as Adam attempts unsuccessfully to rationalize his guilt and convict his Creator. But unlike Satan's soliloquy on Mount Niphates with which it is often compared, Adam's monologue remains formally and tonally a complaint, in which he vainly seeks relief for his miseries in outcries, apostrophes, and agonized questions:

> O miserable of happy! is this the end
> Of this new glorious World, and mee so late
> The Glory of that Glory, who now become
> Accurst of blessed . . .
>
> . . . .
>   O voice once heard
> Delightfully, *Increase and multiply*,
> Now death to hear! for what can I increase
> Or multiply, but curses on my head?
>
> . . . .
>   O fleeting joys
> Of Paradise, dear bought with lasting woes!
>
> . . . .
>   why do I overlive,
> Why am I mockt with death, and length'n'd out
> To deathless pain?
>   (10.720-75)

He concludes with a despairing apostrophe to Death to bring surcease to his hopeless miseries, poignantly contrasting these lyric outbursts to the joyful hymns and pastoral songs of his innocence:

> Thus what thou desir'st,
> And what thou fear'st, alike destroys all hope
> Of refuge, and concludes thee miserable
> Beyond all example and future,
> To *Satan* only like both crime and doom.
> O Conscience, into what Abyss of fears
> And horrors hast thou driv'n me; out of which
> I find no way, from deep to deeper plung'd!
> . . . .
> Why comes not Death,
> Said he, with one thrice acceptable stroke
> To end me? Shall Truth fail to keep her word,
> Justice Divine not hast'n to be just?
> But Death comes not at call, Justice Divine
> Mends not her slowest pace for prayers or cries.
> O Woods, O Fountains, Hillocks, Dales and Bow'rs,
> With other echo late I taught your Shades
> To answer, and resound far other Song.
>   (10.837-62)

In their structure Adam's tragic laments and complaints most closely resemble classical models such as Ovid's *Heroides*,[50] though they also contain echoes of the Psalms, Job, and the Book of Lamentations. The complaint just discussed is replete with biblical echoes, especially from Psalm 77:

> 3. . . . I complained, and my spirit was overwhelmed.
> . . .
> 5. I have considered the days of old. . . .
> 7. Will the Lord cast off for ever? and will he be favourable no more?
> 8. Is his mercy clean gone for ever? doth his promise fail for evermore?

249

But it does not follow the structural paradigm of the lament psalms, as outlined by Mary Ann Radzinowicz:

> A typical [psalm of] lament opens with an invocation, proceeds to a mourning, continues with a supplication, an expression of the motives of the mourner, and ends with an affirmation of confidence or a vow to live better. ... The themes organized by this structural pattern include God giving merited judgment, the servant being tested, his confidence affirmed, his integrity avowed, his sins confessed, and the godly and the wicked contrasted. ... Lament psalms have a common structure which organizes their grief and turns it toward responsiveness and praise.[51]

Instead, Adam's complaint and his other tragic lyrics express only hopelessness and despair.

Unlike Adam's tragic lyrics, Eve's are religious in nature. Her idolatrous hymn to the Tree (9.795-804) anticipates the pagan worship of the ancient world. But her eloquent psalmic prayer begging forgiveness of Adam (10.914-36) begins her redemptive role as type of the Second Eve whose Seed is the Messiah. Tillyard was right to stress the importance of Eve's petition, though it does not (as he suggests) replace the Fall as the true climax of the poem. Rather, Milton makes Eve's psalmic prayer the point at which the classical tragedy of the Fall, eventuating in despair and death, gives way to Christian tragedy. It is at once an appropriate address to the husband she has wronged and a preparation for the repentant prayer Adam and Eve together will address to God at the close of Book Ten.

In this case, interestingly enough, Eve is the perfector of a lyric genre, substituting for Adam's futile complaints a better kind of tragic lyric, the true archetype of the penitential psalms in substance and structure. Her lyric alludes especially to Psalms 38, 51, and 102:

> O Lord, rebuke me not in thy wrath: neither chasten me in thy hot displeasure.

For I will declare mine iniquity; I will be sorry for my
sin.
Forsake me not, O Lord: O my God, be not far from
me.
$$(\text{Ps. } 38{:}1, 18, 21)$$

For I acknowledge my transgressions: and my sin is
ever before me.
Against thee, thee only, have I sinned, and done this
evil in thy sight. . . .
Cast me not away from thy presence. . . .
$$(\text{Ps. } 51{:}3, 4, 11)$$

Hide not thy face from me in the day when I am in
trouble; incline thine ear unto me.
$$(\text{Ps. } 102{:}2)$$

Like the penitential psalms Eve's prayer fully expresses the
misery, grief, and agony of the fallen condition, but also voices
repentance for sin, hope of forgiveness, and desire to make
amends:

> Forsake me not thus, *Adam*, witness Heav'n
> What love sincere, and reverence in my heart
> I bear thee, and unweeting have offended,
> Unhappily deceiv'd; thy suppliant
> I beg, and clasp thy knees; bereave me not,
> Whereon I live, thy gentle looks, thy aid,
> Thy counsel in this uttermost distress,
> My only strength and stay: forlorn of thee,
> Whither shall I betake me, where subsist?
> While yet we live, scarce one short hour perhaps,
> Between us two let there be peace, both joining,
> As join'd in injuries, one enmity
> Against a Foe by doom express assign'd us,
> That cruel Serpent: On me exercise not
> Thy hatred for this misery befall'n,
> On me already lost, mee than thyself
> More miserable; both have sinn'd, but thou
> Against God only, I against God and thee,

And to the place of judgment will return,
There with my cries importune Heaven, that all
The sentence from thy head remov'd may light
On me, sole cause to thee of all this woe,
Mee mee only just object of his ire.
(10.914-36)

Going beyond the psalmic parallel, Eve's prayer also echoes
the words of the Son in the Dialogue in Heaven, as she pro-
poses to take God's entire wrath upon herself.

In prelapsarian Eden Eve invented the love lyric and Adam
raised the kind to its highest perfection, producing a proto-
type of the Bridegroom's song in Canticles. In the fallen world
Adam inaugurates the tragic lament-complaint, while Eve
transforms and perfects the kind, producing a prototype of
the penitential psalms. And since Adam and Eve's prayer of
repentance at the close of Book Ten is not quoted, Eve's lyric
stands as the highest exemplar of the psalmic lament.

As regards that prayer to God, Adam simply describes the
actions and motives which it should exhibit (10.1086-92), and
by repeating Adam's description almost exactly the Miltonic
Bard confirms that the prayer did indeed exhibit those motives
and dispositions:

                    they forthwith to the place
Repairing where he judg'd them prostrate fell
Before him reverent, and both confess'd
Humbly thir faults, and pardon begg'd, with tears
Watering the ground, and with thir sighs the Air
Frequenting, sent from hearts contrite, in sign
Of sorrow unfeign'd, and humilation meek.
(10.1098-1104)

The reasons for this strategy are indicated in the Son's inter-
cessory dialogue with the Father at the beginning of Book
Eleven. The Son notes that of themselves Adam and Eve can
produce only mute sighs and unskillful words, which he as
their Priest and Advocate must interpret and perfect: in their

252

stead and on their behalf he himself voices an eloquent prayer to the Father (11.22-44). Overcome by guilt and remorse and with their regenerate life barely begun, Adam and Eve are not yet able to compose lyrics of prayer and praise to God, even in the tragic mode.

TEN

"Not Less but More Heroic":
Prophecy and the Transformation
of Literary Forms

WITH GOD'S DIRECTIVE to Michael to "reveal / To *Adam* what shall come in future days, / As I shall thee enlighten, intermix / My Cov'nant in the woman's seed renew'd" (11.113-16), the Miltonic Bard changes his notes to prophetic, the mode through which fallen but redeemed humankind can come to terms with the woe of the fallen world. This prophetic mode informs and transforms the several literary genres and modes through which the matter of Books Eleven and Twelve is rendered.[1] Illumined by prophecy, Adam and Eve and their progeny are challenged to redefine and fuse the tragic, georgic, heroic, and pastoral values in their postlapsarian lives. Through prophecy also, they are allowed a prospect of the Apocalypse as a divine comedy in which all things will be made new, though the comedic mode itself no longer fits with human experience in the fallen world. Prophetic dialogue is also transformed: whereas Raphael engaged in "Venial discourse" with Adam, Michael uses dialogue as a sharp corrective instrument to purge Adam's moral blindness and to develop his spiritual understanding. And while prophecy pertaining to the fallen world calls forth the tragic lyrics of lament and complaint, it also makes possible restoration of the higher lyric forms—hymn, love lyric—as an evidence of humankind's redemption.

The genres Michael employs are specifically accommodated to his prophetic purposes: the tragic emblems and pageants through which he presents the antediluvian world, and the typological history and biblical brief epic through which he renders the course of events from Abraham to Apocalypse. As we have seen, Michael invents the prototypes of several mixed-genre works: D'Aubigné's epic-tragic-emblematic poem *Les Tragiques*, which presents biblical and contemporary history as aspects of the apocalyptic conflict of Christ and Antichrist; Augustine's *City of God*, which traces the perpetual warfare between the earthly and heavenly cities and the typological pattern of providential history; and Du Bartas' epic of biblical history, *La Seconde Semaine*.[2]

The principal model for the design of Books Eleven and Twelve as a mixed-genre work in the prophetic mode is the Book of Revelation. In Milton's age it was understood to present the epic conflict of Christ and Antichrist, God and Satan throughout history and at the end of time—a conflict in which the elect are also engaged, "fighting or a warfaring" against the forces of evil.[3] It was also seen as a "most long and dolefull Tragedy, which shall overflow with scourges, slaughters, destructions," and was therefore identified by Milton's contemporaries and by Milton himself as a model for Christian tragedy.[4] In addition, it was perceived as an "ecclesiastical history of the troubles and persecutions of the Church."[5] Pareus (and Milton) described its structure as a sequence of emblematic scenes or pageants requiring interpretation, with angelic hymns interspersed.[6] The book ends with a celestial pastoral scene and an epithalamic celebration of the marriage of the Lamb and his Bride.

THE PROPHETIC MODE

To prepare Adam for prophecy, Michael causes him to ascend a high hill, later termed "the top / Of Speculation" (12.588-89). He then removes from Adam's eyes the film produced by "that false Fruit that promis'd clearer sight," and purges them "with Euphrasy and Rue"—herbs said to cure or quicken the eyesight, and also associated, respectively, with cheerfulness and repentance.[7] Finally, he applies drops from the Well of

Life (grace), which pierce "Ev'n to the inmost seat of mental sight" (11.412-22).

The cure of Adam's vision prepares him for the method Michael employs in the first segment of his prophecy (in Book Eleven) to accomplish his first prophetic purpose, the cure of Adam's moral blindness. Michael shows Adam several tragic masques or pageants from antediluvian history displaying sin and its effects, all of which he must learn to see clearly and interpret properly as emblems. Specifically, these scenes present two of the three root sins commonly associated with the Fall—intemperance and vainglory; the third is ambition.[8] While the traditional "Triple Equation" does not go very far to explain the psychological and spiritual complexity of Milton's treatment of the Fall, the scene does incorporate that motif: Eve's sharp noontime appetite for the fruit and Adam's uxorious love for Eve are varieties of intemperance, Eve's desire to be a God is vainglory, and her desire to know good and evil is ambition.[9] Accordingly, when the pageants of Book Eleven elicit erroneous interpretations from Adam, Michael engages him in rigorous dialogic exchanges, teaching him to read history as a sequence of moral emblems manifesting the ravages of intemperance and vainglory, and also as a series of moral examples embodying the new heroism: Abel, Enoch, Noah. Michael also interprets the scenes apocalyptically, as images of a world given over to sin and subject to divine judgment, through which the Four Horsemen range at will— Death, War, Pestilence, and, in place of Famine, Flood.

Michael completes Adam's moral cure in Book Twelve by a shift in prophetic method. Intemperance and vainglory, sins stemming from blindness as to the true nature of man and his place in the cosmic order, were appropriately treated by forcing Adam to see clearly the effects of those sins. But the third root sin, ambition, involved for Adam and Eve the desire to know good and evil, and thereby to see as God sees. As a corrective to such ambition, Adam is told about but does not see Nimrod, whose unbridled ambition led him to become mankind's first tyrant and to defy God by building a tower intended to reach to heaven. From this point forward, Adam is forced to rely with humility and faith, and without confirmatory vision, upon the revelation of the angel.

There are also more fundamental reasons for Michael's change from vision to narration in the second segment of his prophecy. At the beginning of Book Twelve Michael calls attention to a change in Adam's condition: "I perceive / Thy mortal sight to fail; objects divine / Must needs impair and weary human sense" (12.8-10). Also, the new method is appropriate to Michael's second prophetic purpose: to develop and exercise Adam's faith, leading him to comprehend the typological pattern of history. Michael himself continues to receive his subject from God in visions—"I see him, but thou canst not" (12.128)—but he then presents those visions to Adam by narration and description, the common manner of revelation in scripture.

Adam and Eve's regeneration is presented in Books Ten to Twelve according to the Miltonic paradigm outlined in the *Christian Doctrine*.[10] After the Fall they experience the several degrees of "death" attendant upon sin—guiltiness, shame, terrors of conscience, the obscuration of right reason, and the death of the will. In their prayer at the end of Book Ten they manifest the first effect of regeneration, repentance. They also display faith in the promise proclaimed to them in the woman's Seed, but as yet they understand almost nothing about that promise. At this stage their faith is the "implicit" faith Milton ascribes to "novices and new converts who believe even before they enter upon a course of instruction."[11] They have yet to exhibit the second effect of regeneration, saving faith, defined by Milton as "THE FIRM PERSUASION IMPLANTED IN US BY THE GIFT OF GOD, BY VIRTUE OF WHICH WE BELIEVE, ON THE AUTHORITY OF GOD'S PROMISE, THAT ALL THOSE THINGS WHICH GOD HAS PROMISED US IN CHRIST ARE OURS, AND ESPECIALLY THE GRACE OF ETERNAL LIFE."[12] Michael's biblical narrative and the dialogues it provokes are designed to provide the requisite course of instruction, so as to advance Adam's understanding of and faith in the messianic covenant.

In its substance, Michael's entire prophecy and especially the narrative in Book Twelve expand upon Hebrews 11. As does that epistle, Michael describes a typological progression of exemplary Old Testament heroes of faith, culminating in the antitype, Christ; and he emphasizes the same Pauline examples: Abel, Enoch, Noah (in Book Eleven), and Abraham, Moses, the warring judges and kings, and the multitudes who suffer for their faith (in Book Twelve). The Pauline epistles also provide the explicit rationale for Michael's shift from vision to narrative as a means of developing Adam's faith. Hebrews 11:1 defines faith as "the substance of things hoped for, the evidence of things not seen"; and Romans 10:17 declares that "Faith cometh by hearing" the Word of God.[13] Accordingly, Adam and his progeny receive a revelation addressed not to the eyes but the ears.

Adam does not see the increasingly spiritual manifestations of the Covenant of Grace beginning with Abraham, but his spiritual vision grows keener as his physical vision declines. He now stands before Michael as any Christian stands before the interpreters of the Word of God in scripture: he hears an account of biblical history, he often responds to it inappropriately, he advances under constant correction "From shadowy types to truth" (12.303), and he learns thereby to understand and praise God's providence. Throughout the prophecy, moreover, he identifies very closely with his progeny, and his faith reflects theirs at the appropriate historical stage of development. He denounces the villainy of his murderous son Cain, weeps over Noah's flood, perceives the rigor of the Mosaic Law, and at length attains the fullness of Christian faith as he formally acknowledges his son Jesus as his Redeemer.

When Michael and Adam descend the Mount of Speculation to meet Eve we discover that she has also participated in the prophetic experience through dreams—a lesser but yet important prophetic mode. Michael indicates simply that he has calmed her with "gentle Dreams," directing Adam at fit season to "Let her with thee partake what thou hast heard," so that they may be unanimous in faith (12.595-606). But when Eve greets the returning pair she seems already to have general though not specific knowledge of what has transpired: "Whence thou return'st, and whither went'st, I know; / For God is also in sleep, and Dreams advise, / Which he hath sent propitious, some great good / Presaging" (12.610-13). Between them, Adam and Eve embody the two kinds of prophecy specified in Joel 2:28: "I will pour out my spirit upon all flesh: and your sons and your daughters shall prophesy, your old men shall dream dreams, your young men shall see visions."

CORRECTIVE DIALOGUE: EDUCATION
FOR THE FALLEN WORLD

The scenes and the biblical narratives Michael presents elicit interpretations and questions from Adam, leading to dialogue. In the postlapsarian world, as in Eden, dialogue remains the chief means of education,[14] though it is now a more arduous and painful process. Adam's marred intellect causes him to make much more frequent and more egregious mistakes, necessitating harsher reproofs and more explicit corrections. Nevertheless, Adam is expected and encouraged to take an active role in interpreting the prophecy mediated to him by Michael, and to learn through a strenuous dialogic process of trial and error, faulty formulation and correction.

As Adam views the emblematic historical pageants he responds, often inappropriately, with amazement, dismay, grief, or pleasure. But the dialogues lead him to recognize in all these scenes a reprise of his own sins of intemperance, vainglory, and ambition, and to recognize the many forms of death they cause, as well as to identify with the few just whose virtue challenges the wicked multitude.

The first pageant, Cain's murder of Abel, forces Adam to a vicarious experience of death, the wages of his original sin. Shocked at the brutal scene, he does not at first know what has happened to the devout shepherd, but queries how it can accord with divine justice: "Is Piety thus and pure Devotion

259

paid?" (11.452). Michael, also moved by the sight, declares that God will avenge the murder and reward the just man, and then identifies both murderer and victim as Adam's sons. Adam's vivid imagination makes literal and personal application of this painful new knowledge: "But have I now seen Death? Is this the way / I must return to native dust? O sight / Of terror, foul and ugly to behold, / Horrid to think, how horrible to feel!" (11.462-65).

To correct this too-limited concept of death, Michael shows Adam a lazar house in which loathsome diseases resulting from "th' inabstinence of Eve" cause lingering death. In tears, Adam complains that man as God's image should be spared such degradation, but Michael insists that intemperance has now debased that divine image in man past recognition. Adam is forced to "yield it just," but then asks about other forms of death. In response, Michael urges temperance in food and drink as the means to long life and natural death, but concludes with a grim account of the miseries and decrepitude that attend upon old age. This exchange culminates in Adam's resolve to await his appointed day with patience and Michael's advice to concentrate on living well, "how long or short permit to Heav'n" (11.554).

The next pageant relates more closely to Adam's own form of intemperance: the wedding of the sons of God with the daughters of Cain (Gen. 6:2-4), complete with all manner of sensuous delights—song, dance, feasting, beautiful women. At this sight Adam falls into his old error of overvaluing female charms and supposing them the ends of nature: "True opener of mine eyes, prime Angel blest, / Much better seems this Vision / . . . Here Nature seems fulfill'd in all her ends" (11.598-602). Correcting him, Michael underscores the danger of judging worth by pleasing appearances—"Judge not what is best / By pleasure, though to Nature seeming meet, / Created, as thou art, to nobler end" (11.603-605)—and he proceeds to reveal the licentiousness and wicked wiles of these women. That revelation elicits from Adam a reprise of his earlier accusation of Eve: "But still I see the tenor of Man's woe /

Holds on the same, from Woman to begin" (11.632-33). But Michael (like the Son at the Judgment) gives short shrift to Adam's misogynist blame-shifting, sternly demanding that he face the truth of his situation: "From Man's effeminate slackness it begins, / . . . who should better hold his place / By wisdom, and superior gifts receiv'd" (11.634-36).[15]

The next scene displays vainglory—the desire to be as gods—leading to war and wholesale slaughter. Giants, sprung from the sinful marriages just viewed, transform a peaceful pastoral landscape with fleecy sheep and bleating lambs into a bloody battlefield strewn "With Carcasses and Arms" (11.654). Adam "all in tears," asks the cause, and Michael responds with a scathing denunciation of those who pursue glory through military might, desiring "to be styl'd great Conquerors, / Patrons of Mankind, Gods, and Sons of Gods" (11.695-96). Enoch provides the contrasting model, "The only righteous in a World perverse," transported to heaven in glory.

Adam next sees the entire world depraved by luxury and corruption, and in consequence, the almost total annihilation of life on earth in the great Flood. At this point, Adam identifies very closely indeed with his progeny, experiencing their pain and replicating their Flood in his own tears:

> How didst thou grieve then, *Adam*, to behold
> The end of all thy Offspring, end so sad,
> Depopulation; thee another Flood,
> Of tears and sorrow a Flood thee also drown'd,
> And sunk thee as thy Sons.
> (11.754-58)

To Adam's queries as to whether the Flood will end the race of man, Michael responds by recounting the story of Noah and then pointing to the final pageant: Noah saved in his Ark, the Flood ended, and the sign of the rainbow given. Adam now demonstrates his moral and spiritual progress by his unwitting description of Noah as type of Messiah, and also by his right interpretation of the rainbow as a sign of peace restored between God and humankind. Michael warmly com-

mends his pupil's progress in the interpretation of emblems—
"Dext'rously thou aim'st"—and then reads the emblem more
fully, as a divine covenant never to destroy the earth again by
flood.

Adam's education in the effects of sin and the development
of moral virtue culminates with Nimrod, the mighty hunter
"of proud ambitious heart" who became mankind's first tyrant
(12.24-101). Adam, "fatherly displeas'd," denounces this
"execrable Son" who extended over his fellow man the do-
minion nature gives only over beasts, but Michael, though
commending that judgment, explains that political tyranny has
its roots in the loss of true government over the self caused
by Adam's sin. Adam is to recognize that Nimrod's Tower of
Babel, intended to penetrate heaven, replicates Eve's ambi-
tious desire to know good and evil; he is also to understand
from Nimrod's tyranny that personal and political morality are
inseparable.

Partly overlapping with Michael's program to educate Adam
in moral virtue is his project to develop and exercise Adam's
faith—also through corrective dialogue. Among the pageants
of Book Eleven Adam sees three figures—Abel, Enoch, and
Noah—who are at once examples of rightousness and virtue
in the midst of corruption and also types of the Messiah to
come. Moreover, Adam's last vision is itself a type of the
promised messianic redemption, in that it presents the almost
total destruction of the world, the "one just man" for whose
sake God spared the human race, and a new covenant between
God and man signified by the rainbow. Adam's faith now
parallels and echoes that of his elect son, Noah, who "con-
demned the world" in building the Ark (Hebrews 11:7). Adam
condemns it verbally, as of far less worth than the just Noah
and the new world to come: "Far less I now lament for one
whole World / Of wicked Sons destroy'd, than I rejoice / For
one Man found so perfet and so just, / That God voutsafes to
raise another World / From him, and all his anger to forget"
(11.874-78). Michael concludes this exchange and this seg-
ment of his prophecy by reading the Flood and the subse-

quent restoration of nature anagogically, as types of the Apocalypse and millennium, when fire will "purge all things new, / Both Heav'n and Earth, wherein the just shall dwell" (11.898-901).

Adam's physical vision is adequate to that form of the Covenant of Grace which pertains to his own antediluvian world—the Law of Nature, which is in some measure renewed after the Fall in the hearts of the regenerate.[16] Also, like the patriarchs in the first age, Adam's faith is at first developed through visual types. But Adam cannot see with bodily vision the more spiritual forms of the Covenant of Grace or the typological significance of the various biblical heroes of faith—the substance of Book Twelve. Accordingly, though Michael's own visions continue, he presents them to Adam in narrative form. First, however, he pauses to see "If *Adam* aught perhaps might interpose" (12.4), indicating thereby that he intends the dialogues to continue. As he begins to exercise Adam in the interpretation of biblical revelation, the angel invites him to identify closely with Abraham who was also led by faith: "I see him, but thou canst not, with what Faith / He leaves his Gods, his Friends, and native Soil" (12.128-29).

In describing Abraham, called by God to inhabit Canaan (a type of the Heavenly City), Michael emphasizes the covenant by which God designated Abraham's seed as his chosen people in whom all nations would be blessed. The angel's cryptic comment—"by that Seed / Is meant thy great deliverer, who shall bruise / The Serpent's head; whereof to thee anon / Plainlier shall be reveal'd" (11.148-51)—again underscores the fact that Adam comes to understand the types much as his progeny do at any given historical stage. His faith parallels theirs, and develops through his vicarious identification with them.

In keeping with his emphasis upon the covenant, Michael refers very briefly to Jacob and Joseph, but recounts at length the wonders attending Moses' deliverance of the Israelites from Egyptian slavery: the plagues, the Red Sea crossing; the pillars of cloud and fire; the passage through Jordan into the Promised Land. For these events he supplies an extended typolog-

ical exegesis, noting that Moses foreshadows Christ as Savior
and Mediator, and that the Law delivered on Mount Sinai
foretells,

> by types
> And shadows, of that destin'd Seed to bruise
> The Serpent, by what means he shall achieve
> Mankind's deliverance. But the voice of God
> To mortal ear is dreadful; they beseech
> That *Moses* might report to them his will,
> And terror cease; he grants what they besought,
> Instructed that to God is no access
> Without Mediator, whose high Office now
> *Moses* in figure bears, to introduce
> One greater, of whose day he shall foretell.
> (12.232-42)

Adam interrupts Michael's summary of the conquest of Ca-
naan and of Joshua's role with a joyful cry testifying to but
overestimating his new clarity of spiritual vision. Addressing
the angel as "Enlight'ner of my darkness" he proclaims, "now
first I find / Mine eyes true op'ning" (12.271-74). Again, Ad-
am's faith parallels that of the sons he is observing, in this case
Moses who according to Hebrews 11:27 "endured, as seeing
him who is invisible." Adam alludes to this verse and also
anticipates the cry of Simeon upon beholding the infant Christ
(Luke 2:25-32) as he declares, "but now I see / His day, in
whom all Nations shall be blest" (12.276-79). Adam's growth
in spiritual knowledge is evident when he perceives, untu-
tored, that the multitude of laws argues a multitude of sins,
but he requires Michael to clarify for him the educative func-
tion of the Law in uncovering sins that it cannot remove. At
this juncture, Michael explains very clearly the typological thrust
of Old Testament history, and of his own narrative summa-
rizing that history:

> So Law appears imperfet, and but giv'n
> With purpose to resign them in full time

Up to a better Cov'nant, disciplin'd
From shadowy Types to Truth, from Flesh to Spirit,
From imposition of strict Laws, to free
Acceptance of large Grace, from servile fear
To filial, works of Law to works of Faith.
And therefore shall not *Moses*, though of God
Highly belov'd, being but the Minister
Of Law, his people into *Canaan* lead;
But *Joshua* whom the Gentiles *Jesus* call,
His Name and Office bearing, who shall quell
The adversary Serpent, and bring back
Through the world's wilderness long wander'd man
Safe to eternal Paradise of rest.
                    (12.300-14)

After a brief resumé of the kings, of David's reign, and of
the Babylonian captivity and its aftermath, Michael narrates
the virgin birth of the Messiah. At this juncture Adam pro-
claims forcefully that at last he fully understands the prophecy
concerning the seed of the woman: "O Prophet of glad tid-
ings, finisher / Of utmost hope! now clear I understand / What
oft my steadiest thoughts have searcht in vain" (12.375-77).
But, ironically, he still has one area of spiritual myopia. Even
as his Hebrew progeny expected a warfaring Messiah King to
restore and rule Israel, Adam expects a physical combat be-
tween Messiah and the Serpent: "Needs must the Serpent now
his capital bruise / Expect with mortal pain: say where and when /
Thir fight, what stroke shall bruise the Victor's heel" (12.383-
85). Correcting him firmly but kindly—"Dream not of thir
fight, / As of a Duel"—Michael tells how Jesus will conquer
Satan, Sin, and Death in humankind through obedience and
love which fulfill the Law, and through his death which sat-
isfies God's justice.

Michael's story of Messiah, culminating with his Ascension,
its antitype the Last Judgment, and the eternal bliss of the
faithful, elicits from Adam an ecstatic praise of God's good-
ness. His subsequent perceptive insight as to the fate of Christ's

followers in the world—"will they not deal / Worse with his followers than with him they dealt?" (12.483-84)—is confirmed by Michael's account of the continued ascendancy of evil in the world, until the apocalyptic destruction of "*Satan* with his perverted World" and the millennial restoration of all things. Led by the angel's revelation to comprehend the entire design of God's providence, Adam can now view the long course of human history in prophetic terms, as a "Race of time." His faith now perfected, he takes Jesus as his example for life in the fallen world, and formally acknowledges him "my Redeemer ever blest." But Michael has one further lesson to teach. Commending Adam's perfected faith as the "sum / Of wisdom," he directs Adam to perform "Deeds . . . answerable" to that wisdom, that is, to practice the virtues of faith, patience, temperance, and charity.

PROPHECY AND THE LITERARY MODES

Prophecy also transforms the literary modes used to render postlapsarian human life, and promotes the combination of those modes. In Books Nine and Ten Milton focused upon Adam and Eve as protagonists of an Aristotelian and then a Christian tragedy.[17] In Books Eleven and Twelve the focus widens to epic scale, portraying the impact of this particular tragic Fall upon the course of human history. Specifically, as Adam and Eve learn to define themselves and their lives in the terms set by prophecy, they and their progeny, all humankind, also learn what it is to act heroically, to endure harsh georgic cares and responsibilities, and to seek an internal pastoral *otium* amid the tragic woes that now condition human life.

The terrible changes in nature and in human nature described as the aftermath of the Fall in Book Ten are now shown to blight the external world for all time. Sin and Death, who were static allegorical figures in Book Two, have gained awful power from Satan's victory, and their first ravages in Eden are now multiplied and writ large throughout history. Also, God's adjustments in the cosmos give rise to harsh climatic conditions which render human life and work difficult, rigorous, and painful. These changes are irreversible, despite the spiritual restoration wrought by grace in the regenerate. Moreover, Michael's prophecy shows that the regenerate few cannot work any enduring reformations in the world, since they are always vastly outnumbered by the wicked masses in whom the sins of Adam and Eve reign.

The full horror of these conditions emerges in Book Eleven as Adam and Eve continue the process of discovery, attended by tragic irony. When their repentant prayer produces some spiritual comfort, Eve proposes that they go forth as usual to tend the Garden, not imagining how utterly changed their life will now be: "What can be toilsome in these pleasant Walks? / Here let us live, though in fall'n state, content" (11.178-80). But almost immediately, Michael comes to pronounce the decree of banishment upon them, which Eve laments as an "unexpected stroke, worse than of Death." Adam then witnesses in the historical pageants the extent of the changes wrought by Sin and Death. The first death Adam sees, Cain's brutal murder of Abel, evokes shock and horror. The "racking torture" and "heart-sick Agony" attending the countless varieties of illness in the lazar house wring bitter tears from him. At length he is forced to conclude that all human conditions conduce to evil—war to violence and slaughter, peace to luxury, corruption, and degeneracy (11.783-84).

Michael indicates that the world after the Flood is also permeated by evil and continues to decline: "Thus will this latter, as the former World, / Still tend from bad to worse" (12.105-106). And after Christ's ascension these external conditions remain unchanged: "so shall the World go on, / To good malignant, to bad men benign, / Under her own weight groaning" (12.537-39). We now recognize the precise nature of the tragedy to which the poem's title points: Paradise, the external world shaped to human needs and desires, is forever lost, and the world in which postlapsarian men and women must live and act is fraught with misery, evil, and woe.

But while postlapsarian human life is perceived as tragic by

Adam and the reader, that mode is transformed by prophecy so as to produce a special kind of catharsis. First comes the painful cleansing of Adam's moral vision as the tragic pageants force him to see the fallen world clear: "His eyes he op'n'd"; "He look'd and saw"; "O Visions ill foreseen!" Then, by degrees, the emphasis shifts to the divine *peripeteia* of grace. The parade of the few just who stand apart from the corrupt multitude and serve God—Abel, Enoch, Noah, Abraham, Moses, the disciples of Christ—testifies that the processes of regeneration begun in Adam and Eve continue throughout history. Also, the divine *anagnorisis* begun with the proclamation of the protoevangelion at the judgment of Adam and Eve continues in the biblical revelation summarized by Michael, curing the spiritual blindness produced by sin. And while the pain, loss, and death resulting from the Fall extend the scene of suffering throughout all time, the mental anguish of the regenerate is alleviated through faith and hope, and their despair is transformed into patient endurance as they await the fulfillment of the divine promises in the Apocalypse.

At moments of most intense prophetic insight, Adam experiences a foretaste of comedic joy as he anticipates Messiah's redemption and the apocalyptic re-creation of all things. When Adam views a type of that redemption and restoration in Noah, his sorrow is for the time outweighed by joy: "Far less I now lament for one whole World / Of wicked Sons destroy'd, than I rejoice / For one Man found so perfet and so just, / That God voutsafes to raise another World / From him, and all his anger to forget" (11.874-78). Upon hearing of the birth of Messiah, Adam is "with . . . joy / Surcharg'd" (12.372-73); and upon hearing of the redemption Christ will accomplish and of the final bliss of the faithful he is "Replete with joy and wonder" (12.468).

However, Adam experiences such comedic joy only at moments of special insight: neither he nor Milton's readers can hold that perspective for long. Prophecy does not transform the tragedy of the Fall into comedy or tragicomedy, but rather helps to produce the catharsis of Christian tragedy, whereby our terror and pity are "tempered and reduced" through comprehension of the divine plan and an earnest of future joys.[18] Michael's last words to Adam urge him to meet his future life in such terms: "sad, / With cause for evils past, yet much more cheer'd / With meditation on the happy end." We are to see that faith and hope in that ultimate comedic resolution can sustain and console Adam and Eve in their present and future miseries, allowing them (and us) to go forth from the tragedy just experienced, "sorrowing, yet in peace" (11.117).

The prophetic mode also interpenetrates and transforms the pastoral and the georgic modes. As we have seen, the tragedy of postlapsarian life stems in large part from the entire destruction of Edenic pastoral and the *otium* it fostered. That destruction begins immediately after the Fall as the animals who disported themselves before Adam and Eve in entire harmony are transformed into predators and prey (10.707-14, 11.185-93). At the end of Book Eleven, as Adam witnesses the utter ruin of all earth's loveliness in the Flood, the last vestiges of Edenic pastoral are also obliterated:

> all the Cataracts
> Of Heav'n set open on the Earth shall pour
> Rain day and night, all fountains of the Deep
> Broke up, shall heave the Ocean to usurp
> Beyond all bounds, till inundation rise
> Above the highest Hills: then shall this Mount
> Of Paradise by might of Waves be mov'd
> Out of his place, push'd by the horned flood,
> With all his verdure spoil'd, and Trees adrift
> Down the great River to the op'ning Gulf,
> And there take root an Island salt and bare,
> The haunt of Seals and Orcs, and Sea-mews' clang.
>   (11.824-35)

In the postlapsarian world pastoral is replaced by a harsh and bitter georgic: Adam and Eve must labor in the stony earth for bread and must endure seasonal extremes of climate—"pinching cold and scorching heat" (10.691). Also, they must cultivate the sinful self, not through "venial discourse" but through rigorous corrective dialogue. However, prophecy also enables Adam to come to terms with that postlapsarian georgic world. Michael assuages his dismay at leaving the Edenic places sanctified by God's familiar presence by assuring him that all the earth (not Eden alone) is imbued with the divine Omnipresence and was designed for man's habitation: "surmise not then / His presence to these narrow bounds confin'd / Of Paradise or *Eden*: this had been / Perhaps thy Capital Seat, from whence had spread / All generations, and had hither come / From all the ends of th' Earth" (11.340-45). Also, as Adam witnesses the restoration of the earth and its georgic conditions after the Flood, Michael describes the cyclic patterns of seasonal change and human work as a divine blessing in the fallen world: "Day and Night, / Seed-time and Harvest, Heat and hoary Frost / Shall hold thir course, till fire purge all things new, / Both Heav'n and Earth, wherein the just shall dwell" (11.898-901).

Through prophecy also, Adam can anticipate a millennial pastoral world more perfect that the Edenic pastoral—though that also is a matter of faith and hope, not present experience. Michael's first account of Messiah's mission concludes with a brief reference to the reward of the faithful in pastoral terms: "for then the Earth / Shall all be Paradise, far happier place / Than this of *Eden*, and far happier days" (12.463-65). Later, he supplies a few more details, indicating that at the Apocalypse the Son will dissolve,

> *Satan* with his perverted World, then raise
> From the conflagrant mass, purg'd and refin'd,
> New Heav'ns, new Earth, Ages of endless date
> Founded in righteousness and peace and love,
> To bring forth fruits Joy and eternal Bliss.
> (12.546-51)

Finally, Books Eleven and Twelve are cast in the heroic mode, transformed by prophecy into a new Christian heroism of "Patience and Heroic Martyrdom" appropriate to the fallen world. Michael comes to Adam clad in a "military Vest of purple," and introduces his prophecy with an epic statement of theme: "Expect to hear, supernal Grace contending / With sinfulness of Men; thereby to learn / True patience" (11.359-61). This proposition identifies Michael's prophetic subject as an epic battle transferred to the moral and spiritual plane, a biblical counterpart to Raphael's Homeric brief epic. Adam relates himself to that combat by turning "to the evil" his "obvious breast, arming to overcome / By suffering" (11.373-75).

The old martial heroism is now categorically repudiated as Adam laments in tears the massacres wrought by the giants, and Michael castigates the battle glory sought by the old epic heroes:

> For in those days Might only shall be admir'd,
> And Valor and Heroic Virtue call'd;
> To overcome in Battle, and subdue
> Nations, and bring home spoils with infinite
> Man-slaughter, shall be held the highest pitch
> Of human Glory, and for Glory done
> Of triumph, to be styl'd great Conquerors,
> Patrons of Mankind, Gods, and Sons of Gods,
> Destroyers rightlier call'd, and Plagues of men.
> Thus Fame shall be achiev'd, renown on Earth,
> And what most merits fame in silence hid.
> (11.689-99)

By contrast, Michael's prophecy presents a moral and spiritual battle waged through history, in which not the power but the grace of God is pitted against the plenipotentiaries of Satan, Sin and Death.

In the pageants of Book Eleven Sin and Death are everywhere ascendant, their fearsome power emblematized in the lazar house scene where "triumphant Death his Dart / Shook, but delay'd to strike" (11.491-92). Against them are posed the moral and spiritual victories against evil won by notable heroes of virtue and faith—Enoch, Noah, Moses, David. The

271

battle is joined more directly in Book Twelve, where Nimrod and Abraham are presented as the political architects of Augustine's two cities: Nimrod who instituted tyrannical government in the City of Man; Abraham who founded the elect nation, the City of God on earth, saved by faith in the Promises. The turning point in the vast moral battle is the decisive defeat of Sin and Death at Messiah's crucifixion, followed by the humiliation of Satan who was dragged "in Chains / Through all his Realm" at Christ's Ascension (12.429-55). But despite these victories Sin and Death retain their dominance over the world: ambitious rulers still persecute the Church, wolves infest the Church's sheepfold, and Truth is continually "Bestuck with sland'rous darts." Michael makes very clear that the Kingdom of God will not be established on earth until the Second Coming.

But he also makes clear that in these tragic circumstances the faithful are called to, and are enabled to, exercise some version of the new heroism—unwavering faith and love, moral courage, patient endurance. In the Christian era especially Adam's progeny are armed better than before "With spiritual Armor, able to resist / *Satan's* assaults, and quench his fiery darts," and are empowered to win against their persecutors the victory of the better fortitude (12.485-550). The entire thrust of Michael's prophecy is against any kind of passivity, spiritual, moral, or even political. In every age the few just have the responsibility to oppose, if God calls them to do so, the Nimrods or the Pharaohs or the royalist persecutors of the Church, even though (like the loyal angels) they can win no decisive public victories and can effect no lasting reforms until the Son appears.[19] But prophecy emboldens them for those heroic struggles by strengthening their faith and hope in the final epic victory at the Apocalypse, which will be won by the Son of God fighting for and with Adam's progeny against all the powers of Satan, Sin, and Death.

At the close of Michael's prophecy, Adam proclaims his determination to live in accordance with the transformed and combined heroic-tragic-georgic values defined in that prophecy:

Henceforth I learn, that to obey is best,
And love with fear the only God, to walk
As in his presence, ever to observe
His providence, and on him sole depend,
Merciful over all his works, with good
Still overcoming evil, and by small
Accomplishing great things, by things deem'd weak
Subverting worldly strong, and worldy wise
By simply meek; that suffering for Truth's sake
Is fortitude to highest victory,
And to the faithful Death the Gate of Life.
                    (12.561-71)

Adam also displays his moral growth by taking Christ as model
for that new heroic-tragic-georgic life, and he proclaims his
mature faith by formally acknowledging Christ "my Redeemer
ever blest" (12.573). Warmly approving Adam's declaration
as the "sum of wisdom," Michael indicates that Adam and Eve
can also incorporate a pastoral element in the mixture of modes
that will characterize their new life. Through the practice of
virtue they may attain a paradise within, a new *otium* of con-
tentment and spiritual peace far excelling the external *otium* of
Eden:

                                   only add
Deeds to thy knowledge answerable, add Faith,
Add Virtue, Patience, Temperance, add Love,
By name to come call'd Charity, the soul
Of all the rest: then wilt thou not be loath
To leave this Paradise, but shalt possess
A paradise within thee, happier far.
                    (12.581-87).

PROPHECY AND THE LYRIC GENRES

Michael's prophecy also evokes lyric responses from Adam and
Eve, comprising a large repertoire of postlapsarian lyric kinds.
These embedded lyrics, occurring naturally enough at mo-

273

ments of intense emotional pressure, encapsulate Adam and
Eve's psychological and spiritual progress from bitter grief for
loss, to joy in the anticipated apocalyptic renewal of all things,
to consolation arising from acceptance of the mixed modes of
postlapsarian daily life.

In Book Eleven Michael's prophecy gives rise to tragic lyr-
ics. Eve's "audible lament" upon hearing the decree of banish-
ment is formally an *apobaterion*—a sad leave-taking of home
and country upon going into exile. We should recall Satan's
truncated *apobaterion* for loss of heaven ("Farewell happy
Fields," 1.249-52), and note that unlike Satan Eve can voice
her sorrow for loss of Eden in a poignantly lovely, finished
lyric.[20] Her *apobaterion* also incorporates elements of the fu-
neral dirge, and is thereby a prototype of the funeral poetry
so prominent in the fallen world where death is ubiquitous.
She sees the loss of paradise as worse than death, robbing her
of an identity largely defined through the experiences and as-
sociations of this place, and condemning to death her surro-
gate children, the flowers she named and nurtured from tender
buds:

> O unexpected stroke, worse than of Death!
> Must I thus leave thee Paradise? thus leave
> Thee Native Soil, these happy Walks and Shades,
> Fit haunt of Gods? where I had hope to spend,
> Quiet though sad, the respite of that day
> That must be mortal to us both. O flow'rs,
> That never will in other Climate grow,
> My early visitation, and my last
> At Ev'n, which I bred up with tender hand
> From the first op'ning bud, and gave ye Names,
> Who now shall rear ye to the Sun, or rank
> Your Tribes, and water from th' ambrosial Fount?
> Thee lastly nuptial Bower, by mee adorn'd
> With what to sight or smell was sweet; from thee
> How shall I part, and whither wander down
> Into a lower World, to this obscure

And wild, how shall we breathe in other Air
Less pure, accustom'd to immortal Fruits?
(11.268-85)

Mildly rebuking Eve's overfond attachment to Eden as physical place, the angel reminds her that she does not go forth
alone but with her husband, to find a new native soil.
Adam's characteristic tragic lyric genre remains the complaint.[21] He is moved so profoundly by two of the tragic pageants, the lazar house and the Flood scene, that he pours bitter
"plaints" (11.499, 762), and we recognize that this genre is
also endemic to the fallen world, called forth whenever the
effects of sin and death are encountered with special force.
Recognizing Adam's emotional distress, Michael answers but
does not reprove his implicit questioning of God's ways and
God's justice. Adam's outcry upon seeing the lazar house—
"O miserable Mankind, to what fall / Degraded, to what
wretched state reserv'd! / Better end here unborn" (11.500-
502)—is followed by agonized questions as to why life with
such suffering was given at all or was prolonged, and why
God's image in man is subjected to so great degradation
(11.501-13). Upon viewing the Flood Adam weeps uncontrollably, "as when a Father mourns / His Children, all in view
destroy'd at once" (11.754-62) and then complains bitterly
that the prophecy has brought him such terrible foreknowledge:

O Visions ill foreseen! better had I
Liv'd ignorant of future, so had borne
My part of evil only, each day's lot
Anough to bear; those now, that were dispens't
The burd'n of many Ages, on me light
At once, by my foreknowledge.
(11.763-68)

Ironically, in this complaint Adam unwittingly associates himself with God, as a father also unable to forestall disaster to
his offspring despite his foreknowledge.

At the close of the epic the higher lyric forms are reclaimed by fallen man and woman, who now have a more settled hope of redemption and restoration. When Adam is told of Messiah and at last understands the meaning of the protoevangelion, he voices an ecstataic hymn in some ways reminiscent of verses from the *"Exsultet"* hymn sung in the Holy Saturday liturgy at the blessing of the paschal candle:

> O mira circa nos tuae pietatis dignatio!
> O inestimabilis dilectio caritatis!
> Ut servum redimeres filium tradidisti!
> O certe necessarium Adae peccatum,
> quod Christi morte delectum est!
> O felix culpa, quae talum ac tantum
> meruit habere redemptorem![22]

These verses were variously echoed and paraphrased in several medieval and Renaissance hymns, sermons, and devotional works, including an apostrophe spoken by Mercy in Salandra's tragedy, *Adamo Caduto* (1647): "O happy Sin / O blessed crime / O precious theft / Dear Disobedience / Adam, blest thief not of the Apple / But of Mercy, Clemency, and Glory."[23]

But Adam's hymn in *Paradise Lost* departs significantly from these models. At no point does Adam invoke the paradoxical medieval formula to praise the Fall itself as a "happy fault," nor does he view the Fall in romantic terms as a necessary stimulus to human growth and development. Rather, he expresses mixed emotions, with grief and repentance for his sin outweighed by joy that God has made of the Fall an occasion for manifesting his surpassing goodness in restoring humankind. In Adam's ecstatic lyric, postlapsarian hymnody is fully restored after the perversion of the genre in Eve's idolatrous hymn to the Tree. Adam's hymn conforms to the strictest Christian concept of the kind,[24] since it is directed wholly to the praise of God's goodness:

> O goodness infinite, goodness immense!
> That all this good of evil shall produce,

And evil turn to good; more wonderful
Than that which by creation first brought forth
Light out of darkness! full of doubt I stand,
Whether I should repent me now of sin
By mee done and occasion'd, or rejoice
Much more, that much more good thereof shall spring,
To God more glory, more good will to Men
From God, and over wrath grace shall abound.
(12.469-78)

Then Eve, who composed the first love lyric in Eden (4.639-56), reclaims that genre from its Petrarchan perversions by Satan. When Eve awakens from her prophetic dream and meets Adam returned from the mountain, she voices a love poem appropriate to the fallen world. In substance and tone it echoes Ruth's loving and faithful promise to follow Naomi to another homeland: "whither thou goest, I will go; and where thou lodgest, I will lodge / . . . Where thou diest, will I die, and there will I be buried" (Ruth 1:16-17). Eve's postlapsarian love song is much simpler than her elegant love lyric in Book Four, but it retains some of the same artful rhetorical schemes and it develops the same theme—that Adam is her true Eden:

> In mee is no delay; with thee to go,
> Is to stay here; without thee here to stay,
> Is to go hence unwillling; thou to mee
> Art all things under Heav'n, all places thou,
> Who for my wilful crime art banisht hence.
> (12.615-19)

At this point, in the last words we hear in Eden, Eve rises above lyric, and moves beyond her role as protagonist in the tragedy of the Fall, to embrace her divinely appointed, central role in the epic of Redemption. Illumined by her prophetic dream, she articulates her own version of the new Christian heroism: "though all by mee is lost, / Such favor I unworthy am voutsaf't / By mee the Promis'd Seed shall all restore."

MILTON'S poignant, quiet, marvelously evocative final lines are elegiac in substance and tone. As he describes Adam and Eve led down from the heights of the Garden to the "subjected Plain" he holds in perfect equipose elegiac sadness for loss, and the consolation which the greatest elegies (such as *Lycidas*) traditionally afford. The sense of loss is reinforced by images of "our ling'ring Parents" dropping their "natural tears"; by the flaming brand waved over Paradise "so late thir happy seat"; by their "wand'ring steps and slow" as they make their "solitary" way through Eden. The consolation arises from the wiping of those tears; from the recognition that "The World was all before them, where to choose / Thir place of rest"; from the fact that Providence is still "thir guide"; and from the human comfort of their love as they face the unknown, "hand in hand."

This remarkable elegiac fusion of loss and consolation is also promoted by the adjustments of the perspective glass which the reader (like Adam) must make as the poem ends. Suddenly time, which Adam perceived through prophecy as a brief "Race" compassed all round by the "abyss" of eternity, stretches out before him as an all but impenetrable future. Yet not quite impenetrable. Adam has seen with heightened spiritual vision that his wandering way will end at long last in the Promised Land; that the long struggle of good and evil throughout history will end in heroic victory for Christ-Adam-mankind; that the descent from Eden will culminate in an ascent to the loftier heights of the New Jerusalem; that the destruction and chaos caused by Sin and Death will give way to the re-creation of a new pastoral heaven and earth. But all that is yet to come. From the end of time we are suddenly and startlingly translated back to the beginning again as Adam and Eve go forth to live out all our woe and to await the enactment of all that has been foreseen.

> In either hand the hast'ning Angel caught
> Our ling'ring Parents, and to th' Eastern Gate
> Led them direct, and down the Cliff as fast

To the subjected Plain; then disappear'd.
They looking back, all th' Eastern side beheld
Of Paradise, so late thir happy seat,
Wav'd over by that flaming Brand, the Gate
With dreadful Faces throng'd and fiery Arms:
Some natural tears they dropp'd, but wip'd them soon;
The World was all before them, where to choose
Thir place of rest, and Providence thir guide:
They hand in hand with wand'ring steps and slow,
Through *Eden* took thir solitary way.

(12.637-49)

Notes

CHAPTER 1. *Paradise Lost* AS ENCYCLOPEDIC EPIC:
THE USES OF LITERARY FORMS

1. See especially C. M. Bowra, *From Virgil to Milton* (London: Macmillan, 1944); Davis P. Harding, *The Club of Hercules: Studies in the Classical Background of Paradise Lost* (Urbana: Univ. of Illinois Press, 1962); John M. Steadman, *Milton and the Renaissance Hero* (Oxford: Clarendon Press, 1967); K. W. Gransden, "Paradise Lost and the *Aeneid*," *EIC* 17 (1967), 281-303; Mario A. Di Cesare, "*Paradise Lost* and Epic Tradition," *Milton Studies* 1 (1969), 31-50; Francis C. Blessington, *Paradise Lost and the Classical Epic* (Boston and London: Routledge & Kegan Paul, 1979); G. K. Hunter, *Paradise Lost* (London: George Allen & Unwin, 1980).
2. See, e.g., Martin Mueller, "*Paradise Lost* and the *Iliad*," *CLS* 6 (1969), 292-316; Steadman, *Milton and the Renaissance Hero*, and *Milton's Epic Characters: Image and Idol* (Chapel Hill: Univ. of North Carolina Press, 1968); Manoocher Aryanpur, "*Paradise Lost* and the *Odyssey*," *TSLL* 9 (1967), 151-66; Neil Forsyth, "Homer in Milton: The Attendance Motif and the Graces," *CL* 33 (1981), 137-55; Philip Damon, "*Paradise Lost* as Homeric Epic" (Paper presented at the 100th Annual Meeting of the Modern Language Association, New York, December 27-30, 1983); Blessington, *Paradise Lost and Classical Epic*; Hunter, *Paradise Lost*.
3. See, e.g., Merritt Y. Hughes, "Milton's Celestial Battles and the Theogonies," in *Studies in Honor of T. W. Baldwin*, ed. Don C. Allen (Urbana: Univ. of Illinois Press, 1958), pp. 237-53; rpt. in *Ten Perspectives on Milton* (New Haven: Yale Univ. Press, 1965), pp. 196-219; Stella Purce Revard, *The War in Heaven: Paradise Lost and the Tradition of Satan's Rebellion* (Ithaca and London: Cornell Univ. Press, 1980); Davis P. Harding, *Milton and the Renaissance Ovid* (Urbana: Univ. of Illinois Press, 1946); Louis L. Martz, "*Paradise Lost*: Figurations of Ovid," in *Poet of Exile: A Study of Milton's Poetry* (New Haven and London: Yale Univ. Press, 1980), pp. 203-44; Irene Samuel, *Dante and Milton: The Commedia and Paradise Lost* (Ithaca and London: Cornell Univ. Press,

1966); A. Bartlett Giamatti, *The Earthly Paradise and the Renaissance Epic* (Princeton: Princeton Univ. Press, 1966); Merritt Y. Hughes, "Milton's Limbo of Vanities," and Wayne Shumacher, "*Paradise Lost* and the Italian Epic Tradition," in *Th' Upright Heart and Pure*, ed. Amadeus P. Fiore (Pittsburgh: Duquesne Univ. Press, 1967), pp. 7-24 and 87-100; Edward Weismiller, "Materials Dark and Crude: A Partial Genealogy for Milton's Satan," *HLQ* 31 (1967), 75-93; Edwin Greenlaw, "Spenser's Influence on *Paradise Lost*," *SP* 17 (1920), 320-59; A. Kent Hieatt, "Spenser and Milton," in *Chaucer, Spenser, Milton: Mythopoeic Continuities and Transformations* (Montreal and London: McGill-Queen's University Press, 1975), pp. 153-270; Kathleen Williams, "Milton, Greatest Spenserian," in *Milton and the Line of Vision*, ed. Joseph A. Wittreich (Madison: Univ. of Wisconsin Press, 1975), pp. 25-55; Patricia A. Parker, *Inescapable Romance: Studies in the Poetics of a Mode* (Princeton: Princeton Univ. Press, 1975), pp. 114-58; George C. Taylor, *Milton's Use of Du Bartas* (1934; rpt. New York: Octagon Books, 1967); J. M. Evans, *Paradise Lost and the Genesis Tradition* (Oxford: Clarendon Press, 1968).

4. See, e.g., John M. Steadman, "The Epic as Pseudomorph: Methodology in Milton Studies," *Milton Studies* 7 (1973), 3-25; Joseph A. Wittreich, "Milton and the Tradition of Prophecy," in *Milton and the Line of Vision*, pp. 97-142; Michael Fixler, "The Apocalypse Within *Paradise Lost*," in *New Essays on Paradise Lost*, ed. Thomas Kranidas (Berkeley: Univ. of California Press, 1969), pp. 131-78; T.J.B. Spencer, "*Paradise Lost*: The Anti-Epic," in *Approaches to Paradise Lost: The York Tercentenary Lectures*, ed. C. A. Patrides (Toronto: Univ. of Toronto Press, 1968); Harold E. Toliver, "Milton's Household Epic," *Milton Studies* 9 (1976), 105-20; Joan Webber, *Milton and His Epic Tradition* (Seattle and London: Univ. of Washington Press, 1979). The presence and effects of *genera mixta* in *Paradise Lost* is the burden of several essays (by Earl Miner, Joseph Wittreich, Barbara K. Lewalski, Balachandra Rajan, Richard S. Ide, and Thomas Amorose) in the collection edited by Ide and Wittreich, *Composite Orders: The Genres of Milton's Last Poems, Milton Studies* 17 (Pittsburgh: Univ. of Pittsburgh Press, 1983).

5. See, e.g., James Holly Hanford, "The Dramatic Element in *Paradise Lost*," *SP* 14 (1917), 178-95, rpt. in *John Milton: Poet and Humanist*, ed. John S. Diekhoff (Cleveland: Western Reserve Univ.

NOTES TO CHAPTER 1

Press, 1966), pp. 224-43; Arthur E. Barker, "Structural Pattern in *Paradise Lost,*" *PQ* 28 (1949), 16-36; Ernest Sirluck, *Paradise Lost: A Deliberate Epic* (Cambridge: W. Heffer, 1967); Roger E. Rollin, "*Paradise Lost*: 'Tragical-Comical-Historical-Pastoral,' " *Milton Studies* 5 (1973), 3-37; John M. Steadman, *Epic and Tragic Structure in Paradise Lost* (Chicago: Univ. of Chicago Press, 1976); F. T. Prince, "Milton and the Theatrical Sublime," in *Approaches to Paradise Lost,* ed. Patrides, pp. 53-63; John G. Demaray, *Milton's Theatrical Epic: The Invention and Design of Paradise Lost* (Cambridge and London: Harvard Univ. Press, 1980); Thomas Kranidas, "Adam and Eve in the Garden: A Study of *Paradise Lost,* Book V," *SEL* 4 (1964), 71-83; Alwin Thaler, "Shakespearean Recollections in Milton: A Summing Up," in *Shakespeare and Our World* (Knoxville: Univ. of Tennessee Press, 1966), pp. 139-227; Helen Gardner, "Milton's Satan and the Theme of Damnation in Elizabethan Tragedy," *E&S* 1 (1948), 46-66, rpt. in *A Reading of Paradise Lost* (Oxford: Clarendon Press, 1965), pp. 99-120; Marshall Grossman, "Dramatic Structure and Emotive Pattern in the Fall: *Paradise Lost* IX," *Milton Studies* 13 (1979), 201-19; Richard S. Ide, "On the Uses of Elizabethan Drama: The Revaluation of Epic in *Paradise Lost,*" *Milton Studies* 17 (1983), 121-40; Hunter, *Paradise Lost,* pp. 72-95.

6. The major study is John R. Knott's *Milton's Pastoral Vision: An Approach to Paradise Lost* (Chicago and London: Chicago Univ. Press, 1971). See also Joseph E. Duncan, *Milton's Earthly Paradise: A Historical Study of Eden* (Minneapolis: Univ. of Minnesota Press, 1972); William Empson, "Milton and Bentley: The Pastoral of the Innocence of Man and Nature," in *Some Versions of Pastoral* (London: Chatto & Windus, 1935), pp. 149-94; Northrop Frye, *The Return of Eden* (Toronto: Univ. of Toronto Press, 1965); Roy Daniells, "A Happy Rural Seat of Various View," in *Paradise Lost: A Tercentenary Tribute,* ed. Balachandra Rajan (Toronto: Univ. of Toronto Press, 1967), pp. 3-17; G. Stanley Koehler, "Milton and the Art of Landscape," *Milton Studies* 8 (1975), 3-40; Barbara K. Lewalski, "Innocence and Experience in Milton's Eden," in *New Essays on Paradise Lost,* ed. Kranidas, pp. 86-117; Rollin, " 'Tragical-Comical-Historical-Pastoral.' "

7. See, e.g., Joseph Summers, *The Muse's Method: An Introduction to Paradise Lost* (Cambridge: Harvard Univ. Press, 1962), pp. 71-86; Donald Davie, "Syntax and Music in *Paradise Lost,*" in *The Living*

283

Milton, ed. Frank Kermode (London: Routledge & Kegan Paul, 1960), pp. 70-84; William Haller, "Hail, Wedded Love," *ELH* 13 (1946), 79-97; Gary M. McCown, "Milton and the Epic Epithalamium," *Milton Studies* 5 (1973), 39-66; John Demaray, "Love's Epic Revel in *Paradise Lost*: A Theatrical Vision of Marriage," *MLQ* 38 (1977), 3-20; Lee M. Johnson, "Milton's Blank Verse Sonnets," *Milton Studies* 5 (1973), 129-53; A. K. Nardo, "The Submerged Sonnet as Lyric Moment in Miltonic Epic," *Genre* 9 (1976), 21-35; Richard M. Bridges, "Milton's Original Psalm," *Milton Quarterly* 14 (1980), 12-21; Judy L. Van Sickle, "Song as Structure and Symbol in Four Poems of John Milton" (Ph.D. diss., Brown Univ., 1980), pp. 190-267; Sara Thorne-Thomsen, "Milton's 'adven'rous Song': Lyric Genres in *Paradise Lost*" (Ph.D. diss., Brown Univ. 1985).

8. See, e.g., J. B. Broadbent, *Some Graver Subject: An Essay on Paradise Lost* (London: Chatto & Windus, 1960), pp. 110-20; Broadbent, "Milton's Rhetoric," *MP* 56 (1958-59), 224-42; John M. Steadman, " 'Semblance of Worth': Pandaemonium and Deliberative Oratory," *Neophilologus* 48 (1964), 159-76, rpt. in *Milton's Epic Characters*, 241-62; Steadman, "Ethos and Dianoia: Character and Rhetoric in *Paradise Lost*," in *Language and Style in Milton*, ed. R. D. Emma and John T. Shawcross (New York: Ungar, 1967), pp. 193-232; Dennis Burden, *The Logical Epic: A Study of the Argument of Paradise Lost* (Cambridge: Harvard Univ. Press; London: Routledge & Kegan Paul, 1967); Irene Samuel, "The Dialogue in Heaven: A Reconsideration of *Paradise Lost* III.1-417," *PMLA* 72 (1957), 601-11; Samuel, "Milton on the Province of Rhetoric," *Milton Studies* 10 (1977), 177-93; Elaine B. Safer, "The Use of Contraries; Milton's Adaptation of Dialectic in *Paradise Lost*," *Ariel* 2 (1981), 55-69; H. R. MacCallum, "Milton and Sacred History, Books XI-XII of *Paradise Lost*," in *Essays in English Literature from the Renaissance to the Victorian Age, Presented to A.S.P. Woodhouse*, ed. M. Maclure and F. W. Watt (Toronto: Univ. of Toronto Press, 1964), pp. 149-68; John M. Major, "Milton's View of Rhetoric," *SP* 64 (1967), 685-711; Francis Blessington, "Autotheodicy: The Father as Orator in *Paradise Lost*," *Cithera: Essays in the Judaeo-Christian Tradition* 14 (1975), 49-60.

9. Julius-Caesar Scaliger, *Poetices libri septem*, I.3, III.25 (Geneva, 1561), pp. 5, 113; trans. F. M. Padelford, *Select Translations from Scaliger's Poetics* (New York: Holt, 1905), pp. 20, 54.

10. Rosalie L. Colie, *The Resources of Kind: Genre-Theory in the Renaissance*, ed. Barbara K. Lewalski (Berkeley: Univ. of California Press, 1973), pp. 22-23.

11. Chapman, "The Preface to the Reader," *Homer's Iliad*, in *Chapman's Homer*, ed. Allardyce Nicoll, 2 vols. (Princeton: Princeton Univ. Press, 1967), 1:14; "To the Understander," *Achilles Shield* (1598), in *Chapman's Homer*, ed. Nicoll, 1:549.

12. Scaliger, *Poetices*, III.25, p. 113, Padelford, p. 52.

13. For a survey of this "biblical poetics" tradition, see Lewalski, *Milton's Brief Epic: The Genre, Meaning, and Art of Paradise Regained* (Providence: Brown Univ. Press; London: Methuen, 1966), pp. 10-36, and *Protestant Poetics and the Seventeenth-Century Religious Lyric* (Princeton: Princeton Univ. Press, 1979), pp. 31-71. Also, Joseph A. Wittreich, *Visionary Poetics: Milton's Tradition and His Legacy* (San Marino: Huntington Library, 1979), pp. 9-26.

14. Aristotle, *Poetics* 1459b.8-1460b.5, 1461b.26-1462b.19, trans. S. H. Butcher, *Aristotle's Theory of Poetry and Fine Art*, 4th ed. (1932, rpt. New York: Dover, 1951), pp. 90-97, 106-11; William Webbe, *A Discourse of English Poetrie* (1586), in *Elizabethan Critical Essays*, ed. G. G. Smith, 2 vols. (Oxford: Oxford Univ. Press, 1971), 1:249; Giovambattista Giraldi Cinthio, *Discorso intorno al comporre dei romanzi, delle comedie, e delle tragedie* (Venice, 1554), ed. and trans. Henry L. Snuggs, *On Romances* (Lexington: Univ. of Kentucky Press, 1968), pp. 53, 57; Jacopo Mazzoni, *Della difesa della Comedia di Dante* (Cesena, 1587-1588), cited in Bernard Weinberg, *A History of Literary Criticism of the Italian Renaissance*, 2 vols. (Chicago: Univ. of Chicago Press, 1961), 2:877-83; George Puttenham, *The Arte of English Poesie* (London, 1589), pp. 31-34; Scaliger, *Poetices*, I.2, p. 5; Padelford, pp. 16-17.

15. Sidney, *The Defense of Poesie* (London, 1595), sig. E 3$_v$.

16. Torquato Tasso, *Discorso del poema eroico* (Naples, 1594); *Discourses on the Heroic Poem*, trans. Mariella Cavalchini and Irene Samuel (Oxford, 1973), p. 78. See also pp. 76-77, 191-95.

17. In the Preface to Book 2, *The Reason of Church Government*, *CPW*, 1:813.

18. For an impressive study of intertexuality with reference to ten major "vertical context systems" or "infracontexts," present in *Paradise Lost* but not necessarily by conscious authorial design, see Claes Schaar, *The Full-Voic'd Quire Below: Vertical Context Systems*

285

in Paradise Lost, Lund Studies in English, 60 (Lund: C.W.K. Gleerup, 1982).

19. Thomas M. Greene, *The Light in Troy: Imitation and Discovery in Renaissance Poetry* (New Haven and London: Yale Univ. Press, 1982), esp. pp. 20-27, 32-43.

20. For the counterargument see Harold Bloom, *A Map of Misreading* (New York: Oxford Univ. Press, 1975).

21. For counterarguments, see William Kerrigan, *The Prophetic Milton* (Charlottesville: Univ. of Virginia Press, 1974); Wittreich, *Visionary Poetics*; and John Guillory, *Poetic Authority: Spenser, Milton, and Literary History* (New York: Columbia Univ. Press, 1984).

22. For various reader-response approaches, see Stanley Fish, *Surprised by Sin: The Reader in Paradise Lost* (London: Macmillan; New York: St. Martins, 1967); Robert Crosman, *Reading Paradise Lost* (Bloomington and London: Indiana Univ. Press, 1980); Maureen Quilligan, *Milton's Spenser: The Politics of Reading* (Ithaca and London: Cornell Univ. Press, 1983).

23. *Of Education*, *CPW*, 2:366-79. For the counterargument, see Fish, *Surprised by Sin*.

24. For Renaissance genre theory and practice, the following modern studies are especially useful: Northrop Frye, *Anatomy of Criticism: Four Essays* (Princeton: Princeton Univ. Press, 1957); E. D. Hirsch, *Validity in Interpretation* (New Haven: Yale Univ. Press, 1967); Claudio Guillén, *Literature as System: Essays Toward the Theory of Literary History* (Princeton: Princeton Univ. Press, 1971); Paul Hernadi, *Beyond Genre: New Directions in Literary Classification* (Ithaca and London: Cornell Univ. Press, 1972); Alastair Fowler, *Kinds of Literature: An Introduction to the Theory of Genres and Modes* (Cambridge: Harvard Univ. Press, 1982); Heather Dubrow, *Genre* (London and New York: Methuen, 1982); and Colie, *Resources of Kind*.

25. Italian Renaissance critics of particular importance for genre theory are Scaliger (*Poetices*) and Antonio Sebastiano Minturno (*De Poeta*, Venice, 1559; *L'Arte poetica*, [Venice], 1563 [1564]). Several of the major Italian critical treatises are reprinted in Bernard Weinberg, ed., *Trattati di Poetica e Retorica del Cinquecento*, 4 vols. (Rome: Laterza, 1970-1974); for a general account see Weinberg, *A History of Literary Criticism in the Italian Renaissance*. In England, the major genre theorists are Sidney, Puttenham, and Ben Jonson.

26. See the critique in Guillén, *Literature as System*, pp. 375-419, and especially in Fowler, *Kinds of Literature*, pp. 20-53, 235-55.

27. The division goes back to Plato, *Republic* 392C-394D, and Aristotle, *Poetics* 1447a, 1448a.

28. Minturno, *L'Arte poetica*, p. 3. Also, Guillén calls attention to the development of this triad by Francisco Cascales (*Tablas poéticas*, Murcia, 1617), *Literature as System*, pp. 390-92.

29. Northrop Frye's term is "radicals of presentation," *Anatomy of Criticism*, pp. 246-47.

30. For discussion of this system see James J. Donohue, *The Theory of Literary Kinds: Ancient Classifications of Literature* (Dubuque: Loras College Press, 1943); *The Theory of Literary Kinds: The Ancient Classes of Poetry* (Dubuque: Loras College Press, 1949).

31. Guillén, *Literature as System*, p. 121.

32. Fowler, *Kinds of Literature*, pp. 37-74.

33. Sidney, *Defence of Poesie*, sigs. C 2ᵥ, E 3ᵥ-F.

34. *Reason of Church Government*, CPW 1:813-16.

35. *Defence of Poesie*, sigs C 2ᵥ-3.

36. See Lewalski, *Milton's Brief Epic*, for the brief biblical epic, and see Cinthio, *On Romances*, trans. Snuggs, pp. 18-25.

37. In his Preface to *Samson Agonistes*.

38. Of course, Elizabethan revenge tragedy had classical antecedents, notably Euripides' *Medea*. And Aristotle recognized as an inferior variety of tragedy the "plot of double issue," with an opposite catastrophe for the good and the wicked.

39. This formula descended from two fourth-century grammarians. Diomedes, citing Theophrastus, declared that comedy involves a happy outcome to sad affairs, *Ars grammatica* III.viii.9, ed. Georgius Koebel, *Comicorum graecorum fragmenta* (Berlin, 1899) Vol. I, pp. 57-58. And Evanthus in "De Fabula" proposed that in Comedy "Et illic turbulenta prima, tranquilla ultima" (Koebel, *Com. graec*, Vol. I, pp. 62-71). See Thomas Heywood's paraphrase in *An Apology for Actors* (1612), "Comedies begin in trouble and end in peace," in Allan H. Gilbert, *Literary Criticism, Plato to Dryden* (1940; rpt. Detroit: Wayne State Univ. Press, 1962), p. 555.

40. See Aristotle, *Poetics* 1448a-b, 1449a-b.9, Butcher, pp. 10-21. Scaliger's definition of comedy is: "a dramatic poem which is filled with intrigue, full of action, happy in its outcome, and written in a popular style (poema dramaticum, negotiosum, exitu laeto, stylo populari)," *Poetices* I.5, p. 11; Padelford, p. 38.

41. For the comedy of delight or admiration see Demetrius, *On Style* 3.168-69, trans. W. Rhys Roberts, in *Aristotle, Longinus, and Demetrius* (Loeb, Cambridge: Harvard Univ. Press; London: William Heinemann, 1973), p. 497; Tasso, *Discourses on the Heroic Poem*, 6.34, Samuel and Cavalchini, pp. 171-72; Sidney, *Defence of Poesie*, sig. I$_v$-I 2. See also the discussion by Lester Beaurline, "Comedy of Admiration," in *Jonson and Elizabethan Comedy* (San Marino: Huntington Library, 1978), pp. 35-65.

42. Dante, "Letter to the Can Grande Della Scala," in Gilbert, *Literary Criticism*, p. 204; for the assimilation of the Platonic dialogues to comedy, see Cicero, *De officiis* 1.104-108, and Girolamo Zoppio, *Poetica sopra Dante* (1589), discussed in Weinberg, *Literary Criticism in the Italian Renaissance* 2:895-99.

43. See, e.g., Minturno, *L'Arte Poetica*, pp. 6, 171; Giovanni Antonio Viperano, *De Poetica Libri Tres* (Antwerp, 1579), pp. 149-50; Agnolo Segni, *Lezioni intorno alla poesia* (1581), in Weinberg, ed., *Trattati*, 3:95; Pomponio Torelli, *Trattati della poesia lirica*, in Weinberg, ed., *Trattati*, 4:266.

44. See Donahue, "Lyric," *The Ancient Classes of Poetry*, pp. 48-84.

45. Scaliger, *Poetices*, I.3, I.44-57, III.100-24, pp. 6, 47-54, 150-69.

46. Scaliger did not include biblical or contemporary kinds, but Minturno and Segni, Ronsard and Du Bellay, Sidney and Puttenham, and many others did, usually citing David the Psalmist and Petrarch as primary exemplars. For the biblical lyric tradition, see Lewalski, *Protestant Poetics*, pp. 31-71.

47. See Scaliger, *Poetices*, III.125-27, pp. 169-73; Sidney, *Defence*, sigs. E3$_v$-F2; Puttenham, *Arte*, chaps. 22-31, pp. 36-51. See also Donohue, "Elegiac," *The Ancient Classes of Poetry*, pp. 48-100.

48. Cicero's various orations and treatises, especially the *De Inventione*, were of primary importance for English rhetorical theory and practice, though Quintilian's *Institutio Oratoria*, the pseudo-Ciceronean *Rhetorica ad Herenneum*, and (for the seventeenth-century) Aristotle's *Rhetoric* and the Ramist Logics and Rhetorics were also major influences.

49. See George A. Kennedy, *Classical Rhetoric and Its Christian and Secular Traditions* (Chapel Hill: Univ. of North Carolina Press, 1980), for a discussion of the three major rhetorical traditions (technical, philosophical, and sophistical) as they developed in antiquity and persisted through the Renaissance, and also of various offshoots of the three major rhetorical kinds. In addition, Ovid's

Heroides provided examples of the deliberative oration adapted to poetry and private causes.

50. The ideal is developed in the *Phaedrus*, the *Gorgias*, and the *Republic*, and exemplified throughout the dialogues.

51. See the extended dialogue between Boethius and Lady Philosophy in the *Consolation of Philosophy* and between Franciscus and Augustinus in the *Secretum*, trans. William H. Draper (London: Chatto & Windus, 1911). Several of Dante's dialogues with Beatrice and the saints are poetic versions of this kind of dialogue.

52. Milton's *First Prolusion* indicates that the medieval academic tradition of the debate still flourished at Cambridge in his day. See Louis J. Paetow, "The Arts Course at Medieval Universities, with special reference to grammar and rhetoric," *University Studies of the University of Illinois* 3.7 (1910), 491-624. The debate tradition found its way into many literary works, among them the medieval debates of Body and Soul, to which kind Marvell's elegant "Dialogue between the Soul and Body" belongs. See Michel-André Bossy, "Medieval Debates of Body and Soul," *CL* 28 (1976), 144-63, and Elizabeth Merrill, *The Dialogue in English Literature* (1911; rpt. Hamden, Conn: Archon Books, 1969).

53. See, e.g., Wittreich, ed., *Milton and the Line of Vision*; Leslie Brisman, *Milton's Poetry of Choice and Its Romantic Heirs* (Ithaca and London: Cornell Univ. Press, 1973).

54. M. M. Bakhtin, *The Dialogic Imagination: Four Essays*, ed. Michael Holquist, trans. Caryl Emerson and Michael Holquist (Austin and London: Univ. of Texas Press, 1981).

55. Milton himself had written a "gay elegy" a few months earlier, "Elegy 5," whose florid celebration of nature and its pagan gods is directly reversed in "Elegy 6."

56. Quintilian, *Institutio Oratoria*, 10.1.46-47ff, trans. H. E. Butler, 4 vols. (Loeb, Cambridge: Harvard Univ. Press; London: William Heinemann, 1933), 4:487. See *Iliad* 2.50-397; Tasso, *Gerusalemme*, 2.57-95, 10.25-48.

57. See Fish, *Surprised by Sin*, pp. 59-91. For a fine discussion of the deliberative oratory of the Council in Hell, see Steadman, *Image and Idol*, pp. 241-62.

58. Cicero, *Orator* 3.12, trans. H. M. Hubbell (Loeb, Cambridge: Harvard Univ. Press; London: William Heinemann, 1939), p. 313; *De Oratore* 1.6.20, 1.13.60, 1.8.33-34, 2.8.35, ed. H. Rackham, trans. E. W. Sutton, 2 vols. (Loeb, Cambridge: Harvard Univ.

Press; London: William Heinemann, 1942), 1:17, 45, 25-27, 223; Quintilian, *Institutio*, 1, Pref. 9-12, 2.15.27-36; 2.20-29; 9.1.11-12; 12.1.3-9, 12.2.17; Butler, 1:9-11, 313-17, 353-55; 4:161, 357-61, 391.

59. *Gorgias* 508C, 527C, ed. W.R.M. Lamb (Loeb, Cambridge: Harvard Univ. Press; London: William Heinemann, 1925), pp. 471, 531. *Phaedrus* 277C, ed. Harold North Fowler (Loeb, Cambridge: Harvard Univ. Press; London: William Heinemann, 1943), p. 571. See John M. Steadman, "Milton's Rhetoric: Satan and the 'Unjust Discourse,' " *Milton Studies* 1 (1969), 67-92.

CHAPTER 2. INSPIRATION AND LITERARY ART:
THE PROPHET-POETS OF *Paradise Lost*

1. John Smith, "Of Prophesie," *Select Discourses* (London, 1660), pp. 169-83.
2. *Ibid.*, pp. 273-75.
3. See, e.g., Kerrigan, *Prophetic Milton*, pp. 129-32, for the argument that Milton seeks to surpass Moses and achieve the *visio dei* itself.
4. Smith, "Of Prophesie," p. 173.
5. Spenser's proems to each book of the *Faerie Queene* provide models for proems devoted to such themes. But whereas Spenser sets his proems apart from the narrative as separate poems, Milton incorporates his within the narrative, indicating thereby that the poetic problems he explores in them are an integral part of his poem's subject, the Fall of Man. For a fine analysis of the Bard's voice and self-presentation through metaphor, see Anne Davidson Ferry, *Milton's Epic Voice: The Narrator in Paradise Lost* (Cambridge: Harvard Univ. Press, 1963), pp. 20-43.
6. *Iliad* 1.1-2, *The Iliad of Homer*, trans. Richmond Lattimore (Chicago: Univ. of Chicago Press, 1951). All citations and quotations from the *Iliad* in text and notes are from this edition.
7. *Odyssey* 1.1, *The Odyssey of Homer*, trans. Richmond Lattimore (Chicago: Univ. of Chicago Press, 1965); *Aeneid* 1.1, *Virgil*, trans. H. R. Fairclough, 2 vols. (Loeb, Cambridge: Harvard Univ. Press; London: William Heinemann, 1960). All citations and quotations from the *Odyssey* and the *Aeneid* are from these editions. For the Homeric allegory see, e.g., George Chapman's note to the opening line of the *Odyssey* (*Chapman's Homer*, ed. Nicoll, 2:11): "The in-

NOTES TO CHAPTER 2

formation or fashion of an absolute man, and necessarie (or fatal) passage through many afflictions (according with the most sacred Letter) to his naturall haven and countrey, is the whole argument and scope of this inimitable and miraculous Poeme." For various allegorical readings of the *Aeneid*, see Dominico Comparetti, *Vergil in the Middle Ages*, trans. E.F.M. Benecke (London: S. Sonnenchein; New York: Macmillan, 1895), pp. 60-118.

8. *Aeneid* 1.5-7, Fairclough, 1:241 (italics mine): "dum conderet urbem / inferretque deos Latio; genus unde Latinum / Albanique patres atque altae moenia Romae."

9. Ariosto, *Orlando Furioso*, 1.2.2 (Ferrara, 1516), p. 2.

10. Italics mine.

11. R. W. Condee, "The Formalized Openings of Milton's Epic Poems," *JEGP* 50 (1951), 502-508.

12. Du Bartas' very popular dream-vision poem "Uranie" (1574) established this identity. See Lily B. Campbell, *Divine Poetry and Drama in Sixteenth-Century England* (Cambridge: Cambridge Univ. Press, 1959), pp. 74-92, and E. R. Gregory, "Three Muses and a Poet: A Perspective on Milton's Epic Thought," *Milton Studies* 10 (1977), 35-61.

13. Josuah Sylvester, trans., *The Divine Weeks and Works of Guillaume De Saluste Sieur Du Bartas*, ed. Susan Snyder, 2 vols. (Oxford: Clarendon Press, 1979), I.1.135-39:

My heedful *Muse*, trayned in true Religion,
Devinely-humane keepes the middle Region:
Least, if she should too-high a pitch presume,
Heav'ns glowing flame should melt her waxen plume.

14. Clearly this is not the Holy Spirit of trinitarian theology. In the *De Doctrina Christiana* (chapter 6) Milton finds a limited and somewhat ambiguous role for the Holy Spirit, who is distinctly inferior to the Father and even to the subordinate Son. Milton insists (*CPW*, 6:283), that references to the Spirit in the Old Testament must all refer in the first instance to "the virtue and power of God the Father. For the Holy Spirit had not yet been given, and was not believed in." Milton everywhere ascribes Creation to the power of the Father, the only supreme God. In one place he explains the phrase from Gen. 1:2, "the spirit of God brooded" as perhaps having reference to the agency of the subordinate Son "through whom, as we are constantly told, the Father created all

things" (*CPW*, 6:282), but in the chapter on the Creation he refers this phrase directly to its primary meaning, "the Spirit of God brooded, that is to say, God's divine power, not any particular person" (*CPW*, 6:304).

15. Scaliger, *Poetices*, III.113-15, pp. 162-63; "The Homeric Hymns," in *Hesiod, The Homeric Hymns and Homerica*, trans. Hugh G. Evelyn-White (Loeb, Cambridge: Harvard Univ. Press; London: William Heinemann, 1977), pp. 286-463; "Callimachus: Hymns" in *Callimachus, Lycophron, Aratus*, trans. A. W. and G. R. Mair, ed. E. H. Warmington, 2nd ed. (Loeb, Cambridge: Harvard Univ. Press; London: William Heinemann, 1967), pp. 36-135; Scaliger, "Hymns," in *Poemata ad Illustriss Constantium Rangoniam* (Lyon, 1544).

16. For the literary hymn, see Philip Rollinson, "The Renaissance of the Literary Hymn," *Renaissance Papers*, 1968 (Durham, N.C.: Southeastern Renaissance Conference, 1969), pp. 11-20; "A Generic View of Spenser's *Four Hymns*," *SP* 68 (1971), 292-304; and "Milton's Nativity Poem and the Decorum of Genre," *"Eyes Fast Fixt": Current Perspectives in Milton Methodology*, ed. Albert C. Labriola and Michael Lieb, *Milton Studies* 7 (1975), 165-88. Spenser's "Hymne in Honour of Love" *Poetical Works*, ed. J. C. Smith and E. de Selincourt (Oxford: Oxford Univ. Press, 1970) pp. 590-92, has a narrative purportedly based on the speaker's own experience of love, and his "Hymne of Heavenly Beauty" offers several conceptual and verbal parallels to Milton's hymn in its celebration of God as Beauty and Light, e.g., ll. 176-79:

> With the great glorie of that wondrous light,
> His throne is all encompassed around,
> And hid in his owne brightnesse from the sight
> Of all that looke thereon with eyes unsound.

17. These lines echo the first proof-text Milton cites in the *De Doctrina* in describing God's incomprehensible nature, 1 Tim. 6:16, "dwelling in unapproachable light," *CPW*, 6:133. Other biblical texts that reverberate in this apostrophe are 1 John 1:5, Ps. 104:1-2, and Ps. 36:8. I am unpersuaded by arguments equating this holy light with the Son of God, developed by C. A. Patrides ("*Paradise Lost* and the Language of Theology," in *Language and Style in Milton*, ed. Emma and Shawcross, pp. 102-19, rpt. in *Bright Essence: Studies in Milton's Theology*, by W. B. Hunter, C. A. Pa-

trides, and J. H. Adamson [Salt Lake City: Univ. of Utah Press, 1971], pp. 165-78) and by William B. Hunter, Jr. ("The Meaning of 'Holy Light' in *Paradise Lost* III," *MLN* 74 [1959], 589-92; and "Milton's Urania," *SEL* 4 [1964], 35-42, partly reproduced in "Milton's Muse," *Bright Essence*, pp. 149-56). The reason is not only that Milton's antitrinitarianism would preclude his celebration of the Son as "Coeternal beam" of the Father's light, but especially because the biblical texts echoed in this passage concern light in its relation to God, and the syntax gives no warrant to assume a shift in the object of address at l. 23, when the Bard is clearly speaking of light which is denied him by his blindness. For a judicious summary of the whole issue see, e.g., Merritt Y. Hughes, "Milton and the Symbol of Light," *SEL* 4 (1964), 1-33. Also see Maurice Kelley, *This Great Argument: A Study of Milton's De doctrina Christiana as a gloss upon Paradise Lost* (Princeton, 1941), pp. 92-94, and "Milton's Arianism Again Considered," *HTR* 54 (1961), 195-205.

18. Such a personal myth also relates the hymn to Scaliger's sixth kind, invented or fictional hymns, *Poetices*, III.115, p. 163.

19. For the Orphic "Hymn to Night" see *The Mystical Hymns of Orpheus*, trans. Thomas Taylor, 2nd ed. (London: B. Dobell, 1896), pp. 10-15.

20. See *Paradiso* 33:22-24, trans. Charles S. Singleton (Princeton: Princeton Univ. Press, 1975), p. 372, "Or questi, che da l'infima lacuna / de l'universo infin qui ha vedute." Also, 33:67-72 (p. 374):

> O somma luce che tanto ti levi
>   da' concetti mortali, a la mia mente
>   ripresta un poco di quel che parevi,
>
> e fa la lingua mia tanto possente,
>   ch'una favilla sol de la tua gloria
>   possa lasciare a la futura gente.

For other Dantean parallels see Don C. Allen, "Milton and the Descent to Light," *JEGP* 60 (1961), 614-30.

21. *Paradiso* 30:46-60; Exod. 19:16-20, 24:15-35, especially 24:16: "And the glory of the Lord abode upon mount Sinai, and the cloud covered it six days: and the seventh day he called unto Moses out of the midst of the cloud." The reverberations of the Sinai theophany here and elsewhere in *Paradise Lost* are studied by Jason

Rosenblatt, "The Mosaic Voice in *Paradise Lost*," *Milton Studies* 7 (1975), 207-32.

22. *Aeneid* 7.41-45, Fairclough, 2:4-5:

> dicem horrida bella,
> dicam acies actosque animis in funera reges,
> ....
> maior rerum mihi nascitur ordo,
> maius opus moveo.

23. *Horace: The Odes and Epodes*, trans. C. E. Bennett (Loeb, Cambridge: Harvard Univ. Press; London: William Heinemann, 1921), pp. 187-93. For discussion of Ode III.4, see Edward Fraenkel, *Horace* (Oxford: Clarendon Press, 1957), pp. 273-85.

24. See Horace, Ode III.4.17-36, Bennett, pp. 187-88:

> ut tuto ab atris corpore viperis
> dormirem et ursis, ut premerer sacra
> lauroque conlataque myrto,
> non sine dis animosus infans.
>
> ....
> vestris amicum fontibus et choris
> non me Philippis versa acies retro,
> devota non extinxit arbor,
> nec Sicula Palinurus unda.
> utcumque mecum vos eritis, libens
> insanientem navita Bosphorum
> temptabo et urentes harenas
> litoris Assyrii viator;
> visam Britannos hospitibus feros
> et laetum equino sanguine Concanum,
> visam pharetratos Gelonos
> et Scythicum inviolatus amnem.

25. Bellerophon attempted to fly to heaven on the Muses' winged horse, Pegasus, but was flung to earth by Jove and then wandered on the plains of Aleios distracted and (some said) blind—allegorically a warning against artistic presumption. See *Iliad* 6.200-202, and Natalis Comes, *Mythologiae sive Explicationis Fabularum* (Geneva, 1653), 9.4, pp. 950-54.

26. The songs of Orpheus charmed all savage nature until the frenzied Bacchantes overwhelmed his music with their shrill outcries

and tore him limb from limb—allegorically a portrayal of the civ-
ilizing power of poetry and the danger to it from irrationality and
unbridled passion. See Comes, *Mythologiae*, 7.14, pp. 755-62; Ovid,
Metamorphoses 10-11.66, trans. Frank J. Miller, 2 vols. (Loeb,
Cambridge: Harvard Univ. Press; London: William Heinemann,
1977) 2:64-125; and commentary in George Sandys, *Ovid's Met-
amorphosis Englished, Mythologized, and Represented in Figures*, ed.
K. K. Hulley and S. H. Vandersall (Lincoln: Univ. of Nebraska
Press, 1970), pp. 474-94, 519-21. In the *Ready and Easy Way*
(1660) Milton describes the royalist court about to be restored as
inhabited by "tigers of Bacchus . . . inspir'd with nothing holier
then the Venereal pox," *CPW*, 7:452-53.

27. Psalms 17:3, 8-9; 109:2. For citation of some other psalm echoes
in this passage see James H. Sims, *The Bible in Milton's Epics*
(Gainsville: Univ. of Florida Press, 1962). For psalm categories
see Lewalski, *Protestant Poetics*, pp. 31-53. For discussion of the
psalms of lament with special reference to *Samson Agonistes* see
Mary Ann Radzinowicz, *Toward Samson Agonistes: The Growth of
Milton's Mind* (Princeton: Princeton Univ. Press, 1978), pp. 183-
226, and her forthcoming book on *Paradise Lost* and the Psalms.

28. See, e.g., Juvencus, *Evangeliorum*, ll. 1-24, ed. Johannes Huemer
(*CSEL* 24 [Vienna, 1891]), pp. 1-2; Jacobus Bonus, *De Vita &
Gestis Christi* [Rome, 1562], Dedication; Sylvester, *Du Bartas' Di-
vine Weeks*, ed. Snyder, I.1.1-26, II.1.1-58; Luis Camões, *Lusia-
dos*, trans. Richard Fanshawe (London, 1658), I. cantos 1-18; Tasso,
Gerusalemme Liberata, trans. Edward Fairfax (London, 1600), I.
st. 1-5. In some respects, Milton's proem seems to echo and re-
spond to Abraham Cowley's prefatory remarks concerning his un-
finished *Davideis* (London, 1656), the last significant biblical epic
in English before *Paradise Lost*, and a serious effort to produce a
major neoclassical epic on a biblical martial subject:

> Those mad stories of the *Gods* and *Heroes*, seem in themselves
> so ridiculous; . . . To us who . . . deride their *folly*, and are
> wearied with their *impertinencies*, they ought to appear no bet-
> ter arguments for *Verse*, than those of their worthy *Successors*,
> the *Knights Errant* . . . Are the obsolete threadbare tales of
> *Thebes* and *Troy* half so stored with great, heroical and super-
> natural actions . . . as the wars of *Joshua*, of the *Judges*, of
> *David*, and divers others? Can all the *Transformations* of the

Gods give such copious hints to flourish and expatiate on, as the true *Miracles* of *Christ*. . . . None but a good *Artist* will know how to do it. . . . Sure I am, that there is nothing yet in our *Language* (Nor perhaps in *any*) that is in any degree answerable to the *Idea* that I conceive of it. ("Preface," *Poems* [London, 1656], sig. B2ᵥ-B3)

29. See Steadman's valuable discussion of Aristotle and major Italian neoclassical critics such as Minturno, Castelvetro, and Masenius, in *Epic and Tragic Structure*, pp. 29-40. See also William Davenant, *Gondibert, an Heroick Poeme* (London, 1650), preface; and Theodore Agrippa d'Aubigné, *Les Tragiques*, ed. A. Garnier and J. Plattard, 4 vols. (Paris: E. Droz, 1932).

30. *Iliad* 17.

31. *Aeneid* 7.413-74.

32. Odysseus consciously changes his notes to tragic as he tells (Books 9-12) of his own sufferings and those of the other Argives on their homeward travels: "But now your wish was inclined to ask me about my mournful / sufferings so that I must mourn and grieve even more . . . / Many are the sorrows the gods of the sky have given me." As audience, Alkinoös recognizes Odysseus' narrative as a brief tragic epic: "expertly, as a singer would do, you have told the story / of the dismal sorrows befallen yourself and all of the Argives" (*Odyssey* 9.12-15, 11.368-69, Lattimore, pp. 137, 177). Aeneas also recounts the Fall of Troy for Dido as a tragic narrative: "Beyond all words, O queen, is the grief thou bidst me revive, how the Greeks overthrew Troy's wealth and woeful realm—the sights most piteous that I myself saw and whereof I was no small part" (*Aeneid* 2.3-6, Fairclough, 1:295).

33. In making this choice, the Bard ranges himself against Tasso and the neoclassical critics who urged choice of a martial subject from secular Christian history (e.g., Trissino, Ronsard, Camōens, Tortoletti, Georges de Scudéry) and also against those who proposed or undertook martial epic subjects from the Bible (e.g., Du Bartas in *Judit*, Robert Aylett, Abraham Cowley). He aligns himself rather with those who used or argued for nonmartial subjects, secular and biblical, as appropriate for epic (e.g., Daniello, Varchi, Du Bartas in the *Semaines*, Marino in *Adone*, Jean Chapelain, and Jean Desmarets de Saint-Sorlin). See Lewalski, *Milton's Brief Epic*, pp.

68-101, for discussion of their various positions and prefactory arguments.
34. See Cinthio, "Discorso . . . dei romanzi," *On Romances*, trans. Snuggs. Also, Sir John Harington, "A Preface, or Rather, A Briefe Apologie of Poetrie and of the Author and Translator of this Poem," published with his translation of the *Orlando Furioso* (1591), ed. Robert McNulty (Oxford: Clarendon Press, 1972), pp. 1-15.
35. This Protestant commonplace is often repeated by Milton, and is the starting point of his theological explorations in the *De Doctrina* (Book I, Epistle and Chap. 1), *CPW* 6:117-29. The prophet-poet stands with his audience in their common need for divine illumination in order to know and understand the truths of revelation.
36. See John Smith, "Of Prophesie," pp. 169-70: "For though our own Reason and Understanding carry all *Natural Truth* necessary for *Practice* in any sort, engraven upon themselves . . . yet *Positive Truth* can only be made known to us by a free influx of the Divine Mind upon our Minds and Understandings." For an approach to Miltonic accommodation in terms of fourfold exegesis with special reference to the War in Heaven, see Walter R. Davis, "The Languages of Accommodation and the Styles of *Paradise Lost*," *Milton Studies*, 18 (1983), 103-27.
37. Bloom, *Map of Misreading*, pp. 125-43.
38. Smith, "Of Prophesie," pp. 169-80. The manner of Raphael's illumination resembles but goes beyond Smith's "*gradus Mosaicus*."
39. For discussion of some sources for these ideas see Dennis Saurat, *Milton: Man and Thinker* (London: Jonathan Cape; New York: Dial Press, 1925), pp. 301-309; W. C. Curry, *Milton's Ontology, Cosmogony & Physics* (1957; rpt. Lexington: Univ. of Kentucky Press, 1966), pp. 114-43, 158-82; Kester Svendsen, *Milton and Science* (Cambridge: Harvard Univ. Press, 1956), pp. 9-42, 114-36; Lee A. Jacobus, *Sudden Apprehension: Aspects of Knowledge in Paradise Lost* (The Hague and Paris: Mouton, 1976), pp. 45-88.
40. Lucretius' poem, Empedocles' Περὶ φύσεως, and other philosophical and scientific poems were classified as epic by, e.g., Minturno, *De Poeta*, Bk. 2, p. 146, and Scaliger, *Poetices*, 1.2, pp. 5-6, Padelford, pp. 16-17. Puttenham notes that Lucretius and poets of his type treated noble doctrines and arts "in verse *Exameter* savouring the Heroicall," *Arte of English Poesie*, p. 35.
41. Lucretius, *De Rerum Natura*, 1.54-61, trans. W.H.D. Rouse

(Loeb, Cambridge: Harvard Univ. Press; London: William Heinemann, 1975), p. 6:

> nam tibi de summa caeli ratione deumque
> disserere incipiam, et rerum primordia pandam,
> unde omnis natura creet res auctet alatque
> quove eadem rursum natura perempta resolvat,
> quae nos materiem et genitalia corpora rebus
> reddunda in ratione vocare et semina rerum
> appellare suëmus et haec eadem usurpare
> corpora prima, quod ex illis sunt omnia primis.

[For I shall begin to discourse to you upon the most high system of heaven and of the gods, and I shall disclose the first-beginnings of things (the atoms), from which nature makes all things and increases and nourishes them, and into which the same nature again reduces them when dissolved—which, in discussing philosophy, we are accustomed to call matter, and bodies that generate things, and seeds of things, and to entitle the same first bodies, because from them as first elements all things are.]

42. *Ibid.*, 2.991-1006, pp. 172-73:

> Denique caelesti sumus omnes semine oriundi;
> omnibus ille idem pater est, unde alma liquentis
> umoris guttas mater cum terra recepit,
> feta parit nitidas fruges arbustaque laeta
> et genus humanum, parit omnia saecla ferarum,
> pabula cum praebet quibus omnes corpora pascunt
> et dulcem ducunt vitam prolemque propagant;
> quapropter merito maternum nomen adepta est.
> cedit item retro, de terra quod fuit ante,
> in terras, et quod missumst ex aetheris oris,
> id rursum caeli rellatum templa receptant.
> nec sic interemit mors res ut materiai
> corpora conficiat, sed coetum dissupat ollis;
> inde aliis aliud coniungit, et efficit omnes
> res ita convertant formas mutentque colores
> et capiant sensus et puncto tempore reddant.

[Lastly, we are all sprung from celestial seed; all have that same father, from whom our fostering mother earth receives liquid drops of water, and then teeming brings forth bright corn and luxuriant trees and the race of mankind, brings forth all the generations of wild beasts, providing food with which all nourish their bodies and lead a sweet life and beget their offspring; therefore she has with reason obtained the name of mother. That also which once came from earth, to earth returns back again, and what fell from the borders of ether, that is again brought back, and the regions of heaven again receive it. Nor does death so destroy things as to annihilate the bodies of matter, but it disperses their combination abroad; then it conjoins others with others, and brings it about that thus all things alter their shapes and change their colours and receive sensation and in a moment of time yield it up again.]

43. Cf. Lucretius, *De Rerum Natura*, 1.351-57, p. 30, with *PL*, 5.479-490:

> Trees grow and at their time put forth their fruits, because their food is distributed all over them from the lowest roots through trunks and through branches. . . . But if there were no void there which bodies might pass through . . . you could not see this happen in any way.

> So from the root
> Springs lighter the green stalk, from thence the leaves
> More aery, last the bright consummate flow'r
> Spirits odorous breathes: flow'rs and thir fruit
> Man's nourishment, by gradual scale sublim'd
> To vital spirits aspire, to animal,
> To intellectual, give both life and sense,
> Fancy and understanding, whence the Soul
> Reason receives, and reason is her being,
> Discursive, or Intuitive; discourse
> Is oftest yours, the latter most is ours,
> Differing but in degree, of kind the same.

44. *PL*, 5.491-501:

> Wonder not then, what God for you saw good
> If I refuse not, but convert, as you,
> To proper substance; time may come when men
> With Angels may participate, and find
> No inconvenient Diet, nor too light Fare:
> And from these corporal nutriments perhaps
> Your bodies may at last turn all to spirit,

Improv'd by tract of time, and wing'd ascend
Ethereal, as wee, or may at choice
Here or in Heav'nly Paradises dwell;
If ye be found obedient.

45. See Chapter 1, pp. 4-5 and n. 10.
46. Erasmo di Valvasone, *Angeleida* (Venice, 1590), 2.20, trans. Watson Kirkconnell, *The Celestial Cycle* (Toronto: Univ. of Toronto Press, 1952), p. 81; *The Faerie Queene*, I.7.13, ed. A. C. Hamilton (London and New York: Longman, 1977), p. 99. And see discussion in Revard, *War in Heaven*, pp. 186-90.
47. See Blessington, *Paradise Lost and the Classical Epic*, esp. pp. 8-14.
48. Revard notes (*War in Heaven*, pp. 129-97) that Milton's Battle in Heaven is unique among Renaissance treatments in denying a decisive victory to the angels, and to Michael the central role in achieving that victory. Nor is there precedent for the humiliation and confusion Milton's angels endure at the hands of the rebels. See also Summers, *Muse's Method*, pp. 122-37.
49. See, e.g., Augustine, *Confessions*, in *Basic Writings*, ed. Whitney J. Oates, 2 vols. (New York: Random House, 1948), 1:202; Calvin, *Institutes of the Christian Religion*, ed. John T. McNeill, 2 vols. "Library of Christian Classics" (Philadelphia: Westminster Press, 1960), 1:160. In his *De Doctrina* (I.7) Milton declared that "Anyone who asks what God did before the creation of the world is a fool; and anyone who answers him is not much wiser" (*CPW*, 6:299).
50. Sylvester, *Du Bartas' Divine Weeks*, ed. Snyder, 1:2. *La Semaine* was first published in 1578; the unfinished sequel, *La Seconde Semaine*, dealing with the seven ages of biblical history, was first published in 1584. The standard edition is *The Works of Guillaume de Salluste, Sieur du Bartas*, ed. U. T. Holmes, J. C. Lyons, and R. W. Linker, 3 vols. (Chapel Hill: Univ. of North Carolina Press, 1935-1940). Sylvester's extremely popular translation, the *Divine Weeks and Works*, went through nine editions by 1641, and dedicators ranked the work with, or exalted it above, Homer and Virgil. Gabriel Harvey placed it "even in the next Degree to the sacred and reverend stile of heavenly Divinity it selfe," *Pierce's Supererogation*, in Smith, *Elizabethan Critical Essays*, 2:265. While Tasso's hexaemeral poem, *Le Sette Giornate del Mondo Creato* (Viterbo,

1607) had no such currency, Albert R. Cirillo ("Tasso's *Il Mondo Creato:* Providence and the Created Universe," *Milton Studies* 3 [1971], 83-102) points to some thematic parallels between that poem and Milton's.

51. See esp. *Divine Weeks* I.1.285-90, I.3.533-44, I.5.879-88, and *PL* 7.276-80, 313-19, 442-46. See also Lucretius, *De Rerum Natura*, 5.783-825. For discussion of the use of such sources, and of the imagery of Book Seven, see Taylor, *Milton's Use of Du Bartas*; Grant McColley, *Paradise Lost: An Account of Its Growth and Major Origins* (Chicago: Packard, 1940); Michael Lieb, *The Dialectics of Creation: Patterns of Birth & Regeneration in Paradise Lost* (Amherst: Univ. of Mass. Press, 1969), pp. 56-63.

52. See for example, *Divine Weeks* I.1.51-118, 376-416; I.4.81-180.

53. Galileo, *Dialogo . . . sopra i due massimi sistemi del mondo, tolemaico, e copernicano* (Florence, 1632); trans. Stillman Drake, 2nd ed. (Berkeley: Univ. of California Press, 1967).

54. He is said to "act the part of Copernicus in our arguments, and wear his mask," *ibid.*, p. 131.

55. Sagredo declares, *ibid.*, pp. 59-60: "Has Nature, then, produced and directed all these enormous, perfect, and most noble celestial bodies, invariant, eternal, and divine, for no other purpose than to serve the changeable, transitory, and mortal earth? . . . Take away this purpose of serving the earth, and the innumerable host of celestial bodies is left useless and superfluous."

56. Simplicio declares (*ibid.*, p. 61) that "the goal to which all are directed is the need, the use, the comfort and the delight of men."

57. *Ibid.*, pp. 256, 367-71.

58. Smith, "Of Prophesie," pp. 178-79. The Book of Revelation, attributed to John of Patmos, is described in the Geneva Bible as "a summe of those prophecies, which were writen before, but shulde be fulfilled after the comming of Christ." *The Bible and Holy Scriptures Conteyned in the Olde and Newe Testament* (Geneva, 1560), "Argument" to the Book of Revelation, fol. 114$_v$.

59. Smith, "Of Prophesie," p. 179.

60. For the Book of Revelation as the epic conflict of Christ and Antichrist, God and Satan see, e.g., Franciscus Junius, *The Apocalypse, or Revelation of St. John*, trans. T. Barbar (Cambridge, 1596), p. 247. For the view of it as tragedy see, e.g., Thomas Brightman, *A Revelation of the Apocalypse*, in *Works* (London, 1644), p. 234.

For the view of it as a "history of the troubles and persecutions of the Church" see, e.g., Henry Bullinger, *A Hundred Sermons upon the Apocalypse* (London, 1573), sig. Aiii,. See also Lewalski, "*Samson Agonistes* and the "Tragedy" of the Apocalypse," *PMLA* 85 (1970), 1050-62, and Wittreich, *Visionary Poetics*. Studies of the mix of genres and the historiography of Books Eleven and Twelve include Thomas Amorose, "Milton the Apocalyptic Historian: Competing Genres in *Paradise Lost*, Books XI and XII," *Milton Studies*, 17, 141-62; Michael Cavanagh, "A Meeting of Epic and History: Books XI and XII of *Paradise Lost*," *ELH* 38 (1971), 206-22; MacCallum, "Milton and Sacred History."

61. Pareus referred to Revelation as a "*Propheticall Drama*, show, or representation," in *Commentary upon the Divine Revelation of the Apostle and Evangelist John*, trans. Elias Arnold (Amsterdam, 1644), p. 20. Milton in the *Reason of Church Government* referred to the book as a "high and stately Tragedy, shutting up and intermingling her solemn Scenes and Acts with a sevenfold *Chorus* of halleluja's and harping symphonies" (*CPW*, 1:813-16) and reiterated the description in substantially the same terms in the Preface to *Samson Agonistes*. Demaray, *Milton's Theatrical Epic*, pp. 102-15, explores the masque dimension and backgrounds of Michael's prophecy.

62. See Richard L. Regosin, *The Poetry of Inspiration: Agrippa D'Aubigné's Les Tragiques* (Chapel Hill: Univ. of North Carolina Press, 1970).

63. For further discussion of these Pauline terms as they shape Book Twelve, see Lewalski, "Structure and the Symbolism of Vision in Michael's Prophecy," *Paradise Lost*, Books 11-12," *PQ*, 42 (1963), 25-35.

64. While Augustine traces the origin of the conflict between the earthly and heavenly cities to the companies of rebel and loyal angels in heaven, and on earth to Cain and Abel, he observes that with Abraham the City of God "begins to be more conspicuous, and the divine promises which are now fulfilled in Christ are more fully revealed"; he also identifies Nimrod as both the builder of Babel and the founder of Babylon, that quintessential historical manifestation of the earthly city. See *City of God*, trans. Marcus Dods (New York: Random House, 1950), pp. 526-27, 537.

65. Cf. *ibid.*, p. 477:

Two cities have been formed by two loves: the earthly by the love of self, even to the contempt of God; the heavenly by the love of God, even to the contempt of self. . . . the one seeks glory from men; but the greatest glory of the other is God, the witness of conscience. . . . The one delights in its own strength, represented in the persons of its rulers; the other says to its God, "I will love Thee, O Lord, my strength." And therefore the wise men of the one city [glory] . . . in their own wisdom, and being possessed by pride "they become fools. . . ." But in the other city there is no human wisdom, but only godliness, which offers due worship to the true God, and looks for its reward in the society of the saints.

66. *Divine Weeks*, II.1.9-12, Snyder, 1:316:

Grant me the story of thy Church to sing,
And gests of kinges: Let me this Totall bring
From thy first Sabaoth to his fatall toombe,
My stile extending to the day of doombe.

Du Bartas' overarching scheme of the seven days and ages was also based on Augustine's *City of God*.

CHAPTER 3. "ARGUMENT HEROIC DEEM'D":
THE GENRES OF THE SATANIC HEROIC MODE

1. See, e.g., Bowra, *From Virgil to Milton*; Steadman, *Milton and the Renaissance Hero* and *Milton's Epic Characters*; Di Cesare, "*Paradise Lost* and Epic Tradition"; and Blessington, *Paradise Lost and the Classical Epic*.
2. Renaissance critics were in substantial agreement that the characteristic epic emotion is wonder. The source is Aristotle's argument to the effect that "the irrational, on which the wonderful depends for its chief effects, has wider scope in Epic poetry" (*Poetics* 24, [1460a], Butcher, p. 95). Giraldi Cinthio drew from this precept a definitive conclusion: "Aristotle . . . said that the wonderful was fitting to great heroic compositions and that falsehood serves them much more than truth" (*On Romances*, Snuggs, p. 49). Tasso developed from Aristotle's brief comments a complete "Aristotelian" definition of epic (*Discourses on the Heroic Poem*, Cavalchini and Samuel, pp. 15-17):

The epic poem ought therefore to afford its own delight with
its own effect—which is perhaps to move wonder . . . To move
wonder fits no kind of poetry so much as epic: so Aristotle
teaches, and Homer himself. . . . We shall say that the epic
poem is an imitation of a noble action, great and perfect,
narrated in the loftiest verse, with the purpose of moving the
mind to wonder and thus being useful.

3. Unlike Satan, however, Achilles set a limit on his anger when he
refused the overtures of Agamemnon, Odysseus, and Phoinix: "Still
the heart in me swells up in anger, when I remember / the disgrace
that he wrought upon me before the Argives, / the son of Atreus,
as if I were some dishonoured vagabond. / . . . I shall not think
again of the bloody fighting / until such time as the son of wise
Priam, Hektor the brilliant, / comes all the way to the ships of the
Myrmidons." He also modifies this vow somewhat when he allows
Patroklos to impersonate him: "We will let all this be a thing of
the past; and it was not / in my heart to be angry forever; and yet
I have said / I would not give over my anger until that time came
/ when the fighting with all its clamour came up to my own ships"
(*Iliad* 9.646-652, 16.60-63, Lattimore, pp. 215, 331-32).

4. See *PL*, 1.311-30, 622-62; *Aeneid* 1.124-30, 198-209; *Iliad* 9.9-
28.

5. *Iliad* 12.310-28, Lattimore, pp. 266-67. Also, the parallel calls in
the Councils in Heaven and Hell for a volunteer to undertake a
mission to earth allude to the parallel calls to the Greek and Trojan
armies for a volunteer to undertake a spying mission in the enemy
camp (*Iliad* 10.202-464). In all these cases the audiences were
initially struck mute. We are led to associate Satan, who refused
to allow any other to share the glory of his mission, with the
Trojan spy Dolan who undertook his spying mission alone so as
to be sole recipient of the promised reward. He was captured al-
most immediately, and out of cowardice gave his captors all the
information they sought. The contrasting case was that of the Greek
spy Diomedes, who sought and obtained the company of the wise
Odysseus on his mission declaring, "a man by himself, though he
be careful, / still has less mind in him than two, and his wits have.
less weight" (10.225-26, Lattimore, p. 224).

6. Cf. *Aeneid* 2.274-75: "ei mihi, qualis erat! quantum mutatus ab
illo / Hectore, qui redit exuvias indutus Achilli." Blessington points

out (*Paradise Lost and the Classical Epic*, p. 3) that Aeneas looking on Hector has a vision of death and must learn to accept defeat at the hands of the Greeks, whereas Satan sees on the countenance of Beelzebub the image of spiritual death but does not heed the message.

7. *Aeneid* 1.418-38.

8. *Ibid.*, 5.751, Fairclough, 1:497; *PL*, 2.456-62.

9. *Iliad* 5.633-54; 17.12-42; 22.260-366.

10. *Ibid.*, 6.391-493; 18.70-137; 22.79-93.

11. *Ibid.*, 8.68-77; 208-13. See the discussion of Satan's excessive boasting in Blessington, *Paradise Lost and the Classical Epic*, pp. 10-12.

12. Mueller, "*Paradise Lost* and the *Iliad*," p. 308.

13. *Iliad* 8.24-27, Lattimore, pp. 182-83.

14. *Ibid.*, 22.365-404.

15. Cf. Aeschylus, *Prometheus Bound*, trans. David Grene, in *The Complete Greek Tragedies*, 4 vols. (Chicago: Univ. of Chicago Press, 1959), 1:348.

> Let it not cross your mind that I will turn
> womanish-minded from my fixed decision
> or that I shall entreat the one I hate
> so greatly, with a woman's upturned hands,
> to loose me from my chains; I am far from that.
>   (ll. 1003-1007)

In Aeschylus' version Prometheus is the source of human arts and knowledge and mankind's champion against a tyrant (Zeus) who has overthrown the traditional rule of justice and law; he thereby represents knowledge struggling against brute force. Some of the Satan-Prometheus parallels are explored, to different purpose, in Zwy Werblowski, *Lucifer and Prometheus* (London: Routledge, 1952).

16. Steadman, *Epic and Tragic Structure*, pp. 103-104. Milton's nephew Edward Philips indicated (*The Life of Milton*, rpt. in Hughes, *Complete Poems and Major Prose*, pp. 1034-35) that Milton's projected tragedy on the subject of the Fall began with these lines.

17. For some discussion of Milton's use of Elizabethan tragedies in this soliloquy and elsewhere, see Gardner, "Milton's Satan and the Theme of Damnation in Elizabethan Tragedy"; Rollin, "*Par-*

adise Lost: 'Tragical-Comical-Historical-Pastoral' "; Hanford, "Dramatic Element in *Paradise Lost*."

18. Cf. Marlowe, *Doctor Faustus*, 1.3.76-80, ed. Roma Gill, *The Plays of Christopher Marlowe* (London, Oxford, and New York: Oxford Univ. Press, 1971), p. 343:

> Why, this is hell, nor am I out of it.
> Think'st thou that I who saw the face of God
> And tasted the eternal joys of heaven,
> Am not tormented with ten thousand hells
> In being depriv'd of everlasting bliss?

See also 1.5.127-76, and 5.1.68-70. Also *Hamlet*, 3.3.36-72.

19. See *Macbeth*, 3.1.48-72, 4.1.146-54. Gardner argues that *Macbeth* embodies the same fundamental conception of spiritual self-destruction as does the Faustus myth. See also *Richard III*, 1.1.1-41.

20. Samuel, *Dante and Milton*, pp. 110-66, discusses the parallel in detail. John Wooton, "The Metaphysics of Milton's Epic Burlesque Humor," *Milton Studies* 13 (1979), 255-73 calls attention to some uses of the comic grotesque in Books Two and Three, in the scenes portraying Sin and Death, Chaos, and the Paradise of Fools.

21. Giraldi Cinthio, *On Romances*, Snuggs, p. 57. See also Minturno, *L'Arte Poetica*, p. 29: "Odyssea, alla quale è più simile, che alla Iliada il Romanzo." For a full discussion of the Renaissance debate about whether and on what grounds romances could be considered a species of epic see Weinberg, *Literary Criticism in the Renaissance*, 2:954-1073.

22. Parker, *Inescapable Romance*, p. 4. See also Annabel M. Patterson, "*Paradise Regained*: A Last Chance at True Romance," *Milton Studies* 17 (1983), 187-208.

23. *Odyssey* 1.1, Lattimore, p. 27.

24. In *PL* 2.659-62, Sin and Death are said to be much more abhorrent than "*Scylla* bathing in the Sea that parts / *Calabria* from the hoarse *Trinacrian* shore." And in *PL* 2.1019-20, Satan making his way through Chaos is said to be harder beset than "when *Ulysses* on the Larboard shunn'd / *Charybdis*, and by th' other whirlpool steer'd."

25. *Odyssey* 5.291-457.

26. Cf. *Odyssey* 9.307-536 and *PL* 3.634-4.130.

27. Preparatory to revealing himself to Alkinoös, Odysseus asks the singer Demodokos to sing of Odysseus' strategem and the Fall of Troy, *Odyssey* 8.485-534.

28. Among the several studies of Milton and Spenser, see Greenlaw, "Spenser's Influence on *Paradise Lost*"; Hieatt, "Spenser and Milton," in *Chaucer, Spenser, Milton*, pp. 153-270; Williams, "Milton, Greatest Spenserian," in *Milton and the Line of Vision*, ed. Wittreich, pp. 25-55; Patrick Cullen, *The Infernal Triad: The Flesh, the World, and the Devil in Spenser and Milton* (Princeton: Princeton Univ. Press, 1974). Maureen Quilligan (*Milton's Spenser*, pp. 79-98) cogently discusses the Sin-Death allegory as a Spenserian fiction modelled upon Red Cross's encounter with Errour, identifying that allegory as Milton's formal testimony to his original, and as his engagement with the problem of fiction in his true story.

29. *FQ* 2.30-45.

30. See, e.g., Hughes, "Milton's Limbo of Vanities," in Fiore, ed., *Th' Upright Heart and Pure*, pp. 7-24.

31. *Orlando Furioso*, Bks. 34-35.29.

32. *Ibid.*, 34.73.2, *Orlando Furioso*, trans. Harington (1591), ed. McNulty, p. 396.

33. As Irene Samuel notes, the windblown emptiness of this place and its future inhabitants owes more to the anteroom of Dante's Hell than to Ariosto's Limbo, *Dante and Milton*, pp. 85-93.

34. *Paradiso*, Cantos 10-14.

35. *Le Roman de la Rose*, 129-520, 3357-498; *Faerie Queene*, 4, Canto 10; Luis de Camões, *Os Lusiadas*, Canto 9; *Orlando Furioso*, Cantos 6-8; *Gerusalemme Liberata*, Canto 14, st. 67-Canto 16; *Faerie Queene* 2, Canto 12.

36. For a suggestive exploration of some thematic and structural parallels between Ovid and Milton see Martz, "Figurations of Ovid," in *Poet of Exile*, pp. 203-43. Martz instances the inclusion of antiheroic elements, a structure in which heroic and nonheroic "panels" alternate, and an overall structure which begins with Chaos and ends with history as it is transformed by a superlative hero (Caesar, Christ). See also Harding, *Milton and the Renaissance Ovid*.

37. See, e.g., Brooks Otis, *Ovid as an Epic Poet*, 2nd ed. (Cambridge: Cambridge Univ. Press, 1970); and G. Karl Galinsky, *Ovid's Metamorphoses* (Berkely: Univ. of California Press, 1975). Quintilian complained of Ovid's "lack of seriousness even when he writes epic," but nonetheless linked him with Homer, Virgil, Lucretius,

Ennius, and Lucan as an epic poet (*Institutio* 10.1.88, Butler, 4:50-51). Giraldi Cinthio cited the *Metamorphoses* as precedent for Ariosto and other Romance writers to treat fabulous epic subjects, to use copia and digressions, and to devise a non-Aristotelian epic structure with its own kind of unity and variety:

> In his *Metamorphoses*, Ovid has shown what is fitting for the ingenious poet to do, for abandoning Aristotle's laws of art with admirable mastery, he commenced the work at the beginning of the world and treated in marvelous sequence a great variety of matters; nevertheless he managed to do so in a fewer number of books than Homer did in the *Iliad* and the *Odyssey*, even though both of these embrace a single action. . . . This shows . . . that all poetical compositions that contain deeds of heroes are not bound by the limits that Aristotle set for poets who write poems of a single action. (*On Romances*, Snuggs, p. 20. See also pp. 40-41, 49-50, 53)

Also, Sandys, in his elaborate *Ovid's Metamorphosis Englished*, commented on the epic topoi that define the work's genre and mode: "His Argument first propounded, our Poet according to the custome of the Heroicall, invokes the divine assistance" (Hulley and Vandersall, p. 49).

38. "nihil est toto, quod perstet, in orbe. / cuncta fluunt, omnisque vagens formatur imago; / . . . nam quod fuit ante, relictum est, / fitque, quod haut fuerat," Ovid, *Metamorphoses* 15.178-86, trans. Miller, pp. 10-13; Sandys, 15.179-88, p. 672.

39. Hesiod, *Theogony*, 116-25, 736-66, Evelyn-White, pp. 86-87, 133-35. See, e.g., A. B. Chambers, "Chaos in *Paradise Lost*," *JHI* 24 (1963), 55-84, and Curry, *Milton's Ontology*, pp. 48-91.

40. *Metamorphoses* 1.128-50, Sandys, p. 29.

41. *Ibid*. 13.898-14.74.

42. See *Ovide Moralisé*, 13.4303-14.301, ed. C. De Boer, "Verhandelingen der Koninklijke Nederlandsche Akademie Van Wetenschappen, Afdeeling Letterkunde," Vols. 15, 21, 30, 37, 43 (Amsterdam, 1915-1938), 37:471-78; 43:13-18. Also, *The XV Bookes of P. Ovidius Naso, entytuled Metamorphosis*, trans. Arthur Golding (London, 1567), ed. John F. Nims (New York: Macmillan, 1965), "The Epistle," and "To the Reader," pp. 405-29. Sandys also voices the familiar claim that Ovid's stories had their origins in biblical

stories and so constitute a pagan scripture, "To the Reader," *Ovid's Metamorphosis*, p. 9.

43. Sandys, *Ovid's Metamorphosis*, pp. 645-46:

> *Scylla* represents a Virgin; who . . . once polluted with the sorceries of *Circe*; that is, having rendred her maiden honour to bee deflowred by bewitching pleasure, she is transformed to an horrid monster. And not so only, but endeavours to shipwracke others. . . . This monster *Scylla* was said soone after to have beene changed into a rocke; in regard of the impudency of lascivious women, hardned by custome."

44. Joseph Addison, *Spectator*, #297, in *Criticisms on Paradise Lost*, ed. Albert S. Cook (Boston: Ginn & Co., 1892), p. 36; Samuel Johnson, *Lives of the English Poets*, ed. G. B. Hill, 3 vols. (Oxford: Clarendon Press, 1905), 1:185-86.

45. Quilligan, *Milton's Spenser*, p. 97.

46. See *PL* 9.495-526 for Milton's comparison of Satan's serpentine metamorphosis with those of Ovid's Hermione, Cadmus, Jupiter, and Aesculapius. Several details in the physical description of the Satanic snake—the crested head, the blazing eyes, the upright posture, the "burnisht Neck of verdant Gold"—recall the Ovidian description of Aesculapius as serpent (*Metamorphoses* 15.626-744). Moreover, Sandys' term for his movement as he "Indenteth through the Citie" (15.689, p. 685) is echoed in Milton's description of Satan moving upright on his folds, "not with indented wave, / Prone on the ground, as since." For the typological interpretation, see Sandys, "Annotations" to Book 15, p. 714.

47. *Metamorphoses* 4.576-80.

48. Among the critics who discuss Mosaic and Exodus allusions and motifs in *Paradise Lost* are Harold Fisch, "Hebraic Style and Motifs in *Paradise Lost*," in *Language and Style in Milton*, ed. Emma and Shawcross, pp. 30-64; Shawcross, "*Paradise Lost* and the Theme of Exodus," *Milton Studies* 2 (1970), 3-26; Jason P. Rosenblatt, "Structural Unity and Temporal Concordance: The War in Heaven in *Paradise Lost*," *PMLA* 87 (1972), 31-41; Rosenblatt, "Mosaic Voice in *Paradise Lost*," in *"Eyes Fast Fixt,"* ed. Lieb and Labriola, pp. 207-32.

49. See, e.g., Philo, *De vita contemplativa*, trans. F. H. Colson, *Philo*, 10 vols. (Loeb, Cambridge: Harvard Univ. Press; London: William Heinemann, 1929-1962), 9:163-67; *The Famous and Memo-*

rable Works of Josephus, 1.7, trans. Thomas Lodge (London, 1609), pp. 51-52; Andrew Willet, *Hexapla in Exodum: That is, a Sixfold Commentary upon the Second Booke of Moses called Exodus* (London, 1608), p. 211; Israel M. Baroway, "The Hebrew Hexameter: A Study in Renaissance Sources and Interpretation," *ELH* 2 (1935), 66-91. For Renaissance epic versions see "The Law. The III Part of the III Day," esp. ll. 1-24, in Sylvester, *Du Bartas' Divine Weeks* II, Snyder, 2:545-88; and Michael Drayton, *Moyses in a Map of His Miracles* (London, 1604).

50. This identification is confirmed in the War in Heaven, as the lines describing the rebels' expulsion from heaven (6.834-66) echo Exodus 14:24-31, describing the Lord's destruction of Pharoah's hosts. See Rosenblatt, "Structural Unity and Temporal Concordance," p. 33.

CHAPTER 4. "SEMBLANCE OF WORTH, NOT SUBSTANCE":
THE DISCURSIVE AND LYRIC GENRES
OF THE DAMNED

1. See Chapter 1, pp. 4-6 and nn. 10-12.
2. Cicero declared that deliberative oratory (like epic) demands a style "of more than average grandeur and brilliance" because of the importance of its political subjects and the violent passions it evoked (*De Oratore* 2.82.336-37, Rackham, 1:453). Quintilian agreed, citing as examples the *Philippics* of Demosthenes and Cicero's own public orations (*Institutio* 3.8.64-67, Butler, 1:510-13).
3. *Institutio* 10.1.46-47, Butler, 4:28-29. Quintilian also notes that Homer attributed to Menelaos the qualities of the plain style, to Nestor those of the middle style, and to Odysseus the vehemence and vigor of the grand style, *Institutio* 12.64-65, Butler, 4:486-87. (*Iliad* 3.212-23, 1.247-49.)
4. We may also think of the several dialogues between Hector and the "careful Poulydamas" (*Iliad* 12.60-80, 210-50).
5. The fact that much of Satan's speech is deliberative rhetoric is underscored by the fact that his vehement rhetorical question, "What though the field be lost? / All is not lost" (1.105-106) echoes a phrase from Pluto's formal address to his entire assembly of devils in Tasso's *Gerusalemme*: "We lost the field, yet lost we not our heart," trans. Fairfax, 1.4.15, Nelson, p. 65.

6. Italics mine. Plutarch reports Caesar's statement, "For my part, I had rather be the chiefest man here [in a miserable barbarian village] then the second person in Rome," "The Life of Julius Caesar," in *The Lives of the Noble Grecians and Romanes*, trans. Thomas North (London, 1595), p. 763.

7. Sin's autobiography is the first in a series of such narratives, which includes Eve's and Adam's accounts of their first hours of life, and Satan's feigned account of himself as serpent eating the forbidden fruit.

8. Also, Milton's description of the angelic campfires on the field at night echoes the setting for the nocturnal council in *Iliad* 9.9-172, during which the Greeks, alarmed by Hector's victories, convince Agamemnon to make overtures of reconciliation to Achilles. Cf. *PL* 6.410-16 and *Iliad* 8.560-65, 9.1-3, Lattimore, pp. 197-98.

9. Cf. the scene in which God and the Son ridicule the foolish pretensions of the rebel angels (5.719-42), dramatizing the psalm text, "The Lord shall have them in derision" (Ps. 2:4). But this fully justified divine irony was expressed in private dialogue: God did not make public game of his enemies.

10. Thucydides associated such debasement of language with Civil War (*The Peloponnesian War* 3.82, trans. Benjamin Jowett [New York and Boston: Bantam Books, 1960], p. 199): "The meaning of words had no longer the same relation to things, but was changed by them as they thought proper." Stella Revard points out that we hear also in these exchanges the tone of malign glee ascribed by Milton and his contemporaries to the perpetrators of the Gunpowder Plot (*The War in Heaven*, pp. 86-107).

11. Plato, *Phaedrus* 277C, Fowler, p. 571; *Gorgias* 508C, Lamb, pp. 472-73. In the *Phaedrus* the Platonic Socrates delivers and analyzes two long speeches on love as examples of bad and good rhetoric. In the *Apology* (trans. Henry North Fowler [Loeb, Cambridge: Harvard Univ. Press; London: William Heinemann, 1953], pp. 69-145) Socrates presents his own speech of defense at his trial as a model for judicial rhetoric and a striking contrast to the usual performance. It is lucid, witty, cogently organized; it eschews appeals to emotion and pity as an affront to the court's concern with justice; and it everywhere reveals Socrates' devotion to truth, justice, and the public good. For a suggestive analysis of the Socratic-Aristotelian ideal in *Paradise Lost*, see Steadman, "Satan and the 'Unjust Discourse.'"

12. Cicero, *Orator* 3.12, Hubbell, p. 313; *De Oratore* 1.6.20, 1.13.60, Rackham, 1:17, 45. Quintilian rejects Aristotle's technical definition of rhetoric as the art of persuasion, defining it rather as "the science of speaking well." He elucidates that final term by reference to Plato's precept that the rhetorician "ought to be just, and possess a knowledge of justice," and by reference to the example of Socrates in the *Apology*. See Quintilian, *Intitutio* 2.15.27-36, 2.20.8; 9.1.11-12; 12.1.3-9, 12.2.17, Butler, 1:313-17, 353-55; 4:161, 357-61, 391.

13. *Gorgias* 527C, Lamb, pp. 530-31.

14. *De Oratore* 2.8.35, Rackham, trans. E. W. Sutton, 1:223.

15. *CPW*, 1:816-17.

16. Plato denounced the Sophists for claiming to speak well on all possible subjects and offering to teach others to do so for a fee, when in fact they have only opinions, not true knowledge. They plead cases in the law courts knowing nothing of justice, and advise political assemblies despite their ignorance of virtue. Pandering to their audiences by showy displays of language and playing upon unworthy emotions, they harm rather than benefit the state. *Gorgias* 451-66, Lamb, pp. 287-321; *Phaedrus* 260-63, Fowler, pp. 513-27.

17. Aristotle, *Rhetoric* 1.6 (1362a), *The Basic Works of Aristotle*, ed. Richard McKeon (New York: Random House, 1941), p. 1343: "The deliberative orator's aim is utility: deliberation seeks to determine not ends but the means to ends, i.e., what it is most useful to do." Though Aristotle treats rhetoric as a practical art, a branch of logic, he expects the rhetorician to be a man of learning and virtue. And while he recognizes its potential for abuse he views rhetoric generally as a force for good (1358b-1360a, McKeon, pp. 1335-39).

18. Quintilian, *Institutio* 3.8.25, Butler, 1:493; [pseudo-Cicero], *Ad C. Herennium Libri IV. De ratione dicendi*, trans. Harry Caplan (Loeb, Cambridge: Harvard Univ. Press; London: William Heinemann, 1948), pp. 161-63.

19. Quintilian, *Institutio* 3.8.25, Butler, 1:491-93.

20. *Ibid.*, 3.8.13, 44-47, Butler, 1:485, 501-503.

21. *Ibid.*, 3.8.13, Butler, 1:485.

22. *Aeneid*, trans. Fairclough, 2:260-67:

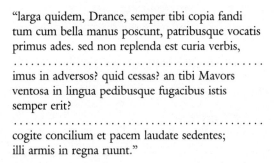

"larga quidem, Drance, semper tibi copia fandi
tum cum bella manus poscunt, patribusque vocatis
primus ades. sed non replenda est curia verbis,

. . . .

imus in adversos? quid cessas? an tibi Mavors
ventosa in lingua pedibusque fugacibus istis
semper erit?

. . . .

cogite concilium et pacem laudate sedentes;
illi armis in regna ruunt."

Similarly, in the council-like scene in Tasso's *Gerusalemme Liberata* in which the pagan ambassadors Argantes and Aletes attempt to dissuade Godfrey from the crusade to recover Jerusalem, Aletes is a worthy precursor of Belial: "a flatterer, a pickthank, and a liar" who delivers "whole streams" of "sugar'd words," appealing especially to ease and safety: "Better sit still, men say, than rise to fall" (2.57-79, trans. Fairfax, pp. 34-39). When Godfrey refuses this plea on the grounds of religious duty, Argantes "Trembling for ire, and waxing pale for rage" calls for war, like a Turnus or a Moloch. See also *Gerusalemme*, 10.34-53. See Weismiller, "Materials Dark and Crude," for discussion of many other echoes of Tasso.

23. Herodotus, *The Persian Wars* 7.8, trans. George Rawlinson (New York: Random House, 1942), p. 498.

24. *Ibid.*, 7.8-18, pp. 496-506.

25. Topics of expediency include: the strength of the armed forces and of the social order of both states, the benefits to be gained from war and from peace, the ease or difficulty of the course proposed. Topics of honor include: the glory of the state, its history and reputation, its rightful ambitions and power. Topics of justice include: revenge for harms suffered, responsibilities to allies. Topics of possibility include: the constraints dictated by things necessary, certain, or fated.

26. All the speakers prefer to account for the security of God's throne in terms of fate rather than divine power.

27. Cf. "To Lollius," ll. 107-12, in *Horace: Satires, Epistles and Ars Poetica*, trans. H. Rushton Fairclough (Loeb, Cambridge: Harvard Univ. Press; London: William Heinemann, 1978), p. 376:

sit mihi quod nunc est, etiam minus, et mihi vivam
quod superest aevi, si quid sueresse volunt di;
sit bona librorum et provisae frugis in annum
copia, neu fluitem dubiae spe pendulus horae.
Sed satis est orare Jovem, qui ponit et aufert,
det vitam, det opes; aequum mi animum ipse parabo.

28. Cf. "Speech of the Consul Lepidus to the Roman People," 24-26, in *Sallust*, trans. John C. Rolfe (Loeb, Cambridge: Harvard Univ. Press; London: William Heinemann, 1920), pp. 392-94:

> If this [Sulla's despotism] seems to you to be peace and order
> ... bow to the laws which have been imposed upon you,
> accept a peace combined with servitude and teach future generations how to ruin their country at the price of their own blood.
> For my own part ... I looked upon freedom united with danger as preferable to peace with slavery (potiorque visa est periculosa libertas quieto servitio).

29. Thucydides, *Peloponnesian War* 2.39, Jowett, p. 117 (Pericles' Funeral Oration).
30. Demosthenes, "The First Olynthiac," "The First Philippic," "The Second Philippic," "The Third Philippic," "The Fourth Philippic," in *Demosthenes 1: Olynthiacs, Philippics, and Minor Orations*, trans. J. H. Vince (Loeb, Cambridge: Harvard Univ. Press; London: William Heinemann, 1970), 1:4-21, 68-99, 123-45, 222-313.
31. "The Third Philippic," 72-76, in *ibid.*, pp. 262-65.
32. Thucydides notes (*Peloponnesian War*, Jowett, p. 131) that Pericles "was able to control the multitude in a free spirit ... for, not seeking power by dishonest arts, he had no need to say pleasant things, but, on the strength of his own high character, could venture to oppose and even to anger them."
33. The subtlety and thoroughness of the manipulation in Milton's council scene may be appreciated by comparing it with Vondel's conception, in which Lucifer's chief ministers concur entirely in and help devise strategy for the revolt, while Beelzebub is concerned only to manipulate the angelic masses. *Vondel's Lucifer*, trans. Charles Van Noppen (New York and London: Continental, 1898; Greensboro, N.C.: C. L. Van Noppen, 1917), pp. 295-327.
34. Satan's scathing question whether the fallen angels are reposing

NOTES TO CHAPTER 4

on the burning lake "for the ease you find / To slumber here . . . /
Or in this abject posture have ye sworn / To adore the Con-
queror?" is somewhat reminiscent of Ajax' scornful exhortation to
the Greeks to save their ships: "Shame, you Argives . . . / Do you
expect if our ships fall to helm-shining Hektor, / You will walk
each of you back dryshod to the land of your fathers? / . . . He is
not inviting you to a dance. He invites you to battle" (*Iliad* 15.502-
508, Lattimore, pp. 322-23).

35. Herodotus, *Persian Wars*, 7.44-46, Rawlinson, pp. 516-17; *Iliad*,
9.9-49.
36. Thucydides, *Peloponnesian War*, 2.59-65, Jowett, pp. 127-30.
37. In a flattering speech to Beelzebub filled with hinted suspicions
regarding the intentions and kingly powers of the Son of God,
Satan directed Beelzebub to lead their forces back to Satan's own
regions, and Beelzebub did so, using "Ambiguous words and jeal-
ousies, to sound / Or taint integrity" (5.703-704).
38. See, e.g., Cicero, "Philippic" 6.7.19, *Philippics*, trans. W.C.A. Ker
(Loeb, Cambridge: Harvard Univ. Press; London: William Hei-
nemann, 1926), p. 333:

> That the Roman people should be slaves is contrary to divine
> law; the immortal Gods have willed it to rule all nations. Mat-
> ters have been brought to the utmost crisis; the issue is lib-
> erty. You must either win victory, Romans, which assuredly
> you will achieve by your loyalty and such unanimity; or do
> anything rather than be slaves. Other nations can endure slav-
> ery; the assured possession of the Roman people is liberty.

39. Lucan, *De bello civili* 1.269-91, *Lucan*, trans. J. D. Duff (Loeb,
Cambridge: Harvard Univ. Press; London: William Heinemann,
1928), pp. 22-25.
40. See Aristotle, *Rhetoric* 2.1 (1377b-1378a), McKeon, pp. 1379-
80; Quintilian, *Institutio* 3.6-13, Butler, 1:482-85. Cicero, *De Or-
atore* 3.59, Rackham, 4:177-79. Milton explicitly invites us to
observe Satan pretending to be so moved by his subject that he
begins without a formal prefatory address to his audience (9.675-
76). The most familiar reference point is Cicero, who was genu-
inely so moved in his first oration against Cataline.
41. See above, Chapter 1, pp. 14-15, and nn. 44, 47.
42. As Helen Gardner notes ("Milton's Satan and the Theme of
Damnation in Elizabethan Tragedy," pp. 46-66) these associations

go far to explain Satan's attractiveness to readers. See also Arnold Stein, "Satan's Metamorphoses: The Internal Speech," *Milton Studies* 1 (1969), 93-113.

43. Scaliger, *Poetices*, 3.125, p. 169; and Puttenham, *Arte of English Poetrie*, pp. 38-39.

44. Scaliger, *Poetices*, 3.122-23, pp. 167-68; and see the discussion in O. B. Hardison, *The Enduring Monument: A Study of the Idea of Praise in Renaissance Literary Theory and Practice* (Chapel Hill: Univ. of North Carolina Press, 1962), pp. 113-18.

45. In several laments mixed with complaint, Hector is urged to refrain from battle by his wife Andromache (6.407-39), and his aged parents Priam and Hecabe (22.38-76, 82-89). Other laments are for the dead and those fated to die: Thetis and her Nereids grieve for the slain Patroklos and for Achilles' imminent death (18.52-64). Achilles and Briseis voice mournful laments for Patroklos (18.324-42; 19.287-300, 315-337). Hecabe and Andromache lament when they learn that Hector is slain (22.431-36, 477-514). And as the funeral dirge is chanted over Hector's body, Andromache, Hecabe, and Helen in turn "lead the lamentations" with monodies (24.718-75).

46. Dido delivers several anguished tirades in the tragic mode as Aeneas departs and she prepares her suicide (4.305-330, 365-87, 534-52, 590-629). In the *Orlando Furioso* the love complaint, with some mixture of lament, is the dominant lyric kind, but here it is used for comic and ironic effect, as all the major characters complain of their lovers and their misfortunes at great length and in much the same terms.

47. Puttenham analyzes this curative effect at some length (*Arte of English Poetrie*, pp. 37-38): "Lamenting is altogether contrary to rejoising, every man saith so, and yet is it a peece of joy to be able to lament with ease. . . . This was a very necessary devise of the Poet . . . to play also the Phisitian, and not onely by applying a medicine to the ordinary sicknes of mankind, but by making the very greef it selfe (in part) cure of the disease."

48. See esp. *Aeneid* 2.274-76, Fairclough, 1:312: "quantum mutatus ab illo / Hectore, qui redit exuvias indutus Achilli, / vel Danaum Phrygios iaculatus puppibus ignis!" Blessington discusses the allusion in *Paradise Lost and the Classical Epic*, p. 3.

49. See Scaliger, *Poetices*, 3.107, p. 259. Satan's words recall Scaliger's example of the *apobaterion*, Aeneas' farewell to Andromache

and Helenus (3.493-505) as he leaves their settlement to continue searching for his destined kingdom: "Fare ye well, ye whose own destiny is already achieved; we are still summoned from fate to fate." Aeneas, however, takes consolation in the prospect of future links of friendship between the society he leaves and that which he will found, whereas Satan only anticipates, solipsistically, that his new realm will be the image of his own mind. See also Thorne-Thomsen, "Milton's 'advent'rous Song,' " pp. 136, 162, 181.

50. See *Faustus*, 5.2.126-84, esp. ll. 138-40, 174-76, *Plays of Marlowe*, ed. Gill, pp. 387-88:

> O I'll leap up to my God! Who pulls me down?
> See, see, where Christ's blood streams in the firmament!
> One drop would save my soul, half a drop. Ah my Christ!
> . . . .
> Curs'd be the parents that engender'd me!
> No, Faustus, curse thyself, curse Lucifer,
> That hath depriv'd thee of the joys of heaven.

Also see *Hamlet* 3.3.36-98, esp. ll. 46-47, 65-72:

> Whereto serves mercy
> But to confront the visage of offense?
> . . . .
> Try what repentance can. What can it not?
> Yet what can it when one cannot repent?
> Oh, wretched state! O bosom black as death!
> Oh, limèd soul, that struggling to be free
> Art more engaged! Help, angels! Make assay!
> Bow, stubborn knees, and heart with strings of steel,
> Be soft as sinews of the newborn babe!
> All may be well.

51. See below, Chapter 5, pp. 120-21 and nn. 21-23.

52. See, e.g., Cicero, *De Inventione* 1.11.14-15, trans. H. M. Hubbell (Loeb, Cambridge: Harvard Univ. Press; London: William Heinemann, 1949), p. 31.

53. See Irene Samuel, "Satan and the 'Diminisht' Stars," *MP* 59 (1962), 239-47.

54. Cicero, *De Inventione* 1.24.34-26.37, Hubbell, pp. 71-75.

55. See *Rhetorica ad Herennium* 2.17.26, Caplan, p. 105: "When we

wish to Reject the Responsibility, we shall throw the blame for our crime either upon some circumstance or upon another person."

56. Cicero, *De Inventione* 1.55.106-109, Hubbell, pp. 157-61: "*Conquestio* [lament or complaint] is a passage seeking to arouse the pity of the audience. . . ."

57. The topic of *Indignatio*. Cicero, *De Inventione* 1.51.98-54.106, Hubbell, pp. 147-57.

58. *Ibid.*, 1.56.109, p. 161.

59. See *Richard III*, 1.1.1-40, and *Othello*, 1.3.389-410; 2.1.295-321.

60. Cicero, *De Inventione* 2.25.78, Hubbell, pp. 243-45: "A retort of the charge occurs when the defendant admits the act of which he is accused, but shows that he was justified in doing it because he was influenced by an offence committed by the other party."

61. See Plato's argument in *Republic* 3.399a that music in the sober Dorian mode best prepares men for battle.

62. Demodokos sang two such epic songs about the Trojan War (*Odyssey* 7.72-95, 487-542). And Achilles sang in his tent as he held himself apart from the battle, "delighting his heart in a lyre, clear-sounding, / splendid and carefully wrought . . . singing of men's fame" (*Iliad* 9.186-89, Lattimore, p. 203).

63. McCown, "Milton and the Epic Epithalamium," pp. 59-60, discusses Satan as a surrogate choragus for the epithalamic wedding sequence which is one of the formal patterns developed in Book Four. See also Thorne-Thomsen, " 'Milton's advent'rous Song,' " pp. 32-42.

64. Cf. Canticles 2:10-13:

> . . . Rise up, my love, my fair one, and come away.
> For, lo, the winter is past, the rain is over and gone.
> The flowers appear on the earth; the time of the singing of birds is come, and the voice of the turtle is heard in our land.
> The fig tree putteth forth her green figs, and the vines with the tender grape, give a good smell.

Other perverse notions in Satan's serenade are these: that night is the proper time for waking; that the moon's shadowy light is preferable to the sun (which reveals the beauties of creation); that all the stars of heaven shine only to behold Eve's beauty. See also Howard Schultz, "Satan's Serenade," *PQ* 27 (1948), 17-26.

65. The trophies carried in a triumphal procession were valuable, beautiful, or curious objects from the conquered land (coins, statues, weapons, armor, etc.), together with models of the cities or forts captured. Sin's point is that this curious and remarkable bridge is itself a trophy of Satan's victory since that victory empowered Death to build it. And, since the victor returns to his city over this structure, it also serves as a triumphal arch.
66. The other two were the goods of nature (health, strength, beauty), and the goods of fortune (family, wealth). See, e.g., Cicero, *De Oratore* 2.342-49; *Rhetorica ad Herennium* 3.7.13-17; Quintilian, *Institutio* 3.7.10-18.
67. Behind the imperator in his triumphal chariot stood a slave who was to whisper from time to time, *Respice post te, hominem memento*. Also, the soldiers of the imperator were allowed total freedom of speech and exercised it by interspersing their shouts of *Io Triumphe* with coarse ribaldry at the imperator's expense. *Harper's Dictionary of Classical Literature and Antiquities*, ed. H. T. Peck (New York: Harper & Row, 1962), pp. 1609-11.
68. Following this, Satan parodies the Father's commission of the Son as his "Vicegerent" to exercise judgment on earth (10.55-56), proclaiming Sin and Death his viceroys "Plenipotent on Earth" (403-404)—sent as by a Roman emperor to rule a newly conquered territory. His final directive, "If your joint power prevail, th' affairs of Hell / No detriment need fear, go and be strong" (10.408-409), evokes better associations: the charge given to Roman consuls to save the Republic from "detriment" by assuming supreme power in time of crisis; and God's reiterated charge to Joshua to "be strong" in leading the Israelites into the Promised Land (See Hughes, p. 416; Joshua, 1:1-9). The Satanic contrast to all these missions is absolute: Sin and Death are not sent to rule, or to defend, or to found a society, but to ravage the social order and nature itself.
69. Satan first assumes his throne disguised as a "Plebian Angel" and then reveals himself in a blaze of permissive glory—recalling similar scenes of new glory shed upon Odysseus by Athena, and upon Aeneas by Venus, before they enter the courts of Alkinoös and Dido (*Odyssey* 8.18-24; *Aeneid* 1.586-95). The analogues remind us that both heroes recounted their adventures only at the importunity of their hosts, and as sad tales of suffering and struggle, not as triumphs. In a parallel scene in *Gerusalemme Liberata*, 10.49-52,

Soliman suddenly appears and recounts his past victories—but to hearten his allies, not to glorify himself. By other specific references (to Xerxes' bridge spanning the Hellespont and to the fallen angels as "Sophi" and their council as a "Divan," 10.306-11, 431-36, 457), we are invited to recall Xerxes' premature triumph over the conquest of Athens, and to anticipate for Satan a rout more disastrous than Xerxes' experiences at Salamis (Herodotus, *The Persian Wars*, 7.33-9.70, and especially 8.97-99, Rawlinson, pp. 511-691). The explicit comparison brings full circle the Satan-Xerxes analogue begun with the reference in Book One to Satan weeping (like Xerxes) over his assembled troops.

70. *Harper's Dictionary*, pp. 1609-10.
71. *Ibid.*, p. 1610.

CHAPTER 5. "OTHER EXCELLENCE":
GENERIC MULTIPLICITY AND MILTON'S LITERARY GOD

1. Joseph Addison, *Spectator* #315, *Criticisms on Paradise Lost*, ed. Cook, pp. 61-62; Shelley, "On the Devil, and Devils," in *The Romantics on Milton: Formal Essays and Critical Asides*, ed. Joseph A. Wittreich, Jr. (Cleveland and London: Case Western Reserve Univ. Press, 1970), pp. 534-35; William Empson, *Milton's God* (London: Chatto & Windus, 1961); A.J.A. Waldock, *Paradise Lost and Its Critics* (1947; rpt. Cambridge: Cambridge Univ. Press, 1967), p. 103; Douglas Bush, *English Literature in the Earlier Seventeenth Century, 1600-1660* (Oxford: Clarendon Press, 1945), p. 381.
2. See, e.g., C. A. Patrides, "Paradise Lost and the Theory of Accommodation," *TSLL* 5 (1963), 58-63, rpt. in *Bright Essence*, pp. 159-63; Charles G. Shirley, Jr., "The Four Phases of the Creation: Milton's Use of Accommodation in *Paradise Lost* VII," *SAB* 45 (1980), 51-61; Michael Lieb, *Poetics of the Holy: A Reading of "Paradise Lost"* (Chapel Hill: Univ. of North Carolina Press, 1981); Dennis R. Danielson, *Milton's Good God: A Study in Literary Theodicy* (Cambridge: Cambridge Univ. Press, 1982); Georgia B. Christopher, *Milton and the Science of the Saints* (Princeton: Princeton Univ. Press, 1982), pp. 3-29, 89-133.
3. Stanley Fish, *Surprised by Sin*, pp. 62-87; William Kerrigan, *The Sacred Complex: On the Psychogenesis of Paradise Lost* (Cambridge:

Harvard Univ. Press, 1983); Andrew Milner, *John Milton and the English Revolution* (London: Macmillan, 1981).

4. *De Doctrina*, 1.2, *CPW*, 6:133.

5. *Ibid.*, pp. 133-34.

6. *Ibid.*, pp. 134-35. For a review of the literature on Milton's anthropomorphic (or anthropopathic) God, see Sister Hilda Bonham, "The Anthropomorphic God of *Paradise Lost*," *Papers of the Michigan Academy of Science, Arts and Letters* 53 (1968), 329-35.

7. See Sims, *The Bible in Milton's Epics*, pp. 17-20, and his index of Bible references, pp. 259-78.

8. Michael Murrin in "The Language of Milton's Heaven," *MP* 74 (1977), 350-65, points to Milton's fusion of biblical prophetic images in such a way as to prevent distinct visualization of God or heaven—ascribing this to Milton's iconoclasm. I suggest that the mix of genres performs a somewhat similar function, by preventing reductive or presumptuously comprehensive conceptions of God. But the generic patterns and paradigms also assist our understanding of God by directing us to clarify our perceptions through comparisons, contrasts, and emphases.

9. *De Doctrina* 1.5, *CPW*, 6:205-11, 227, 261-64.

10. *Ibid.*, pp. 236-39, 267-70. This is substantially the position of Maurice Kelley in *This Great Argument* and "Milton's Arianism Again Considered"; also, Christopher Hill in *Milton and the Engish Revolution* (London: Faber & Faber, 1977), pp. 285-305. For further consideration of Milton's antitrinitarianism with special application to *Paradise Regained* see Lewalski, *Milton's Brief Epic*, pp. 133-63. For the counterargument see essays in *Bright Essence*.

11. For a study of this epic motif in reference to the Council in Hell see Mason Hammond, "Concilia Deorum from Homer through Virgil," *SP* 30 (1933), 1-16; and O. H. Moore, "The Infernal Council," *MP* 16 (1918), 169-93. For an argument that both councils are transformed by Milton's prophetic impulse, see Joseph Wittreich, " 'All Angelic Natures Joined in One': Epic Convention and Prophetic Interiority in the Council Scenes of *Paradise Lost*," in *Composite Orders*, pp. 43-74.

12. *Odyssey* 1.32-34, Lattimore, p. 28.

13. *Aeneid*, trans. Fairclough, 2:141. Several of Milton's editors, including Newton and Todd, have noted this allusion.

14. In the romances erotic love is central and occasionally heroic, as when Edward and Gildippes fight and die side by side in battle

(Tasso, *Gerusalemme*, trans. Fairfax, 20.32-43, 94-100), or Brito-
mart rescues her spouse-to-be Artegall from enslavement by Radi-
gund (*FQ* 5.5-8). For a discussion of Milton's revaluation of several
heroic virtues see Steadman, *Milton and the Renaissance Hero*.

15. Cf. *PL* 3.56-71, and Ovid, *Metamorphoses* 2.31-32: "Ipse loco
medius rerum novitate paventem / Sol oculis juvenem, quibus ad-
spicit omnia."

16. Ovid, *Metamorphoses* 2.42-43; Sandys, ed. Hulley and Vandersall,
pp. 80-81.

17. Milton's sketch in the Trinity College manuscript for a drama on
"Paradise Lost" (*John Milton: Poems* [facs. ed., Menston: Scolar
Press, 1972], p. 35), has a version of the Parliament of Heaven,
with Justice and Mercy "debating what should become of man if
he fall." The debate was evidently to be resolved by the next listed
character, Wisdom. For a review of this motif in drama and in
allegorical narratives, see Hope Traver, *The Four Daughters of God:
A Study of the Versions of this Allegory* (Philadelphia: J. C. Winston,
1907). Studies of Milton's Dialogue in Heaven with some refer-
ence to this tradition include Merritt Y. Hughes, "The Filiations
of Milton's Celestial Dialogue," *Ten Perspectives on Milton* (New
Haven and London: Yale Univ. Press, 1965), pp. 104-35; and
Irene Samuel, "The Dialogue in Heaven."

18. The thematic development of the speeches in Milton's Dialogue
in Heaven resembles most closely the Coventry cycle *Salutatio and
Conception*, and the morality, *The Castell of Perseverence*, in which
Truth (rather than Mercy as is more usual) opens the debate. See
Traver, *Four Daughters of God*, pp. 138-40.

19. As Milton did in his Preface to *Samson Agonistes*, Renaissance
critics found ancient precedent for Christian tragedy based on the
Passion in the *Christus Patiens*, commonly though perhaps erro-
neously attributed to the fourth-century bishop Gregory Nazian-
zen. Hugo Grotius' neo-Latin play, *Tragoedia Christus patiens*
(Monachii, 1627) provides a contemporary example.

20. On this point see also Anthony Low, "Milton's God: Authority
in *Paradise Lost*," *Milton Studies* 4 (1972), 19-38. For the counter-
argument, see Fish, *Surprised by Sin*, pp. 62-87.

21. Cicero, *De Inventione* 1.11.14-15, 2.28.86-87, Hubbell, pp. 31,
253; *Rhetorica ad Herennium* 1.14.24-26, 2.17.26, Caplan, pp. 43-
49, 105.

22. Cicero, *De Inventione* 1.16.22, 1.19.27, Hubbell, pp. 45, 55; *Ad Herennium* 1.6.9-1.8.13, Caplan, pp. 17-25.
23. Cicero, *De Inventione* 2.29.88, Hubbell, p. 255; *Ad Herennium* 1.15.25, Caplan, pp. 47-49.
24. See also Moses' plea to God for the backsliding Israelites in Num. 14:15-16:

> Now if thou shalt kill all this people as one man, then the nations which have heard the fame of thee will speak, saying, Because the Lord was not able to bring this people into the land which he sware unto them, therefore he hath slain them in the wilderness.

Compare *PL* 3.162-65:

> or wilt thou thyself
> Abolish thy Creation, and unmake
> For him, what for thy glory thou hast made?
> So should thy goodness and thy greatness both
> Be question'd and blasphem'd without defense.

25. Plato, *Apology*, Fowler, pp. 69-145. At his trial, Socrates held forth his speech of defense as a model for forensic rhetoric. See Chapter 4, n. 11. For discussion of some adaptations of Socratic dialectic in the Councils in Hell and Heaven, and in the Abdiel-Satan debate, see Safer, "The Use of Contraries."
26. See esp. *Iliad* 8.5-27, Lattimore, p. 182:

> Hear me, all you gods and all you goddesses: hear me
> while I speak forth what the heart within my breast urges.
> Now let no female divinity, nor male god either,
> presume to cut across the way of my word, but consent to it
> all of you, so that I can make an end in speed of these matters.
> And any one I perceive against the gods' will attempting
> to go among the Trojans and help them, or among the Danaans,
> he shall go whipped against his dignity back to Olympos;
> . . . .
> Then he will see how far I am strongest of all the immortals.

27. See, e.g.,

> Heb. 1:5: For unto which of the angels said he at any time, Thou art my son, this day have I begotten thee? And again, I will be to him a Father, and he shall be to me a Son?

Ps. 2:6-7: Yet have I set my king upon my holy hill of Zion.
I will declare the decree: The Lord hath said unto me, Thou art
my Son: this day have I begotten thee.

Ps. 110:1: The Lord said unto my Lord, Sit thou at my right
hand, until I make thine enemies thy footstool.

Coloss. 2:10: And ye are complete in him, which is the head of
all principality and power.

Gen. 22:16: By myself have I sworn, saith the Lord . . .

Philip. 2:10-11: That at the name of Jesus every knee should bow,
of things in heaven, and things in earth, and things under the earth;
And that every tongue should confess that Jesus Christ is Lord, to
the glory of God the Father.

28. See above, Chapter 4, pp. 83-84.
29. *Iliad* 16.49-100, Lattimore, pp. 332-33. Achilles urges Patroklos
to "win, for me, great honour and glory," but commands him not
to attempt a definitive victory against the Trojans, lest the gods
crush him. However, he relishes the idea of universal slaughter as
glorious: "if only / not one of all the Trojans could escape destruc-
tion, not one / of the Argives, but you and I could emerge from
the slaughter / so that we two alone could break Troy's hallowed
coronal."
30. The scene of investiture is presented as an infusion of divine
power: The Father "on his Son with Rays direct / Shone full; hee
all his Father full exprest / Ineffably into his face receiv'd" (6.719-
21).
31. See Rom. 12:10; also Ps. 94:1, Deut. 32:35, and Heb. 10:30.
32. *Iliad* 21.214-15.
33. *Iliad* 22.205-207.
34. We are not to conclude from Milton's critique of war in *Paradise
Lost* that he has repudiated the Civil War, or the Lord's battles in
the Old Testament, or the very idea of war. What he had repu-
diated is the notion that war is in itself glorious—however neces-
sary it may sometimes be as an instrument of God's judgment or
providential design. For various views on the issue, see Jackie Di
Salvo, "The Lord's Battles: *Samson Agonistes* and the Puritan Rev-
olution," *Milton Studies* 4 (1972), 39-62. See also Boyd M. Berry,
Process of Speech: Puritan Religious Writing and Paradise Lost (Bal-
timore and London: Johns Hopkins Univ. Press, 1976).
35. Hesiod, *Theogony*, ll. 674-81, Evelyn-White, pp. 128-29. For

discussion of these and other Hesiodic elements, see Merritt Y. Hughes, "Milton's Celestial Battle and the Theogonies." See also Philip J. Gallagher, "*Paradise Lost* and the Greek Theogony," *ELR* 9 (1979), 121-48, for the questionable argument that Milton intends by these allusions to ridicule Hesiod's poem as a Satanic epic.

36. *Theogony*, ll. 687-712, Evelyn-White, pp. 128-31. Hesiod's description of Zeus' warfare is especially suggestive:

> From heaven and from Olympus he came forthwith, hurling his lightning: the bolts flew thick and fast from his strong hand together with thunder and lightning, whirling an awesome flame. The life-giving earth crashed around in burning, and the vast wood crackled loud with fire all about. All the land seethed, and Ocean's streams and the unfruitful sea. The hot vapour lapped round the earthborn Titans: flame unspeakable rose to the bright upper air: the flashing glare of the thunderstone and lightning blinded their eyes for all that they were strong.

Other analogues in the two poems are the response of Chaos to the Battle, and the fall of the rebels to Tartarus. Compare *Theogony*, ll. 700-21, and *PL* 6.867-74.

37. The Miltonic God's omnipotence is further emphasized by the fact that in other Christian epics treating the Battle in Heaven, Michael and the loyal angels are able to defeat and cast out the Satanic forces. See, e.g., Erasmo di Valvasone, *Angeleida* (Venice, 1590). And see Revard, *The War in Heaven*, pp. 235-63.

38. Ps. 24:8. For a discussion of Hebrew exegetical tradition treating the Exodus as an epiclike event, see Harold Fisch, "Hebraic Style and Motifs in *Paradise Lost*," in *Language and Style in Milton*, ed. Emma and Shawcross, pp. 37-39; and Jason Rosenblatt, "Structural Unity and Temporal Concordance," pp. 31-41. For discussion of Exodus motifs in other parts of the poem see Shawcross, "*Paradise Lost* and the Theme of Exodus."

39. Cf. Exod. 19:16, 18, and *PL* 6.56-60:

> And it came to pass on the third day in the morning, that there were thunders and lightnings, and a thick cloud upon the mount, and the voice of the trumpet exceeding loud; so that all the people that was in the camp trembled.

. . . .

> And mount Sinai was altogether on a smoke, because the
> Lord descended upon it in fire.

> So spake the Sovran voice, and Clouds began
> To darken all the Hill, and smoke to roll
> In dusky wreaths, reluctant flames, the sign
> Of wrath awak't: nor with less dread the loud
> Ethereal Trumpet from on high gan blow.

The analogue is noted by Murrin, "Language of Milton's Heaven,"
pp. 252-53. See also Exod. 20:18.

40. For discussion of the parallels, see Rosenblatt, "Structural Unity
and Temporal Concordance," pp. 31-41. For the theory of the
epiclike meter in Exodus 15, see Philo, *De vita contemplativa*, in
Philo, trans. F. H. Colson (Loeb, Cambridge: Harvard Univ. Press;
London: William Heinemann, 1929-1962), pp. 9:163-67; and
Andrew Willet, *Hexapla in Exordium: that is, a Sixfold Commentary
upon the Second Book of Moses Called Exodus* (London, 1608), pp.
210-11. We should also recall the simile (*PL* 1.339-46) in which
Satan as a perverse Moses calls up the rebel angels from the burn-
ing lake of hell as a plague of locusts.

41. We are directed to the great epic battle and cataclysm at the
Apocalypse by the rebel angels' wish that "the Mountains now
might be again / Thrown on them as a shelter from his ire" (6.843-
44), echoing the cry of the wicked at the Last Judgment "to the
mountains and rocks, Fall on us, and hide us from the face of him
that sitteth upon the throne" (Rev. 6:16). For the argument that
the three-day Battle in Heaven is primarily typological, looking
forward to the Apocalyptic warfare of Christ and Antichrist, see
William Madsen, *From Shadowy Types to Truth: Studies in Milton's
Symbolism* (New Haven: Yale Univ. Press, 1968), pp. 99-111; and
for the argument that it foreshadows Christ's death and resurrec-
tion, see W. H. Hunter, "Milton on the Exaltation of the Son:
The War in Heaven in *Paradise Lost*," *ELH* 36 (1969), pp. 215-
31. While the first victory of the Son clearly foreshadows those to
come, I think we are intended to focus on this battle primarily as
literal event, accommodated to us by reference to all other ac-
counts of the Son's warfare against Satan throughout all time.

42. See Ezekiel 1:4-28. Kitty Cohen, *The Throne and the Chariot:
Studies in Milton's Hebraism* (The Hague: Mouton, 1975), pp. 103-
32, emphasizes Milton's strategies for portraying the divine power

as essentially spiritual. The Chariot of Paternal Deity as war char-
iot may also owe something to Isaiah 66:15: "For, behold, the
Lord will come with fire, and with his chariots like a whirlwind,
to render his anger with fury, and his rebuke with flames of fire."
43. See *Iliad* 15.320-27, Lattimore, pp. 317-18:

But when he stared straight into the eyes of the fast-mounted
Danaans
and shook the aegis, and himself gave a great baying cry, the spirit
inside them was mazed to hear it, they forgot their furious valour.
And they, as when in the dim of the black night two wild beasts
stampede a herd of cattle or big flock of sheep, falling
suddenly upon them, when no herdsman is by, the Achaians
fled so in their weakness and terror, since Apollo drove
terror upon them.

Cf. Matt. 8:28-34, Mark 5:1-13, Luke 8:26-33. Milton's substi-
tution of goats for Homer's cattle or sheep and the Gadarene swine
is no doubt dictated by the traditional image of the wicked as goats
at the Last Judgment. His metaphor presents those goats rendered
timorous as sheep by the manifestation of divine power.
44. The language of mission makes this distinction clear: "This I
perform, speak thou, and be it done" (7.164).
45. See Sims, *The Bible in Milton's Epics*, pp. 33-35, 266-67; Ernst
Häublein, "Milton's Paraphrase of Genesis: A Stylistic Reading of
Paradise Lost, Book VII," *Milton Studies* 7 (1975), 101-25.
46. "When he prepared the heavens, I was there: when he set a
compass upon the face of the depth."
47. See above, Chapter 2, pp. 44-46. For specific parallels with Du
Bartas and Sylvester's translation, see Taylor, *Milton's Use of Du
Bartas*, and the introduction to Snyder's edition of Sylvester's *Du
Bartas*, 1:72-95.
48. For discussion of this image and its implications see, e.g., Lieb,
Dialectics of Creation, pp. 56-68; Summers, *Muse's Method*, pp. 137-
46; Shirley, "Four Phases of the Creation," pp. 51-61; Gardner,
Reading of Paradise Lost, pp. 70-75; O. B. Hardison, Jr., "Written
Records and Truths of Spirit in *Paradise Lost*," *Milton Studies* 1
(1969), 147-65.
49. *PL* 7.243-49:

Let there be Light, said God, and forthwith Light
Ethereal, first of things, quintessence pure

Sprung from the Deep, and from her Native East
To journey through the airy gloom began,
Spher'd in a radiant Cloud, for yet the Sun
Was not; shee in a cloudy Tabernacle
Sojourn'd the while. God saw the Light was good.

50. See Lucretius, *De Rerum Natura* 5.1-854. See above, Chapter 2, pp. 40-41 and nn. 40-43. Milton also lays under contribution Ovid's stories of Creation and Flood, *Metamorphoses* 1.1-437.

51. For discussion of Adam's question and its significance, see below, Chapter 8, pp. 209-10, and Lewalski, "Innocence and Experience in Milton's Eden."

52. *De Rerum Natura*, 5.168-69, Rouse, pp. 390-91:

quidve novi potuit tanto post ante quietos
inlicere, ut cuperent vitam mutare priorem?

53. *De Rerum Natura* 2.992-95, Rouse, pp. 172-73:

omnibus ille idem pater est, unde alma liquentis
umoris guttas mater cum terra recepit,
feta parit nitidas fruges arbustaque laeta
et genus humanum, parit omnia saecla ferarum.

Cf. Ovid, *Metamorphoses* 1.417-21, Miller, 1:30-33:

postquam vetus umor ab igne
percaluit solis, caenumque udaeque paludes
intumuere aestu, fecundaque semina rerum
vivaci nutrita solo ceu matris in alvo
creverunt faciemque aliquam cepere morando.

54. *De Rerum Natura* 5.781-91, Rouse, pp. 438-41:

novo fetu . . .

. . . .

Principio genus herbarum viridemque nitorem
terra dedit circum collis camposque per omnis,
florida fulserunt viridanti prata colore,
arboribusque datumst variis exinde per auras
crescendi magnum inmissis certamen habenis.
ut pluma atque pili primum saetaeque creantur
quadripedum membris et corpore pennipotentum,

sic nova tum tellus herbas virgultaque primum
sustulit.

55. *De Rerum Natura* 5.795-924, Rouse, pp. 440-42, 450-51, esp.
ll. 806-13, 916-17:

multus enim calor atque umor superabat in arvis.
hoc ubi quaeque loci regio opportuna dabatur,
crescebant uteri terram radicibus apti;
quos ubi tempore maturo patefecerat aetas
infantum, fugiens umorem aurasque petessens,
convertebat ibi natura foramina terrae
et sucum venis cogebat fundere apertis
consimilem lactis.

. . . .

nam quod multa fuere in terris semina rerum
tempore quo primum tellus animalia fudit.

56. The structural centrality of the Creation was first argued by Arthur Barker, "Structural Pattern in *Paradise Lost*," *PQ* 23 (1949), 16-30.
57. See commentaries on Gen. 3:8-24, in Willet, *Hexapla in Genesim*; Calvin, *A Commentarie of John Calvine, upon the first book of Moses, called Genesis*, trans. Thomas Tymme (London, 1578); Luther, *Lectures on Genesis*, in *Works*, ed. Jaroslav Pelikan and Helmut E. Lehmann, 51 vols. (St. Louis: Condordia Publishing House, 1955-1975), Vol. 1. See also Arnold Williams, *The Common Expositor: An Account of the Commentaries on Genesis, 1527-1633* (Chapel Hill: Univ. of North Carolina Press, 1948).
58. *Metamorphoses* 1.160-416, Miller, 1:12-31.
59. *Metamorphoses* 1.166-67: "ingentes animo et dignas Iove concipit iras / conciliumque vocat." Cf. Sandys, ed. Hulley and Vandersall, p. 30: "Just anger, worthy *Jove*, inflam'd his brest. / A Synod call'd."
60. *Metamorphoses* 1.244-49, Miller, 1:18-19.
61. *Ibid.*, 1.230-443.
62. Sylvester's *Du Bartas*, "The Furies," 2.1, pt. 3, ll. 112-72, Snyder, 1:360-62.
63. *Metamorphoses* 1.262-91.
64. For discussion of the major exegetical traditions regarding the curse on nature and Milton's distinctive conception of it in *Para-*

dise Lost, see Ellen Goodman, "The Design of Milton's World" (Ph.D. diss., Brown Univ., 1966).

65. *PL* 11.22-30:

> See Father, what first fruits on Earth are sprung
> From thy implanted Grace in Man, these Sighs
> And Prayers, which in this Golden Censer, mixt
> With Incense, I thy Priest before thee bring,
> Fruits of more pleasing savor from thy seed
> Sown with contrition in his heart, than those
> Which his own hand manuring all the Trees
> Of Paradise could have produc't, ere fall'n
> From innocence.

66. See Gen. 3:22-23:

> And the Lord God said, Behold, the man is become as one of us, to know good and evil: and now, lest he put forth his hand, and take also of the tree of life, and eat, and live for ever:
>
> Therefore, the Lord God sent him forth from the garden of Eden, to till the ground from whence he was taken.

67. In Ovid Jove argues the need to cut away with a knife that which is incurable "lest the untainted part also draw infection"—the demigods and rustic divinities dwelling on earth (*Metamorphoses* 1.187-95, Miller, 1:14-15). Milton's God also speaks of the "filth / Which man's polluting Sin with taint hath shed / On what was pure" (10.630-32), but he explains the sealing off of Eden by the Cherubim's swords in part by the need to protect man: "Lest Paradise a receptácle prove / To Spirits foul, and all my Trees thir prey, / With whose stol'n Fruit Man once more to delude" (11.123-25).

CHAPTER 6. "OUR HAPPY STATE":
LITERARY FORMS FOR ANGELIC WHOLENESS

1. Leland Ryken, *The Apocalyptic Vision in Paradise Lost* (Ithaca and London: Cornell Univ. Press, 1970), pp. 75-87.
2. Knott, *Milton's Pastoral Vision*, pp. 62-87.
3. In *The Greek Bucolic Poets*, trans. J. M. Edmonds (Loeb, Cam-

bridge: Harvard Univ. Press; London: William Heinemann, 1970), pp. 91-107.

4. See Virgil, *Georgics* 2.458-542, and for the daily round, ll. 513-31, in *Virgil*, Fairclough, 1:148-58. Other major examples are Horace's "Epode 2, Beatus ille" (*Horace*, Bennett, pp. 364-69); Palinode's paeon to May Day in Spenser's *Shepheardes Calendar*, "Maye," ll. 1-16, *Poetical Works*, p. 436; and the "Sixth Nymphall" in Drayton's *Muses Elizeum* (*Works*, ed. J. William Hebel, 5 vols. [Oxford: B. Blackwell, 1931-1941], 3:293-300). See the account of this tradition traced with reference to "L'Allegro" and "Il Penseroso" in Sara Ruth Watson, "Milton's Ideal Day: Its Development as a Pastoral Theme," *PMLA* 44 (1942), 404-20.

5. See Demaray, *Milton's Theatrical Epic*, pp. 92-96.

6. *PL* 8.618-30, and discussion below, Chapter 8, pp. 217-18.

7. *Iliad* 1.595-611, Lattimore, pp. 74-75; *Aeneid* 6.637-65, Fairclough, 1:550-53; Theocritus, "Idyl 7," in *Greek Bucolic Poets*, Edmonds, pp. 105-107. Mary Thomas Crane has called my attention to the jewelled cup topos in Juvenal, "Satire X," ll. 25-27, with associations of vice and danger entirely foreign to the angelic feasting.

8. *Odyssey* 9.82-102, 10.460-77, Lattimore, pp. 139-40, 164; Tasso, *Gerusalemme Liberata*, trans. Fairfax, 15.57-16.35, pp. 314-26; *Faerie Queene* 2.12. For a discussion of the ways in which the sensuous gardens of romance and their pleasures are reflected in Milton's epic, see Giamatti, *Earthly Paradise*, pp. 295-355.

9. The comparison, "Like *Maia's* son he stood," explicitly associates Raphael with Mercury, as does Adam's epithet for him, "Divine Interpreter" (7.72), which literally translates Virgil's "*interpres divum*" (4.378), applied to Mercury. For discussion of further parallels, see Harding, *Club of Hercules*, pp. 101-103; Thomas Greene, *The Descent from Heaven: A Study in Epic Continuity* (New Haven and London: Yale Univ. Press. 1963), pp. 363-87; and Blessington, *Paradise Lost and the Classical Epic*, pp. 25-34.

10. Revard (*War in Heaven*) underscores the significant ways in which Milton has departed from the tradition, perhaps most notably in portraying the loyal angels forced to come to terms with their own limitations. The point is also noted by Summers, *Muse's Method*, pp. 122-37; Fish, *Surprised by Sin*, pp. 180-207; and Dick Taylor, Jr., "The Battle in Heaven in *Paradise Lost*," *Tulane Studies in English* 3 (1952), 69-92.

11. James A. Freeman, *Milton and the Martial Muse: Paradise Lost and European Traditions of War* (Princeton: Princeton Univ. Press, 1980), argues that *Paradise Lost* presents a thoroughgoing and absolute condemnation of war, directly opposing and challenging Renaissance and seventeenth-century military values, conventions, and techniques. But Milton's presentation of the loyal angels as warriors creates some difficulties for that thesis.

12. Cf. *Iliad* 2.459-63, and *Aeneid* 7.699-701.

13. Arnold Stein's seminal essay, "The War In Heaven," in *Answerable Style: Essays on Paradise Lost* (Minneapolis: Univ. of Minnesota Press, 1953), pp. 20-23, interprets the entire battle as mock-epic, laden with irony and comic excess directed against epic heroism. Similarly, B. A. Wright, *Milton's "Paradise Lost"* (London: Methuen, 1962), pp. 131-37, sees the battle as an "extravagant satire" on warfare as such, and on belief in its heroism. I suggest rather that the tone remains substantially heroic until the invention of the cannon, despite the ongoing critique of martial heroism and the modifications in epic warfare occasioned by the angelic invulnerability and immortality. Milton shifts the generic frame to mock-epic at just this moment to signal a decline from the flawed heroism of Homeric battle to the thoroughly ignoble warfare fought with "demonic" modern weapons.

14. Lieb, *Dialectics of Creation*, pp. 118-20.

15. Hesiod, *Theogony*, ll. 674-78, 713-20, Evelyn-White, pp. 128-31.

16. Gardner, *A Reading of Paradise Lost*, pp. 67-68, has pointed to the tragic dimension in Milton's portrayal of warfare.

17. Madsen, *From Shadowy Types to Truth*, pp. 85-113. See also Jon S. Lowry, *The Shadow of Heaven* (Ithaca: Cornell Univ. Press, 1968), pp. 199-202; and Austin C. Dobbins, *Milton and the Book of Revelation* (University: Univ. of Alabama Press, 1975), pp. 26-27.

18. *CPW*, 2:554-56. Cf. Num. 11:29, "Would God that all the Lord's people were prophets, and that the Lord would put his Spirit upon them."

19. *De Doctrina*, 1.15, 19, *CPW*, 6:432, 572. See William Perkins' manual on preaching called *The Arte of Prophecying*, trans. Thomas Tuke, *Workes*, Vol. 2 (London, 1612-1613). And see discussion in Kerrigan, *The Prophetic Milton*, pp. 93-108.

20. *An Apology Against a Pamphlet, CPW*, 1:899-901.

21. See above, Chapter 5, pp. 122-24.

22. See, e.g., *Phaedrus*, trans. Fowler, pp. 568-75; *Republic* 7.532-40, trans. Paul Shorey, 2 vols. (Loeb, Cambridge: Harvard Univ. Press; London: William Heinemann, 1982), 2:196-233.

23. See Boethius, *The Consolation of Philosophy*, ed. Irwin Edman (New York: Modern Library, 1943), for the dialogues between Boethius and Lady Philosophy. Another model for the dialogic method of Milton's angels is provided by the Dante-Beatrice exchanges in the *Divine Comedy*.

24. Cf. Ps. 8:5-6:

> For thou hast made him a little lower than the angels, and hast crowned him with glory and honour.
>
> Thou madest him to have dominion over the works of thy hands: thou hast put all things under his feet.

25. See, e.g., Ps. 106.2: "Who can utter the mighty acts of the Lord? who can show forth all his praise?" Also Ps. 111.4: "He hath made his wonderful works to be remembered." Uriel's unqualified assertion of authority as an eyewitness—"I saw when at his Word the formless Mass, / This world's material mould, came to a heap: / Confusion heard his voice, and wild uproar / Stood rul'd, stood vast infinitude confin'd" (3.708-711)—contrasts with Raphael's comment that he did not see the creation of man.

26. See above, Chapter 2. And see below, Chapter 8, pp. 208-10 for discussion of Adam's role in these dialogues.

27. See above, Chapter 2, p. 44 and n. 49.

28. Sallust, *The War with Cataline*, 20.1-17, trans. J. C. Rolfe (Loeb, Cambridge: Harvard Univ. Press; London: William Heinemann, 1965), pp. 35-39.

29. Lucan, *De bello civili*, 1.299-351, Duff, pp. 24-29, esp. ll. 350-51: "Nam neque praeda meis neque regnum quaeritur armis: / Detrahimus dominos urbi servire paratae."

30. See Aristotle, *Politics* 3.13-15, McKeon, *Basic Works*, pp. 1197-1200:

> Some one who is pre-eminent in virtue—what is to be done with him? . . . he ought not to be a subject—that would be as if mankind should claim to rule over Zeus, dividing his offices among them. The only alternative is that all should joyfully obey such a ruler, according to what seems to be the order of nature, and that men like him should be kings in their state for life. (1284b.28-34)

NOTES TO CHAPTER 6

Let us assume that they are the freemen, and that they never act in violation of the law, but fill up the gaps which the law is obliged to leave. . . . Aristocracy will be better for states than royalty, whether the government is supported by force or not, provided only that a number of men equal in virtue can be found. (1286a.37-1266b.9)

31. *CPW*, 3:198-99:

No man who knows ought, can be so stupid to deny that all men naturally were borne free, being the image and resemblance of God himself, and were by privilege above all the creatures, born to command and not to obey: and that they liv'd so. Till from the root of *Adams* transgression, falling among themselves to doe wrong and violence, . . . they saw it needfull to ordaine som authoritie . . . King . . . [and] Magistrates. Not to be thir Lords and Maisters . . . but, to be thir Deputies and Commissioners.

32. This is the only angelic soliloquy in the poem, but its presence indicates that soliloquy is not in itself a fallen genre, as is sometimes suggested. Abdiel uses it properly, to work out from true principles the action he should take and the results likely to follow from it.

33. Demaray, *Milton's Theatrical Epic*, pp. 85-101, classifies four major ceremonial occasions in heaven as Triumphs. However, in a strict generic sense only the Son's return from the Battle in Heaven and from the Creation are presented as Triumphs.

34. See Menander, *Rhetores Graeci*, ed. Leonhard von Spengel, 3 vols. (Leipzig, 1856), 3:33-43; J.-C. Scaliger, *Poetices*, 1.44-45, pp. 47-49. See discussion in Rollinson, "Milton's Nativity Poem," pp. 165-88; and Hardison, *Enduring Monument*, pp. 95-102.

35. Major models were the fourth-century poet Prudentius, *Cathemerinon* and *Peristephanon Liber*, trans. C. J. Thomson, 2 vols. (Loeb, Cambridge: Harvard Univ. Press; London: William Heinemann, 1969); Marco Girolamo Vida, *Poemata Omnia* (Cremona, 1550); and Julius-Caesar Scaliger, *Poemata ad Illustriss Constantiam Rangoniam* (Lyon, 1544).

36. See articles by Phillip Rollinson cited in Chapter 2, n. 16. Rollinson's distinction between the literary (heroic) and the public (lyric) hymn traditions is challenged by Paul H. Fry in *The Poet's*

Calling in the English Ode (New Haven and London: Yale Univ. Press, 1980), pp. 1-14, who reserves the hymn category to public, communal praise. But his argument does not meet Rollinson's historical case for the dual tradition, or the strong evidence of the distinction in Renaissance theorists and poets.

37. See, e.g., Jerome, "Hieronymus Paulino," *Biblia Sacra* (Venice, [1616]), sig. [*6]: "David Simonides noster. Pindarus & Alcaeus Flaccus quoque Catullus, atque Serenus"; Franciscus Gomarus, *Davidis Lyra: seu nova Hebraea S. Scripturae Ars Poetica* (Lyon, 1637); Henry Hammond, *A Paraphrase and Annotations upon the Books of the Psalms* (London, 1659). And see Baroway, "The Hebrew Hexameter," pp. 66-91, and "The Lyre of David: A Further Study in Renaissance Interpretation of Biblical Form," *ELH* 8 (1941), 119-42.

38. Puttenham, *Arte of English Poesie*, pp. 21-23.

39. George Wither, *A Preparation to the Psalter* (London, 1619), pp. 54, 77. And see discussion in Lewalski, *Protestant Poetics*, pp. 46-47.

40. For discussion of the exalted hymns in Exodus, Isaiah, and Revelation see, e.g., Nehemiah Rogers, *A Strange Vineyard in Palaestina* (London, 1623), pp. 8, 23; Brightman, *A Revelation of the Apocalyps*, pp. 65, 254; Bullinger, *Sermons upon the Apocalips*, pp. 172, 177, 474, 559-62; George Gifford, *Sermons upon the Whole Book of the Revelation* (London, 1599), pp. 232, 234, 365, 370.

41. On the "solemn day" in heaven the angels spent the daylight hours "in song and . . . Mystical dance" resembling the spheres in their movement and harmony, and during the night angelic choirs alternated "Melodious Hymns about the sovran Throne" (5.618-57). Adam tells Eve that Angels "with songs / And choral symphonies, Day without Night, / Circle his [God's] Throne rejoicing" (5.162-64); and throughout Eden Adam hears "Cherubic Songs by night from neighboring Hills" (5.547). The Son also refers to what seems to be a customary ceremony in which he and the angels "circle" God's holy Mount, singing "Unfeigned *Halleluiahs*" and "Hymns of high praise" (6.743-45).

42. See discussion above, Chapter 3, pp. 107-109.

43. The obvious texts for such development, the hymn of triumph in Rev. 5:3-4 celebrating the Lamb's victory over the Beast, and Psalm 24, celebrating the Lord of Hosts as a "Man of War" vic-

torious over all his enemies, are reserved for the celebration of God's Creation.

44. "And I heard as it were the voice of a great multitude, and as the voice of many waters, and as the voice of mighty thunderings, saying, Alleluia: for the Lord God omnipotent reigneth." Earlier, the angels also accompany the Son in solemn procession as he goes forth to judge Adam and Eve.

45. In that ceremony the four beasts first shout "Holy, holy, holy, Lord God Almighty, which was, and is, and is to come" (4:8); then the elders "fall down before him that sat on the throne . . . and cast their crowns before the throne." In Milton's scene this sequence is followed, though all the actions are performed by the choir of angels.

46. Brightman, *Revelation of the Apocalips*, p. 62. The text of the hymn in Rev. 4:11 is: "Thou art worthy, O Lord, to receive glory and honour and power: for thou hast created all things, and for thy pleasure they are and were created."

47. See, e.g., Hymns 8, 10, 12, and 23, "To Ares," "To Aphrodite," "To Hera," and "To the Son of Chronos, Most High," in *Hesiod, the Homeric Hymns and Homerica*, Evelyn-White, pp. 433-35, 447-52. Also, the Miltonic hymn contains verbal echoes of Exod. 24:15, Isaiah 6:1-4, Sylvester's Du Bartas, *Divine Weeks* 1.1.46, and Spenser's "Hymne of Heavenly Beautie," ll. 170-79.

48. Rev. 5:9-14 records the "new Song" sung by several choirs of elders, angels, and all the creatures, singing antiphonally:

9. And they sung a new song, saying, Thou art worthy to take the book, and to open the seals thereof: for thou wast slain, and hast redeemed us to God by thy blood out of every kindred, and tongue, and people, and nation.

. . . .

11. And I beheld, and I heard the voice of many angels round about the throne . . .

12. Saying with a loud voice, Worthy is the Lamb that was slain to receive power, and riches, and wisdom, and strength, and honour, and glory, and blessing.

13. And every creature which is in heaven, and on the earth, and under the earth, and such as are in the sea, and all that are in them, heard I saying, Blessing, and honour, and glory, and power, be unto him that sitteth upon the throne, and unto the Lamb for ever and ever.

49. Bullinger, *Hundred Sermons on the Apocalips*, p. 172. See also Junius, *Apocalyps*, pp. 17-18.

50. The ceremony is reported in *Aeneid* 8.280-305, and the hymn is an embedded lyric, quoted in full.

51. See for this structure, Hymns 17 and 28, "To Artemis" and "To Athena," in *Hesiod, the Homeric Hymns, and Homerica*, Evelyn-White, pp. 452-55.

52. See Hymn 3, "To Delian Apollo," *ibid.*, pp. 336-37. Also the peroration to the "Hymn to Hercules," *Aeneid* 8. 301-302: "salve, vera Jovis proles, decus addite divis, / et nos et tua dexter adi pede sacra secundo."

53. *Reason of Church Government, CPW*, 1.816.

54. The angels' nativity hymn was often paraphrased in Renaissance collections of biblical psalms and songs, for example in George Wither's *Hymnes and Songs of the Church* (London, 1623), p. 33. Wither describes the hymn as celebrating "the unspeakable good will, and deere Communion, . . . established betweene the God head, the Manhood, and Them" [the angels]—suggesting some basis for Milton's use of that text in the Creation sequence.

55. The ancient liturgical hymn of praise based on the Luke text, the "Gloria in Excelsis," may have suggested some elements of the Miltonic hymn. The book of Common Prayer (1599) renders the first verses as follows: "Glory be to God on high. And in earth peace, good will toward men. We praise thee, we bless thee, we worship thee, we glorify thee, we give thanks to thee for thy great glory."

56. *PL* 7.205-209: "Heav'n op'n'd wide / Her ever-during Gates, Harmonious sound / On golden Hinges moving, to let forth / The King of Glory in his powerful Word / And Spirit coming to create new Worlds." Cf. Ps. 24:7: "Lift up your heads, O ye gates; and be ye lift up, ye everlasting doors; and the King of glory shall come in."

57. See Exod. 15, esp. verses 3, 7, 8, 11:

> 3. The Lord is a man of war: the Lord is his name.
>
> . . . .
>
> 7. And in the greatness of thine excellency thou hast over-thrown them that rose up against thee: thou sentest forth thy wrath, which consumed them as stubble.
>
> 8. And with the blast of thy nostrils the waters were gath-

ered together, the floods stood upright as an heap, and the
depths were congealed in the heart of the sea.

. . . .

11. Who is like unto thee, O Lord, among the gods? who
is like thee, glorious in holiness, fearful in praises, doing won-
ders?

58. Gen. 1:26: "And God said, Let us make man in our image, after
our likeness: and let them have dominion . . . over all the earth."
Ps. 8:6: "Thou madest him to have dominion over the works of
thy hands: thou hast put all things under his feet."

59. *Georgics* 2.458-60:

> O fortunatos nimium, sua si bona norint,
> agricolas! quibus ipsa, procul discordibus armis
> fundit humo facilem victum iustissima tellus.

CHAPTER 7. "A HAPPY RURAL SEAT
OF VARIOUS VIEW": PASTORAL IDYL AND
THE GENRES OF EDENIC INNOCENCE

1. For discussion of many pastoral themes and topoi in the poem,
see Knott, *Milton's Pastoral Vision.*
2. See the discussion of Theocritan or Arcadian pastoral in Thomas
G. Rosenmeyer, *The Green Cabinet: Theocritus and the European
Pastoral Lyric* (Berkeley and London: Univ. of California Press,
1969), esp. pp. 3-129. Also, Hallett Smith, *Elizabethan Poetry: A
Study in Conventions, Meaning, and Expression* (Cambridge: Har-
vard Univ. Press, 1952); and Renato Paggioli, *The Oaten Flute:
Essays on Pastoral Poetry and the Pastoral Ideal* (Cambridge: Har-
vard Univ. Press, 1975), pp. 1-63.
3. This view is set forth in Scaliger, *Poetices* 1.3, 1.4, pp. 6-10, *Select
Translations,* trans. Padelford, pp. 20-29; in E. K.'s introduction
and notes to Spenser's *Shepheardes Calendar*; and in William Webbe,
Discourse of English Poesie (1586), in Smith, ed. *Elizabethan Critical
Essays,* 1:262. See the resumé of theories of pastoral in J. E. Con-
gleton, *Theories of Pastoral Poetry in England, 1684-1798* (Gaines-
ville: Univ. of Florida Press, 1952), pp. 3-65.
4. Minturno, *De Poetica,* Bk. II, p. 146; Tasso, *Gerusalemme Liberata*
7.1-22; *Faerie Queene* 6.9-10.

5. See, e.g., Thomas Sebillet, *L'Art poétique françoys* (1548), ed. Felix Gaiffe (Paris: Droz, 1932), pp. 159-61; Juan Luis Vives, Preface to Virgil's *Eclogues*, trans. William Lisle (London, 1628), p. 10; Sir Philip Sidney, *Defense of Poesie*, sigs. E 3ᵥ-E 4; Guillaume Colletet, *Discours du poème bucolique, Où il est traitté, de l'eglogue, de l'idyle, et de la bergerie* (Paris, 1657), rpt. in *L'Art Poetique* (Paris, 1658), pp. 15, 16, 45.

6. Giambattista Guarini, *Il Pastor Fido*, published with *Compendio della poesia tragicomica, tratti dai due verati* (Venice, 1601), pp. 13, 46-53; George Chapman, Commendatory poem to Fletcher's *Faithful Shepherdess*, in *The Works of Francis Beaumont and John Fletcher*, 10 vols., ed. Arnold Glover and A. R. Waller (Cambridge: Cambridge Univ. Press, 1905-1912), 2:520.

7. René Rapin, "Dissertatio de Carmine Pastorali," Preface to *Eclogae Sacrae*, trans. Thomas Creech, *The Idylliums of Theocritus* (Oxford, 1684), pp. 2-6.

8. I have argued this point in "Innocence and Experience in Milton's Eden," in *New Essays*, ed. Kranidas, pp. 86-117.

9. Scaliger, *Poetices* 1.5, pp. 10-11 (Padelford, pp. 33-38) argues that comedy evolved from village revels.

10. Frye, *Anatomy of Criticism*, pp. 285-87.

11. For the romance dimension of the Garden, see Giamatti, *Earthly Paradise*, pp. 295-351. The tainted qualities of the romance garden are, I suggest, associated with the Satanic perspective and adventures, not (as Giamatti proposes) with the Garden itself.

12. *FQ* 2.12; *Gerusalemme Liberata*, Bks. 14-15.

13. See Colletet, *Discours . . . de l'idyle*, pp. 21-44; Edward Phillips, *The New World of English Words* (London, 1658), sig. T 2. And see "idyl" in *Princeton Encyclopedia of Poetry and Poetics*, ed. Alex Preminger (Princeton: Princeton Univ. Press, 1974), pp. 362-63.

14. Puttenham, *Arte of English Poesie*, p. 200, defines *Topographia* as "counterfeit place," a set description of "any true place, citie, castell, hill, valley or sea, & such like," or any feigned place, as "heaven, hell, paradise, the house of fame, the pallace of the sunne, the denne of sheepe, and such like which ye shall see in Poetes." See James Turner's discussion of the use of perspective and prospect in this passage, *The Politics of Landscape: Rural Scenery and Society in English Poetry, 1630-1660* (Cambridge: Harvard Univ. Press, 1979), pp. 8-35.

15. C. S. Lewis, *A Preface to Paradise Lost* (1942; rpt. London: Oxford Univ. Press, 1960), pp. 49-50.
16. Ernst Curtius, *European Literature and the Latin Middle Ages*, trans. Willard R. Trask (New York: Pantheon Books, 1953), pp. 183-202, esp. p. 195.
17. Cf. Dante, *Purgatorio*, 28.1-51; Sidney, *The Countesse of Pembrokes Arcadia (1590)* (facs. ed., Kent: Kent State Univ. Press, 1970), pp. 7-8; Spenser, *FQ* 3.6.30-31, 42-44; Ovid, *Metamorphoses* 5.385-96; Ovid, *Fasti* 4.425-42, ed. Sir James Frazer (Loeb, Cambridge: Harvard Univ. Press; London: William Heinemann, 1931), p. 221. See John R. Knott, "Symbolic Landscape in *Paradise Lost*," *Milton Studies* 2 (1970), 42-43; and Koehler, "Milton and the Art of Landscape," 5-9.
18. From Alkinoös' door, Odysseus sees the courtyard and beyond it a great orchard with ever-bearing fruit, fig, and olive trees; the vineyard beside it; the planted garden at the bottom of the field; and two springs watering all the garden and jetting by the courtyard (*Odyssey* 7.112-25). Aeneas at the entrance to the Elysian fields sees some heroes engaged in war games and others feasting in laurel groves; from a mountain ridge he see Anchises deep in a green vale; and from that retired vale he sees "a sequestered grove and rustling forest thickets, and the river of Lethe drifting past" (*Aeneid* 6.637-705).
19. For the gardenist material see Koehler, "Milton and the Art of Landscape," pp. 3-40; Charlotte F. Otten, " 'My Native Element': Milton's Paradise of English Gardens," *Milton Studies* 5 (1973), 249-67; John Dixon Hunt, "Milton and the Making of the English Landscape Garden," *Milton Studies* 15 (1981), 81-105.
20. For the influence of landscape painting on Milton's Eden see Knott, "Symbolic Landscape," p. 47; and Mario Praz, "Milton and Poussin," in *Seventeenth Century Studies Presented to Sir Herbert Grierson* (Oxford: Clarendon Press, 1938), pp. 192-210. Sir Kenneth Clark, *Landscape into Art* (London: J. Murray, 1949), pp. 68-69, points to Poussin's "Spring" as "a perfect illustration for *Paradise Lost*." Also see illustrations of "The Garden of Eden" by Jan Bruegel the Elder, reproduced as plates 158 and 159 in Roland M. Frye, *Milton's Imagery and the Visual Arts* (Princeton: Princeton Univ. Press, 1978).
21. Milton evokes these various gardens and groves by verbal echo and at times by direct reference, accommodating Eden to us through

the many familiar literary images we know, but at the same time insisting that it bears no real comparison with any of these, being the true garden of which they are only shadows:

> Others whose fruit burnisht with Golden Rind
> Hung amiable, *Hesperian* Fables true,
> If true, here only. (4.249-51)

> Not that fair field
> Of *Enna*, where *Proserpin* gath'ring flow'rs
> Herself a fairer Flow'r by gloomy *Dis*
> Was gather'd, which cost *Ceres* all that pain
> To seek her through the world; nor that sweet Grove
> Of *Daphne* by *Orontes*, and th' inspir'd
> *Castalian* Spring might with this Paradise
> Of *Eden* strive. (4.268-75)

22. Milton's Field of Enna simile evokes the familiar description in Ovid (*Fasti* 4.427-42, Frazer, pp. 220-21):

> valle sub umbrosa locus est aspergine multa
> uvidus ex alto desilientis aquae.
> tot fuerant illic, quot habet natura, colores,
> pictaque dissimili flore nitebat humus.
> . . . .
> ipsa [Proserpina] crocos tenues liliaque alba legit.

23. Cf. *Odyssey* 5.63-74.
24. See Ovid, *Fasti* 5.195-222. And see the discussion of the *Primavera* and the Neoplatonic allegories it draws upon in Edgar Wind, *Pagan Mysteries in the Renaissance* (New York: Norton, 1968), pp. 113-27.
25. Italics mine. Broadbent, *Some Graver Subject*, p. 184, remarks the association, but finds it "almost laughable"—one more indication that modern criticism has paid too little attention to the deliberateness and sophistication of Milton's generic strategy.
26. Ben Jonson, "To Penshurst," esp. ll. 85-102, in *The Complete Poetry of Ben Jonson*, ed. William B. Hunter (New York: Norton, 1963), pp. 77-81.
27. Puttenham, *Arte of English Poesie*, pp. 204-205. See also Henry Peacham, *The Garden of Eloquence* (London, 1577), sigs. U 2- U 2ᵥ.
28. See the reproductions of Lucas Cranach, *Paradise*, and Albrecht

Dürer, *The Fall*, in Frye, *Milton's Imagery and the Visual Arts*, pls. 163 and 164. In Spenser, the first six stanzas of Book I, Canto 1, are especially iconic.

29. See the entry, "Blason," in the *Princeton Encyclopedia*, p. 81. And see discussion in Sebillet, *Art poétique françoys*, pp. 169-70. As an independent lyric the genre had its origin in Clement Marot's blason "Du beau tétin," in *Les Epigrammes en deux livres, Les Oeuvres* (Lyon, 1538), f. 16ᵥ-17.

30. See, e.g., J. Wooton, "Damaetas Madrigall in praise of his Daphnis"; Robert Greene, "Doron's description of his faire Sheepheardesse Samela"; and [Edward Vere], Earl of Oxford, "The Sheepheards commendation of his Nimph," in *England's Helicon* (1600), ed. Hugh MacDonald (1949; rpt. London: Routledge & Kegan Paul, 1962), pp. 60-63, 79-81.

31. See, e.g., Spenser, "Aprill," *The Shepheardes Calendar*, esp. ll. 46-72. For a survey of this literature see Elkin Calhoun Wilson, *England's Eliza* (Cambridge: Harvard Univ. Press, 1939), pp. 126-66.

32. See, e.g., Cornelius à Lapide, *Commentarius in Ecclesiasten, Canticum Canticorum, et Librum Sapientiae* (Antwerp, 1726), sigs. **4-**4ᵥ, who describes the book as a five-act pastoral drama with the Spouse as pastoral virgin and the Bridegroom as a shepherd. Others saw it as an epithalamion in eclogic form. Gervase Markham, *The Poem of Poems, or Sions Muse, Contayning the Divine Song of King Solomon, divided into eight Eclogues* (London, [1596]) presents, as his title suggests, a verse paraphrase in eclogues. Milton in the *Reason of Church Government* describes the Song of Songs as a "divine pastoral drama," *CPW*, 1:815.

33. We are to recall that Athena endowed Ulysses with hyacinthine flowing locks to make him more attractive to Nausikaä (*Odyssey* 6.229-31).

34. Giamatti, *Earthly Paradise*, pp. 295-351.

35. Tasso, *Gerusalemme Liberata*, trans. Fairfax, 16.17-26, pp. 322-24; Longus, *Daphnis and Chloe*, 1.9-14, 24-26, 2.8-11, trans. George Thornley, rev. J. M. Edmonds (London: William Heinemann; New York: Putnam's, 1926), esp. pp. 20-31, 46-50, 79-85. Sidney, *Arcadia* [The Old Arcadia], ed. Jean Robertson (Oxford: Clarendon Press, 1973), pp. 196-202, 306.

36. Theocritus, 1.12-14, and "A Country Singing-March," 6.1-5, Edmonds, pp. 8-9, 84-5; Baptista Mantuan, Eclogue 1, "Faustus,"

ll. 1-4, *The Eclogues of Mantuan*, trans. George Turberville, ed. Douglas Bush (New York: Scholars Facsimiles, 1937), sig. B i.

37. Milton obviously intends his readers to recall Ovid's version of the story (*Metamorphoses* 3.343-510). Indeed, God's speech recalling Eve from her self-regarding gaze in the water echoes Ovid's apostrophe to Narcissus (3.432-36, Miller, 1:154-55):

> credule, quid frustra simulacra fugacia captas?
> quod petis, est nusquam; quod amas, avertere, perdes!
> ista repercussae, quam cernis, imaginis umbra est:
> nil habet ista sui; tecum venitque manetque;
> tecum discedet, si tu discedere possis!

O fondly foolish boy, why vainly seek to clasp a fleeting image? What you seek is nowhere; but turn yourself away, and the object of your love will be no more. That which you behold is but the shadow of a reflected form and has no substance of its own. With you it comes, with you it stays, and it will go with you—if you can go.

Cf. *PL* 4.468-72:

> What thou seest,
> What there thou seest fair Creature is thyself,
> With thee it came and goes: but follow me,
> And I will bring thee where no shadow stays
> Thy coming. . . .

38. Even Faustus' narration in Mantuan's Eclogue 1, which ends with an account of his marriage to Galla, focuses upon the griefs and frustrations he endured during his long courtship, and the brevity of his happiness, once attained (*Eclogues of Mantuan*, ed. Bush, sig. B i).

39. Eve presents her autobiographical narrative in accordance with the recommendations of many contemporary Puritan theologians for meditations on personal experience, or spiritual autobiography. See, e.g., Richard Sibbes, *The Soules conflict with it selfe, and Victorie over it selfe by Faith* (London, 1635), p. 302: "If we were well read in the story of our own lives, wee might have a divinity of our own, drawne out of the observations of God's particular dealing toward us." Isaac Ambrose, *Prima, Media, and Ultima, The First, Middle, and Last Things* (London, 1659), pp. 164-81, offers very

detailed analyses of and recommendations for such meditation. See discussion in Lewalski, *Protestant Poetics*, pp. 160-62.

40. Virgil's *Georgics* is the primary model for the fusion of pastoral with georgic, especially in the "golden age" passage, *Georgics* 2.458-540.

41. See discussion of this point in Lewalski, "Innocence and Experience," in *New Essays on Paradise Lost*, ed. Kranidas, pp. 86-117.

42. See Johnson, "Milton's Blank Verse Sonnets," and Nardo, "Submerged Sonnet as Lyric Moment."

43. William Drummond of Hawthornden, *Poems* (n.p., [1614]), (facs. ed., Menston: Scolar Press, 1969), p. 330a. Milton's editor H. J. Todd (1801; 1809) notes the analogue. Drummond's *volta* is, however, in the final couplet.

44. Theocritus, "Thyrsis," 1.1-3, 7-8, Edmonds, pp. 8-9.

45. The point has not been fully appreciated by some feminist critics, for example, Marcia Landy, "Kinship and the Role of Women in *Paradise Lost*," *Milton Studies* 4 (1972), 3-18.

46. See discussion in McCown, "Milton and the Epic Epithalamium," pp. 39-66, and Thorne-Thomsen, "Milton's 'advent'rous Song,' " pp. 1-42. McCown notes the presence of epithalamic topics throughout Book Four: several references to Hesperus, the evening star; praises of the couple's beauty and accomplishments; references to their dalliance; description of their supper feast and the entertainment accompanying it (here by the Edenic animals). He suggests that Milton incorporated into Book Four material he had planned to use in his drama on the Fall: the third sketch in the Trinity ms. has as characters Heavenly Love, Evening Starre, and a chorus singing the marriage song of Adam and Eve. Adam's joyous and sensuous epithalamic description of his own wedding day (8.510-20) recalls Spenser's rapturous poem celebrating his wedding day. The passage of postlapsarian love-making (9.1027-45) focuses on the powerful sexual desire of Adam for Eve—a central epithalamic topic for Scaliger—and the wanton "play" which is its concomitant. That passage explicitly recalls Zeus' and Hera's love play (*Iliad* 14.292-353), instigated by a treacherous love potion. And Michael's description of the degenerate marriages of the daughters of Cain and the sons of God emphasizes the element of overwhelming sexual desire (11.586-92).

47. Puttenham, *Arte of English Poesie*, p. 41.

48. The point is left deliberately obscure by Milton, so as to reinforce

the notion that life, growth, and development in Eden was a genuine possibility, that Paradise was not lost (as most commentators thought) almost immediately. Eve, accordingly, refers to the day of her creation as "That day I oft remember" (4.449), suggesting some passage of time.

49. For an account of the genre, see Virginia Tufte, *The Poetry of Marriage: The Epithalamium in Europe and Its Development in England* (Los Angeles: Tinnon-Brown, 1970).

50. *The Poems of Gaius Valerius Catullus*, trans. F. W. Cornish, in *Catullus, Tibullus, and Pervigilium Veneris* (Loeb, Cambridge: Harvard Univ. Press; London: William Heinemann, 1914), pp. 69-85. The hymnic section praising Hymen (esp. ll. 46-75) declares him matchless among the gods by reason of his vast powers over the bride and bridegroom and their families, and details the great social benefits he brings to humankind: without him homes are destitute of children, parents are barren of offspring, and the state is left defenseless. See esp. ll. 66-75:

> nulla quit sine te domus
> liberos dare, nec parens
> stirpe nitier: ac potest
> te volente. quis huic deo
> compararier ausit?
>
> quae tuis careat sacris,
> non queat dare praesides
> terra finibus: at queat
> te volente. quis huic deo
> compararier ausit?

51. Menander, *Rhetores Graeci*, ed. Aldus Manutius, 2 vols. (Venice, 1508), 1:594-641; *Menander Rhetor*, ed. and trans. H. A. Russell and N. G. Wilson (Oxford: Clarendon Press, 1981), pp. 135, 139, 145.

52. Scaliger, *Poetices*, 3.101, pp. 150-54. Scaliger emphasized the use of elevated (heroic) style for celebrating the nuptials of the great, and proposed a six-part structure: description of the passionate desires of the couple; praises of their country, race, intellect, beauty; predictions of good fortune; delivery of gentle fescennine jests emphasizing wantonness and dalliance; promise of offspring; exhortations to the guest to sleep and to the bridal couple to spend the

night in love-making (*allocutio sponsalis*). Subsidiary topics to be used include: praise of the bridal couch; comparison of this marriage to the union of the gods; dispraise of unworthy loves. See the discussion of Scaliger's influence on the development of the genre in Thorne-Thomsen, "Milton's 'advent'rous Song,' " pp. 7-9.

53. Theocritus, *Greek Bucolic Poets*, Edmonds, pp. 224-31; Catullus, *Poems*, Cornish, pp. 84-91; *Old Arcadia*, ed. Robertson, pp. 244-48.

54. See above, n. 32. See also Origen, "First Homily," *The Song of Songs, Commentary and Homilies*, trans. R. P. Lawson (London: Longmans, 1957), p. 258; Simon Patrick, *The Song of Salomon Paraphrased* (London, 1710), p. 38; Joseph Hall, *An Open and Plaine Paraphrase upon the Song of Songs* (London, 1609), sigs. N2-N2$_v$; Matthew Henry, *An Exposition of the Five Poetical Books of the Old Testament* (London, 1710), sig. iv.

55. Catullus, *Poems*, Cornish, pp. 98-129. Virgil employs epithalamic elements to highlight the unsanctioned and inauspicious union between Aeneas and Dido (*Aeneid* 4.160-72). Spenser adapts such elements to celebrate the wedding of the Thames and Medway rivers as an emblem of concord (*FQ* 4.11.8-53).

56. Sylvester, *Du Bartas' Divine Weeks*, 1.6.1054-78, ed. Snyder, 1:291-92:

> O blessed Bond! O happy Mariage!
> Which doost the match twixt Christ and us presage!
> O chastest friendship, whose pure flames impart
> Two Soules in one, two Harts into one Hart!
> O holy knot, in *Eden* instituted
> (Not in this Earth with blood and wrongs poluted,
> Prophan'd with mischiefes, the pre-Scæne of Hell
> To cursed Creatures that 'gainst Heav'n rebell)
> . . . .
>   By thy deere Favour, after our Decease
> We leave behind our living Images:
> Change Warre to Peace, in kindred multiplie,
> And in our Children, live eternallie.
> By thee, we quench the wilde and wanton Fiers,
> That in our Soule the *Paphian* shot inspires:

And taught (by thee) a Love more firme and fitter
We find the Mel more sweet, the Gall less bitter,
Which heere (by turnes) heape up our humane Life
Even now with joyes, anon with jarres and strife.

McCown ("Milton and the Epic Epithalamium," pp. 49-50) also
calls attention to the long lyric epithalamium in Andrew Ramsay's
Poemata Sacra, sung for Adam and Eve by a phoenix. Based on
Catullus #61, its subject is the praise of marriage for its many benefits—chaste kisses, offspring, and the enhancement of trade through
population growth.

57. Giamatti, *Earthly Paradise*, pp. 449-52 calls attention to a source
for Adam and Eve's bower in the "Venus Bower" motif first used
by Statius in his "Epithalamion in Stellum et Violentillam" (*Silvae*
1.2.51-54), and by Claudian in his "Epithalamium de Nuptiis
Honorii Augusti" (ll. 49-96).

58. See, e.g., Wither, *Preparation to the Psalter*, p. 77; "Athanasius in
Psalmos," quoted in [Matthew Parker], *The Whole Psalter translated into English Metre* (London, 1657), sig. B 4ᵥ; Luther, *A Manual of the Book of Psalms*, trans. Henry Cole (London, 1835), pp.
5-7; Calvin, *The Psalms of David and Others*, trans. [Arthur Golding], (London, 1571), sig. [*6ᵥ]; Donne, *Sermons*, ed. G. F. Potter
and Evelyn Simpson, 10 vols. (Berkeley: Univ. of California Press,
1953-1962), 5:288, 299. See discussion in Lewalski, *Protestant
Poetics*, pp. 41-53.

59. Petrarch, *Trionfi* (1470); See Henry Parker, Lord Morley, trans.,
The Tryumphes of Fraunces Petrarcke [1553-1556?], ed. D. D. Carnicelli (Cambridge: Harvard Univ. Press, 1971), pp. 80-108; *FQ*
3.12.

60. The topic was proposed by Scaliger and often used in Christian
epithalamia. See above, n. 52.

CHAPTER 8. "OUR PLEASANT LABOR": GEORGIC AND
COMEDIC MODES AND GENRES IN EDEN

1. *Georgics* 2.538, Fairclough 1:152-53: "aureus hanc vitam in terris
Saturnus agebat."
2. *Georgics* 2.458-501, Fairclough, 1:148-53:

O fortunatos nimium, sua si bona norint,
agricolas! quibus ipsa, procul discordibus armis,
fundit humo facilem victum iustissima tellus.
. . . .
Me vero primum dulces ante omnia Musae,
quarum sacra fero ingenti percussus amore,
accipiant caelique vias . . .
. . . .
sin, has ne possim naturae accedere partis,
frigidus obstiterit circum praecordia sanguis,
rura mihi et rigui placeant in vallibus amnes,
. . . .
Felix, qui potuit rerum cognoscere causas,
atque metus omnis et inexorabile fatum
subiecit pedibus strepitumque Acherontis avari.
fortunatus et ille, deos qui novit agrestis,
. . . .
quos rami fructus, quos ipsa volentia rura
sponte tulere sua, carpsit.

3. Though readers sometimes overlook this point, the Miltonic Bard
insists upon it: "Yet went she not, as not with such discourse /
Delighted, or not capable her ear / Of what was high: such pleas-
ure she reserv'd, / *Adam* relating, she sole Auditress" (8.48-51).
4. See Chapter 1, pp.13-14, and n. 39. See also Dante's justification
for the title of his poem, "Letter to the Can Grande della Scala,"
in Gilbert, *Literary Criticism*, p. 204: "Comedy . . . at the begin-
ning deals with the harsh aspect of some affair, but its matter
terminates prosperously. . . . From this it is clear why the present
work is called *Comedy*. For if we consider the material, at the be-
ginning it is horrible and fetid, since it begins with Hell, but at
the end it is attractive and pleasing, since it ends with Heaven."
5. Demetrius, *On Style* 3.168-69, Roberts, p. 407; Tasso, *Discourses
on the Heroic Poem* 6.34, Samuel and Cavalchini, pp. 171-72; Sid-
ney, *Defence of Poesie*, sigs. I$_v$-I 2.
6. For comedy based on intrigue plots and the ridicule of vices and
follies in common or base characters, see Aristotle, *Poetics* 1448a-
b 9; Giraldi Cinthio, *Discorsi intorno . . . delle comedie, e delle tra-
gedie*, pp. 206-208; and Scaliger, *Poetices*, 1.5, 7, pp. 10-14, trans.
Padelford, pp. 33-38. See also A. P. McMahon, "On the Second

Book of Aristotle's *Poetics*," and "Seven Questions on Aristotelian Definitions of Tragedy and Comedy," *Harvard Studies in Classical Philology* 28 (1917), 1-46; 40 (1929), 97-198; and Mary H. Grant, *The Ancient Rhetorical Theories of the Laughable* (Madison: Univ. of Wisconsin Press, 1924), pp. 132-39. The primary models for this kind of comedy were Plautus and Terence.

7. See discussion in Beaurline, *Jonson and Elizabethan Comedy*, pp. 35-65.

8. Sidney, *Defence of Poesie*, sigs. I$_v$-I 2. See the discussion of the relevant Neoplatonic tracts by Diason Denores, Francisco Patrizi, Vincenzo Maggi, and Giovanni Pigna in Weinberg, *History of Literary Criticism*, 1:427, 412-17, 451-52, 622; 2:774.

9. Sidney, *Defense of Poesie*, sig. I$_v$: "If we marke them [the ancients] well, wee shall finde that they never or verie daintily matche horne Pipes and Funeralls. So falleth it out, that having indeed no right Comedie in that Comicall part of our Tragidie, wee have nothing but scurrillitie."

10. See, e.g., Cicero, *De Officiis* 1.104-108, Miller, pp. 106-11: "There are, generally speaking, two sorts of jest: The one, coarse, rude, vicious, indecent; the other, refined, polite, clever, witty. With the latter sort not only our own Plautus and the Old Comedy of Athens, but also the books of Socratic philosophy abound. . . . Socrates was fascinating and witty, a genial conversationalist; he was what the Greeks call Εἴρων." See also *De Officiis* 1.134-35, pp. 136-39; *De Oratore* 2.269-71; and Frye, *Anatomy of Criticism*, pp. 40, 286.

11. See discussion in Weinberg, *History of Literary Criticism*, 2:895-99. Zoppio defines poetry as dialogue: "le Poesie pure sono tutte imitatione per via di Dialogi, contrasti & dispute intorno à gli affari humani." He likens Plato's dialogue to the scenes of dramas which are nothing more than "Ragionamenti & Dialogi tra persone argomentanti & disputanti di cose, & negocii con proposte, & riposte in forma Dialettica."

12. The *alba* or *aube* originated in Provence, in dialogues of lovers parted by the dawn. In English poetry examples can be found in Chaucer's *Troilus and Criseyde* and *The Reeve's Tale*, and in *Romeo and Juliet*. Donne's lyric "Break of Day" offers a seventeenth-century example with the woman as speaker. See Alfred Jeanroy, *La Poésie lyrique des troubadours*, 2 vols. (Toulouse: E. Privat, 1934), 2:292-97, and *Les Origines de la poésie lyrique en France au moyen*

âge, 3d ed. (Paris: H. Champion, 1925), pp. 61-83, 145-51; Arthur T. Hatto, ed., *EOS: An Inquiry into the Theme of Lovers' Meetings and Partings at Dawn in Poetry* (The Hague and London: Mouton, 1965), pp. 271-98, 344-89, 428-72, 505-31; and Jonathan Saville, *The Medieval Erotic Alba: Structure as Meaning* (New York: Columbia Univ. Press, 1972). See also *Princeton Encyclopedia*, p. 8.

13. Jean Frappier, *La Poésie lyrique française aux xii⁰ et xiii⁰ siècles, les auteurs et les genres* (Paris: Centre de documentaire universitaire [1966]), p. 41. And see discussion in Thorne-Thomsen, "Milton's 'advent'rous Song,' " pp. 77-90, 105-115.

14. See, e.g., Theodore Beza, *Sermons upon the Three First Chapters of Canticles*, trans. John Harmer (Oxford, 1587), sig. *2ᵥ, who pronounced the Song of Songs "the most heavenliest and excellentest ditty, concluded in terms and phrases of speach altogether enigmaticall and allegoricall." Robert Aylett, *The Song of Songs, which was Solomon's* (London, 1643), p. [96], declared, "No Men nor Angel ever yet did hear / Diviner musick from a mortal tongue." Also see *Annotations upon all the Books of the Old and New Testament* by . . . Certain learned Divines (London, 1645), sig. FFFv. The Song of Songs was not literally a dawn song (see Hatto, *EOS*, pp. 212-13), but English translations suggested that generic association, "Rise up, my love . . ."

15. Origen, *Songs of Songs*, trans. Lawson, p. 268. Paraeus, *Commentary upon . . . Revelation*, p. 20.

16. Lapide, *Commentarius . . . Canticum Canticorum* (Antwerp, 1725), sigs. *4-**4ᵥ. Milton, *Reason of Church Government*, *CPW*, 1:815.

17. See, e.g., John Dove, *The Conversion of Solomon* (London, 1613). John Robotham, *An Exposition on the whole booke of Solomons Song* (London, 1651), esp. pp. 711 ff. William Gouge, *An Exposition of the Song of Solomon* (London, 1615), pp. 75-76.

18. Scaliger, *Poetices*, 1.3, p. 6, trans. Padelford, p. 20: "Now in our treatment of poetry we can follow either the order of excellence or the chronological order. The most excellent kinds of poetry are hymns and paeans [to the Gods]." Cf. Puttenham, *Arte of English Poesie*, p. 23: "These hymnes to the gods was the first forme of Poesie and the highest & the stateliest, & they were song by the Poets as priests, and by the people or whole congregation as we sing in our Churchs the Psalmes of *David*, but they did it commonly in some shadie groves of tall tymber trees." Sidney, *Defence*

of Poesie, sig. C$_v$-C 2: "The chiefe both in antiquitie and excellencie, were they that did imitate the unconceivable excellencies of God. Such were *David* in his *Psalmes*, *Salomon* in his song of songs . . . *Moses* and *Debora*, in their Hymnes. . . . In this kinde, though in a full wrong divinitie, were *Orpheus*, *Amphion*, *Homer* in his himnes."

19. See Plato, "Ion," trans. W.R.M. Lamb, *The Statesman, Philibus, Ion* (Loeb, Cambridge: Harvard Univ. Press; London: William Heinemann, 1925), pp. 407-47, for the influential description of the poet as Vates. In *The Republic* (10.607), hymns to the gods and praises of good men are the only forms of poetry Socrates allows in his ideal state.

20. Thorne-Thomsen, "Milton's 'advent'rous Song,' " pp. 231-41.

21. Summers, *Muse's Method*, p. 155.

22. See Callimachus, Hymns 1-3, "To Zeus," "To Apollo," "To Artemis," and Hymn 6, "To Demeter," in *Callimachus, Lycophron, and Aratus*, ed. G. A. Mair (Loeb, Cambridge: Harvard Univ. Press; London: William Heinemann, 1977), pp. 36-83, 125-35.

23. Cf. Callimachus, *ibid.*, Hymn 1, "To Zeus," ll. 90-95: "Hail! greatly hail! most high Son of Cronus, giver of good things, giver of safety. Thy works who could sing? There hath not been, there shall not be, who shall sing the works of Zeus. Hail! Father, hail again! and grant us goodness and prosperity. Without goodness wealth cannot bless men, nor goodness without prosperity. Give us goodness and weal." And see Homeric Hymns 5 and 6, "To Aphrodite"; and Hymns 7, 8, and 18, "To Dionysus," "To Ares," and "To Hermes," in *Hesiod, The Homeric Hymns, and Homerica*, ed. Evelyn-White, pp. 406-447.

24. See Menander's discussion of eight kinds of hymns (with possibilities for mixtures of kinds), in "Treatise II, Division of Epideictic Speeches," 1.333-334, in *Menander Rhetor*, ed. Russell and Wilson, pp. 7-29. Also, Scaliger's discussion of hymnic kinds based on Menander, in *Poetices*, 3.109-116, pp. 47-49. See discussion in Rollinson, "Renaissance of the Literary Hymn," pp. 11-17.

25. Scaliger, *Poetices*, 3.116, p. 6. See Rollinson, "Renaissance of the Literary Hymn," pp. 12-13.

26. The suggestion is made in Thorne-Thomsen, "Milton's 'advent'rous Song,' " p. 232. See *Horace: The Odes and Epodes*, trans. Bennett, pp. 350-57.

27. See, e.g., Beza, *The Psalmes of David*, trans. Anthonie Gilbie (London, 1581), pp. 304-305; Donne, *Sermons*, ed. Potter and

Simpson, 6:293; Wither, *Preparation to the Psalter*, pp. 54, 77. David Dickson, *A Brief Explication upon the last fifty Psalms from Psalm 100 to the end*, 2nd ed. (London, 1655), pp. 366-67. Rogers, *Strange Vineyard in Palaestina*, pp. 8-9.

28. Augustine's commentary on Psalm 148 contains his definition of hymn: "A hymn then containeth these three things, song, and praise, and that of God. Praise then of God in song is called a hymn," *Expositions on the Psalms*, trans. J. Tweed et al., 6 vols. (Oxford: J. H. Parker, 1847-1857), 6:577.

29. Dickson, *The Last Fifty Psalms*, pp. 366, 370.

30. See Lewalski, *Protestant Poetics*, pp. 31-53; Campbell, *Divine Poetry and Drama*, pp. 9-54; Coburn Freer, *Music for a King: George Herbert's Style and the Metrical Psalms* (Baltimore and London: Johns Hopkins Univ. Press, 1972), pp. 1-115.

31. John Hollander, *The Figure of Echo: A Mode of Allusion in Milton and After* (Berkeley and London: Univ. of California Press, 1981), p. 37.

32. See David M. Bergeron, *English Civic Pageantry, 1558-1642* (Columbia: Univ. of South Carolina Press, 1971).

33. See Greene, *Descent From Heaven*, pp. 363-418; Blessington, *Paradise Lost and the Classical Epic*, pp. 25-34.

34. In this discussion I follow Jason Rosenblatt, "Celestial Entertainment in Eden: Book V of *Paradise Lost*," HTR 62 (1969), 411-27, who points out the parallels and allusions. See also Sims, *Bible in Milton's Epics*, pp. 202-204, 210.

35. Thomas Kranidas, "Adam and Eve in the Garden: A Study of *Paradise Lost*, Book V," SEL 4 (1964), 71-83.

36. See above, Chapter 2, pp. 39-50; Chapter 6, pp. 152-54.

37. See discussion in Lewalski, "Innocence and Experience," *New Essays*, ed. Kranidas, pp. 86-117.

38. See above, Chap. 7, pp. 185-86, and n. 39.

39. The spiritual autobiography flourished in the seventeenth century. Some notable examples include Joseph Hall, *Some Specialties of Divine Providence in his Life*, in *The Shaking of the Olive Tree* (London, 1660); Richard Baxter, *Autobiography*, in *Reliquiae Baxterianae* (London, 1696); John Bunyan, *Grace Abounding to the Chief of Sinners* (London, 1666); Henry More, *Autobiography* (London, 1679); Thomas Ellwood, *History of the Life of Thomas Ellwood* (London, 1714). See Paul Delany, *British Autobiography in*

the Seventeenth Century (London: Routledge & Kegan Paul; New York: Columbia Univ. Press, 1969).

40. See above, n. 18.

41. See, e.g., Boccaccio, *Genealogia Deorum Gentilium* 14.8, in *Boccaccio on Poetry*, ed. Charles G. Osgood (New York: Liberal Arts Press, 1956), pp. 42-47.

42. See above, Chapter 5, pp. 123-24.

43. Plato, *Symposium*, in *Lysis, Symposium, Gorgias*, ed. W.R.M. Lamb (Loeb, Cambridge: Harvard Univ. Press; London: William Heinemann, 1975), pp. 74-245; Leone Ebreo, *The Philosophy of Love [Dialoghi d'Amore]*, trans. F. Friedeberg-Seeley and Jean H. Barnes (London: Soncino Press, 1937); *Ficino's Commentary on Plato's Symposium*, trans. Sears R. Jayne, University of Missouri Studies, no. 19, 1 (Columbia: Univ. of Missouri Press, 1944); Baldassare Castiglione, *Il Libro del Cortegiano* ([Venice], 1528), trans. Sir Thomas Hoby, *The Courtyer* (London, 1561).

44. *Il Cortegiano*, Bk. 4, 225-42, Hoby, sigs. Ss 4ᵥ-Yy 2.

45. For the counterargument, see Stein, *Answerable Style*, p. 100; Robert H. West, *Milton and the Angels* (Athens: Univ. of Georgia Press, 1955), p. 173; E.M.W. Tillyard, *Studies in Milton* (London: Chatto & Windus, 1951), pp. 12-13.

46. See for example, Dante, *Paradiso* 31.13-14: "Le facce tutte avean di fiamma viva / e l'ali d'oro" (They [the angels] had their faces all of living flame, and their wings of gold). See also Teresa of Avila, *The Flaming Hart*, trans. M. T. [Toby Matthew?] (Antwerp, 1642), p. 419: "But in this Vision, Our Lord was pleased, that I should see the Angell. . . . His face was so inflamed, that he appeared to be of those most Superiour Angells, who seem to be, all in a fire; and he might well be of them, whome we call Seraphins."

47. For such readings see Frye, *Return of Eden*, pp. 61-62 and John Peter, *A Critique of Paradise Lost* (London: Longmans; New York: Columbia Univ. Press, 1960), pp. 108-109.

CHAPTER 9. "I NOW MUST CHANGE THOSE NOTES TO TRAGIC": THE FALL AND THE TRAGIC GENRES

1. See above, Chapter 2, pp. 36-38.

2. Joseph Addison, *Spectator #297*, in *Criticism on Paradise Lost*, ed. Cook, p. 35.

3. On this point, see Steadman, *Epic and Tragic Structure*, pp. 41-104, and Hanford, "Dramatic Element in *Paradise Lost*," pp. 224-43. Also, Beverley Sherry, "Speech in *Paradise Lost*," *Milton Studies* 8 (1975), 247-66; and Grossman, "Dramatic Structure and Emotive Pattern in the Fall," pp. 201-19.

4. E.g., Waldock, *Paradise Lost and Its Critics*, pp. 25-64; Peter, *Critique of Paradise Lost*. See the critique of such dramatic readings by Ferry, *Milton's Epic Voice*, pp. 1-66.

5. Walter Raleigh, *Milton* (London: Edward Arnold, 1900), pp. 81-82.

6. See, e.g., Tillyard, *Studies in Milton*, pp. 8-44.

7. See Guarini's defense of the new genre, *Compendio della Poesia Tragicomica*, pp. 1-64, esp. pp. 22-23, 38. See discussion in Weinberg, *History of Literary Criticism* 2:1074-1105.

8. *Works of Beaumont and Fletcher*, ed. Glover and Waller, 2:522.

9. For an exploration of tragicomedy in such terms, with Shakespeare's *Measure for Measure* as a central example, see Cyrus Hoy, *The Hyacinth Room: An Investigation of the Nature of Comedy, Tragedy & Tragicomedy* (New York: Knopf, 1964).

10. Aristotle, *Poetics* 1453a. 30-40, McKeon, *Basic Works*, p. 1467.

11. See the title page of George Gascoigne's *The Glasse of Government* (London, 1575): "A tragicall Comedie so entituled, bycause therein are handled aswell the rewardes for Vertues, as also the punishment for Vices"; Cinthio, *Discorso . . . delle comedie, e delle tragedie*, pp. 211-13, 219, 221.

12. Beza, *Abraham Sacrifiant* (Geneva, 1550); trans. Arthur Golding, *A Tragedie of Abrahams Sacrifice* (London, 1577), ed. Malcolm W. Wallace (Toronto: Univ. of Toronto Press, 1906), p. 7.

13. For some discussion of Milton's idea of Christian tragedy in reference to *Samson Agonistes*, see Lewalski, "*Samson Agonistes* and the 'Tragedy' of the Apocalypse," 1050-62; A.S.P. Woodhouse, "Tragic Effect in *Samson Agonistes*," rpt. from *UTQ* 28 (1958-1959) in Arthur Barker, *Milton: Modern Essays in Criticism* (New York: Oxford Univ. Press, 1965), pp. 464-66; and Radzinowicz, *Toward Samson Agonistes*, pp. 8-66, 261-65, 359-64.

14. Tertullian, *De spectaculis* 30, trans. T. R. Glover (Loeb, Cambridge: Harvard Univ. Press; London: William Heinemann, 1931), pp. 296-301.

15. On this point, and on the Fall as reference point for subsequent Christian tragedy, see William Lewis, " 'Trie thy braines to gain a

deity': Christian Tragedy of the Fall" (Ph.D. diss., Harvard Univ., 1978).

16. See, e.g., Hugo Grotius, *Sacra in Quibus Adamus Exul Tragoedia* (The Hague, 1601), Act 5, pp. 71-72; Serafino Della Salandra, *Adamo Caduto, Tragedia Sacra* (Cosenza, 1647), Act 5, pp. 243-51.

17. The point is discussed by John N. King, *English Reformation Literature: The Tudor Origins of the Protestant Tradition* (Princeton: Princeton Univ. Press, 1982), pp. 271-318, and in his unpublished essay, "Providential Comedy: The Emergence of a Reformation Mode."

18. Martin Bucer, "De Honestis Ludis," from *De Regno Christi* (1550), trans. Glynne Wickham, in *Early English Stages 1300-1600*, 2 vols. in 3 (New York: Columbia Univ. Press, 1963), Vol. 2, pt. 1, Appendix C.

19. Kirchmeyer, *Pammachius* (Wittenberg, 1538). John Bale translated the work in a version no longer extant, for production at Lambeth Palace during Christmas 1539. See David Bevington, *Tudor Drama and Politics: A Critical Approach to Topical Meaning* (Cambridge: Harvard Univ. Press, 1968), pp. 97-98.

20. John Bale labelled his *Kynge Johan* (c. 1538) and his *Tragedye Manyfestyng the Chefe Promyses of God unto Man* (Wesel, c. 1547) tragedies, evidently because the first focuses on the struggles and sufferings of the reforming monarch, King John, and of all the elect in forwarding the Reformation (seen as a type of the Last Judgment); and the second treats the Fall and the covenantal promises of God to a succession of Old Testament prophets and patriarchs, looking forward to a Messiah who has not yet come. Nicholas Grimald termed his *Archipropheta: tragoedia* (Cologne, 1548) a tragedy evidently because of its central concern with the martyrdom of John Baptist, even though Jehovah explains the ironic "hidden victory" which Christ's ministry will bring about. On the other hand, plays that Bale labels comedies (*A Brefe Comedy concernynge the Temptacyon of our Lorde* [Wesel, 1547], and *A Comedy concernynge Thre Lawes* [Wesel, c. 1548]) conclude with some actual realization, not simply expectation, of the victory of grace. And John Foxe's *Christus Triumphans* (Basel, 1556) is labelled a "comoedia apocalyptica" even though this dramatic version of the Book of Revelation incorporates the "unspeakable tragedies of the suffering faithful" (*dicendas tragoedias*) at the hands of Satan and

Antichrist, evidently because it concludes with the comedic epi-
thalamion of Bride and Bridegroom (John Hazel Smith, trans.,
Two Latin Comedies by John Foxe the Martyrologist [Ithaca and Lon-
don: Cornell Univ. Press, 1973], p. 212).

21. *CPW*, 1:815.

22. Pareus, *Commentary upon . . . Revelation*, pp. 20-26, 84, 105,
134. See also, among many others, Bullinger, *Sermons upon the
Apocalypse*, sigs. Aii$_v$-Aiii$_v$; Brightman, *Revelation of the Apocalypse*,
sig. A 2$_v$, pp. 194, 234, 332.

23. *Poetics* 1452b.30-1453a.17, McKeon, pp. 1466-67.

24. See the classic discussion of the genre in Fredson Bowers, *Eliz-
abethan Revenge Tragedy* (Princeton: Princeton Univ. Press, 1940).

25. *Poetics* 1453a.7-17, McKeon, p. 1467.

26. *Poetics* 1453a.9. See Steadman, *Epic and Tragic Structure*, pp. 34-
35.

27. *Poetics* 1452a.22-25, McKeon, p. 1465.

28. *Poetics* 1452a.30-32, ibid.

29. Steadman, *Epic and Tragic Structure*, p. 68.

30. *Poetics* 1453a.5-7, McKeon, p. 1467.

31. *PL* 4.374, 9.404, 10.23-25.

32. *Poetics* 1452b.10-12, McKeon, p. 1466.

33. Steadman, *Epic and Tragic Structure*, pp. 74-88.

34. Italics mine. See Steadman, " 'Passions Well Imitated,': Rhetoric
and Poetics in the Preface to *Samson Agonistes*," in *Calm of Mind:
Tercentenary Essays on Paradise Regained and Samson Agonistes in
Honor of John S. Diekhoff*, ed. Joseph A. Wittreich (Cleveland and
London: Case Western Reserve Univ. Press, 1971); and Alan
Kimbrough, "Passions Well Imitated" (Ph.D. diss, Brown Univ.,
1974).

35. See Steadman, *Epic and Tragic Structure*, pp. 89-104.

36. Grotius, *Adamus Exul*; Andreini, *L'Adamo. Sacra Rapresentatione*
(Milan, 1613); Salandra, *Adamo Caduto*; Joost van den Vondel,
Adam in Ballingschap (Amsterdam, 1664).

37. William Lauder, *An Essay on Milton's Use and Imitation of the
Moderns, in His Paradise Lost* (London, 1750).

38. Grotius, Act 4, pp. 39-50; Salandra, Act 2, Scene 5, pp. 66-68;
Vondel, Act 4, Scene 1-2, pp. 42-45.

39. Adam's language here seems to echo verses from Ecclesiastes 4
often cited in such tracts, as John Reichert has pointed out to me:

9. Two are better than one . . .

10. For if they fall, the one will lift up his fellow: but woe to him that is alone when he falleth; for he hath not another to help him up.

. . . .

12. And if one prevail against him, two shall withstand him . . .

40. Grotius, Act 4, p. 41; Andreini, Act 2, Scene 6, p. 70; Vondel, Act 4, Scene 2, p. 47.

41. Grotius, Act 4, pp. 47-50; Vondel, Act 4, Scene 2, pp. 49-50.

42. *De Doctrina*, 1.11, *CPW*, 6:388:

Each type of sin, common and personal, has two subdivisions, whether we call them degrees or parts or modes of sin, or whether they are related to each other as cause and effect. These subdivisions are evil desire, or the will to do evil, and the evil deed itself. James i. 14, 15: *every man is tempted when he is drawn on and enticed by his own lust: then, when lust has conceived, it brings forth sin. . . .*

It was evil desire that our first parents were originally guilty of.

43. The Satanic argument leading Eve to make false analogies between her own expectations and the falsely reported effects of the fruit on the serpent is evidently original with Milton.

44. Italics mine.

45. Cf. *PL* 5.792-93.

46. Cf. Grotius, Act 4, pp. 50-55; Vondel, Act 4, Scene 3, pp. 50-55; Andreini, Act 3, Scene 1, pp. 65-75.

47. See, e.g., Viperano, *De Poetica*, p. 150: "si gravem, aliquam actionem imitetur, a Tragoedia et Epopoeia non differet; nec si humilem et jocosam effingat, a Comœdia nihilo distabit." Others who divide lyric into tragic and comic are Trissino, *Sesta Divisione della poetica*, in *Trattati di Poetica*, ed. Weinberg, 2:89-90, and Robortello, *In Librum Aristotelis de Arte Poetica Explicationes* (Florence, 1548), pp. 22-23, 42-43, 55.

48. See above, Chapter 4, pp. 103-105.

49. *Princeton Encyclopedia*, p. 148.

50. Ovid, *Heroides and Amores*, trans. Grant Showerman (Loeb, Cambridge: Harvard Univ. Press; London: William Heinemann,

1963). See esp. *Heroides* 2, "Phylllis to Demophoon"; 7, "Dido to Aeneas"; and 11, "Canace to Macareus," all of which portray the speaker sinking ever more deeply into despair and looking toward death.

51. Radzinowicz, *Toward Samson Agonistes*, pp. 208-210.

CHAPTER 10. "NOT LESS BUT MORE HEROIC":
PROPHECY AND THE TRANSFORMATION OF LITERARY FORMS

1. See Wittreich, *Visionary Poetics*, and Kerrigan, *The Prophetic Milton*, for other views of the literary status of prophecy in Milton's poem. For discussion of various generic elements in those books, see, e.g., Amerose, "Milton the Apocalyptic Historian"; MacCallum, "Milton and Sacred History"; Balachandra Rajan, "*Paradise Lost*: The Hill of History," *HLQ* 31 (1967), 43-63; and Lawrence A. Sasek, "The Drama of *Paradise Lost*, Books XI and XII," *Studies in English Renaissance Literature*, ed. Waldo F. McNeir (Baton Rouge: Louisiana State Univ. Press, 1962), pp. 181-96.

2. See above, Chapter 2, pp. 50-54.

3. See, e.g., Junius, *Apocalypse, or Revelation*, p. 247.

4. See, e.g., Brightman, *Revelation of the Apocalypse*, sig. A 2$_v$, pp. 194, 234, 332. And see above, Chapter 9, pp. 222-24.

5. See, e.g., Bullinger, *Sermons upon the Apocalypse*, sig. Aiii$_v$.

6. Pareus, *Commentary upon . . . Revelation*, p. 20. See also Hezekiah Holland, *An Exposition . . . Upon the Revelation of Saint John* (London, 1650), p. 146. In the *Reason of Church Government* Milton, citing "the grave autority of *Pareus*," described the Apocalypse as "the majestick image of a high and stately Tragedy, shutting up and intermingling her solemn Scenes and Acts with a sevenfold *Chorus* of halleluja's and harping symphonies," *CPW*, 1:815.

7. For the medicinal effects of these herbs, see Gerard's *Herball*, pp. 537, 1074 (cited in Hughes, p. 442). Euphrasy derives from the Greek "cheerfulness," and one meaning of rue is sorrow, repentance (see OED entries and Alastair Fowler's note on this passage, *Milton: Paradise Lost* [London: Longman, 1968], p. 585). See also Ophelia's speech (*Hamlet* 4.5.175-76: "There's rue for you, and here's some for me. We may call it herb of grace a Sundays").

8. See Elizabeth Pope's valuable study of this "triple equation" tra-

dition in *Paradise Regained: The Tradition and the Poem* (Baltimore: Johns Hopkins Univ. Press, 1947).

9. *PL* 9.786-90: "Intent now wholly on her taste, naught else / Regarded, such delight till then, as seem'd, / In Fruit she never tasted, whether true / Or fancied so, through expectation high / Of knowledge, nor was God-head from her thought."

10. *De Doctrina*, 1.chaps. 12-13, 17-25, *CPW*, 6:393-414, 453-514.

11. *Ibid.*, 1.chap. 20, *CPW* 6:472.

12. *Ibid.*, p. 471.

13. For further discussion see Lewalski, "Structure and the Symbolism of Vision in Michael's Prophecy, *Paradise Lost*, Books XI-XII," *PQ* 42 (1963), 25-35; and Raymond B. Waddington, "The Death of Adam: Vision and Voice in Books XI and XII of *Paradise Lost*," *MP* 70 (1972), 9-21.

14. For other views of the education of Adam in *PL* 11-12, see, e.g., Fish, *Surprised by Sin*, pp. 300-31; F. T. Prince, "On the Last Two Books of *Paradise Lost*" *E&S* 11 (1958), 36-52; Mary Ann Radzinowicz, "Man as a Probationer of Immortality: *Paradise Lost* XI-XII," in *Approaches to Paradise Lost: The York Tercentenary Lectures*, ed. C. A. Patrides (Toronto: Univ. of Toronto Press, 1968), pp. 31-51; George Williamson, "The Education of Adam," *MP* 61 (1963), 96-109.

15. See above, Chapter 9, pp. 241-42. Cf. *PL* 10.126-56.

16. *De Doctrina*, 1.26, *CPW*, 6:516: "The unwritten law is the law of nature given to the first man. A kind of gleam or glimmering of it still remains in the hearts of all mankind. In the regenerate this is daily brought nearer to a renewal of its original perfection by the operation of the Holy Spirit. . . . The manifestation of this free covenant under the law took place partly in Moses' time and partly before."

17. See above, Chapter 9, pp. 221-32.

18. The argument that the mode and effect of Milton's epic are comic rather than tragic is developed by John Shawcross in "The Balanced Structure of *Paradise Lost*," *SP* 62 (1965), 696-718, and "The Son in His Ascending: A Reading of *Paradise Lost*," MLQ 27 (1966); the argument that the poem modulates from tragedy to tragicomedy is developed by Rollin, "*Paradise Lost*: 'Tragical-Comical-Historical-Pastoral.' " In the Preface to *Samson Agonistes*, Milton describes tragic catharsis as part of his definition of the effect of tragedy, "by raising pity and fear, or terror, to purge the

mind of those and such like passions, that is to temper and reduce them to just measure."

19. A common view of Milton's life emphasizes his disillusion with political action after the Restoration, and his final, total withdrawal from public concerns. Books Eleven and Twelve of *Paradise Lost* are often read as a manifestation of this disillusion, directing the regenerate to attend solely to the "paradise within." See, e.g., William R. Parker, *Milton: A Biography*, Vol. 1 (Oxford: Clarendon Press, 1968), pp. 588-95, and Broadbent, *Some Graver Subject*, pp. 278-84. Several recent critics have challenged this interpretation of Milton's biography, though with primary reference to the political implications of *Samson Agonistes*. See, e.g., Radzinowicz, *Toward Samson Agonistes*, pp. 67-179, and Hill, *Milton and the English Revolution*, pp. 380-488.

20. See Chapter 4, p. 99 and n. 49.

21. See Chapter 9, pp. 248-50.

22. In Louis Duchesne, *Christian Worship: Its Origin and Evolution: A Study of the Latin Liturgy up to the Time of Charlesmagne*, trans. M. L. McClure, 5th ed. (London: Society for Promoting Christian Knowledge; New York: Macmillan, 1923), p. 254: "O wonderful condescension of thy mercy towards us! / O inestimable affection of charity! / That thou might redeem a slave, Thou didst deliver up Thy Son! / O truly needful sin of Adam / which was blotted out by the death of Christ! / O happy fault, that was worthy of so great a Redeemer." See also discussion of the *Exsultet* in the *New Catholic Encyclopedia*, 15 vols. (New York: McGraw-Hill, 1967), 5:765-66.

23. Salandra, *Adamo caduto*, Act 2, Scene 14, p. 105:

> O Fortunata colpa,
> O delitto gradito,
> O furto pretioso,
> Cara inubedienza.
> Ladro, bene Ladro, Adam, non già del Pomo,
> Ma di pietà, ma di clemenza, e gloria.

And see other examples cited by A. O. Lovejoy, "Milton and the Paradox of the Fortunate Fall," *ELH* 4 (1937), 161-79, rpt. in *Essays in the History of Ideas* (Baltimore: Johns Hopkins Univ. Press, 1948), 277-95.

24. See above, Chapter 6, pp. 160-62, and nn. 34-40.

Index

Adamson, J. H., *see Bright Essence*
Addison, Joseph, 74, 110, 220; *Spectator #297*, 309(44), 353(2); *Spectator #315*, 320(1)
Aeschylus, 13; *Prometheus Bound*, 62-63, 305(15)
Agrippa d'Aubigné, Theodore, *Les Tragiques*, 36, 52, 255, 296(29)
Alexandrian *Canons*, 10
Allen, Don C., "Milton and the Descent to Light," 293(20)
Ambrose, Isaac, *Prima, Media, and Ultima*, 343-44(39)
Amorose, Thomas, 282(4); "Milton the Apocalyptic Historian," 302(60), 358(1)
Amphion, 351(18)
Anacreon, 14
Andreini, Giambattista, 232; *Adamo*, 356(36), 357(40)(46)
Annotations . . . by . . . learned Divines [English Annotations], 350(14)
Ariosto, Lodovico, 3, 12, 13, 20, 29, 69, 308(37); *Orlando Furioso*, 12, 21, 69-70, 291(9), 307(31)(33)(35), 316(46); trans. Sir John Harington, 297(34), 307(32)
Aristotle, 9, 13, 15, 80, 85, 157, 225, 227-29, 287(38), 296(29); *Poetics*, 285(14), 287(27)(40), 303(2), 348(6), 354(10), 356(23)(25)(26)(27)(28)(30)(32); *Politics*, 333-34(30); *Rhetoric*, 288(48), 312(17), 315(40)

Aryanpur, Manoocher, "*Paradise Lost* and the *Odyssey*," 281(2)
Athanasius, "In Psalmos," 347(58)
Augustine, *City of God*, 53, 255, 302(64)(65), 303(66); *Confessions*, 211, 300(49); *Expositions on the Psalms*, 352(28)
Aylett, Robert, 296(33); *The Song of Songs, which was Solomon's*, 350(14)

Bakhtin, M. M., 17; *The Dialogic Imagination*, 289(54)
Bale, John, 355(19); *A Brefe Comedy concernynge the Temptacyon of our Lorde*, 355(20); *A Comedy concernynge Thre Lawes*, 355(20); *Kynge Johan*, 223, 355(20); *Tragedye Manyfestyng the Chefe Promyses of God unto Man*, 355(20)
Barker, Arthur E., "Structural Pattern in *Paradise Lost*," 283(5), 329(56)
Baroway, Israel M., "The Hebrew Hexameter," 310(49), 335(37); "The Lyre of David," 335(37)
Baxter, Richard, *Autobiography*, 352(39); *Reliquiae Baxterianae*, 352(39)
Beaumont, Joseph (and John Fletcher), *Philaster*, 221
Beaurline, Lester, *Jonson and Elizabethan Comedy*, 288(41), 349(7)
Bergeron, David M., *English Civic Pageantry*, 352(32)
Berry, Boyd M., *Process of Speech*, 324(34)

332(19), 357(42), 359(10)
(11)(12)(16); *Samson Agonistes*,
230, "Preface," 13, 224, 229-30,
231, 287(37), 302(61), 321(19),
359-60(18)
Miner, Earl, 282(4)
Minturno, Antonio Sebastiano, 9,
14, 288(46), 296(29); *De Poeta*,
286(46), 296(29); *L'Arte Poetica*,
286(25), 287(28), 288(43),
306(21)
Moore, O. H., "The Infernal Coun-
cil," 321(11)
More, Henry, *Autobiography*,
352(39)
Mueller, Janel, x
Mueller, Martin, 60; "*Paradise Lost
and the Iliad*," 281(2), 305(12)
(13)(14)
Murrin, Michael, "The Language of
Milton's Heaven," 321(8),
326(39)
Musaeus, 18

Nardo, A. K., "The Submerged
Sonnet as Lyric Moment in Mil-
tonic Epic," 284(7), 344(42)
Nazianzen, *see* Gregory

Origen, 11, 201; *Song of Songs*,
350(15), "First Homily,"
346(54)
Orpheus, 18, 32, 34, 351(18);
"Hymn to Night," 32, 293(19)
Orwell, George, 84
Otis, Brooks, *Ovid as an Epic Poet*,
307(37)
Otten, Charlotte, " 'My Native Ele-
ment': Milton's Paradise of Eng-
lish Gardens," 340(19)
Ovid, 3, 6, 45, 56, 110, 117, 136,
138, 179, 180; *Heroides*, 249,
288-89(49), 357-58(50), 2.
"Phyllis to Demophoon,"

358(50), 7. "Dido to Aeneas,"
358(50), 11. "Canace to Maca-
reus," 358(50); *Metamorphoses*, 5,
56, 71-76, 117-18, 136-39,
295(26), 308(37)(38)(40)(41),
322(15)(16), 328(50)(53),
329(58)(59)(60)(63), 330(67),
340(17), 343(37); *Fasti*,
340(17), 341(22)(24); *see also*
Golding, Arthur; and Sandys,
George
Ovide Moralisé, 308(42)

Paetow, Louis J., "The Arts Course
at Medieval Universities,"
289(52)
Paggioli, Renato, *The Oaten Flute*,
338(2)
Pareus, David, 224; *Commentary
upon . . . Revelation*, 51, 302(61),
350(15), 356(22), 358(6)
Parker, Patricia A., 65; *Inescapable
Romance*, 282(3), 306(22)
Parker, William R., *Milton: A Biog-
raphy*, 360(19)
Patrick, Simon, *The Song of Salomon
Paraphrased*, 346(54)
Patrides, C. A., 110; "*Paradise Lost
and the Language of Theology*,"
292(17); "Paradise Lost and the
Theory of Accommodation,"
320(2); *see also Bright Essence*
Patrizi, Francisco, 349(8)
Patterson, Annabel M., "*Paradise
Regained*: A Last Chance at True
Romance," 306(22)
Peacham, Henry, *The Garden of Elo-
quence*, 241(27)
Perkins, William, *The Arte of Proph-
ecying*, 332(19)
Peter, John, *A Critique of Paradise
Lost*, 353(47), 354(4)
Petrarch, 5; *Secretum*, 16, 289(51);

Sherry, Beverley, "Speech in *Paradise Lost*," 354(3)
Shirley, Charles G., Jr., "The Four Phases of the Creation," 320(2), 327(48)
Shumacher, Wayne, "*Paradise Lost* and the Italian Epic Tradition," 282(3)
Sibbes, Richard, *The Soules conflict with it selfe*, 343(39)
Sidney, Sir Philip, 5, 10, 11, 12, 14, 179, 198, 286(25), 288(46); *Arcadia [New Arcadia]*, 6, 12, 173, 340(17); *Arcadia [Old Arcadia]*, 342(35), "Epithalamium for Lalus and Kala," 191, 346(53); *Defense of Poesie*, 285(15), 287(33)(35), 288(41)(47), 339(5), 348(5), 349(8)(9), 350-51(18)
Sims, James H., *The Bible in Milton's Epics*, 295(27), 321(7), 327(45), 352(34)
Sirluck, Ernest, *Paradise Lost: A Deliberate Epic*, 283(5)
Smith, Hallett, *Elizabethan Poetry*, 338(2)
Smith, John, 25, 27, 38, 39, 50; "Of Prophesie," 290(1)(2)(4), 297(36)(38), 301(58)(59)
Snyder, Susan, 44, 327(47); *see also* Du Bartas
Sophocles, 11, 13
Spencer, T.J.B., "*Paradise Lost*: The Anti-Epic," 282(4)
Spenser, Edmund, 3, 20, 29, 59, 143, 193; "Epithalamium," 191-92, 344(46); *Faerie Queene*, 6, 12, 42, 68-69, 173, 177, 178, 179, 182, 194, 290(5), 300(46), 307(29)(35), 322(14), 331(8), 338(4), 339(12), 341(28), 346(55); *Four Hymns*, 31, "Hymne in Honour of Love,"

292(16), "Hymne of Heavenly Beautie," 292(16), 336(47); *Shepheardes Calendar*, E. K.'s "Introduction," 338(3), "Aprill," 342(31), "Maye," 331(4)
Statius, "Epithalamion in Stellum et Violentillam," *Silvae*, 347(57)
Steadman, John M., 63, 228, 229; *Epic and Tragic Structure in Paradise Lost*, 283(5), 284(8), 296(29), 305(16), 354(3), 356(26)(29)(33)(35); "Epic as Pseudomorph: Methodology in Milton Studies," 282(4); *Milton and the Renaissance Hero*, 281(1)(2), 303(1), 322(14); *Milton's Epic Characters: Image and Idol*, 281(2), 284(8), 289(57), 303(1); "Milton's Rhetoric," 290(59); " 'Passions Well Imitated,' " 356(34); "Satan and the Unjust Discourse," 311(11); " 'Semblance of Worth': Pandaemonium and Deliberative Oratory," 284(8)
Stein, Arnold, *Answerable Style*, 332(13), 353(45); "Satan's Metamorphoses: The Internal Speech," 316(42)
Summers, Joseph, 203; *The Muse's Method*, 283(7), 300(48), 327(48), 331(10), 351(21)
Svendsen, Kester, *Milton and Science*, 297(39)
Sylvester, Josuah, *see* Du Bartas

Tasso, Torquato, 6, 11, 14, 20, 29, 132, 143, 198, 229, 296(33); *Discorso del poema eroico [Discourses on the Heroic Poem]*, 285(16), 288(41), 303(2), 348(5); *Gerusalemme Liberata*, 6, 12, 289(56), 307(35), 313(22), 319-20(69),

INDEX

Library of Congress Cataloging in Publication Data

Lewalski, Barbara Kiefer, 1931-
Paradise lost and the rhetoric of literary forms.

Includes index.
1. Milton, John, 1608-1674. Paradise lost.
2. Literary form. I. Title.
PR3562.L385 1985   821'.4   84-24819
ISBN 0-691-06642-6 (alk. paper)

Barbara Kiefer Lewalski is Willaim R. Kenan Professor of English Literature and History at Harvard University. Among her works are *Donne's "Anniversaries" and the Poetry of Praise: The Creation of a Symbolic Mode* (Princeton) and *Protestant Poetics and the Seventeenth-Century Religious Lyric* (Princeton), which won the James Russell Lowell Prize of the Modern Language Association in 1979.